Lecture Notes in Computer Science 15382

Founding Editors

Gerhard Goos
Juris Hartmanis

AF167716

The series Lecture Notes in Computer Science (LNCS), including its subseries Lecture Notes in Artificial Intelligence (LNAI) and Lecture Notes in Bioinformatics (LNBI), has established itself as a medium for the publication of new developments in computer science and information technology research, teaching, and education.

LNCS enjoys close cooperation with the computer science R & D community, the series counts many renowned academics among its volume editors and paper authors, and collaborates with prestigious societies. Its mission is to serve this international community by providing an invaluable service, mainly focused on the publication of conference and workshop proceedings and postproceedings. LNCS commenced publication in 1973.

Helmut Degen · Stavroula Ntoa
Editors

HCI International 2024 – Late Breaking Papers

26th International Conference on
Human-Computer Interaction, HCII 2024
Washington, DC, USA, June 29 – July 4, 2024
Proceedings, Part IX

 Springer

Editors
Helmut Degen
Siemens Corporation
Princeton, NJ, USA

Stavroula Ntoa
Foundation for Research
and Technology – Hellas (FORTH)
Heraklion, Crete, Greece

ISSN 0302-9743 ISSN 1611-3349 (electronic)
Lecture Notes in Computer Science
ISBN 978-3-031-76826-2 ISBN 978-3-031-76827-9 (eBook)
https://doi.org/10.1007/978-3-031-76827-9

This Springer imprint is published by the registered company Springer Nature Switzerland AG
The registered company address is: Gewerbestrasse 11, 6330 Cham, Switzerland

If disposing of this product, please recycle the paper.

Foreword

This year we celebrate 40 years since the establishment of the HCI International (HCII) Conference, which has been a hub for presenting groundbreaking research and novel ideas and collaboration for people from all over the world.

The HCII conference was founded in 1984 by Prof. Gavriel Salvendy (Purdue University, USA, Tsinghua University, P.R. China, and University of Central Florida, USA) and the first event of the series, "1st USA-Japan Conference on Human-Computer Interaction", was held in Honolulu, Hawaii, USA, 18–20 August. Since then, HCI International is held jointly with several Thematic Areas and Affiliated Conferences, with each one under the auspices of a distinguished international Program Board and under one management and one registration. Twenty-six HCI International Conferences have been organized so far (every two years until 2013, and annually thereafter).

Over the years, this conference has served as a platform for scholars, researchers, industry experts and students to exchange ideas, connect, and address challenges in the ever-evolving HCI field. Throughout these 40 years, the conference has evolved itself, adapting to new technologies and emerging trends, while staying committed to its core mission of advancing knowledge and driving change.

As we celebrate this milestone anniversary, we reflect on the contributions of its founding members and appreciate the commitment of its current and past Affiliated Conference Program Board Chairs and members. We are also thankful to all past conference attendees who have shaped this community into what it is today.

The 26th International Conference on Human-Computer Interaction, HCI International 2024 (HCII 2024), was held as a 'hybrid' event at the Washington Hilton Hotel, Washington, DC, USA, during 29 June – 4 July 2024. It incorporated the 21 thematic areas and affiliated conferences listed below.

A total of 5108 individuals from academia, research institutes, industry, and government agencies from 85 countries submitted contributions, and 1271 papers and 309 posters were included in the volumes of the proceedings that were published just before the start of the conference. Additionally, 222 papers and 104 posters were included in the volumes of the proceedings published after the conference, as "Late Breaking Work". The contributions thoroughly cover the entire field of human-computer interaction, addressing major advances in knowledge and effective use of computers in a variety of application areas. These papers provide academics, researchers, engineers, scientists, practitioners and students with state-of-the-art information on the most recent advances in HCI. The volumes constituting the full set of the HCII 2024 conference proceedings are listed on the following pages.

I would like to thank the Program Board Chairs and the members of the Program Boards of all thematic areas and affiliated conferences for their contribution towards the high scientific quality and overall success of the HCI International 2024 conference. Their manifold support in terms of paper reviewing (single-blind review process, with a minimum of two reviews per submission), session organization and their willingness to act as goodwill ambassadors for the conference is most highly appreciated.

This conference would not have been possible without the continuous and unwavering support and advice of Gavriel Salvendy, founder, General Chair Emeritus, and Scientific Advisor. For his outstanding efforts, I would like to express my sincere appreciation to Abbas Moallem, Communications Chair and Editor of HCI International News.

September 2024   Constantine Stephanidis

HCI International 2024 Thematic Areas and Affiliated Conferences

- HCI: Human-Computer Interaction Thematic Area
- HIMI: Human Interface and the Management of Information Thematic Area
- EPCE: 21st International Conference on Engineering Psychology and Cognitive Ergonomics
- AC: 18th International Conference on Augmented Cognition
- UAHCI: 18th International Conference on Universal Access in Human-Computer Interaction
- CCD: 16th International Conference on Cross-Cultural Design
- SCSM: 16th International Conference on Social Computing and Social Media
- VAMR: 16th International Conference on Virtual, Augmented and Mixed Reality
- DHM: 15th International Conference on Digital Human Modeling & Applications in Health, Safety, Ergonomics & Risk Management
- DUXU: 13th International Conference on Design, User Experience and Usability
- C&C: 12th International Conference on Culture and Computing
- DAPI: 12th International Conference on Distributed, Ambient and Pervasive Interactions
- HCIBGO: 11th International Conference on HCI in Business, Government and Organizations
- LCT: 11th International Conference on Learning and Collaboration Technologies
- ITAP: 10th International Conference on Human Aspects of IT for the Aged Population
- AIS: 6th International Conference on Adaptive Instructional Systems
- HCI-CPT: 6th International Conference on HCI for Cybersecurity, Privacy and Trust
- HCI-Games: 6th International Conference on HCI in Games
- MobiTAS: 6th International Conference on HCI in Mobility, Transport and Automotive Systems
- AI-HCI: 5th International Conference on Artificial Intelligence in HCI
- MOBILE: 5th International Conference on Human-Centered Design, Operation and Evaluation of Mobile Communications

Conference Proceedings – Full List of Volumes

69. LNCS 15380, HCI International 2024 - Late Breaking Papers: Part VII, edited by Aaron Marcus, Elizabeth Rosenzweig, Marcelo M. Soares, Pei-Luen Patrick Rau and Abbas Moallem

70. LNCS 15381, HCI International 2024 - Late Breaking Papers: Part VIII, edited by Don Harris, Wen-Chin Li and Heidi Krömker

71. LNCS 15382, HCI International 2024 - Late Breaking Papers: Part IX, edited by Helmut Degen and Stavroula Ntoa

72. CCIS 2319, HCI International 2024 - Late Breaking Posters: Part I, edited by Constantine Stephanidis, Margherita Antona, Stavroula Ntoa and Gavriel Salvendy

73. CCIS 2320, HCI International 2024 - Late Breaking Posters: Part II, edited by Constantine Stephanidis, Margherita Antona, Stavroula Ntoa and Gavriel Salvendy

74. CCIS 2321, HCI International 2024 - Late Breaking Posters: Part III, edited by Constantine Stephanidis, Margherita Antona, Stavroula Ntoa and Gavriel Salvendy

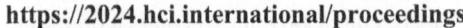

https://2024.hci.international/proceedings

26th International Conference on Human-Computer Interaction (HCII 2024)

The full list with the Program Board Chairs and the members of the Program Boards of all thematic areas and affiliated conferences of HCII2024 is available online at:

http://www.hci.international/board-members-2024.php

HCI International 2025 Conference

The 27th International Conference on Human-Computer Interaction, HCI International 2025, will be held jointly with the affiliated conferences at the Swedish Exhibition & Congress Centre and Gothia Towers Hotel, Gothenburg, Sweden, June 22–27, 2025. It will cover a broad spectrum of themes related to Human-Computer Interaction, including theoretical issues, methods, tools, processes, and case studies in HCI design, as well as novel interaction techniques, interfaces, and applications. The proceedings will be published by Springer. More information is available on the conference website: https://2025.hci.international/.

General Chair
Prof. Constantine Stephanidis
University of Crete and ICS-FORTH
Heraklion, Crete, Greece
Email: general_chair@2025.hci.international

https://2025.hci.international/

Contents – Part IX

AI for Decision Making and Sentiment Analysis

Human-Centered AI

Multimodal Referring Expression Generation for Human-Computer Interaction

Nada Alalyani$^{(\boxtimes)}$ (ID) and Nikhil Krishnaswamy (ID)

Colorado State University, Fort Collins, USA
{nadahass,nkrishna}@colostate.edu

Abstract. Using both verbal and non-verbal modalities in generating definite descriptions of objects and locations is a critical human capability in collaborative interactions. Despite recent advancements in AI, embodied interactive virtual agents (IVAs) are not equipped to intelligently mix modalities to communicate their intents as humans do, which hamstrings naturalistic multimodal HCI. We introduce **SCMRE**, a corpus designed for training generative AI systems in multimodal HCI, focusing on multimodal referring expressions. Our contributions include: 1) Developing an interactive virtual agent (IVA) platform that interprets human multimodal instructions and responds with language and gestures; 2) Providing 24 participants with 10 scenes, each involving ten equally-sized blocks randomly placed on a table. These interactions generated a dataset of 10,408 samples; 3) Analyzing SCMRE, revealing that the utilization of pointing significantly reduces the ambiguity of prompts and increases the efficiency of IVA's execution of humans' prompts; 4) Augmenting and synthesizing SCMRE, resulting in 22,159 samples to generate more data for model training; 5) Using LLaMA 2-13B to conduct parameter-efficient finetuning for generating contextually-correct and situationally-fluent multimodal referring expressions; 6) Integrating the fine-tuned model into the IVA to evaluate the success of the generative model-enabled IVA in communication with humans; 7) Establishing the evaluation process which applies to both humans and IVAs and combines quantitative and qualitative metrics.

Keywords: Embodied agents · non-verbal behaviours · multimodality · referring expression generation

1 Introduction

As human-computer interaction (HCI) systems become more advanced and sophisticated, there is an increasing expectation for them to behave more like humans in integrating modalities to communicate their intents. Humans fluently communicate in various non-verbal modalities with verbal modalities, a capability that even advanced multimodal models are unable to achieve [34]. While modern chatbots, powered by generative large language models (LLMs) such

© The Author(s), under exclusive license to Springer Nature Switzerland AG 2024
H. Degen and S. Ntoa (Eds.): HCII 2024, LNCS 15382, pp. 3–22, 2024.
https://doi.org/10.1007/978-3-031-76827-9_1

as OpenAI's ChatGPT, have demonstrated remarkable abilities in generating coherent and context-relevant text, learning from and generating text alone fails to demonstrate an understanding of the meaning that connects utterance to communicative intent [6].

Agent embodiment provides a structure to demonstrate language understanding in context [25]. If a particular mode of expression, such as language, is inadequately communicative, another mode, such as gesture, can be used to disambiguate intents and targets. AI advancements have developed language models, e.g., GPT-4, that enable humans to interact with computers multimodally [34], but to date embodied interactive virtual agents (IVAs) cannot typically intelligently mix modalities to communicate their intents as humans do, which hamstrings naturalistic multimodal HCI. Due to the fact that objects within a shared situated context as anchors for establishing mutual understanding between interlocutors, *Multimodal Referring Expressions* (MREs), leveraging information about both object characteristics and locations, have emerged as a valuable case study for understanding multimodal language use in context [26, 32].

In this paper, we present SCMRE, a Situated Corpus of Multimodal Referring Expressions, and leverage it to train and evaluate generative AI models for embodied HCI. Our aim is advancing the development of IVAs capable of utilizing non-verbal and verbal behavior bidirectionally and symmetrically in interactions with humans. Our key contributions are:

- Developing an embodied IVA with the capability to interpret and respond using language and gestures to collect MREs from humans.
- Collecting the SCMRE corpus via bidirectional and symmetrical human-IVA interaction.
- Implementing a fine-tuned LLM for generating contextually correct and situationally fluent MREs.
- Applying quantitative and qualitative metrics to evaluate MRE generation for both humans and the IVA.

2 Related Work

Recent advancements in embodied HCI indicate the potential for enabling human-like interactions with users [14, 22]. Nonetheless, it is argued that HCI systems lack of bidirectional and symmetrical recognition and generation of multimodal communication mechanisms [50]. Therefore, IVAs, such as the Diana system [27, 28] built on then VoxWorld platform [29, 30] to support embodied HCI in recognizing both virtual and physical environments [50–52], enabling collaboration with humans in task-based interactions. Embodiment plays a significant role in representing and interpreting objects in a scene [53], in mutual understanding [26], and in evaluating the outputs of interactive systems [1, 33]. This emphasizes the importance of IVAs in not solely recognizing but also generating multimodal communication, particularly in the domain of referring expressions (REs).

Referring Expression Generation. Despite the significant contribution of deictic gesture to the successful communication of intent, [17,46], early RE generation research prioritized linguistic descriptions, including object properties [16,63] and spatial references [12,35,43]. Non-verbal cues like deictic gesture were more explored in RE comprehension [39,54,58]. Agent embodiment features were rarely integrated into generation [23,24], with most studies treating generation and comprehension separately [13].

Multimodal Generative LLMs. Recent AI advances have led to the development of multimodal foundation models (MFMs) for multimodal generation [68]. Multimodal transformers, such as CLIP [55], ViLBERT [41], VisualBERT [38], SimVLM [67], BLIP-2 [37] and Flamingo [2], process inputs from various modalities like text, images, and point clouds. Other models focus on processing video, audio, or 3D data understanding [3,19,70]. These models are pre-trained on large multimodal datasets containing images, audios and language.

Datasets. Various datasets contain human-generated descriptions of objects in visual scenes, such as Bishop [18], Drawer [64], GRE3D3 [65], TUNA [16], RS-VS [43], and other recent collections [12,35]. Other datasets focus on verbal references only [9,10,45], gestures only [57,59,60], or embodied multimodal referring expressions comprehension [32,56]. These multimodal expressions are generated either by simulators, such as VoxSim [32], and CAESAR [21], or by humans referring to images [57] or outdoor objects [8].

Metrics. Overlap in the properties of human and machine descriptions can been computed according to Dice Coefficient [11], MASI [48], Levenshtein Distance [36], BLEU [47], ROUGE [40], or METEOR [4]. Alternatively, human judges can evaluate generated REs according to adequacy of reference or naturalness. While adequacy is evaluated by object identification tasks [12,13,15,35], naturalness is evaluated by (1) metrics such as error rate, identification time, and reading time [5] or (2) human ranking of generated references for objects in images or videos [1,12,31,35].

In this study, we developed an IVA to elicit MREs from humans in real-time interaction, trained a MRE generative model focusing on gesture and language, and evaluated how non-verbal strategies complement verbal strategies for situated HCI, both quantitatively and qualitatively.

3 SCMRE Dataset

This section outlines the collection process of SCMRE, aimed at developing generative models for multimodal HCI combining both language and gestures. It covers the IVA development, participants recruitment, human-IVA collaboration, and data statistics.

3.1 Development of the Interactive Virtual Agent (IVA)

We developed a standalone version of the Diana system [27,50], a virtual agent designed for task-based interactions with humans using live gestures and speech.

In this implementation, humans interact with randomly positioned objects, providing both verbal (relational, historical) and non-verbal (deictic), references in response to Diana's prompts. As depicted in Fig. 1a, Diana asks questions such as "Which object should we focus on?" while the human points using the mouse/trackpad, with the purple reticle fluctuating in location and size to approximate the noise inherent in live deictic gesture detection, as in the original Diana system. We created algorithms to parse and interpret human-generated multimodal referring expressions, including *attributive REs*, which describe objects properties, *relational REs*, which define objects by their relations to other objects, and *historical REs*, which uses previous events to describe objects, aligning them with deictic gestures, as shown in Fig. 1b-f. Diana generates verbal and non-verbal behaviors, e.g., in Fig. 1h, to enhance social fluency [66], using text-to-speech and animation for gestures, confirming understanding, responding to prompts, and displaying emotions. This system improves naturalistic human-computer interaction by accurately integrating speech and gestures. Further details can be found in [1,50].

3.2   Human-IVA Collaboration Data Collection

To investigate human MRE generation, we organized human-IVA interaction sessions, consisting of 24 participants from Colorado State University (CSU)'s Computer Science Department. Participants, aged 18–35 (mean = 27, SD = 4.21) and fluent in English, included both males and females with diverse native languages. The study was approved by CSU's IRB. Participants received compensation in the form of Amazon gift cards or extra course credit. Each participant downloaded the IVA executable and engaged in an object identification task across 10 scenes, using language, deixis, or both to identify 10 target blocks per scene. Successful referencing occurred when Diana correctly identified the intended object. During the interaction, the IVA's and participants' movements were logged, including parameters outlined in [25].

3.3   Data Statistics

The SCMRE corpus is organized by incorporating each generated event, including actions and referring expressions, as a distinct sample. As shown in Table 1, the elicitation process resulted in a total of 10,408 events, including 7,681 pointing-only references, 551 transitive attributive events, 641 attributive events, 369 relational events, 27 historical events, 453 non-executed events, and 686 non-referencing events—which include 428 undoing events, 118 refusal events, and 117 affirmative events. In terms of modalities used by humans, 575 events were generated multimodally by mixing deixis and language, 7,681 events were generated using pointing-only, and 2,152 events were generated using speech-only. The number of events generated by each participant varied from 258 to 801 (mean = 444, SD = 171). Additionally, the data includes 194 recorded videos spanning approximately 36 h, ranging from 24 min to 4 h (mean = 01:27:52, SD = 0.04). The IVA, *Diana*, responded to each human-generated event, totaling 10,408

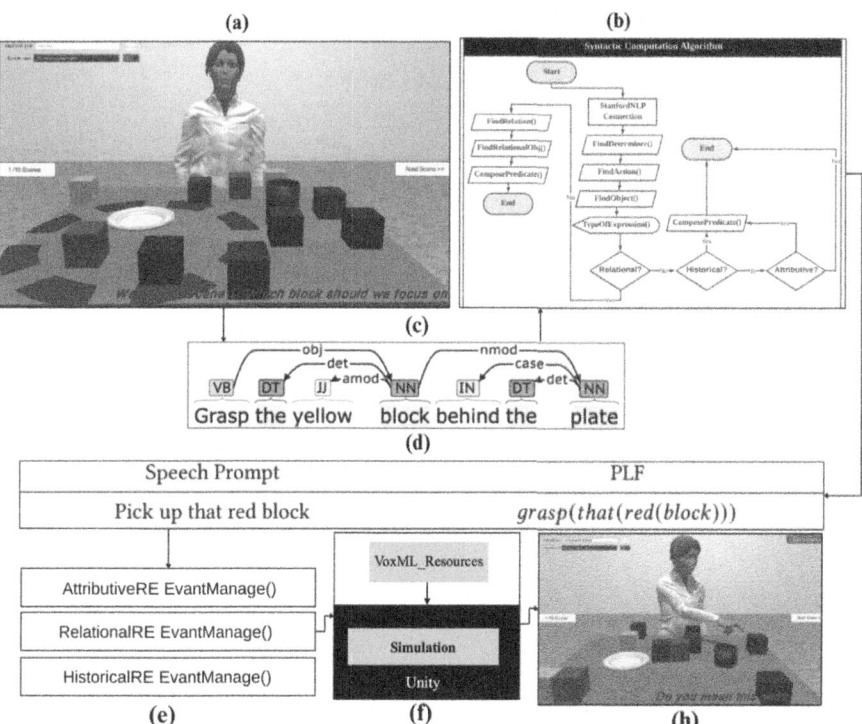

Fig. 1. Human-IVA interaction. a) Diana asks: "Which object should we focus on?" with a fluctuating purple circle indicating the pointing gesture; b) Speech parsing using Stanford CoreNLP [44]; c) Syntactic transformation of speech to Predicate Logic Format (PLF); d) Example of speech converted to PLF; e) Interpretation algorithms for complex MREs; f) Simulation of PLFs using VoxWorld platform; g) Diana acts on human prompts.

IVA responses. She generated 5,271 multimodal actions for 539 multimodal events, 3,628 pointing-only events, 686 non-referencing events, and 418 speech-only events. Moreover, she reacted unimodally: using deictic gestures for 4,053 pointing events to confirm understanding and using language to request more information for 1,084 events.

4   MRE Generation Model

4.1   Data Preparation

To create a robust and diverse dataset that ensures that an LLM trained over it can contextually generate MREs, four key preparation steps were applied to the SCMRE dataset: annotation, augmentation, synthesizing, prompting and splitting, as illustrated in Fig. 2. Dataset before and after preparation is publicly available in GitHub[1].

---

[1] https://github.com/nadahass/SCMRE_Dataset.

8   N. Alalyani and N. Krishnaswamy

Table 1. Quantities of human-generated events based on modalities used, including deictic gesture, speech only, or both.

Humans' Used Modalities			
Events	Modalities	Quantity	Total
Attributive Multimodal Events	Multimodal	186	575
Transitive Attributive Multimodal Events		302	
Relational Multimodal Events		48	
Historical Multimodal Events		3	
Not executed multimodal events		36	
Focus and target pointing	Pointing-Only	7,681	7,681
Attributive Speech Only Events	Speech-Only	455	2,152
Transitive attributive speech only events		249	
Relational speech-only events		321	
Historical speech-only events		24	
Non-referencing speech-only		686	
Not executed speech-only events		416	
Total			**10,408**

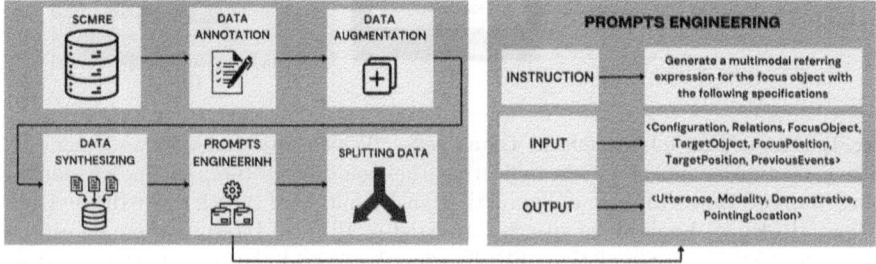

Fig. 2. The main steps of data preparation, including annotation, augmentation, synthesizing, prompting, and splitting.

Data Annotation. This step addressed 453 prompts that were not executed because they could not be parsed by the IVA's parser component. One such example is "move blue block in corner to pink block," where failure to correctly parse "in corner" resulted in an invalid PLF form. This failure prevented the identification of target objects and associated parameters. The parameters that were logged for these prompts include timestamps, utterances, relations, configurations, and previous events. To effectively explore human referential behaviors and train our model, we included the remaining parameters: focus objects (focus of discourse), destination objects (objects to which other objects are moved), focus positions, target positions, and demonstratives. We systematically review these prompts and their corresponding videos to predict the focus and target objects, extract their positions from the generated configurations, and identify the demonstratives within the linguistic prompts.

Table 2. Quantities of original, augmented, and synthesized datasets

Dataset	Speech-Only REs	Multimodal REs	Pointing-Only REs	Total
Original Dataset	2,152	575	7,681	**10,408**
Augmented Dataset	**6,550**	**2,296**	7,681	**16,527**
Synthesized Dataset	6,550	**7,928**	7,681	**22,159**

Data Augmentation. A data augmentation method was utilized to increase both the size and diversity of SCMRE. Specifically, we employed the Synonym Augmentation technique from the NLPAug library [42] to expand the range of multimodal and speech-only referring expressions. Each original expression was augmented to produce three similar expressions. To maintain semantic similarity to the ground truth MRE, we systemically reviewed and adjusted the augmented expressions by replacing less popular or informative words to align with our specific requirements. We then used BERT Score [69] to assess semantic similarity between augmented REs to human REs using the cosine similarity of their respective embedding vectors. We achieve an average BERT-Precision of 97.1%, BERT-Recall of 97.6%, and BERT-F1 97.3%. The dataset was expanded to include 16,527 events, comprising 2,296 multimodal REs, 6,550 speech-only REs, and 7,681 pointing-only REs. Both multimodal REs and speech-only REs obtained significant increases compared to their original counts (Table 2).

Data Synthesis. Despite the expansions resulting from augmentation, the dataset remained imbalanced, particularly in multimodal REs, potentially affecting the robustness of MRE generative model training. To augment the dataset with diverse multimodal samples, we synthesized individual pointing-only and speech-only samples to create new multimodal RE samples. This process involved identifying instances where both deictic gestures and speech were used to refer to the same object at the same spatial location. By aligning these expressions based on their shared focus object and position, we created composite samples that incorporate both modalities. Consequently, an additional 5,632 multimodal RE samples were incorporated, expanding the multimodal samples to 7,928 and increasing the total dataset size from 16,527 to 22,159, as shown in Table 2.

Prompt Engineering. We used Alpaca [61] as the basis for our MRE-generating model. Alpaca's Instruction-following models require structuring the data in a way that aligns with the model's architecture, incorporating instructions, inputs, and outputs consistently throughout the dataset. This involved concatenating a set of columns for both the input and output components as shown in Fig. 2. The input tuple includes configuration, relations, focus object, target object, and previous events, while the output tuple comprises the utterance, modality, demonstrative, and pointing location.

Data Splitting. For training experiments, we split the original and enhanced dataset into three subsets: a training set, validation set and a testing set. The training set, comprising 80% of the total data, was used to train models. The validation set, consisting of 20% of the total data, was reserved for evaluating the model's performance. The testing data, comprising 20% of the validation data, was used to assess the model's generalization ability on unseen data. Table 3 illustrates the resulting number of samples in each set for both original and enhanced datasets. To ensure an unbiased representation of the data, the datasets were shuffled and the division was performed randomly.

Table 3. Training, Validation, and Testing Sets

LLaMAModels	Train. Set	Valid. Set	Test. Set	Total
Original Dataset	8,325	1,665	417	10,407
Enhanced Dataset	17,727	3,545	887	22,159

4.2 Model Architecture

We used open-weight LLaMA models [62] to conduct parameter-efficient fine-tuning for generating contextually-correct and situationally-fluent referring expressions, including language and gesture. As illustrated in Fig. 3, the model takes a query, representing the target object O, its position P, relations R, configurations C, and previous events H; and outputs a descriptor tuple, $\langle Modality,$ $Utterance, Location, Demonstratives\rangle$. $M \in \{$Gesture, Language, Ensemble$\}$, U is a decoded sentence embedding, L is the location the gesture grounds to, and $D \in \{the, this, that\}$. Depending on the value of M, some of the other parameters may be empty by default. The query constitutes a description of the environment in which the agent is situated, along with an utterance prompting for a referring expression, and the model is optimized to generate output that approximates what a human would say in response to the prompt, while remaining situationally-grounded, fluent, natural, and referring to the correct object. The query $\langle O = $ RedBlock, $P = <X, Y, Z>$, $R = [$Right(RedBlock, Green-Block),...], $C = [<X', Y', Z'>, ...]$, $H = [$Put(YellowBlock),...$] \rangle$, represents the target object (the red block), the current spatial arrangement, associated relations and previous events. The corresponding output, $\langle$ multimodal, pick the red block, $<X'', Y'', Z''>$, the $\rangle$, contains the elements of the generated multimodal referring expression. Here, this output prompts the agent to utter "pick the red block" while pointing to location $<X'', Y'', Z''>$.

4.3 Learning Experiments

We fine-tuned multiple LLMs using Low-Rank Adapters (LoRA [20]) to enhance parameter and memory efficiency. LLaMA [62], developed by Meta AI, includes large-scale language models available in four parameter sizes: 7B, 13B, 33B, and 65B, and empirical studies indicate that even the LLaMA-13B model, with just $\frac{1}{10}$ of the parameters, surpasses GPT-3 (175B) [7] in most benchmark evaluations. For this study, we selected LLaMA-7B and LLaMA-13B as our foundational experimental models. To enable loading these models, fitting them into memory, and speeding up inference, we employed 8-bits quantization to represent weights with lower-precision data types. We use LLaMA 2 in this study, which for convenience is hereafter simply referred to as "LLaMA."

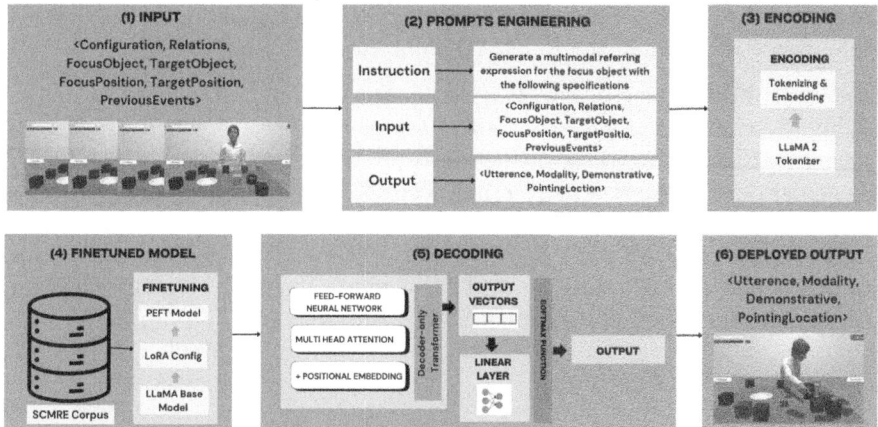

Fig. 3. The architecture of multimodal referring expressions generation model

Table 4. Hyper-parameters of Fine-tuning and Training Time for LLaMA Models

Models	Dataset	Learning rate	Epochs	Steps	Training Time (hh:mm:ss)
LLaMA-13B	8,325	3×10^{-4}	0.14	300	$3 : 54 : 29$
LLaMA-13B	17,727	3×10^{-4}	0.07	300	$6 : 49 : 15$
LLaMA-7B	17,727	2×10^{-5}	0.25	1,107	$9 : 00 : 35$
LLaMA-13B	17,727	3×10^{-4}	1	4,432	$48 : 30 : 10$

According to the code implementation of Alpaca-LoRA, we applied patches to the LoRA modules for the key, query, and value matrices, setting their rank to 8, a scaling factor to 16, a dropout rate of 0.05, and task type to `CAUSAL_LM`. This setting reduced the trainable parameters from $13,022,417,920$ parameters to $6,553,600$ parameters, allowing models to be processed on 2 NVIDIA RTX A6000-49GB GPUs.

We utilized a learning rate of 2×10^{-5} for LLaMA-7B and 3×10^{-4} for LLaMA-13B. The fine-tuning process included one LLaMA-7B model that was fine-tuned for $1,107$ steps, and three LLaMA-13B models were fine-tuned, two for 300 steps each, and one for $4,432$ steps. We applied *AdamW* as a stochastic optimization method with a global batch size of 4 and precision of $fp16$. We incorporated warm-up steps of 100 and validation steps of 100 for all models. The checkpoint with the best cross-entropy on development set was retained. Table 4 lists the hyper-parameters, training sets and training time that are related to each fine-tuned model.

4.4 Results

Loss Entropy. The loss curve for LLaMA-13B in Fig. 4a, trained for 4,430 steps (1 epoch), shows faster convergence and achieves lower loss values compared to LLaMA-7B in Fig. 4c, which was trained for 1,107 steps (0.25 epochs).

The fine-tuned LLaMA-13B reached training and evaluation losses of 0.517 and 0.515, respectively, while the LLaMA-7B obtained 0.576 and 0.575.

Perplexity. As depicted in Fig. 4b, d, the perplexity of both models decreases steadily as training progresses, indicating that both fine-tuned models are learning and improving their predictions over time. Nonetheless, the LLaMA-13B model demonstrates a more rapid decrease in perplexity compared to the LLaMA-7B model. The fine-tuned LLaMA-7B achieved training and evaluation perplexity values of 1.777 and 1.779, respectively, whereas the LLaMA-13B recorded values of 1.676 and 1.674. This suggests that LLaMA-13B converges faster and achieves better performance more quickly.

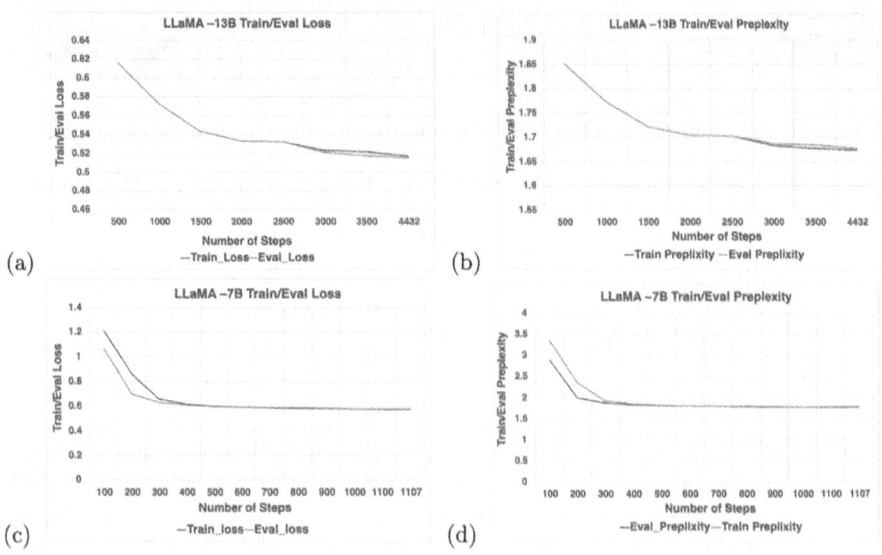

Fig. 4. The loss (a) and perplexity (b) of LLaMA-13B after one epoch of training. The loss (c) and perplexity (d) of LLaMA-7B after 1,107 steps of training

Comparisons Between Human and LLM Utilization of Referring Strategies. We tested the performance of fine-tuned Alpaca LoRA-based models—namely LLaMA-7B and LLaMA-13B—in integrating gesture and speech for referential behaviors across various parameterizations. Using datasets of 10K and 22K samples and varying training epochs and step counts (see Table 4), it was observed that the performance improved with larger datasets, models, and more training steps. The LLaMA-13B model, trained for one epoch on a test set of 887 samples, demonstrated the best performance in mixing modalities for generating referring expressions as depicted in Fig. 5d. It generates 40.61% of multimodal REs, 13.91% speech-only REs, and 45.48% of pointing-only REs, closely resembling human utilization of modalities when generating REs as in Fig. 5e: 43.55%, 22.29%, 34.16%, respectively. Nevertheless, pointing-only REs dominate with the tuned LLaMA-13B model trained on the original dataset. In Fig. 5a, they account for 96% of outputs. On the LLaMA-7B model (Fig. 5b), they account for 55.13%, and on the enhanced dataset with fewer steps (Fig. 5c), they account for at 54.31%.

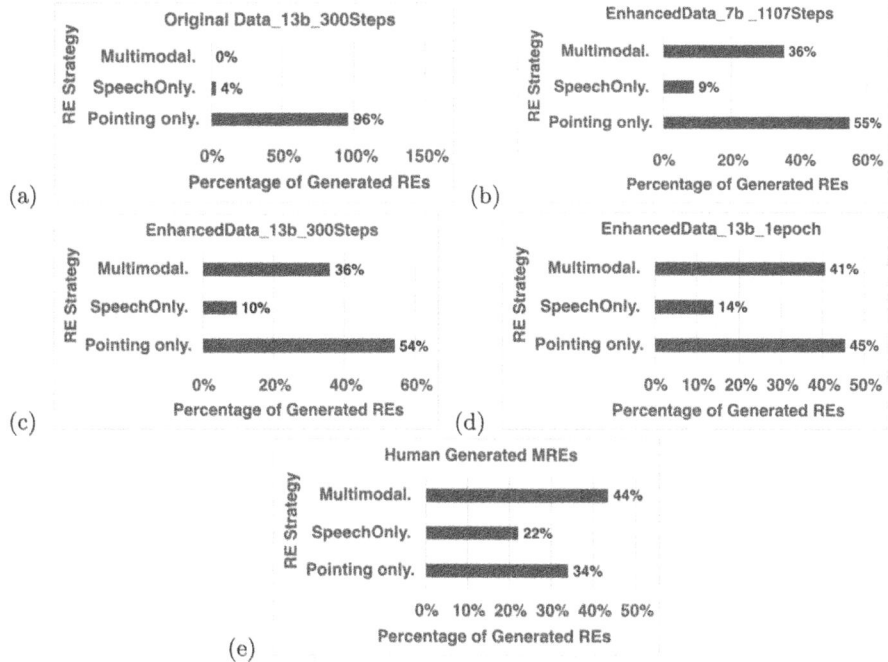

Fig. 5. Quantities of Human and LLM Generated Pointing, Linguistic and Multimodal Referring Expressions.

Similarity Between Human-Generated and LLM-Generated MREs. Successful generation results in a descriptor tuple that includes speech, demonstrative, gesture, and the target location for the specified target object and scene configuration. The multimodal generated description should maintain semantic similarity to the ground truth MRE. Semantic similarity must be attained at both the speech and position levels. The tuned LLaMA-13B model for one epoch surpasses all models in achieving similarity to human outputs on both the tuple and speech levels. It achieves an average BERT-Precision of 93%, BERT-Recall of 93%, BERT-F1 of 93%, and IoU of 72% on the tuple level, and an average BERT-Precision of 91%, BERT-Recall of 92%, and BERT-F1 of 91% on the speech level. Figure 6 depicts the distribution of similarity results of BERT-F1 between human-generated tuples and the dominant LLaMA-13B model-generated tuples. Approximately 350 samples exhibit similarity results ranging from 98% to 100%. The remaining low-similarity results occur due to the divergence in generated modalities compared to human samples.

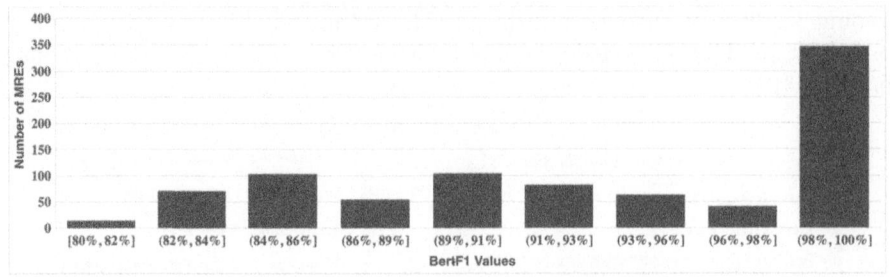

Fig. 6. The distribution of BERT-F1 similarity results between human-generated and LLM-generated MREs

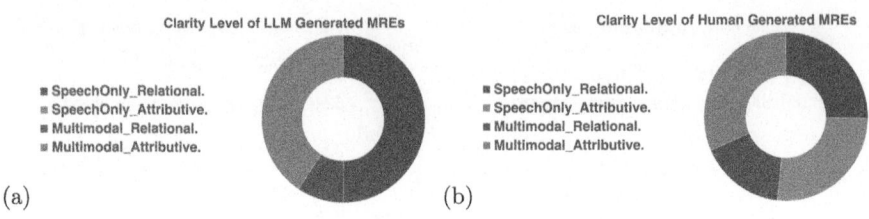

(a)   (b)

Fig. 7. Clarity level of the (a) LLM-generated and (b) human generated referring expressions

Clarity of Generated MREs. Based on the significant reduction in ambiguity levels observed when humans used co-gestural referring expressions (REs) while interacting with the IVA (see Sect. 5.1), we evaluate whether LLM-generated references maintain this level of clarity. We compared human and LLM-generated REs based on the information provided to communicate their intents. Figure 7 categorizes the combined strategies used by human and LLM to convey information about the target object. Humans utilized multimodal relational REs, multimodal attributive REs, speech-only relational REs, and speech-only attributive REs. The fine-tuned model utilized all the above strategies except speech-only attributive REs. This is a feature of the fine-tuned model, as using only object attributes without additional clarification often requires interlocutors to seek disambiguation, leading to inefficient communication of intent. Figure 8 presents examples of all combinations of RE strategies for both humans and the fine-tuned model when referring to the same target objects in identical situations.

Correctness of Generated Positions. The fine-tuned LLaMA-13B, trained for one epoch, achieved remarkable performance, with an average accuracy, precision, recall, and F1-score of 99% for correctly generated positions. Performance for LLaMA-13B with fewer steps and LLaMA-7B was notably lower, reaching 86% and 97% respective for the LLaMA-13B models, and 87% for LLaMA-7B, as shown by Fig. 9.

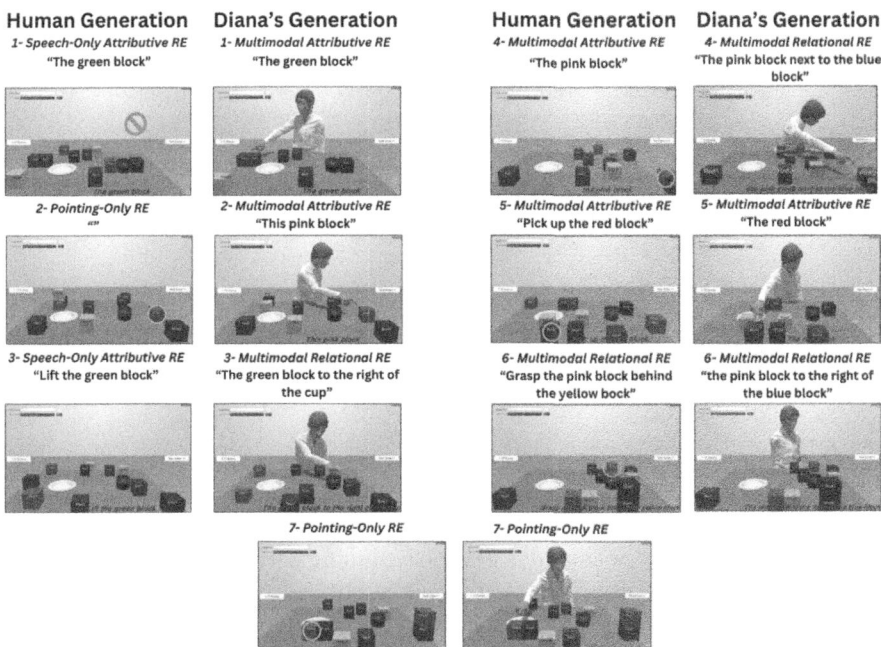

Fig. 8. Comparing human and IVA-generated REs for identical configurations.

5 Evaluation

To enable bidirectional communication between IVAs and humans using multimodal referring expressions, we previously proposed quantitative and qualitative metrics to assess if an IVA's non-verbal behavior generation aids human understanding. These metrics cover the following aspects: task completion efficiency, software reliability, understanding diverse communications, and meaningful content contribution by the agent as detailed in [1].

5.1 Automated Quantitative Evaluation

Using quantitative metrics in [1], we assessed *Multimodal Prompt Completion Efficiency* (MPCE) and *Linguistic Prompt Completion Efficiency* (LPCE) by measuring differences in target identification and task completion times for multimodal versus verbal-only REs. *Human Interpretation Efficiency of Machine Communication* (HIEMC) measured the time from the machine's reference generation to human target identification, and *Agent Pointing Success Rate* (APSR) tracked the success rate of the agent pointing to the target object. The subsequent analysis of SCMRE showed that multimodal referring expressions significantly reduce prompt ambiguity (p-value $< .001$, χ^2-test) and enhance IVA response efficiency (p-value $< .001$, ANOVA test; see Fig. 10a,b). This is evidenced by the IVA's ability to correctly identify referenced objects and

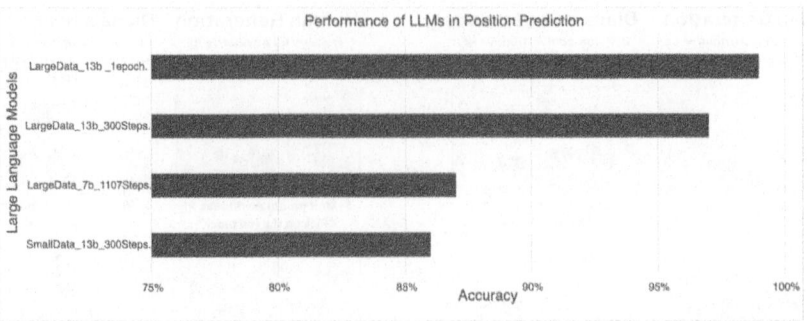

Fig. 9. The performance of LLaMA models in predicting positions of target objects

execute human prompts, demonstrating bidirectional communicative efficiency (see Fig. 10c, d). Additional quantitative metrics, along with their corresponding results, for evaluating the model's generation capability are detailed in Sect. 4.4. These results show the capacity of a generative model within HCI systems to contextually integrate gestures and language, thereby enhancing task-based interactions and facilitating more natural human-computer communication.

5.2   Human Based Evaluation

Alongside the automatic quantitative evaluations, we conducted two human-based experiments on Amazon Mechanical Turk (AMT) to assess the fluency and clarity of IVA and human-generated MREs. We proposed two criteria for evaluating the generated MREs: 1) A qualitative comparison of IVA with human-generated MREs, using *Machine References Fluency Rate* (MRFR), the rate of top-rated machine references based on third-party human judgments, and *Human References Fluency Rate* (HRFR), the rate of top-rated human references based on third-party human judgments, through preference ordering, 2) quantitative comparison of IVA with human-generated MREs, using *Machine Object Identification Success Rate* (MOISR), the rate of correctly identified objects (by machine), and *Human Object Identification Success Rate* (HOISR), the rate of correctly identified objects (by humans), through task completion [1]. Evaluation data and results are publicly available on GitHub[2].

Study Design. We selected 50 human MREs from the SCMRE dataset. These were compared with 50 REs generated by the virtual agent in the same situation when driven by a generative model trained over the human data. A total of 100 videos were collected. The referencing strategies examined for each of human and IVA generation are pointing only REs, relational speech-only REs, attributive speech-only REs, relational multimodal REs and attributive multimodal REs. Videos were used in a set of AMT human intelligence tasks (HITs), wherein workers rated 1 video for *both* fluency and clarity, including 1 machine generated

---

[2] https://github.com/nadahass/Human-based-Evaluation-MREG.git.

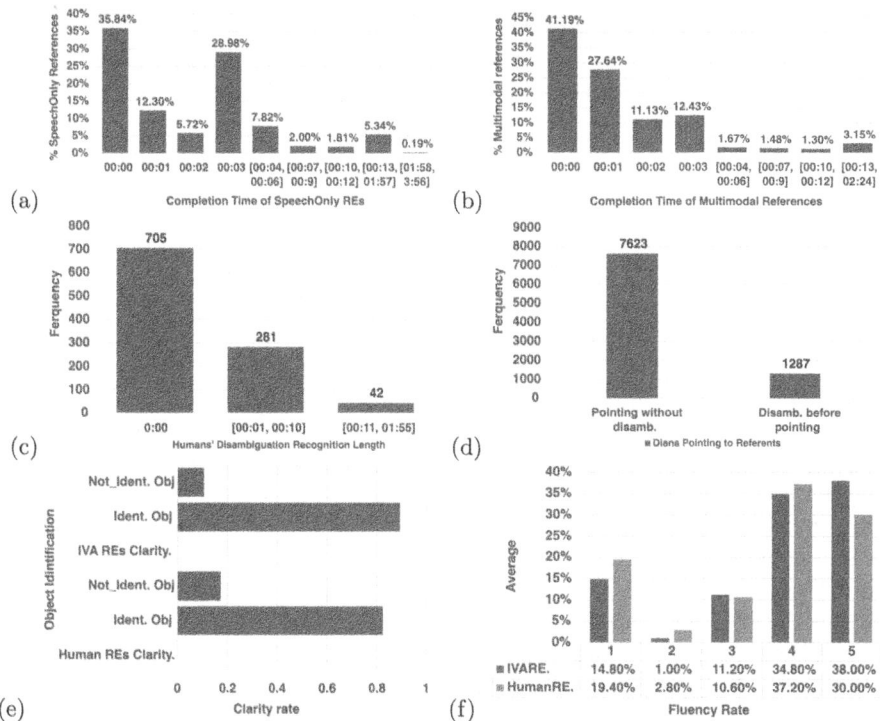

Fig. 10. Diana's completion time of (a) Speech Event (LPCE); (b) Multimodal Event (MPCE); (c) Human Interpretation Efficiency of Machine Communication (HIEMC); (d) Agent Pointing Success Rate (APSR); (e) Machine Object Identification Success Rate (MOISR) and Human Object Identification Success Rate (HOISR), and (f) Machine References Fluency Rate (MRFR) and Human References Fluency Rate (HRFR)

RE or 1 human RE, for a total of 100 HITs. Workers first identified the target object mentioned, then, they rate the fluency of each video description on a Likert scale (5 = best, 1 = worst). Each video was completed by 10 workers, for a total of 1,000 individual judgments. We recruited workers fluent in English between 18 and 60 years old. They were given 1 h per task and were compensated $0.75 per HIT.

Results and Analysis. Upon analyzing 1,000 assignments, it was found that 300 were rejected for not following instructions or attempting to game the system, and were subsequently republished. Workers, with an average lifetime approval rate of 100%, invested approximately 30 min on average to complete the tasks, indicating thorough engagement. The accuracy rates of identifying objects referred to by humans and IVA were compared to the intended objects in the dataset. As shown in Fig. 10e, the overall HOISR and MOISR were 82.6% and 89.4%, respectively, demonstrating that the clarity level of IVA-generated

MREs strongly competes with human-generated MREs (p-value $< 2.2e - 16$ using Pearson's χ^2-test [49]). For the fluency task, Fig. 10f shows MRFR of 73% and HRFR of 67% , with ratings at "4" and "5". These results indicate that both human-generated and IVA-generated MREs are perceived similarly in terms of and fluency (p-value $= 0.5529$ using Pearson's χ^2-test). This suggests that IVAs are capable of generating REs of comparable quality to those of humans.

6   Conclusion

Given the advancements in interactive agents, there is a growing expectation that they will contribute to interactions in ways that resemble human behavior, rather than just performing tasks. This study showcases significant advancements in multimodal HCI capabilities, specifically in bridging the gap between human and IVA communication capabilities in generating referring expressions. The developed SCMRE corpus, coupled with the fine-tuned generative model and comprehensive evaluation framework, enables more effective and naturalistic interactions between humans and IVAs. Our findings demonstrate a means by which IVAs can close the gap with human in generating contextually appropriate multimodal referring expressions, which is one crucial capacity for more naturalistic HCI. Future work will focus on refining the IVA's ability to handle more complex and bidirectional interaction scenarios, enhancing real-time processing capabilities, and integrating these models into diverse application domains. Further research is also needed to explore long-term user adaptation and the IVA's ability to learn from ongoing interactions.

Acknowledgments. We express our gratitude to our reviewers for their valuable comments. Additionally, we extend our thanks to our participants for their contributions in providing the SCMRE data.

References

1. Alalyani, N., Krishnaswamy, N.: A methodology for evaluating multimodal referring expression generation for embodied virtual agents. In: Companion Publication of the 25th International Conference on Multimodal Interaction, pp. 164–173 (2023)
2. Alayrac, J.B., et al.: Flamingo: a visual language model for few-shot learning. In: Advances in Neural Information Processing Systems, vol. 35, pp. 23716–23736 (2022)
3. Alayrac, J.B., et al.: Self-supervised multimodal versatile networks. In: Advances in Neural Information Processing Systems, vol. 33, pp. 25–37 (2020)
4. Banerjee, S., Lavie, A.: Meteor: an automatic metric for MT evaluation with improved correlation with human judgments. In: Proceedings of the ACL Workshop on Intrinsic and Extrinsic Evaluation Measures for Machine Translation And/Or Summarization, pp. 65–72 (2005)
5. Belz, A., Gatt, A.: Intrinsic vs. extrinsic evaluation measures for referring expression generation. In: Proceedings of ACL-08: HLT, Short Papers, pp. 197–200 (2008)

6. Bender, E.M., Koller, A.: Climbing towards NLU: on meaning, form, and understanding in the age of data. In: Proceedings of the 58th Annual Meeting of the Association for Computational Linguistics, pp. 5185–5198 (2020)
7. Brown, T., et al.: Language models are few-shot learners. In: Advances in Neural Information Processing Systems, vol. 33, pp. 1877–1901 (2020)
8. Chen, Y., et al.: Yourefit: embodied reference understanding with language and gesture. In: Proceedings of the IEEE/CVF International Conference on Computer Vision, pp. 1385–1395 (2021)
9. Chen, Z., Wang, P., Ma, L., Wong, K.Y.K., Wu, Q.: Cops-ref: a new dataset and task on compositional referring expression comprehension. In: Proceedings of the IEEE/CVF Conference on Computer Vision and Pattern Recognition, pp. 10086–10095 (2020)
10. De Vries, H., Strub, F., Chandar, S., Pietquin, O., Larochelle, H., Courville, A.: Guesswhat?! Visual object discovery through multi-modal dialogue. In: Proceedings of the IEEE Conference on Computer Vision and Pattern Recognition, pp. 5503–5512 (2017)
11. Dice, L.R.: Measures of the amount of ecologic association between species. Ecology **26**(3), 297–302 (1945)
12. Doğan, F.I., Kalkan, S., Leite, I.: Learning to generate unambiguous spatial referring expressions for real-world environments. In: 2019 IEEE/RSJ International Conference on Intelligent Robots and Systems (IROS), pp. 4992–4999. IEEE (2019)
13. Fang, R., Doering, M., Chai, J.Y.: Embodied collaborative referring expression generation in situated human-robot interaction. In: Proceedings of the Tenth Annual ACM/IEEE International Conference on Human-Robot Interaction, pp. 271–278 (2015)
14. Foster, M.E.: Enhancing human-computer interaction with embodied conversational agents. In: Stephanidis, C. (ed.) UAHCI 2007, Part II. LNCS, vol. 4555, pp. 828–837. Springer, Heidelberg (2007). https://doi.org/10.1007/978-3-540-73281-5_91
15. Gatt, A., Belz, A., Kow, E.: The tuna-reg challenge 2009: overview and evaluation results. Assoc. Comput. Linguist. (2009)
16. Gatt, A., Van Deemter, K.: Lexical choice and conceptual perspective in the generation of plural referring expressions. J. Logic Lang. Inform. **16**(4), 423–443 (2007)
17. Goldin-Meadow, S.: The role of gesture in communication and thinking. Trends Cogn. Sci. **3**(11), 419–429 (1999)
18. Gorniak, P., Roy, D.: Grounded semantic composition for visual scenes. J. Artif. Intell. Res. **21**, 429–470 (2004)
19. Han, L., Zheng, T., Xu, L., Fang, L.: OccuSeg: occupancy-aware 3D instance segmentation. In: Proceedings of the IEEE/CVF Conference on Computer Vision and Pattern Recognition, pp. 2940–2949 (2020)
20. Hu, E.J., et al.: LoRa: low-rank adaptation of large language models. arXiv preprint arXiv:2106.09685 (2021)
21. Islam, M.M., Mirzaiee, R., Gladstone, A., Green, H., Iqbal, T.: Caesar: An embodied simulator for generating multimodal referring expression datasets. In: Advances in Neural Information Processing Systems, vol. 35, pp. 21001–21015 (2022)
22. Kalinowska, A., Pilarski, P.M., Murphey, T.D.: Embodied communication: how robots and people communicate through physical interaction. Annu. Rev. Control Robot. Auton. Syst. **6**, 205–232 (2023)
23. Krahmer, E., van der Sluis, I.: A new model for generating multimodal referring expressions. In: Proceedings of the ENLG, vol. 3, pp. 47–54 (2003)

24. Kranstedt, A., Kopp, S., Wachsmuth, I.: MurML: a multimodal utterance representation markup language for conversational agents. In: AAMAS'02 Workshop Embodied Conversational Agents-Let's Specify and Evaluate Them! (2002)
25. Krishnaswamy, N., Alalyani, N.: Embodied multimodal agents to bridge the understanding gap. In: Proceedings of the First Workshop on Bridging Human–Computer Interaction and Natural Language Processing, pp. 41–46 (2021)
26. Krishnaswamy, N., Alalyani, N.: Embodied multimodal agents to bridge the understanding gap. In: Proceedings of the First Workshop on Bridging Human–Computer Interaction and Natural Language Processing, pp. 41–46. Association for Computational Linguistics, Online (2021)
27. Krishnaswamy, N., et al.: Diana's world: a situated multimodal interactive agent. In: Proceedings of the AAAI Conference on Artificial Intelligence, vol. 34, pp. 13618–13619 (2020)
28. Krishnaswamy, N., et al.: Communicating and acting: understanding gesture in simulation semantics. In: Proceedings of the 12th International Conference on Computational Semantics (IWCS)-Short papers (2017)
29. Krishnaswamy, N., Pickard, W., Cates, B., Blanchard, N., Pustejovsky, J.: The voxworld platform for multimodal embodied agents. In: Proceedings of the Thirteenth Language Resources and Evaluation Conference, pp. 1529–1541 (2022)
30. Krishnaswamy, N., Pustejovsky, J.: Voxsim: a visual platform for modeling motion language. In: Proceedings of COLING 2016, the 26th International Conference on Computational Linguistics: System Demonstrations, pp. 54–58 (2016)
31. Krishnaswamy, N., Pustejovsky, J.: An evaluation framework for multimodal interaction. In: Proceedings of the Eleventh International Conference on Language Resources and Evaluation (LREC 2018) (2018)
32. Krishnaswamy, N., Pustejovsky, J.: Generating a novel dataset of multimodal referring expressions. In: Proceedings of the 13th International Conference on Computational Semantics-Short Papers, pp. 44–51 (2019)
33. Krishnaswamy, N., Pustejovsky, J.: The role of embodiment and simulation in evaluating hci: Experiments and evaluation. In: International Conference on Human-Computer Interaction, pp. 220–232 (2021)
34. Krishnaswamy, N., Pustejovsky, J.: Affordance embeddings for situated language understanding. Front. Artif. Intell. **5**, 774752 (2022)
35. Kunze, L., Williams, T., Hawes, N., Scheutz, M.: Spatial referring expression generation for HRI: algorithms and evaluation framework. In: 2017 AAAI Fall Symposium Series (2017)
36. Levenshtein, V.I., et al.: Binary codes capable of correcting deletions, insertions, and reversals. In: Soviet Phys. Doklady, vol. 10, pp. 707–710. Soviet Union (1966)
37. Li, J., Li, D., Savarese, S., Hoi, S.: Blip-2: bootstrapping language-image pretraining with frozen image encoders and large language models. arXiv preprint arXiv:2301.12597 (2023)
38. Li, L.H., Yatskar, M., Yin, D., Hsieh, C.J., Chang, K.W.: VisualBERT: a simple and performant baseline for vision and language. arXiv preprint arXiv:1908.03557 (2019)
39. Li, X., Guo, D., Liu, H., Sun, F.: Reve-CE: remote embodied visual referring expression in continuous environment. IEEE Robot. Autom. Lett. **7**(2), 1494–1501 (2022)
40. Lin, C.Y., Hovy, E.: Automatic evaluation of summaries using n-gram co-occurrence statistics. In: Proceedings of the 2003 Human Language Technology Conference of the North American Chapter of the Association for Computational Linguistics, pp. 150–157 (2003)

41. Lu, J., Batra, D., Parikh, D., Lee, S.: ViLBERT: pretraining task-agnostic visi-olinguistic representations for vision-and-language tasks. In: Advances in Neural Information Processing Systems, vol. 32 (2019)
42. Ma, E.: NLP augmentation (2019). https://github.com/makcedward/nlpaug
43. Magassouba, A., Sugiura, K., Kawai, H.: Multimodal attention branch network for perspective-free sentence generation. In: Conference on Robot Learning, pp. 76–85. PMLR (2020)
44. Manning, C., Surdeanu, M., Bauer, J., Finkel, J., Bethard, S., McClosky, D.: The Stanford CoreNLP natural language processing toolkit. In: Proceedings of 52nd Annual Meeting of the Association for Computational Linguistics: System Demon-strations, pp. 55–60. Association for Computational Linguistics, Baltimore, Mary-land (2014)
45. Mao, J., Huang, J., Toshev, A., Camburu, O., Yuille, A.L., Murphy, K.: Generation and comprehension of unambiguous object descriptions. In: Proceedings of the IEEE Conference on Computer Vision and Pattern Recognition, pp. 11–20 (2016)
46. McNeill, D.: So you think gestures are nonverbal? Psychol. Rev. **92**(3), 350 (1985)
47. Papineni, K., Roukos, S., Ward, T., Zhu, W.J.: Bleu: a method for automatic evaluation of machine translation. In: Proceedings of the 40th Annual Meeting of the Association for Computational Linguistics, pp. 311–318 (2002)
48. Passonneau, R.: Measuring agreement on set-valued items (MASI) for semantic and pragmatic annotation (2006)
49. Pearson, K.: X. on the criterion that a given system of deviations from the probable in the case of a correlated system of variables is such that it can be reasonably supposed to have arisen from random sampling. The London, Edinburgh, and Dublin Philos. Mag. J. Sci. **50**(302), 157–175 (1900)
50. Pustejovsky, J., Krishnaswamy, N.: Embodied human-computer interactions through situated grounding. In: Proceedings of the 20th ACM International Con-ference on Intelligent Virtual Agents, pp. 1–3 (2020)
51. Pustejovsky, J., Krishnaswamy, N.: Situated meaning in multimodal dialogue: human-robot and human-computer interactions. Traitement Automatique des Langues **61**(3), 17–41 (2020)
52. Pustejovsky, J., Krishnaswamy, N.: Embodied human computer interaction. KI-Künstliche Intelligenz **35**(3), 307–327 (2021)
53. Pustejovsky, J., Krishnaswamy, N.: Multimodal semantics for affordances and actions. In: Kurosu, M. (ed.) HCII 2022. LNCS, vol. 13302, pp. 137–160. Springer, Cham (2022). https://doi.org/10.1007/978-3-031-05311-5_9
54. Qi, Y., et al.: Reverie: remote embodied visual referring expression in real indoor environments. In: Proceedings of the IEEE/CVF Conference on Computer Vision and Pattern Recognition, pp. 9982–9991 (2020)
55. Radford, A., et al.: Learning transferable visual models from natural language supervision. In: International Conference on Machine Learning, pp. 8748–8763. PMLR (2021)
56. Schauerte, B., Fink, G.A.: Focusing computational visual attention in multi-modal human-robot interaction. In: International Conference on Multimodal Interfaces and the Workshop on Machine Learning for Multimodal Interaction, pp. 1–8 (2010)
57. Schauerte, B., Richarz, J., Fink, G.A.: Saliency-based identification and recognition of pointed-at objects. In: 2010 IEEE/RSJ International Conference on Intelligent Robots and Systems, pp. 4638–4643. IEEE (2010)
58. Shridhar, M., Mittal, D., Hsu, D.: Ingress: interactive visual grounding of referring expressions. Int. J. Robot. Res. **39**(2–3), 217–232 (2020)

59. Shukla, D., Erkent, O., Piater, J.: Probabilistic detection of pointing directions for human-robot interaction. In: 2015 International Conference on Digital Image Computing: Techniques and Applications (DICTA), pp. 1–8. IEEE (2015)
60. Shukla, D., Erkent, Ö., Piater, J.: A multi-view hand gesture rgb-d dataset for human-robot interaction scenarios. In: 2016 25th IEEE International Symposium on Robot and Human Interactive Communication (RO-MAN), pp. 1084–1091. IEEE (2016)
61. Taori, R., et al.: Stanford alpaca: an instruction-following llama model (2023). https://github.com/tatsu-lab/stanford_alpaca
62. Touvron, H., et al.: Llama: open and efficient foundation language models (2023). arXiv preprint arXiv:2302.13971 (2023)
63. Van Deemter, K.: Generating referring expressions that involve gradable properties. Comput. Linguist. **32**(2), 195–222 (2006)
64. Viethen, J., Dale, R.: Algorithms for generating referring expressions: do they do what people do? In: Proceedings of the Fourth International Natural Language Generation Conference, pp. 63–70 (2006)
65. Viethen, J., Dale, R.: The use of spatial relations in referring expression generation. In: Proceedings of the Fifth International Natural Language Generation Conference, pp. 59–67 (2008)
66. Wang, I., Smith, J., Ruiz, J.: Exploring virtual agents for augmented reality. In: Proceedings of the 2019 CHI Conference on Human Factors in Computing Systems, pp. 1–12 (2019)
67. Wang, Z., Yu, J., Yu, A.W., Dai, Z., Tsvetkov, Y., Cao, Y.: SimVLM: simple visual language model pretraining with weak supervision. arXiv preprint arXiv:2108.10904 (2021)
68. Xu, M., et al.: A survey of resource-efficient LLM and multimodal foundation models. arXiv preprint arXiv:2401.08092 (2024)
69. Zhang, T., Kishore, V., Wu, F., Weinberger, K.Q., Artzi, Y.: Bertscore: evaluating text generation with BERT. In: International Conference on Learning Representations (2019)
70. Zhu, L., Yang, Y.: ActBERT: learning global-local video-text representations. In: Proceedings of the IEEE/CVF Conference on Computer Vision and Pattern Recognition, pp. 8746–8755 (2020)

Ethics in the Use of Artificial Intelligence in the Media

Deniz Çupi[✉]

Faculty of Human Sciences and Law, Ismail Qemali University, Vlorë, Albania
dxhoga@yahoo.com, deniz.cupi@univlora.edu.al

Abstract. The use of artificial intelligence and robotics in the media is no longer a novelty and is rapidly entering all areas of life, including the media. Now, a robot can replace the news anchor, the moderator of TV shows, and more. Artificial intelligence can write the text of a news story, select news sources, and also edit the footage of a television news report. Is it ethical for the public to be informed by a robot or artificial intelligence machine? To what extent is it moral and acceptable to use artificial intelligence technology and robotics in the production and serving of news content? A declaration of authorship, indicating that the content was created by artificial intelligence or a journalist, would be one of the ethical solutions, but not everyone can be transparent and conscientious. The use of artificial intelligence also brings a series of ethical and moral implications to the media, which you need to anticipate so that tomorrow does not return to us as a boomerang. This urgent need has prompted various governance proposals, including the "OECD Recommendation on Artificial Intelligence" in 2019. In 2022, the United Nations member states published the "Principles for Ethical Use of Artificial Intelligence in the United Nations System." In 2021, UNESCO also published the "Recommendation on the Ethics of Artificial Intelligence," and the EU has established the European Group on Ethics in Science and New Technologies. But these initiatives need to extend to lower levels of governance as well, and the establishment of ethics committees on the use of artificial intelligence in media and beyond should be undertaken by every state.

Keywords: AI in social media · artificial intelligence · media · ethics · authorship · ethics committees

1 Introduction

Nothing is inherently bad; it depends on how and for what purpose it is used. AI technology is increasingly emerging as a transformative force, reshaping industries and offering unprecedented opportunities for innovation. However, its integration into various aspects of society, especially in the media, raises various ethical issues. Media in the era of AI includes ethical issues of morality, accountability, transparency, privacy, bias, and the spread of news through algorithms, bringing about a broader societal impact of media in directions predetermined by AI (Jones et al. 2022). While the dimensions of AI

H. Degen and S. Ntoa (Eds.): HCII 2024, LNCS 15382, pp. 23–37, 2024.
https://doi.org/10.1007/978-3-031-76827-9_2

have attracted the attention of academics, policymakers, industry leaders, and the public, sparking a broad discussion on the balance that should exist between technological development and human values, in a small and economically weak country like Albania, the use of AI systems is still in its early stages. If one day these technologies become widespread, and in countries with fragile democracies like Albania, where media ethics leave much to be desired, the use of AI in the media becomes truly dangerous for society. Setting the rules for the game is an immediate necessity. The media system in Albania is characterized by problems stemming from a lack of transparency in ownership and media financing. Owners' interventions in editorial content are a common phenomenon, making it difficult to create a common front from the media community to defend ethical standards (Londo 2023a).

The implementation of some ethical principles in the use of AI is urgent (Fernohlz et al. 2024), such as declaring the authorship of every news item if it is prepared by AI or a human author. Following this, responsibility for reporting, respect for privacy, security, transparency, non-discrimination, and the promotion of human values begin. Despite the statements of media leaders and the growing consensus, studies show that (Stahl 2021) there are still differences in the interpretation and application of these principles by different media outlets. Ensuring responsible development and application of AI requires a multidisciplinary approach with expertise from fields such as computer science, economics, philosophy, ethics, jurisprudence, sociology, and psychology.

2 Literature

The argumentation of the issues is based on the literature, on researchers and journalists who have addressed the use of artificial intelligence in the media, such as Michael Kearns, Aaron Roth, and Nicholas Diakopoulos, who examine the intersection of AI and journalism, weighing the ethical implications of producing and distributing algorithmic news. Other authors, such as Müller, have addressed the ethical issues of using robotics in the media, while Alice Marwick and Rebecca Lewis have addressed the ethical implications of using AI and manipulating the media through it. The executive steps of the implementation of ethics in AI have been reviewed, starting with the reports and guidelines prepared by the IEEE Global Initiative and the UNESCO report "World Trends in Freedom of Expression and Media Development." In addition to the Code of Ethics of the Society of Professional Journalists (SPJ), the AI4People Ethical Framework for a Good AI Society is an Act of the European Parliament.

2.1 The Issues Addressed

The use of artificial intelligence in news production and distribution is advancing more rapidly than we expected. The establishment of ethics committees at local governance levels by each state is imperative. The use of artificial intelligence also raises a series of ethical and moral implications in the media.

Is it ethical for the public to be informed by a robot or artificial intelligence machine?

To what extent is it moral and acceptable to use artificial intelligence technology and robotics in the production and serving of news content? A declaration of authorship, indicating that the content was created by artificial intelligence or a journalist, would be one of the ethical solutions.

What are the legal mechanisms that ensure transparency in authorship and news sources?

3 Methodology

In this study, a qualitative and quantitative research method was used. The treatment of this topic is based on media monitoring, focusing on the issues raised as well as on a survey of 50 professional journalists conducted by the author. A comparison is made between the development of automatic journalism in the Albanian media and those used in other countries or international media. The work done and the inclusion of the use of AI in the code of ethics in European countries, as well as the implementation of this code by the Albanian media, Furthermore, this study uses the qualitative method of in-depth interviews with 10 respondents and thematic analysis to present the findings of the study.

4 Results

News organizations in many developed countries are increasingly using new ways of producing news through automated journalism and are facing new challenges related to technology (Thorne & Vlachos 2018). The relationship between journalists and automation can change significantly in different sociocultural contexts, which is why it is necessary to study how automated journalism affects media freedom, especially when it raises legal and ethical issues. While the impact of automated journalism on media freedom in many Western democratic countries is questionable, it is essential to examine its impact on media freedom in authoritarian and post-authoritarian regimes or in transitional countries such as Albania, which continues to have a fragile democracy. This analysis is necessary to prepare Albanian journalists for the practice of automated journalism and to develop a regulatory framework that can recognize the changes brought about by automation in journalism. According to the survey carried out in the framework of this study, 26.7% of the journalists surveyed stated that AI-generated news is often published in the media; 20% responded to the question of whether the media has published AI-generated news more than once; and another 20% affirm that the media has never used AI-generated news (Fig. 1).

The survey of journalists shows a range of perspectives on the frequency with which websites publish news generated by Artificial Intelligence (AI). 36.7% of journalists believe that AI-generated news is published frequently on websites. This indicates that a significant portion of journalists observe a high usage of AI in online news content. 26.7% of journalists think that websites have published AI-generated news more than once, suggesting a moderate level of AI content without it being overly dominant. Another 26.7% of journalists reported that websites have not published AI-generated news at all. This demonstrates that for a notable portion of journalists, AI-generated news has yet to make a noticeable impact on certain websites. Lastly, 9.9% of journalists indicated that websites have published AI-generated news only once. This shows a minimal level of AI-generated news exposure for some journalists. These results suggest that there's

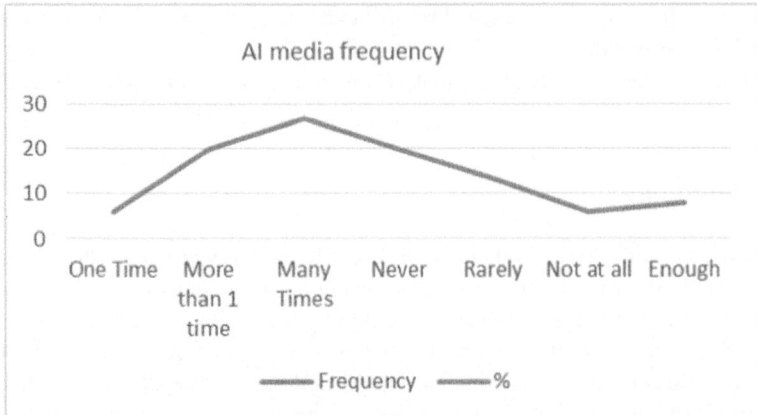

Fig. 1. AI media frequency

a considerable variance in how journalists perceive the adoption of AI-generated news across websites, with some reporting frequent use and others noting little to no AI-generated news (Fig. 2).

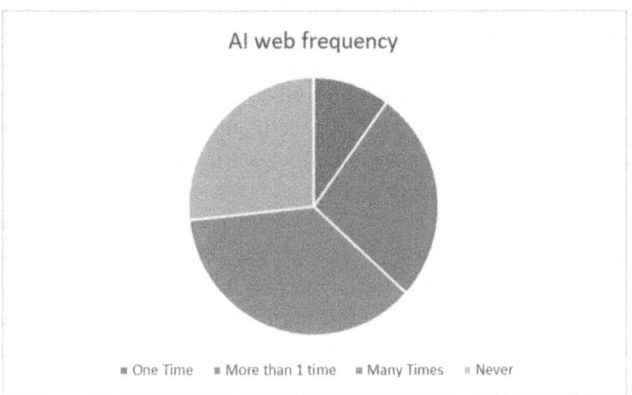

Fig. 2. AI web frequency

36.7% of the journalists surveyed said that AI had only been used once on television. This refers to Euronews TV, where a robotic presenter presented a news edition, and this happened only once. Here we see that Albanian journalists still cannot distinguish the use of AI systems from the use of robotics. Meanwhile, another 30% said that AI systems had been used in the media more than once, and 20% of them said that they had not been used at all. This percentage suggests a segment of journalists perceives little to no use of AI in media, which could reflect either limited exposure or knowledge gaps. Regarding the use of AI through social media, the distribution of the percentage of journalists surveyed is clearer, with 56.7% stating that AI has been used many times. This high percentage underscores a recognition of AI's significant role in social media platforms, whether through content recommendation algorithms, automated moderation, or other applications. As for the question of which social networks are used the most, 30% say that TikTok is used the most, followed by Facebook with 26.7% and Instagram with 20%, and less Twitter. This distribution aligns with broader trends showing TikTok's rapid growth and AI-driven content recommendations, as well as the established roles of Facebook and Instagram in social media. There are also journalists who answer that AI systems are not used at all on social networks, with 16.7%. This may again reflect differing interpretations of AI's presence or an awareness gap (Fig. 3).

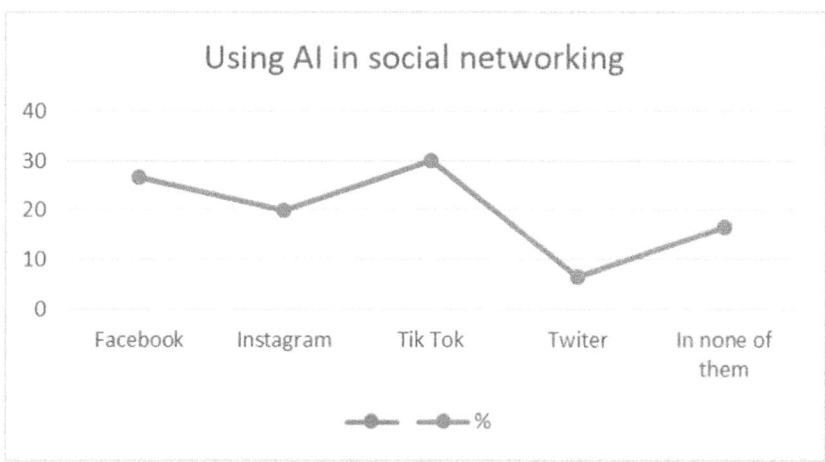

Fig. 3. Using AI in social media networking

These results show that Albanian journalists have a low understanding of the use of AI systems by the media, as well as ambiguity and confusion. Overall, this survey data points to a landscape where AI-generated content is being integrated into different forms of media at different rates. While social media platforms appear to be embracing AI more quickly, traditional media such as television and news websites are adopting it at a slower pace. In the in-depth interviews, five journalists expressed that AI is not yet widely used in the media. "In Albania, AI is used in the field of medicine, and the government has issued tenders for the introduction of AI systems in the provision of government services through the E-Albania system," says journalist Rovena Rrozhani (2023). Meanwhile, TOP News presenter Dafina Hysa (2024) explains that AI systems are used in documentaries for processing TV, video, and photo material, but under the full supervision of journalists. Web journalist Elberta Spaho (2024) expresses that in the case of the murder of Liridona Ademi, where the suspected perpetrator is the spouse, videos of the victim were taken from her Instagram account and the voice was modified. In this video, she expresses regret for the orphaned children. The video circulated on social networks for only 1 h, then was deleted by the authors due to the protests of the audience on the networks. "It was not professional work; it was noticeable that the lip movement belonged to other words," says Spaho (2024). Another journalist, Blerina Goce (2024), remembers only one case when a portal published inappropriate photos for the blogger Zh. Lekatari, generated by AI. Journalist Rivjera Dedja (2024) expresses that in 2023, the news spread that a video implicating two TV presenters with a criminal gang was circulating on the Sky platform. This information spread on social media, but soon other information was provided that the images were created with artificial intelligence systems. These are the only concrete cases brought up by journalists regarding the use of AI systems in Albania. So, among the 50 journalists, 25 of them express that one of the reasons for the non-introduction of AI in the Albanian media is the lack of sufficient budgets of the owners to purchase AI systems. In addition, 27 of them state that the generation familiar with AI systems has not yet been sufficiently trained to use them extensively in the media, while 3% express that they do not know the reason.

Although Albanian journalists may not be familiar with the use of AI, the media in which they work and especially their social networks are forced to submit to the developments of information technology and especially the use of AI. Thus, AI systems now play a central role in social media. They are used to index, search, and exploit social media content. Text, images, and videos on social media, along with the information they contain, are analyzed using AI (Draper & Joseph 2019). Most social media companies have a business model based on targeted advertising. AI is used through algorithms to profile advertisements and distribute them to audiences according to recommendation systems (Anonymous, Business Wire 2017). AI is also being used to monitor, filter, and remove content that violates the company's policies and threatens its image (Christodoulou et al. 2021). In addition, through algorithms used in social media, AI is helping to gather opinions and discover public trends (Buernfil et al. 2019).

5   Media Challenges in the Age of Artificial Intelligence

Artificial intelligence is transforming the news media. At its simplest, AI is used to create stories from data (automated journalism). Journalists input information, and AI constructs the news story, adhering to the 5 Ws (who, what, where, when, and why) and the structure of the news. This helps online journalists keep up with the pace of news production. For example, on a local news site, a journalist may need to publish a new story every 10 min, while on a national or international media outlet, the pace is even faster. This workflow is designed to keep the audience's attention. The journalist gains time to work on a story that requires more effort and time to write while simultaneously publishing "cheap news" written by AI on the website (Paris & Donovan 2019). In addition to helping journalists in online media, AI also helps television journalists write simple news scripts, collect data, analyze large datasets, track news, identify the most followed news stories throughout the day, produce and distribute videos, visualize data, and automatically fact-check (Diakopoulos 2019a).

AI can be used both to generate fresh news and to detect and eliminate fake news. Potentially, these AI applications can enhance the capacity of journalists and newsrooms and increase audience engagement. But some of their uses also raise ethical questions. Let us consider the simplest and most common case of AI writing a news story. The text has no author's name and no disclaimer that the news was written by artificial intelligence. But can the news be dehumanized and made fit for human consumption? "Algorithms lack animus; they are inert," said Diakopoulos (2019b). Another concern is that automated journalism, which includes the collection and analysis of data and the production of stories, does not necessarily adhere to journalistic values. Algorithms can be biased, they can deceive, and audiences can draw false conclusions (even if there are correlations). The rights of subjects used as sources may be violated, and the rights of parties involved in the automatically generated event may be harmed (Zhow et al. 2023). The dehumanization of news leads to the dehumanization of news sources. Thus, AI does not support journalism but harms it. Studies show that several standards that are the foundations of journalism, such as impartiality, accuracy, independence, humanism, and accountability, are violated.

Transparency, an important value in journalism, is also at risk. *"What animates algorithms are the people who design, develop, operate, and manage them. It is people who define, measure, and sample data to feed and train algorithms. And it is people who consume and are impacted by algorithmic outputs and decisions,"* said Diakopoulos (2019c). The names of the people who design the systems of automated journalism and the algorithms are not published anywhere; the philosophical and ethical principles on which the content is based are not published; and who and on what ethical-moral parameters the network of these systems is built is not published. AI systems are built by people. In any case, it is humans who are in charge (Kaur et al. 2023). AI systems are built by humans; AI produces content that is consumed by humans. So, humans are still at the center (Anderson et al. 2018). Artificial intelligence systems do not disclose the methodology of data collection and analysis; on the contrary, with the amount of information they have, they can control the world (Beckett 2019). But these software systems have owners like any other material or intellectual asset, and they certainly reflect the ethical and moral principles and interests of their owners. Their personal interests do not necessarily represent the interests of the public; in the worst case, they may even undermine public interest. Ethical-moral principles and the interests of the broader public are balanced on very fragile boundaries (Chen, Chekam 2021).

Another concern is that AI could bring "poverty" to journalism (Latar 2015). Small newsrooms currently cannot afford expensive AI systems. As a result, larger newsrooms may gain a competitive advantage by using AI technology to generate news that competes in quantity and timeliness with news generated by small local newsrooms but produced by journalists themselves. At the same time, an AI system can produce much more news than a human or a newsroom (Liu 2017). Another issue is hyperpersonalization; risks may arise from the application of AI and machine learning to generate personalized news sources and even news stories for users according to their preferences and beliefs (Drunen et al. 2019). The personalization of news sources and information carries the risk of trapping individuals in "filter bubbles" (Jansen, Brey et al. 2019). This is particularly worrisome when their knowledge is limited; these narrowly personalized news stories only confirm these individuals' biases. The influence of media organizations on public polarization and radicalization has always been a concern (Van Stekelenburg 2014; Bakshy, Messing, & Adamic 2015). Also, another concern is the use of AI to generate and spread fake news. Today, AI programs can generate very convincing news stories that are even more trustworthy than stories written by humans (Schoenherr 2022). The dissemination of fake news, whether for the purpose of attacking political opponents, corporations, or groups and individuals seeking to profit from clicks and audience growth

(Landon-Murray et al. 2019), harms society by corrupting democratic processes and undermining trust in the news media (Schoenherr 2022). Deepfakes produced by AI combine images and videos to create fake images and videos, which are often very difficult to identify as false (Satarino and Mozur 2023). Deepfakes not only spread fake news and create false beliefs, but they can also cast doubt on any image or movie produced by the media (Jasen 2019).

5.1   The Pros and Cons of the AI Journalist

We face the fact that journalists around the world are increasingly using artificial intelligence applications, such as OpenAI's ChatGPT. According to a survey by the World Association of Newspapers and News Publishers (WAN-IFRA), 49 percent of respondents said their newsrooms use AI systems (Tema 2023). News Corp. Australia is producing 3,000 articles a week using generative artificial intelligence, CEO Michael Miller revealed (The Guardian 2023). These are thousands of local stories about the weather, fuel prices, and traffic conditions produced each week by AI, according to a report in Media Week (2023). A spokesperson for News Corp Australia says that these news stories are produced by AI but monitored by humans (The Guardian 2023).

The existing literature offers various suggestions on how AI journalists (and their programmers) could make news content more acceptable to audiences (Schiffrin 2019). Some studies suggest that source credibility generally does not differ between AI journalists, human journalists, or a combination of both (Wolker and Powell 2021). However, when the same news article is attributed to either a human or an AI, the human journalist is perceived as more trustworthy. Meanwhile, when the audience is presented with different articles, each written by either an AI journalist or a human journalist, the AI journalist is seen as more trustworthy (Graefe and Bohlken 2020). This depends very much on the topic and the content of the articles. In general, when the source of information is AI, there is a tendency to be more objective than when it is written by a human, regardless of the perceived decrease in credibility (Edison, Tandoc, Yao, and Wu 2020). An AI journalist reduces emotional engagement with the partisan story (Liu and Wei 2018). Other evidence suggests that an AI journalist does not activate emotional involvement, but this does not improve perceptions of the objectivity of news content (Opdahl et al. 2023), while human authors risk speculating on a topic with high emotional involvement (Połońska, & Beckett (Eds.). 2019).

On the contrary, attributing authorship to AI may reduce perceptions of news bias if the article is claimed to come from a network that is ideologically opposed to the audience's position. However, since AI journalists work with templates, they are more likely to have heuristic biases than a human journalist (Cloudy et al. 2023). In any case, the audience should at least be aware of the authorship of the news, whether it is AI, human, or mixed. Well-known media such as Bayerischer Rundfunk (BR) in Germany, the BBC in the UK, Aftonbladet and VG from Sweden and Norway, ANP, the Dutch News Agency, Reuters, The Guardian, CBC, and News Corporations in Canada all claim to use AI in news production, but no news is published without strict supervision by editors, i.e., humans. However, as these authors point out, the methods of using AI, the degree of AI involvement in news, and human oversight vary from one media outlet to another (Cools and Diakopoulos 2023).

News organizations also reject the idea of replacing journalists with machines and emphasize the importance of human decision-making when using generative AI tools. There is a point at which their interests converge; AI companies want to be paid for their contribution, and media organizations seem unwilling to take sole responsibility, even for mistakes made by AI. Last year, discussions began between OpenAI, Google, Microsoft, and Adobe executives and media leaders to discuss copyright issues related to their products, such as chatbots and image generators. *"Sources for the Financial Times have revealed that publishers including News Corp., Axel Springer, The New York Times, and The Guardian have been in discussions with at least one of the technology companies"* (Xhelili 2023).

6   The Norms of Ethics and Software Engineering

Until a few years ago, it seemed that the computer technology industry preferred the self-regulatory way of the media, "Partnership for AI" (Metz 2019). In fact, researcher Haapanen (2022) emphasizes that the media does not need urgent self-regulatory measures; it is enough to review the procedures for public complaints, give it more space to express itself, and efficiently address concerns from the audience. While today, when academic debates have increased and AI ethics have turned into a concern for society, attitudes have changed: *"time for citizens of other democratic societies to request that their rights be protected as well."* (Bauer and Dubljević 2020a). The formulation of binding standards and the monitoring of their implementation are on the agenda of international organizations such as the EU and the United Nations. However, despite accountability systems and empirical studies, practice shows that the ethical influence on AI decision-making by software engineers is currently very modest and, in some cases, nonexistent. Hagendorff notes: *"Currently, AI ethics is failing in many cases. Ethics lacks an enforcement mechanism. Violators of various ethical codes face no consequences. And in cases where ethics is integrated into institutions, it serves primarily as a marketing strategy"* (Hagendoff 2020). An empirical study conducted by a group of European researchers in 2019 shows that developers *"see ethics as an impractical construct, far removed from the problems they face in their work"* (Evas 2020a). AI needs to be governed and managed according to well-considered and clear rules (Waltz et al. 2019).

7   Discussion

Efforts for self-regulation of the media system in Albania have been a long and difficult process, and the results have not been satisfactory. Despite the efforts to establish a self-regulation system based on professional standards in the media, "so far there is no concrete example or instrument that can be considered a successful achievement and serve as an example for self-regulation in the media" (Londo 2023b). The current media system is characterized by problems stemming from a lack of transparency in media ownership and financing, as well as the interference of owners in editorial content. This situation makes it difficult for the media community to form a common front to protect ethical standards. Meanwhile, these standards are constantly being tested by new developments, including the significant increase in the number of online media outlets and the pressure of competition among them. This leads to a secondary focus on respecting professional standards (Zguri 2017, IDRA 2019, Londo 2023c). As mentioned above, the implementation of AI systems in Albania is still in its early stages, but the current lack of adherence to the code of ethics and the absence of a self-regulatory system for professional standards in the media could have dangerous and hard-to-repair consequences for the Albanian media once the application of AI becomes widespread.

A positive development in Albania was also the amendment of the Law on Audio-visual Media in 2023, which added a separate provision on self-regulation and co-regulation of the media. According to this law, the regulatory authority must require media outlets to develop codes of professional conduct with standards and practices to ensure respect for human rights and dignity. (AMA 2023) These provisions also require regular monitoring of the objectives set out in these codes to ensure satisfactory compliance with these standards, including effective and proportionate sanctions. However, this law has not yet been implemented in Albania. The resolution of ethical issues in the Albanian media is urgent because "*you cannot have AI ethics without ethics,*" said Lauer (2020). One of the conclusions of Londo (2023d) is that current *codes and guidelines do not adequately address online media, while professional debate on new developments, such as alignment with EU standards or the impact of algorithms and artificial intelligence on the media, is at a minimal level. Similarly, there has been no professional debate or specific initiative on new phenomena such as algorithms and artificial intelligence (AI). There have been very few articles in the media on these topics, and usually only articles from foreign media are published,*" the study says. The survey conducted as part of the study showed that journalists and editors of online media are aware of the role of algorithms, but they mainly use this knowledge to attract as large an audience as possible for the materials they post on their social platforms, and there is no reflection on the impact that the development of technology, and especially AI, may have on their profession. At the same time, interviewees emphasize that, along with the novelty, there is a sense of insecurity about these issues, which also explains the lack of internal debate on these issues (Londo 2023e).

In other countries, the use of AI in the media is progressing rapidly. "*Nearly 60% of news articles across all outlets are indexed to industry products, initiatives, or announcements. 33% of unique sources across all articles are affiliated with industry, nearly twice as many as those from academia and six times as many as those from government. Nearly 12% of all articles reference Elon Musk*" (Brennen et al. 2018). In this context, the Albanian media is not far from using AI systems. By presenting AI as a relevant and competent solution to a variety of audience-related issues, the media continuously emphasizes its impact on all areas of public life, as well as the ongoing debates about the possible effects of AI. Just as AI itself is an evolving public issue, the implications and consequences of its use are still not fully understood. "Media can't survive without the support of technology. And artificial intelligence has ushered in a new age of journalism. Now, news can be produced and distributed with the help of artificial intelligence" (Kaushik et al. 2022).

The ethics of AI received a major boost after the development of the Fall 2005 AI Symposium on Machine Ethics. Machine ethics, or the morality of machines, lies at the intersection of ethics and computer science (Guzman 2021). However, machine ethics is only one part of AI ethics. Since 2015, there has been an explosion of publications on AI ethics. One of the historical milestones in the development of AI ethics is the IEEE Global Initiative on Ethics of Autonomous and Intelligent Systems, which aims to establish ethical standards for AI in the fields of computer science, IT, and electrical engineering (Piscataway 2017). The European Parliament published the study "European framework on ethical aspects of artificial intelligence, robotics, and related technologies" in 2020. *"An analysis of the current regulatory framework conducted in this study shows that there is no binding, horizontal legal instrument that specifically defines a regulatory framework for AI ethics in the EU or globally"* (Evas 2020b).

Global corporate investments in the technology sector pose a potential risk to the balance and protection of public interests and may potentially undermine competition. Finally, the current framework, characterized by "soft" initiatives for AI ethics, negatively impacts the consistency, implementation, and oversight of the expansion of AI in journalism (Baldini et al. 2018; Bauer and Dubljević 2020b; Chuan et al. 2019). International organizations support the conduct of studies and reports in this area, such as the UNESCO report "World Trends in Freedom of Expression and Media Development," supported by the IEEE Global Initiative, the Society of Professional Journalists' Code of Ethics, and AI4People: An Ethical Framework for a Good AI Society: Opportunities, Risks, Principles, and Recommendations. However, this is a self-regulatory process carried out by the media itself. Every national and international media outlet is required to publish its Code of Ethics or Ethical Charter on its website, but in Albania, this is done only by the Albanian Public Radio Television. After the European Commission presented the proposal for an EU regulatory framework on artificial intelligence (AI) in April 2021 as a first attempt to adopt a horizontal regulation on AI based on a risk-based approach, where AI systems posing "unacceptable" risks would be banned and others posing "lower risk" would be subject to a set of requirements and obligations to gain access to the EU market, the Parliament voted on its position in June 2023. EU lawmakers will now begin negotiations to finalize the new legislation (European Parliament 2023). Following the events of June 2023, the Summit on Protection from Artificial Intelligence Risks was held in London in November 2023. Delegates from 28 countries, including the United States and China, agreed to work together to mitigate the potentially "catastrophic" risks posed by advances in artificial intelligence (AI Safety Summit 2023).

8 Conclusion

In conclusion, while AI is still in its early stages in the Albanian media, the understanding of AI is similar to that of journalists around the world, as there is uncertainty and confusion in the journalistic community. While this case study approach is not representative of the diversity of journalists nationally or globally, one thing is clear: traditional media values such as balance, trustworthiness, transparency of sources, and authorship are being undermined. It is now widely accepted that algorithmic systems embody a new typology of values and provoke new distributions of power in journalism. This requires experts to make specific ontological and epistemological commitments that seem different from those of traditional journalism. The development and implementation of ethical codes adapted to this new space that AI brings to the media would enhance, or at least not further minimize, the role the media has traditionally played in serving the public.

References

AI safety Summit (2023). https://www.aisafetysummit.gov.uk/#:~:text=1st%20and%202nd% 20November%202023%20at%20Bletchley%20Park&text=The%20UK%20hosted%20the% 20first,frontier%20AI%20around%20the%20world

AMA. Low nr.-30-2023, AMA on line (2023). https://ama.gov.al/wp-content/uploads/2020/07/ Ligji-nr.-30-2023-Per-disa-ndryshime-dhe-shtesa-ne-ligjin-nr.-97-2013-Per-mediat-Audiov izive-ne-Republiken-e-Shqiperise-te-ndryshuar.pdf

Anderson, J., Rainie, L., Luchsinger, A.: Artificial intelligence and the future of humans. Pew Research Center, Israel (2018). https://www.pewresearch.org/internet/2018/12/10/artificial-int elligence-and-the-future-of-humans/

Baldini, G., Botterman, M., Neisse, R., Tallacchini, M.: Ethical design in the internet of things. Sci. Eng. Ethics **24**, 905–925 (2018)

Bauer, W.A., Dubljević, V.: AI assistants and the paradox of internal automaticity. Neuroethics **13**, 303–310 (2020). https://doi.org/10.1007/s12152-019-09423-6

Beckett, C.: New powers, new responsibilities: a global survey of journalism and artificial intelligence. London School Econ. **18** (2019)

Brennen, J.S., Howard, P.N., Nielsen, R.K.N.: An industry-led debate: how UK media cover artificial intelligence. London (2018). https://doi.org/10.60625/risj-v219-d676

Buenfil, J., Arnold, R., Abruzzo, B., Korpela, C.: Artificial intelligence ethics: governance through social media. In: 2019 IEEE International Symposium on Technologies for Homeland Security (HST), pp. 1–6. IEEE (2019)

Chen, C., Chekam, G.A.: Algorithms and media ethics in the AI age. In: Ward, S.J.A. (eds.) Handbook of Global Media Ethics. Springer, Cham (2021). https://doi.org/10.1007/978-3-319-32103-5_16

Christodoulou, E., Iordanou, K.: Democracy under attack: challenges of addressing ethical issues of AI and big data for more democratic digital media and societies. Front. Politic. Sci. **3**, 682945 (2021)

Chuan, C.-H., Tsai, W.-H., Cho, S.: Framing artificial intelligence in American newspapers. AI, ethics, and society. AAAI workshops. AAAI Press, AAAI workshop (2019)

Cloudy, J., Banks, J., Bowman, N.D.: The STR (AI) GHT scoop: artificial intelligence cues reduce perceptions of hostile media bias. Digit. J. **11**(9), 1577–1596 (2023)

Cools, H., Diakopoulos, N.: Writing guidelines for the role of AI in your newsroom? Here are some, er, guidelines for that. July, Nieman Lab (2023). https://generative-ai-newsroom.com/ towards-guidelines-for-guidelines-on-the-use-of-generative-ai-in-newsrooms-55b0c2c1d960

Dedja, R.: journalist on Report TV, 12 Janunary, author's interview D. Ç (2024)

Diakopoulos, N.: Automating the News: How algorithms are rewriting the Media. Harvard University Press, Cambridge (2019). https://doi.org/10.4159/9780674239302

Draper, N.A., Joseph, T.: The corporate cultivation of digital resignation. New Media Soc. **21**(8), 1824–1839 (2019). https://doi.org/10.1177/1461444819833331

Drunen, M.V., Helberger, N., Bastian, M.: Know your algorithm: what media organizations need to explain to their users about news personalization. Int. Data Priv. Law **9**(4), 220–235 (2019). https://doi.org/10.1093/idpl/ipz011

Tandoc, E.C., Yao, L.J., Wu, S.: Man vs. Machine? the impact of algorithm authorship on news credibility. Dig. J. **8**:4, 548–562 (2020). https://doi.org/10.1080/21670811.2020.1762102

European Parliament. EU AI Act: first regulation on artificial intelligence, Jun, European Parliament on line (2023). https://www.europarl.europa.eu/topics/en/article/20230601STO93804/eu-ai-act-first-regulation-on-artificial-intelligence

Evas. T.: European framework on ethical aspects of artificial intelligence, robotics and related technologies, Brussels, September, European Parliament (2020). https://www.europarl.europa.eu/RegData/etudes/STUD/2020/654179/EPRS_STU (2020) 654179_EN.pdf

Fernholz, Y., Ermakova, T., Fabian, B., Buxmann, P.: User-driven prioritization of ethical principles for artificial intelligence systems. Comput. Hum. Behav. Artific. Hum. (2024). https://doi.org/10.1016/j.chbah.2024.100055

Graefe, A., Bohlken, N.: Automated journalism: a meta-analysis of readers' perceptions of human-written in comparison to automated news. Media Commun. **8**(3), 50–59 (2020). https://doi.org/10.17645/mac.v8i3.3019

Goce, B.: Journalist on MCN TV, 13 Janunary, author's interview D. Ç (2024)

Guzman, A.L.: Should machines write about death? Questions of technology, humanity, and ethics in the automation of journalism. In: Ward, S.J.A. (eds.) Handbook of Global Media Ethics. Springer, Cham (2021). https://doi.org/10.1007/978-3-319-32103-5_28

Haapanen, L.: Adapting media self-regulation to the era of news automation. In: Manninen, V.J.E., Niemi, M.K., Ridge-Newman, A. (eds.) Futures of Journalism. Palgrave Macmillan, Cham (2022). https://doi.org/10.1007/978-3-030-95073-6_6

Hagendorff, T.: The ethics of AI ethics: an evaluation of guidelines. Mind. Mach. **30**, 99–120 (2020). https://doi.org/10.1007/s11023-020-09517-8

Hysa, D.: Journalist on Top News TV, 11 Janunary, author's interview D. Ç (2024)

IDRA: Studim për profesionistët e medias: Panoramë e medias në Shqipëri. (Study for media professionals: Panorama of the media in Albania). IDRA (2019). https://www.idrainstitute.org/files/Panoram%C3%ABn%20e%20Medias%20n%C3%AB%20Shqip%C3%ABri.pdf

Jansen, P., Brey, P. et al.: D4.4: Ethical Analysis of AI and Robotics Technologies, SIENNA project, of European Union (EU), pp. 161–163 (2019). https://www.sienna-project.eu/digitalAssets/801/c_801912-l_1-k_d4.4_ethical-analysis--ai-and-r--with-acknowledgements.pdf

Jones, B., Jones, R., Luger, E.: AI 'everywhere and nowhere': addressing the AI intelligibility problem in public service journalism. Digit. J. **10**(10), 1731–1755 (2022). https://doi.org/10.1080/21670811.2022.2145328

Kaur, D., Uslu, S., Rittichier, R., Durresi, A.: Trustworthy artificial intelligence: a review. ACM Comput. Surv. **55**, 2, Article 39, 38 (2023). https://doi.org/10.1145/3491209

Kaushik E., Rishi. R., Sharma A.: Artificial intelligence: media for the future, Jaipur (2022). https://www.researchgate.net/lab/Amit-Sharma-Lab-6

Landon-Murray, M., Mujkic, E., Nussbaum, B.: Disinformation in contemporary U.S. foreign policy: impacts and ethics in an era of fake news, social media, and artificial intelligence. Public Integrity **21**:5, 512–522 (2019). https://doi.org/10.1080/10999922.2019.1613832

Latar, N.L.: The robot journalist in the age of social physics: the end of human journalism? In: Einav, G. (eds.) The New World of Transitioned Media. The Economics of Information, Communication, and Entertainment. Springer, Cham (2015). https://doi.org/10.1007/978-3-319-09009-2_6

Lauer, D.: You cannot have AI ethics without ethics. AI Ethics **1**, 21–25 (2021). https://doi.org/10.1007/s43681-020-00013-4

Liu, B., Wei, L.: Reading machine-written news: effect of machine heuristic and novelty on hostile media perception. n: Kurosu, M. (eds.) Human-Computer Interaction. Theories, Methods, and Human Issues. HCI 2018. LNCS, vol. 10901. Springer, Cham (2018). https://doi.org/10.1007/978-3-319-91238-7_26

Liu, X., Nourbakhsh, A., Li, Q., Shah, S., Martin, R., Duprey, J.: Reuters tracer: toward automated news production using large scale social media data. In: 2017 IEEE International Conference on Big Data (Big Data) (2017). https://doi.org/10.1109/bigdata.2017.8258082

Londo, I.: Low priority for ethical issues media self-regulation in Albania, Foundation "Mediacentar", Sarajevo & Albanian Media Institute, Tirana & Peace Institute, Ljubljana (2023). https://www.institutemedia.org/research-low-priority-for-ethical-issues/

Mediaweek: Michael Miller tells publishers how News Corp Australia had best year in a decade (2023). July, accessed on the on line. https://www.mediaweek.com.au/michael-miller-tells-pub lishers-how-news-corp-australia-had-best-year-in-a-decade/

Metz, C.: Is ethical A.I. even possible? The New York Times. March, The New York Times accessed on line (2019). https://www.nytimes.com/2019/03/01/business/ethics-artificial-intell igence.html

Opdahl, A.L., et al.: Trustworthy journalism through AI. Data Knowl. Eng. **146**, 102182 (2023)

Paris, B., Donovan, J.: Deepfakes and cheap fakes. The Manipulation of Audio and Visual Evidence, Data & Society, SHBA (2019). https://datasociety.net/wpcontent/uploads/2019/09/DS_ Deepfakes_Cheap_FakesFinal-1-1.pdf

Piscataway, N.J.: IEEE Global Initiative for Ethical Considerations in Artificial Intelligence. 11 Oct, Anonymous Business Wire on line (2017). https://www.businesswire.com/news/home/ 20170719005136/en/IEEE-Global-Initiative-for-Ethical-Considerations-in-Artificial-Intell igence-AI-and-Autonomous-Systems-AS-Drives-Together-with-IEEE-Societies-New-Standa rds-Projects-Releases-New-Report-on-

Połońska, E., Beckett, C. (eds.): Public service broadcasting and media systems in troubled European democracies. Springer (2019). https://doi.org/10.1007/9783030027100

Rrozhani, R.: Journalist on Top Channel TV, 10 August, author's interview D. Ç (2023)

Satariano, A., Mozur P.: The people onscreen are fake. the disinformation is real. The New Yourk Times (2023). https://www.nytimes.com/2023/02/07/technology/artificial-intelligence- training-deepfake.html

Schoenherr, J.R.: Ethical artificial intelligence from popular to cognitive science: trust in the age of entanglement (1st edn.). Routledge (2022). https://doi.org/10.4324/9781003143284

Schiffrin, 2019. Schiffrin, A.: Credibility and trust in journalism. In: Oxford Research Encyclopedia of Communication (2019). https://doi.org/10.1093/acrefore/9780190228613.013.794

Spaho, E.: Web journalist on focusnews web, 13 Janunary, author's interview D. Ç (2024)

Stahl, B.C.: Concepts of ethics and their application to AI. Artific. Intell. Better Future **18**, 19–33 (2021). https://doi.org/10.1007/978-3-030-69978-9_3. PMCID: PMC7968613

Tema: Inteligjenca artificiale në botën e medias, (Artificial intelligence in the world of media) (2023). 3 June, accessed on the on line. https://www.gazetatema.net/hi-tech/inteligjenca-artifi ciale-ne-boten-e-medias-i392791

The Gardian: News Corp using AI to produce 3,000 Australian local news stories a week (2023). 31 Jul, accessed on the on line. https://www.theguardian.com/media/2023/aug/01/news-corp- ai-chat-gpt-stories

Thorne, J., Vlachos, A.: Automated fact checking: task formulations, methods and future directions (2018). arXiv preprint arXiv:1806.07687

Van Stekelenburg, J.: Going all the way: politicizing, polarizing, and radicalizing identity offline and online. Sociol. Compass **8**(5), 540–555 (2014). https://doi.org/10.1111/soc4.12157

Walz, A., Firth-Butterfield, K.: AI governance: a holistic approach to implement ethics into AI. WEF White Paper (2019). https://hdl.handle.net/21.11116/0000-0005-790E-5

Wölker, A., Powell, T.E.: Algorithms in the newsroom? News readers' perceived credibility and selection of automated journalism. Journalism **22**(1), 86–103 (2021). https://doi.org/10.1177/ 1464884918757072

Xhelili, S.: Inteligjenca artificiale dhe kompanitë e medias negociojnë marrëveshje historike mbi përmbajtjen e lajmeve, (AI and media companies negotiate historic news content deal) (2023) Albanian Post. June, accessed on the on line. https://albanianpost.com/inteligjenca-artificiale-dhe-kompanite-e-medias-negociojne-marreveshje-historike-mbi-permbajtjen-e-lajmeve/

Zguri, R.: Relations between media and politics in Albania. Albanian Media Institute, Tirane (2017). https://www.institutemedia.org/wp-content/uploads/2020/05/anglisht-marred heniet-mes-medias.pdf

Zhow, J., Zhang, Y., Luo, Q., Parker, A., Choudhury, M.: Synthetic lies: understanding AI-generated misinformation and evaluating algorithmic and human solutions. In: CHI 2023: Proceedings of the 2023 CHI Conference on Human Factors in Computing Systems, Hamburg, Germany (2023). https://doi.org/10.1145/3544548.3581318

Are Fair Machine Learning Models More Useful?

Anurata Prabha Hridi$^{(\boxtimes)}$ and Benjamin Watson

North Carolina State University, Raleigh, USA
{aphridi,bwatson}@ncsu.edu

Abstract. Over the last few years, machine learning (ML) fairness has been widely studied: both its impacts on society, and methods for making it fairer. Yet, interestingly, the relationship between fairness and utility (usefulness) has remained underexplored. The small amount of existing research assumes that fairness and usefulness are conflicting goals, requiring compromise. In contrast, we reason that data and models describing a group of people are often used by those same people, and therefore, models that better describe users will be more useful. In particular, when groups of people are more diverse, the data and models describing them must also be more diverse: fair machine learning models should be more useful (not less). We tested this hypothesis by modeling human color naming—which varies significantly by gender—using datasets with different gender balances and varying fairness. We then compared the model results to actual human naming behavior, finding good evidence that fairer data and models that better represent users are more useful to those users in that they agree with them more often. We conclude with result discussion followed by potential future work.

Keywords: User-centered utility · Fairness · Gender

1 Introduction

Many have studied fairness and diversity in machine learning (ML) [10], focusing on quantitative, data-focused measures of fairness (e.g., [11,28,49]). The goal of this work is diversity itself, which certainly has intrinsic value. This paper examines a proposition about diversity in ML modeling: that fair models are more useful. Veda Bawo, director of data governance at financial services company Raymond James, said, *"If the data quality is not good, you're nowhere"* [36]. If data will be used by the population it describes, good quality data should accurately describe that population. With this in mind, we investigated the possibility that ML models trained with data that is a demographic match to their user population will better model and, indeed, be preferred by that population.

To test this hypothesis, we used a color-naming task, in which people name a color they are shown. Females and males perform color naming differently [6,7,20,21], making it sensitive to gender demographics. At the same time, unlike many tasks that vary by demographics, color naming is not politically or personally sensitive, avoiding many unnecessary impacts on experimental participants. Moreover, a large color naming dataset is readily available, the XKCD dataset [39], which contains the names given to over five million colors by 222,500 respondents. This data has been used by many researchers in various fields (e.g., [24,25,35,42,43]).

We then built several ML models of human color naming using data sampled from the XKCD set with different gender balances. Next, we asked a group of gender-balanced experimental participants to choose between the colors produced by these models by having them select the color swatch that most closely matched a given color name. We hypothesized that as a group, participants would choose the colors output by models built using data with a gender balance most similar to their own.

We received partial confirmation that participants often preferred the colors produced by the model built with demographically matching data. In the rest of this paper, we discuss these results and their interpretation in more detail and propose possibilities that might lead to stronger evidence for our hypothesis.

2   Related Work

As ML spreads throughout our daily lives, model fairness is becoming increasingly relevant. Cai et al. introduced the challenge of addressing disparities in ML models' performance across different demographic groups due to a lack of representation in the training data [9]. The authors also highlighted the importance of tailored data collection strategies for achieving equitable outcomes. Research on fairness and diversity in ML [10] has often focused on quantitative fairness measures (e.g., [11,28]). Many have raised concerns about potential discrimination in algorithmic decisions towards specific population groups or minorities [2,4,5,8,17]. Caton & Haas [10] provided an overview of various approaches to mitigate social biases produced by ML models, organized into pre-processing, in-processing, and post-processing methods, with further subcategories. We use pre-processing—resampling of data to adjust demographic makeup—to enable us to examine our experimental hypothesis.

2.1   ML Model Bias and Mitigation

Over the years, researchers have noted that ML models themselves can be unfair [23] due to various kinds of human bias captured in the data used to train the models, including race, sex, age, politics, disability, and religion, among others [3,13–15,27]. Sometimes, the protected attributes of samples in a dataset are unavailable or inaccessible, which makes them prone to bias generation by disallowing fair usage [1,37]. Addressing these biases to promote fairness in AI/ML applications is crucial. To promote tackling such uneven representation in dataset collections, researchers have begun proposing methods for reducing biases. Bird et al. proposed visualization combined with algorithm change [3], while Goel and

Faltings [21] described extensive algorithmic changes. Hube et al. [27] proposed model training methods to improve data quality, while Zou and Schiebinger suggested both data and model improvements [53]. As part of post-processing bias mitigation, DiCiccio et al. proposed calibrating models to ensure that the model interpretation and expected outcomes are the same [16].

Despite all these works, few have evaluated the relationship between fairness and user-centered utility in ML modeling. With the little research found, it is commonly considered that they can sometimes conflict with each other—with Menon and Williamson, among others, stating utility as the price to achieve a desired degree of fairness [38]. One apparent exception is the work by Li and Liu [31], which described a data reweighing method for achieving "fairness at no utility cost", asserting that the conventional fairness-utility tradeoff could be relaxed in most cases. Yet their work still focuses on analytic accuracy in the model itself rather than user assessment of the model. Others working in the area [18, 26, 30, 46, 47, 51] have a similar focus on fairness vs. model accuracy and utility, rather than usefulness.

2.2   Color Naming and Its Use in This Research

The anthropology of colors has intrigued humans for decades [34]. Color vocabulary and/or preference can vary largely based on gender [6, 12, 19, 20, 22, 40, 41, 45, 50], language [29, 32], and age [7, 48]. Women are more accurate and consistent when naming color and have a larger color vocabulary [40]. In addition to being better at color naming, women do better at matching colors to names [12, 41].

Color naming's strong relationship to gender and other demographics makes it a good experimental context for us to examine our research question. Moreover, unlike many other tasks with demographic sensitivities, color naming is not a topic fraught with social sensitivities, and so it reduces risks for experimental participants. One convenient and widely used color naming dataset was produced for the online comic XKCD [39]. Maheshwari et al. used it extensively for text-to-color representation [35], inverting the XKCD data's color-to-name mapping to learn 11 basic colors to represent queries in search engines. Heer & Stone developed a probabilistic model for color naming [25], as Maheshwari et al. did in [35]. They applied scaling techniques to reduce XKCD survey data to a small set of "maximally information preserving color terms". Havasi et al. focused on semantic knowledge for the color assignment [24]. They used a crowd-sourced semantic net called *ConceptNet* for the color selection task. Setlur & Stone determined the linguistic relationship between color terms and basic colors for visualization [42] using the same model created in [25]. While Havasi et al. did the same calculation using ConceptNet [24], the authors here used n-gram analysis. Simon et al. [43] created ML models from XKCD color data using Decision Tree classifiers, which also influenced our model creation. Therefore, even though we explored other color datasets (e.g., [33, 52]), we also decided to use XKCD color survey data in our work.

3 Research Question

Our research question is: **Do models built on datasets with demographics that match user populations better model those populations and are therefore more useful to them?** We describe our experiment, examining this question below.

4 Experiment with a Balanced Model and an Unbalanced Model

In this experiment, we built two color naming models that, given a name, produced a color: one with the raw XKCD data containing roughly three male responses for every female response and one with resampled XKCD data with one male response for every female response. Given a color name, we asked experimental participants to indicate which model they preferred both by *choosing* between two colors produced by each of the models and less directly by having them input a color that matched the name—*picking*. We then compared the participants' colors to the model colors algorithmically.

4.1 Design

To address these research questions, we used a 2 (participant gender) x 2 (interaction order) between-participants design.

Independent Variables. Our first independent variable was *gender*, either **male** or **female** (no non-binary people elected to participate in our study). For the same color name, participants were asked to first choose one of two model colors and then input RGB values using a color picker or vice versa, depending on *interaction order* (our second). Half of our participants were randomly assigned to a **choose first** order and half to a **picker first** order.

Dependent Measures. We had two dependent measures. One was *choice*. If the participant chose the color produced by the balanced model, `choice = +1`; if they chose the color produced by the unbalanced model, `choice = -1`. We also let the participants choose neither model, in which case `choice = 0`. The second was *distance*. If `pcolor`, `bcolor`, `ucolor` are the RGB color coordinates of the colors picked by the participant, the balanced model and the unbalanced model, respectively, then -

$$bdist = d(pcolor, bcolor)$$
$$udist = d(pcolor, ucolor)$$
$$distance = udist - bdist$$

where `d` is the Euclidean distance between two 3D coordinates in RGB color space. If distance is positive, then the participant has picked a color closer to the balanced model's color. If it is negative, then the picked color is closer to the unbalanced model's color.

Hypotheses. Because our participants were balanced across genders, we expected that they would choose colors produced by the balanced model (choice > 0) and pick colors closer to the balanced model (distance > 0). Similarly, we expected that choice and distance would be positive for our female participant subpopulation, while for our male subpopulation, they would be negative. We did not expect these subpopulation preferences to be as strong as those for the overall population since neither of our two color models was built with data that closely matched the demographics of these subpopulations.

4.2 Data and Equipment

Below, we describe how we built our color naming models and the system we set up for surveying our participants.

Dataset Description. The XKCD data does not have any non-binary responses and is heavily dominated by males (73% male, 27% female). When naming colors distributed across the 3D RGB color space, roughly 150K respondents produced 3.4M rows of naming data, where 183,398 color names were unique. There were a total of 3,083,876 unique RGB tuples and at least 143,107 rows that had no information about colors (participants put random information) out of approximately 3M entries. Figure 1 shows a 2D (fully saturated) projection of the colors named in the 3D space.

Fig. 1. A fully saturated 2D projection of the colors named in the XKCD data. (Color figure online)

Processing Data. We eliminated color names that had no relevant interpretation, contained stray characters, or were misspelled—therefore had no meaningful contribution to the experiment, e.g., *i-don't-like-this-survey, when will it end?*, etc. Next, we created a list of stopwords:

1. basic colors (violet, indigo, blue, green, yellow, orange, red, purple, black, white, brown, grey, gray). We did not use these color names because they are categorical, matching a wide range of RGB colors.

2. anything that starts with 'bright', 'dark', 'light', 'pale'. These darkening and lightening modifiers are largely synonymous with one another and still not very specific.
3. combination of two basic colors ('red orange'). These combinations connect two very categorical descriptors and, again, are not very specific.
4. flesh, skin. These are widely ranging and disjoint color references.

Building Color Models. From the processed XKCD data, we created two subsets to train our models: an unbalanced dataset and a balanced dataset. Both datasets contained 20000 rows, with colors in the unbalanced dataset chosen randomly to reproduce the gender ratio of the original XKCD data and colors in the balanced dataset produced with randomly chosen male-female row pairs. There were 2680 and 2706 unique color names in the unbalanced and balanced datasets, of which 2310 were shared.

Next, we created two ML models based on these two datasets, using the decision tree method [43]. We split the two datasets, 80–20, into training and test subsets. Since we were more focused on how participants interact with visual colors given color names, we used the color names as features and the RGB values/hex codes (e.g., RGB = 255,0,0 = #FF0000) as the labels.

To generate colors for participants to interact with, we chose the 64 most frequently named colors from the 2310 shared names on which the models were trained. Using our balanced and unbalanced color naming models, we then generated the hex codes for the 64 color names and rendered these as 128 patches, which we called "swatches".

We divided the 64 swatches generated by each of the two models into four sets of 16 (participants interacted with 16 colors each). Figs. 2, 3, 4 and 5 show the four color sets we used in this study, with unbalanced swatches on top, and balanced below. Swatches are sorted by hue across each set (participants saw the questions in random order).

Preparing the Survey. Next, we built a Flask application to survey participants about their color preferences. The application used React JavaScript and NPM, and relevant code was uploaded to the lab GitHub repository for code review. We used our own application rather than a standard survey tool to support the use of a color picker. We used an SQLite database to store the responses on our server.

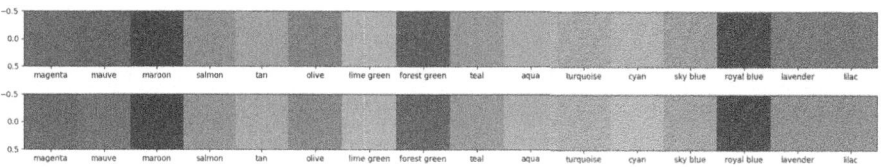

Fig. 2. First color set. The top and bottom rows contain unbalanced and balanced swatches, respectively. (Color figure online)

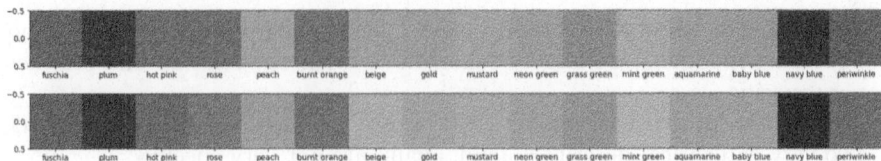

Fig. 3. Second color set. The top and bottom rows contain unbalanced and balanced swatches, respectively. (Color figure online)

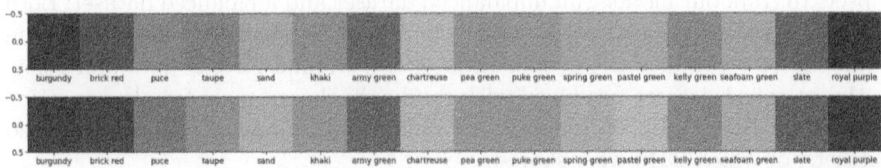

Fig. 4. Third color set. The top and bottom rows contain unbalanced and balanced swatches, respectively. (Color figure online)

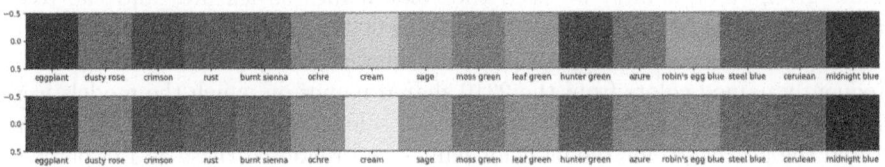

Fig. 5. Fourth color set. The top and bottom rows contain unbalanced and balanced swatches, respectively. (Color figure online)

4.3 Participants

Participants had to be at least 18 years of age to be eligible for our study. We recruited 128 female and 128 male participants through Mechanical Turk, who were compensated for their time with $4. These participants gave informed consent per our approved IRB protocol. While we allowed our participants to identify their gender broadly (e.g., as reported by Spiel et al. [44]), none of them identified as non-binary. We also did not have participants who self-reported having a color deficiency. Each participant answered questions about one of the four color sets, with Table 1 showing how they were distributed across the color set and our independent variables.

Table 1. How participants were distributed across gender, color set, and interaction order.

Gender	Color Set#	Interaction Order	# of Participants
Male	1	Picker first	16
Male	1	Choose first	16
Male	2	Picker first	16
Male	2	Choose first	16
Male	3	Picker first	16
Male	3	Choose first	16
Male	4	Picker first	16
Female	4	Choose first	16
Female	1	Picker first	16
Female	1	Choose first	16
Female	2	Picker first	16
Female	2	Choose first	16
Female	3	Picker first	16
Female	3	Choose first	16
Female	4	Picker first	16
Female	4	Choose first	16

4.4 Procedure and Tasks

Figure 6 shows the complete flowchart of participant tasks. Depending on the interaction order independent variable, each participant followed one of two paths, consisting of a few demographic questions, followed by picking and choosing 16 colors (or choosing and picking).

Participants consented online and were instructed not to seek assistance from any external or online sources (Fig. 7). They were asked about their gender, nationality, language, and whether they had a color-deficient vision as part of demography questions (Fig. 8). Next, participants chose the swatch that best matched a given color name and picked a color (defined by an RGB coordinate) that matched that name (Fig. 9). Figure 10 shows the 10-s timer used before each of the color questions appeared and the confirmation code after the successful completion of the survey needed to be paid. Three trap questions (Fig. 11) were introduced to gauge participants' attention.

Rejection Criteria. We rejected eight responses. These were responses that were incomplete, failed two of the three trap questions, or repeatedly picked inappropriate colors (e.g., input red when given a color name containing "green").

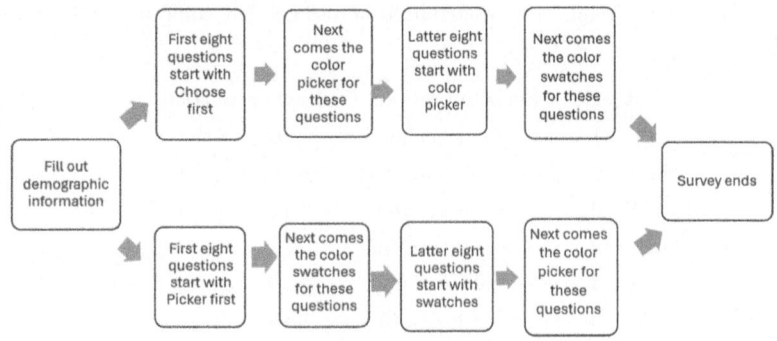

Fig. 6. Tasks in the survey.

You are being asked to complete a study for research purposes. The survey is about choosing the color that best matches a given color name, from among several potentially matching colors shown. Completing this study is voluntary and you can stop at any time by closing this window.

You must be 18 years of age or older to participate in this study.

There are minimal risks associated with your participation in this study. You will receive $4 for completing this study. In order to receive full compensation for completing the study, you must complete the survey, and enter the provided random number code at the end of the study into the MTurk HIT window. We expect you to carefully answer the questions and pay attention to the questions asked.

Please note that because you are participating in this research via MTurk, your participation will be listed on your MTurk profile. However, MTurk will not have access to your responses on the survey. Further, while we will have access to your MTurk ID, we will only use this information to pay you and then your ID will be deleted from our records and will no longer be associated with your responses.

If you have any questions about the study itself, how it is implemented, or study compensation, please contact AP Hridi at aphridi@ncsu.edu or B Watson at bwatson@ncsu.edu . Please reference study number 24051 when contacting anyone about this project.

If you have questions about your rights as a participant or are concerned with your treatment throughout the research process, please contact the NC State University IRB Director at IRB-Director@ncsu.edu, 919-515-8754, or fill out this confidential form online.

If you consent to complete this survey, please click the "Yes, I consent" button to continue.

Additional instructions: Please do not Google the colors while doing the survey. Some phones may make this task difficult, we recommend using a desktop or laptop. Before you begin, please consider keeping your browser extensions turned off for the duration of the experiment.

Yes, I consent

Fig. 7. Landing page.

4.5 Results

We calculated descriptive statistics such as mean and standard deviation and performed one-sampled, two-sided T-tests to determine if the choice and distance means differed significantly from zero, indicating a preference for a certain ML color naming model. We performed these tests for the entire participant population, as well as the male and female subpopulations. To compare means and test for interactions of our independent variables, we also performed two-way ANOVAs. Interaction order did not interact with gender, so we do not discuss it further in this analysis. We report the significant results in Table 2.

Choice Measure. We graph the choice results in Fig. 12 (left). While male participants chose swatches produced by both models with similar frequency ($\mu = -0.033$, $\sigma = 0.373$, $T(127) = -1.02$, $p = 0.31$), female participants more

What is your gender?

○ Male

◉ Female

○ Other

Where do you live?

United States of America (the)   ⌄

What is your native language?

Bengali

Do you have color deficiency or identify yourself as colorblind? Answering YES will not affect your participation in this study.

○ Yes

◉ No

○ Not sure/prefer not to answer

Fig. 8. Demographic information page.

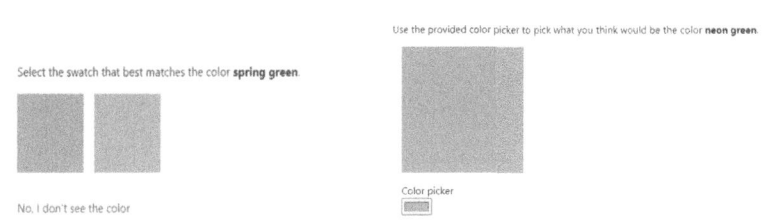

Use the provided color picker to pick what you think would be the color **neon green**

Select the swatch that best matches the color **spring green**

No, I don't see the color

Color picker

Fig. 9. Color swatch and color picker page, respectively. (Color figure online)

frequently chose the swatches produced by the balanced model ($\mu = 0.061$, $\sigma = 0.321$, $T(127) = 2.15$, p = 0.03 < 0.05). Overall, across both females and males, participants chose swatches produced by both models with similar frequency ($\mu = 0.014$, $\sigma = 0.35$, $T(255) = 0.62$, p = 0.53). In an ANOVA by gender, the model swatch choices for males and females differed significantly ($F(1, 254) = 4.741$, p = 0.0304 < 0.05).

Distance Measure. We graph the distance results in Fig. 12. Females picked colors with similar distances to the colors produced by both models ($\mu = -0.002$, $\sigma = 0.014$, $T(127) = -1.59$, p = 0.11). Males picked colors closer to those produced by the unbalanced model ($\mu = -0.004$, $\sigma = 0.015$, $T(127) = -3.4$, p = 0.0009 < 0.05). Overall, across both females and males, participants picked colors closer to those produced by the unbalanced model ($\mu = -0.003$, $\sigma = 0.015$, $T(255) = -3.35$, p = 0.0005 < 0.001). In an ANOVA by gender, the distances of the colors picked by males were similar to the distances of colors picked by females ($F(1, 254) = 1.866$, p = 0.173).

Think of the color **neon green** before you click on the Next button below.

Thank you for participating! Your completion code is:

33513

Fig. 10. A 10-s timer for each color question and survey ends with a confirmation code.

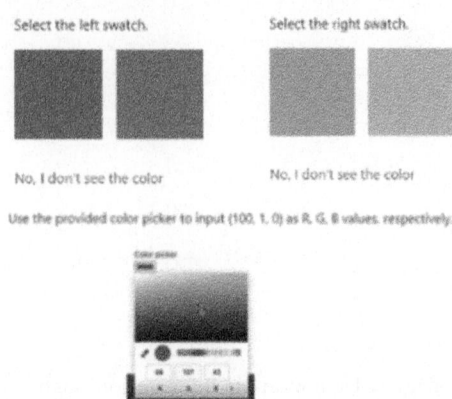

Fig. 11. Sample trap questions. The top ones asked participants to choose the left and right swatches, respectively. The question at the bottom asked them to input specific RGB values from the color picker. (Color figure online)

Table 2. Significant Experimental Results

Test	Gender	Dependent Measure	Mean, Standard Deviation	Test Statistic	p-value
T	Females	Choice	0.061, 0.321 Balanced preferred	$T(127) = 2.153$	<0.05
ANOVA	Males vs. Females	Choice	Females: 0.061, 0.321 Males: −0.033, 0.373	$F(1, 254) = 4.741$	<0.05
T	Males	Distance	−0.004, 0.015 Unbalanced preferred	$T(127) = -3.4$	<0.001
T	Both	Distance	−0.003, 0.015 Unbalanced preferred	$T(255) = -3.35$	<0.001

4.6   Discussion

We anticipated that the overall participant population would choose and pick colors that indicated a preference for the balanced model, since the gender makeup of participants and balanced model data matched. In fact, participants chose colors produced by both models with equal frequency and picked colors closer to the unbalanced model's colors.

We also expected that males would choose colors from and pick colors like the unbalanced model's, while females would favor the balanced model's colors. This proved partially true, with males picking colors closer to the unbalanced model (but not favoring that model when choosing), while females chose colors from the balanced model (but not favoring that model when picking). Male and female choices did differ significantly.

One plausible explanation for the only partial confirmation of our hypotheses was the demographic similarity of the training data in our models (73% male vs 27% female for unbalanced compared to 50% vs 50% for balanced). This could have made the colors they produced more similar, weakening the preferences of male and female participants among models. Since the preferences of the overall participation population are comprised of the preferences of the male and female subpopulations, the overall population's preferences also became weaker and noisier.

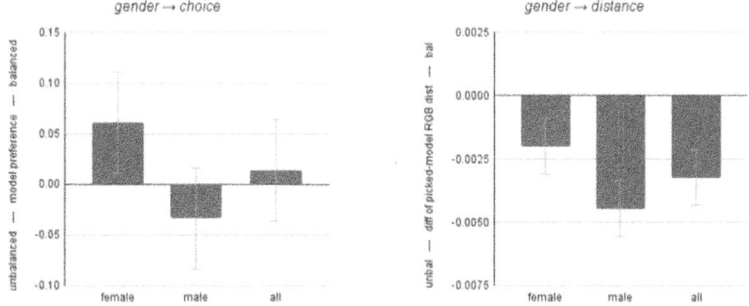

Fig. 12. Means and standard error across gender for dependent variables choice (left) and distance (right).

5 Limitations

Because we asked participants to match the colors most frequently named in the XKCD data, colors were not broadly distributed through the RGB color space, limiting generality—and perhaps distorting results. Figure 13 shows that 13 equally sized sub-regions of the RGB space were not used in the experiment.

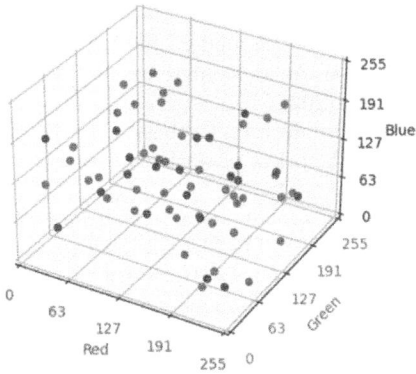

Fig. 13. 13 sub-regions out of 64 in the RGB space did not contain color names that participants matched. (Color figure online)

6   Conclusions and Future Work

We conducted an experiment to explore whether models that were fairer—that is, trained using data with demographics that matched the user population—were more useful. Our experiment offered some support for our hypothesis. As we continue our efforts, we plan to use colors generated by three ML models trained using data with very distinct demographics: balanced in gender, all male, and all female. These demographics would closely match our overall participant population and its male and female subpopulations. We will also ask participants to rank their preferences instead of just choosing.

To follow up more on this work, we see three paths. First, we might sample the color space more broadly. Second, we might give participants a true color naming task, asking them to provide a name rather than choosing or picking a color. This would be a more significant change, possibly requiring a linguistic measure of naming similarity as a distance measure. Third, we want to test our fairness and usefulness hypothesis in other domains, e.g., law or medicine. This might involve different demographics than gender, including but not limited to language or ethnicity.

Training ML models to accommodate diverse opinions can significantly enhance the utility of these models across a wide range of fields where user needs and perspectives play a substantial role. This paper illustrates that training ML models to account for diverse opinions could have value beyond improving ML performance metrics. It is a step towards creating models that align with the needs and perspectives of the diverse user base they are intended to serve. The challenges and insights highlighted in the paper can guide future efforts in building more accurate, inclusive, and adaptable ML models across various domains.

References

1. Awasthi, P., Beutel, A., Kleindessner, M., Morgenstern, J., Wang, X.: Evaluating fairness of machine learning models under uncertain and incomplete information. In: Proceedings of the 2021 ACM Conference on Fairness, Accountability, and Transparency, pp. 206–214 (2021)
2. Besse, P., del Barrio, E., Gordaliza, P., Loubes, J.M., Risser, L.: A survey of bias in machine learning through the prism of statistical parity. Am. Stat. **76**(2), 188–198 (2022)
3. Bird, S., et al.: Fairlearn: a toolkit for assessing and improving fairness in AI. Microsoft, Technical report MSR-TR-2020-32 (2020)
4. Blease, C., Kharko, A., Locher, C., DesRoches, C.M., Mandl, K.D.: US primary care in 2029: a Delphi survey on the impact of machine learning. PLoS ONE **15**(10), e0239947 (2020)
5. Bommasani, R., et al.: On the opportunities and risks of foundation models. arXiv preprint arXiv:2108.07258 (2021)
6. Bonnardel, V., Miller, S., Wardle, L., Drews, E.: Gender differences in colour-naming task. Perception **31**, 71 (2002)
7. Bornstein, M.H.: On the development of color naming in young children: data and theory. Brain Lang. **26**(1), 72–93 (1985)

8. Brewer, R.N., Harrington, C., Heldreth, C.: Envisioning equitable speech technologies for black older adults. In: Proceedings of the 2023 ACM Conference on Fairness, Accountability, and Transparency, pp. 379–388 (2023)
9. Cai, W., et al.: Adaptive sampling strategies to construct equitable training datasets. In: Proceedings of the 2022 ACM Conference on Fairness, Accountability, and Transparency, pp. 1467–1478 (2022)
10. Caton, S., Haas, C.: Fairness in machine learning: a survey. arXiv preprint arXiv:2010.04053 (2020)
11. Celis, L.E., Deshpande, A., Kathuria, T., Vishnoi, N.K.: How to be fair and diverse? arXiv preprint arXiv:1610.07183 (2016)
12. Chapanis, A.: Color names for color space. Am. Sci. **53**(3), 327–346 (1965)
13. Cook, A.M., Polgar, J.M.: Assistive Technologies-e-Book: Principles and Practice. Elsevier Health Sciences (2014)
14. Corbett-Davies, S., Pierson, E., Feller, A., Goel, S., Huq, A.: Algorithmic decision making and the cost of fairness. In: Proceedings of the 23rd ACM SIGKDD International Conference on Knowledge Discovery and Data Mining, pp. 797–806 (2017)
15. Daugherty, P.R., Wilson, H.J., Chowdhury, R.: Using artificial intelligence to promote diversity. MIT Sloan Manag. Rev. **60**(2), 1 (2019)
16. DiCiccio, C., Hsu, B., Yu, Y., Nandy, P., Basu, K.: Detection and mitigation of algorithmic bias via predictive parity. In: Proceedings of the 2023 ACM Conference on Fairness, Accountability, and Transparency, pp. 1801–1816 (2023)
17. Digital, M., the McKinsey Institute for Black Economic Mobility: the impact of generative AI on black communities. https://www.mckinsey.com/bem/our-insights/the-impact-of-generative-ai-on-black-communities
18. Dutta, S., Wei, D., Yueksel, H., Chen, P.Y., Liu, S., Varshney, K.: Is there a trade-off between fairness and accuracy? A perspective using mismatched hypothesis testing. In: International Conference on Machine Learning, pp. 2803–2813. PMLR (2020)
19. Fider, N.A., Komarova, N.L.: Differences in color categorization manifested by males and females: a quantitative world color survey study. Palgrave Commun. **5**(1) (2019)
20. Frank, J.: Gender differences in color naming: direct mail order advertisements. Am. Speech **65**(2), 114–126 (1990)
21. Goel, N., Faltings, B.: Crowdsourcing with fairness, diversity and budget constraints. In: Proceedings of the 2019 AAAI/ACM Conference on AI, Ethics, and Society, pp. 297–304 (2019)
22. Greene, K.S., Gynther, M.D.: Blue versus periwinkle: color identification and gender. Percept. Mot. Skills **80**(1), 27–32 (1995)
23. Gu, J., Oelke, D.: Understanding bias in machine learning. arXiv preprint arXiv:1909.01866 (2019)
24. Havasi, C., Speer, R., Holmgren, J.: Automated color selection using semantic knowledge. In: 2010 AAAI Fall Symposium Series (2010)
25. Heer, J., Stone, M.: Color naming models for color selection, image editing and palette design. In: Proceedings of the SIGCHI Conference on Human Factors in Computing Systems, pp. 1007–1016 (2012)
26. Hort, M.: Investigating trade-offs for fair machine learning systems. Ph.D. thesis, UCL (University College London) (2023)
27. Hube, C., Fetahu, B., Gadiraju, U.: Understanding and mitigating worker biases in the crowdsourced collection of subjective judgments. In: Proceedings of the 2019 CHI Conference on Human Factors in Computing Systems, pp. 1–12 (2019)

28. Iosifidis, V., Fetahu, B., Ntoutsi, E.: Fae: a fairness-aware ensemble framework. In: 2019 IEEE International Conference on Big Data (Big Data), pp. 1375–1380. IEEE (2019)

29. Kay, P., Regier, T.: Language, thought and color: recent developments. Trends Cogn. Sci. **10**(2), 51–54 (2006)

30. Li, P.: Harmonizing Fairness with Utility in Data and Learning. Ph.D. thesis, Brandeis University, Graduate School of Arts & Sciences (2024)

31. Li, P., Liu, H.: Achieving fairness at no utility cost via data reweighing with influence. In: International Conference on Machine Learning, pp. 12917–12930. PMLR (2022)

32. Lin, H., Luo, M.R., MacDonald, L.W., Tarrant, A.W.: A cross-cultural colour-naming study. Part I: using an unconstrained method. Color Research & Application: Endorsed by Inter-Society Color Council, The Colour Group (Great Britain), Canadian Society for Color, Color Science Association of Japan, Dutch Society for the Study of Color, The Swedish Colour Centre Foundation, Colour Society of Australia, Centre Français de la Couleur **26**(1), 40–60 (2001)

33. Liu, S., et al.: Fashion parsing with weak color-category labels. IEEE Trans. Multimedia **16**(1), 253–265 (2013)

34. MacLaury, R., Paramei, G., Dedrick, D.: Anthropology of Color: Interdisciplinary Multilevel Modeling. John Benjamins Publishing Company (2007)

35. Maheshwari, P., Ghuhan, M., Vinay, V.: Learning colour representations of search queries. In: Proceedings of the 43rd International ACM SIGIR Conference on Research and Development in Information Retrieval, pp. 1389–1398 (2020)

36. Mayor, T.: 3 challenges for chief data officers in finance. https://mitsloan.mit.edu/ideas-made-to-matter/3-challenges-chief-data-officers-finance

37. Mehrabi, N., Morstatter, F., Saxena, N., Lerman, K., Galstyan, A.: A survey on bias and fairness in machine learning. ACM Comput. Surv. (CSUR) **54**(6), 1–35 (2021)

38. Menon, A.K., Williamson, R.C.: The cost of fairness in binary classification. In: Conference on Fairness, Accountability and Transparency, pp. 107–118. PMLR (2018)

39. Munroe, R.: Color survey results. https://blog.xkcd.com/2010/05/03/color-survey-results/

40. Mylonas, D., Paramei, G.V., MacDonald, L.: Gender differences in colour naming. Colour studies: a broad spectrum, pp. 225–239 (2014)

41. Nowaczyk, R.H.: Sex-related differences in the color lexicon. Lang. Speech **25**(3), 257–265 (1982)

42. Setlur, V., Stone, M.C.: A linguistic approach to categorical color assignment for data visualization. IEEE Trans. Visual Comput. Graph. **22**(1), 698–707 (2015)

43. Simon, J., Bilodeau, G.-A., Steele, D., Mahadik, H.: Color inference from semantic labeling for person search in videos. In: Campilho, A., Karray, F., Wang, Z. (eds.) ICIAR 2020. LNCS, vol. 12131, pp. 139–151. Springer, Cham (2020). https://doi.org/10.1007/978-3-030-50347-5_13

44. Spiel, K., Haimson, O.L., Lottridge, D.: How to do better with gender on surveys: a guide for HCI researchers. Interactions **26**(4), 62–65 (2019)

45. Steckler, N.A., Cooper, W.E.: Sex differences in color naming of unisex apparel. Anthropol. Linguist. **22**(9), 373–381 (1980)

46. Tang, H., Cheng, L., Liu, N., Du, M.: A theoretical approach to characterize the accuracy-fairness trade-off pareto frontier. arXiv preprint arXiv:2310.12785 (2023)

47. Wang, H., Wu, Z., He, J.: Fairif: boosting fairness in deep learning via influence functions with validation set sensitive attributes. In: Proceedings of the 17th ACM International Conference on Web Search and Data Mining, pp. 721–730 (2024)
48. Wijk, H., Berg, S., Sivik, L., Steen, B.: Color discrimination, color naming and color preferences in 80-year olds. Aging Clin. Exp. Res. **11**, 176–185 (1999)
49. Zafar, M.B., Valera, I., Gomez Rodriguez, M., Gummadi, K.P.: Fairness beyond disparate treatment & disparate impact: Learning classification without disparate mistreatment. In: Proceedings of the 26th International Conference on World Wide Web, pp. 1171–1180 (2017)
50. Zaragoza, I.E.: Colour and gender: language nuances. Feminismo-s (38), 115 (2021)
51. Zhang, S., et al.: Towards better fairness-utility trade-off: a comprehensive measurement-based reinforcement learning framework. arXiv preprint arXiv:2307.11379 (2023)
52. Zheng, L., Shen, L., Tian, L., Wang, S., Wang, J., Tian, Q.: Scalable person re-identification: a benchmark. In: Proceedings of the IEEE International Conference on Computer Vision, pp. 1116–1124 (2015)
53. Zou, J., Schiebinger, L.: AI can be sexist and racist-it's time to make it fair (2018)

A Human-Centered Algorithmic Management Framework: A Literature Review

Yunshan Jiang[1], Shixin Fan[1], Yifan Zhu[1], Long Wang[1], Kunhui Ye[1], Jia Zhou[1]([✉]),
Liangqing Zhang[1], Zhixiu Wang[1], Liu Wu[2], and Pei-Luen Patrick Rau[3]

[1] School of Management Science and Real Estate, Chongqing University, Chongqing,
People's Republic of China
zhoujia07@gmail.com
[2] School of Economics and Management, Chongqing Jiaotong University, Chongqing,
People's Republic of China
[3] Department of Industrial Engineering, Tsinghua University, Beijing,
People's Republic of China

Abstract. Algorithmic management has become an important tool for most organizations to improve operational efficiency and decision-making quality, and has attracted the attention of many traditional organizations. However, the key challenge is how to design and effectively apply algorithmic management to ensure that it is applicable to different organization types, while protecting the rights of employees in the process. As a result, a human-centered algorithmic management (HCAM) framework has been developed to address the current challenges. The framework: (1) outlined the current main issues of algorithmic management, including inflexible, intrusive, inscrutable, unfair, and unsustainable; (2) identified the goals to be achieved and the corresponding strategies, including the goals of autonomous, collaborative, fair, satisfactory, sustainable, trustworthy, transparent, interpretable, and understandable; (3) verified by comparing the application of the framework in two different work environments in digital and traditional organizations. The human-centered algorithmic management framework is not only more likely to be effectively implemented in diverse organizational environments, but also enables algorithmic design to be competent in more complex management tasks, facilitates multi-party collaboration and satisfaction, and at the same time supports employee autonomy, innovation, and long-term sustainable development of the organization, among others.

Keywords: Human-centered · Algorithmic management · Human interaction · User-centered design · Human resources management

1 Introduction

Algorithmic management (AM) has gradually become indispensable, as over 88% of companies worldwide determined to use artificial intelligence for human resource management by 2024 [1]. An earlier work by Lee et al. [2] highlights that the heart of algorithmic management is utilizing algorithmic techniques to automate decision-making

H. Degen and S. Ntoa (Eds.): HCII 2024, LNCS 15382, pp. 54–71, 2024.
https://doi.org/10.1007/978-3-031-76827-9_4

and control, employed for partially or fully executing human resources management functions [3, 4]. It is prevalent in the digital organization, where platforms like Uber and Deliveroo employ algorithms to manage and monitor their global workforce.

However, the application of algorithmic management in some traditional organizations is still difficult. Traditional organizations are typically characterized by conventional business models that often embody bureaucracy, hierarchy, integration, co-location, stability, and an adversarial stance, it emphasize financial capital, mechanization, automation, economies of scale, and fixed employment [5]. Traditional organizations, which are also deeply rooted in conventional sectors such as automotive, manufacturing, construction, tourism, and banking, have historically enjoyed financial prosperity. Traditional organizations often restrict the role of algorithms in management to assisting with specific management tasks, such as wage calculation or optimizing recruitment procedures [6]. However, many algorithmic management mechanisms extensively used in platform work systems are not properly implemented when transferred to traditional work environments [7]. The majority of algorithmically governed subjects under platform organizations are gig workers, with permanent employment in traditional industries making up the majority [8]. Given the temporary and highly replaceable nature of casual workers, algorithms are used in platform organizations to carry out typical human resource processes such as work allocation and performance management [9]. The use of direct employment (i.e. a fixed employer-employee relationship) in traditional organizations may render these mechanisms inapplicable [10], which possesses a larger number of participants and a more complex composition of personnel than the crowd sourced type of work content in platform organizations. Platform organizations, acting as intermediaries between employees and customers, tend to distance managerial personnel, from direct engagement with the workplace [11]. The self-positioning and management of work in platform organizations bring with it separateness and decentralized characteristics [8] that do not require face-to-face interaction[12]. Traditional industries are mainly characterized by centralized production, not only in terms of production space but also in terms of time schedule. The above evidence suggests that there are differences between different organizations in terms of composition, management relationships, and organizational forms. This implies that current algorithmic management may not be fully applicable in some traditional organizations.

Besides inapplicability in traditional organizations, algorithmic management is subject to several challenges. As the practical application of artificial intelligence continues to grow in human resource management, challenges related to bias, lack of transparency, and ethics may ascend [13]. For example, foreign job seekers are 42% less likely to get contracts from Spanish employers through online labor platforms compared to the traditional labor market [14]. Algorithmic management may not fully benefit employees' well-being; instead, it is often treated as intrusive control over employees [11].

However, many of the current challenges in algorithmic management and the main reasons for its inapplicability in traditional organizations stem from a lack of human-centered design. While there have been studies proposing concepts such as Human-Centered Artificial Intelligence (HCAI) [15], Human-Centered Algorithmic Services (HCAS) [16], and Human-Centered Interactive Artificial Intelligence (IHCAI) [17], these concepts and frameworks do not emphasize that human resources management.

The HCAI was proposed to reinforce human capabilities in the process of cooperation between humans and automation systems [15]. But in human resource management, algorithmic management adds an employment relationship to the cooperative relationship between the automated system and the human [9]. Meanwhile, the HCAS focus on matching food donations with nonprofit organizations, and no employment relationships among the people involved [16]. Moreover, although the IHCAI focuses on the collaboration between humans and automated systems [17], but it is difficult to form effective feedback links between humans and algorithmic management systems according to the complex relationship between employees and managers [18, 19]. In light of the above evidence, directly introducing the above concepts or frameworks may not effectively address the challenges currently faced in algorithmic management.

Therefore, the research aim is: (1) to identify the current issues in the application of algorithmic management in various fields; (2) to propose a framework of human-centered algorithmic management by combining the current issues and other related frameworks; (3) to validate the proposed framework in different organizations to address the current issues in algorithmic management.

2   Methods

The retrieval process of the literature covered three phases. Relevant studies published between 2000 and 2023 were included in the review.

Phase 1: Retrieve literature based on the topic. A comprehensive search of electronic databases, including Web of Science, SpringerLink, ACM Digital Library, IEEE Xplore Digital Library, Project MUSE, and Google Scholar, was conducted using keywords such as "artificial intelligence", "human-centered", "worker-centered", "algorithmic management", "algorithmic decision", "algorithm", "perception,", "fairness", "trust", "intelligent systems", "platform labor", "platform economy", "gig economy", "construction" and "engineering project management".

Phase 2: Retrieve literature based on the reference. The cited references, citing documents and relevant literature of each paper were collected.

Phase 3: Retrieve literature based on authors. Further tracking and retrieval were conducted for authors who repeatedly appear and for authors whose research fields highly match the content.

Since this study covers computer science, information science, management, construction, social science, ergonomics, and other disciplines, the source journals were diverse, including *MIS Quarterly, Journal of the Association for Information Systems, Harvard Business Review, Journal of Management Studies, Human Resource Management, Big Data & Society, Information and Organization, Journal of Construction Engineering and Management, International Journal of Human-Computer Interaction*, and other reputable publications. Relevant conference papers were also collected, including those from prominent events such as the *ACM CHI Conference on Human Factors in Computing Systems* and the *International Conference on Information Systems*.

3   Current Main Issues for AM

Current algorithmic management has issues such as inflexible, intrusive, inscrutable, unfair, and unsustainable, which can have various negative impacts on employees, managers, and organizations (Table 1).

3.1   Inflexible

AM may make employees and work practices mechanistic. Current AM limits employee creativity and motivation, reduces employee motivation and well-being, and may not apply to more complex work environments and work tasks. AM does not provide employees with the flexibility, freedom, and autonomy that the platform organization advertises [6]. The majority of employees managed by algorithms do not have a combination of work intensity, security, and flexibility [20]. The mechanized work practices deprive employees of their autonomy and creativity, making them simple executives rather than subjects capable of exercising their abilities and innovations [21]. Self-determination theory (SDT) recognizes that people in work scenarios have three basic psychological needs (autonomy, relatedness, and competence) [22]. Over time, the frustration of not satisfying these three basic psychological needs translates into lower performance and reduced work motivation and employee well-being [23, 24]. In addition, AM eliminates the ability to think differently that managers have in traditional management, destroying balanced working relationships and making it difficult for individuals to establish trustworthy working relationships.

3.2   Intrusive

Algorithmic management realizes algorithmic authoritarianism by exerting surveillance and control over workers, limiting their freedom and value. As a result of the authoritarianism of algorithmic management, workers have lost their freedom of control over what they do, when they do it, and how they are paid [26]. Won et al. found through surveys and interviews that the delivery platforms restricted the freedom of the delivery workers about time and activities [27]. Moreover, the authoritarianism of AM simultaneously limits the pecuniary and non-pecuniary values that workers can access. Monetary values include things like automating wage theft and limiting the leeway workers have to make the best decisions for themselves [28, 29]. Non-pecuniary values include personal growth, experiencing a sense of fulfillment, etc. [20, 30]. This may trigger an adversarial relationship of control and counter-control between employers/managers and workers [18, 19].

3.3   Inscrutable

AM has obvious ethical, legal, and institutional issues (including invasion of employee privacy, increased employee insecurity and mistrust, etc.) while increasing management efficiency. The data and manipulation of the results of AM decisions are incomprehensible or untraceable for both managers and employees. The increasing use of algorithms and AI in HRM (human resources management) can be a manipulation burden and a privacy burden for employees [23]. Employees who are unfamiliar with algorithms may overestimate the transparency and objectivity of AM systems, and such employees will suffer more from systemic bias, unequal power, and privacy intrusion [31]. In addition, highly opaque AM systems prevent workers from having a clear perception of their behavior, skills, and contributions [32]. Previous research has shown that employees exposed to algorithmic tools report greater job insecurity [33]. A study of interviews with executives and engineers at Uber suggests that platform workers experience tension related to salary and belonging [34].

3.4 Unfair

The phenomenon of AM making incorrect predictions or decisions about employees due to datasets, design flaws in algorithms, and human factors can lead to a variety of fairness issues. The fairness, biased, discriminatory, or marginalized character of AM places workers at a systemic disadvantage in AM practices [35], such as pay fairness [36]. From a socio-technical perspective, Schulze et al. organized online focus groups with employees who had experience working with AM systems and found that workers experienced systemic inequities in the form of devaluation, limitation, and exclusion [35]. Previous studies have shown that online employment platforms have exacerbated discrimination in the labor market.

3.5 Unsustainable

Sustainability in algorithmic management can lead to several problems, including a lack of defined career paths for employees, a lack of employee stability, unsustainable business success, and difficulty in applying to traditional organizations. Algorithmic management often emphasizes flexibility and ad hoc work arrangements, which can leave employees with a lack of stability in their positions and limited opportunities for career paths [37, 38]. For organizations using algorithmic management, people risk is business risk. Without employee sustainability, it is difficult to achieve sustainable business success [36]. Currently, AM achieves monitoring and control of employees but is unable to coordinate multiple workers to support their co-creation of more complex products or services [39]. This new form of Taylorism can affect the sustainability of the firm. The current AM system has high requirements for the application scenario and presents an algorithmic system-centric management model in platform organizations [20]. Traditional organizations need to shift the business model of the AM system. However, how traditional organizations transfer their business and management functions to AM systems has not been effectively addressed yet [20].

Table 1. Summary of current main issues for AM

Main issues	Negative impacts
Inflexible	• Limiting employee autonomy and creativity [6, 20, 21] • Reduced employee motivation and happiness [23, 24]
Intrusive	• Restrictions on the freedom of employees [18, 19, 27–29] • Limiting the value of employees [20, 30]
Inscrutable	• Invasion of employee privacy [23, 31] • Increased employee insecurity [33, 34] • Increased employee distrust of algorithms [32] • Increased managerial distrust of algorithms [34]
Unfair	• Putting employees at a disadvantage [35] • Increased bias and discrimination against employees [14]
Unsustainable	• Lack of stability and defined career progression for employees [37, 38] • Difficulty in sustainable business development [36] • Difficult to apply to traditional organizations [20, 39]

4   A HCAM Framework

4.1   Goals of HCAM

With the various issues present in current algorithmic management, there has been a growing discussion around Human-Centered Algorithmic Management (HCAM) [41]. Concepts related to HCAM include Human-Centered Artificial Intelligence (HCAI), Human-Centered Algorithmic Services (HCAS), and Interactive Human-Centered Artificial Intelligence (IHCAI), among others. However, HCAI primarily focuses on the interaction between individuals and artificial intelligence [42], while HCAS primarily targets the collaboration among organizations through Algorithm systems, and IHCAI concentrates on the information exchange between intelligent systems and humans [44]. These concepts have received less discussion in the context of organizational management and cannot directly address the main issues in current algorithmic management. Direct application of these concepts may lead to uncertainty among designers and practitioners of algorithmic governance regarding which actions to take when addressing the problems and challenges encountered in their work.

Therefore, this section proposed the following goals for HCAM by analyzing relevant frameworks and combining them with the issues identified in the second section, as shown in Table 2.

4.2   A HCAM Framework Summarized the Issues, Solutions, and Goals

The HCAM framework is summarized as follows (Fig. 1). This framework draws upon UCD (user-centered design) concepts and methodologies [59, 60], constructing the HCAM framework from three aspects: user needs, algorithmic design and development, and system evaluation [61]. The user needs are derived from the previously

Table 2. HCAM goals were proposed by integrating current issues and related frameworks

HCAI			Goals of HCAM
References	Issues	Goals	
[42, 45–47]	Autonomy challenge/Privacy challenge/Prejudice and inequality/Right-to-work insecurity challenge	Reliability/Safe/Trustworthy/Privacy and accountability/ Fairness/Supporting human self-efficacy	• Autonomous [45, 46, 48] • Fair [42, 49, 50] • Sustainable
HCAS			• Collaborative [52, 53] • Understandable [44, 54–58]
References	**Issues**	**Goals**	• Interpretable [44, 54–58]
[52, 53]	The challenge of discriminatory decision-making /Uncertainty and ambiguity challenges/Explainable and accountable organizational challenges	Collaboration/Coordination/Reliability	• Satisfactory [44, 54–58] • Trustworthy [42] • Transparent [42]
IHCAI			
References	**Issues**	**Goals**	
[44, 54–58]	The challenge of uncertainty/The challenge of complexity/The abstraction challenge/The quality consistency challenge	Interpretable/Effective/Efficient/Satisfying/understandable	

summarized current issues in algorithmic management, while algorithmic design and development and system evaluation are the two main directions for achieving the goal of human-centered algorithmic management.

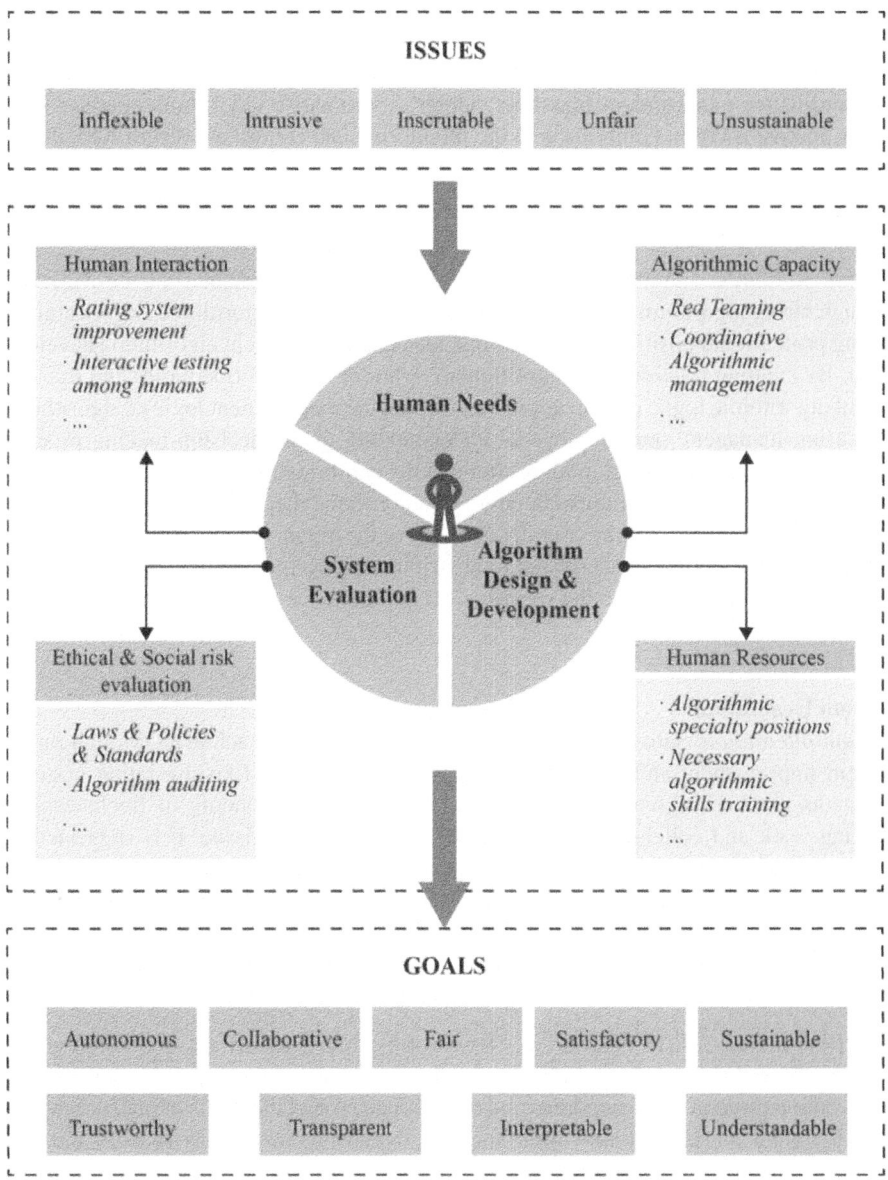

Fig. 1. The framework for HCAM

Algorithm Design and Development

Algorithmic Capacity. Autonomous, collaborative, satisfactory, sustainable, and trustworthy can be achieved through red teaming and coordinated algorithmic management. Red teaming serves to augment user trust and satisfaction by simulating adversarial attacks within algorithmic management, thereby enhancing system security through the identification and rectification of potential vulnerabilities, and fortifying the robustness of algorithms against cyber threats [62]. Algorithms should evolve along the lines of coordinative management functions, namely coordinative algorithmic management (Coordinative AM). In comparison to the monitoring and control aspects of AM, Coordinative AM emphasizes supporting employees rather than segmenting them, achieving collectively beneficial outcomes by guiding interactions and work among employees [39].

Human Resources. Transparent, understandable, and interpretable can be achieved through hiring algorithmic specialty positions and necessary algorithmic skills training. Hiring professional positions in algorithmic management can help algorithmic development. By creating roles such as algorithmists, who serve as intermediaries and translators of algorithmic logic, organizations can explain the management logic of algorithms, increasing managers' and employees' understanding of the decision-making process [68, 69]. Necessary training in algorithmic skills can bridge the gap in organizational workforces by fostering an understanding of algorithms, thereby enhancing collaboration among employees and the overall efficiency of the organization. Specifically, digital literacy enhancement courses related to algorithm management can be conducted both online and offline, tailored to the specific skill requirements of the job roles in question [63, 64].

System Evaluation

Human Interaction. Satisfactory, collaborative, and fair can be achieved through rating system improvement and interactive testing among humans. Existing rating systems may compromise the work experience and diminish the autonomy of freelancers in seeking work and collaborating with clients. To address this issue, it is suggested to adopt a more qualitative rating approach, using textual descriptions rather than numerical ratings to showcase evaluations of workers [65]. Current algorithmic management lacks an assessment of human-to-human interaction [61], which is critical for the operation of organizations in certain work environments. There is a need to focus on work scenarios and content that require high levels of collaboration between individuals.

Ethical and Social Risk Evaluation. Trustworthy, transparent, fair, and autonomous can be achieved through laws, policies, standards, and algorithm auditing. Government intervention through laws, standards and policies can protect the rights of platform workers. Governments should find ways to increase freelancers' autonomy in work and life, enabling them to better balance work and personal life [65]. Providing material features and policies to achieve and enhance the autonomy of gig workers is recommended [66]. Policymakers are advised to strengthen regulatory frameworks in the gig economy sector, which may involve significant adjustments and revisions to labor laws [67]. Clarifying the definition of "employment," creating a new category of "independent workers," and reexamining the concept of "employer" are suggested [68]. On the other hand, companies often refrain from disclosing specific details about their algorithmic management practices to protect confidentiality, leading workers to perceive algorithms as highly opaque "black boxes," hindering their understanding and acceptance of algorithmic management [69]. Conducting algorithm audits through third-party organizations can systematically examine potential discriminatory outcomes in algorithms [70], thereby reducing the risks associated with transparency.

5 Examples of Application and Popularization of HCAM

This section takes the gig economy in digital organizations and engineering projects with more complex management tasks in traditional organizations as examples to validate the proposed human-centered algorithmic management framework for its applicability in different organizations. The "gig economy" is one of the main areas where algorithmic management is currently applied, characterized by flexible working hours, locations, methods, and fragmented work content. Engineering projects are a more specific type of traditional organization, characterized by high costs, high complexity, and uncertainty [71].

5.1 The Difference Between the Gig Economy and Engineering Projects

There are significant differences between engineering projects and the gig economy, primarily in terms of the complexity, uncertainty, and ambiguity of work content, personnel characteristics, and management aspects. To apply algorithmic management to engineering projects, these differences and characteristics must be taken into consideration.

Work Aspect
Work Content. Simple vs. Complex. In the gig economy, work tasks are often clear, involving simple and limited types of work. The characteristics of project tasks mainly manifest in the uncertainty of project requirements, time constraints, and uncertainty in risk sharing [72]. Engineering projects consist of multiple tasks divided into different stages, each managed by multiple stakeholders with different functional roles. In the same stage of a project, various tasks involve stakeholders performing different functions, including individuals, organizations, and business departments, among other actors [73].

Work Mode: Independent Work vs. Coordination and Collaboration Across Multiple Job Types. In the algorithm-managed gig economy, independent work is prevalent, whereas engineering project management requires coordination and collaboration across various job types. Engineering projects are highly complex, involving multiple departments, units, and various professions such as mechanical and electrical engineering, civil engineering, business management, etc. If effective communication and coordination among these professions cannot be achieved, it can severely impact the quality of the engineering project.

Personnel Characteristics Aspect

Composition of Stakeholders: Simple vs. Complex. In the gig economy, participants include the gig suppliers (such as gig workers and the relevant enterprises providing gig labor) and the gig demanders (such as gig consumers and businesses with gig-related demands), while third-party stakeholders consist of government regulatory agencies, financial institutions, and advertisers [74]. In contrast, the stakeholders involved in engineering projects are much more complex. According to the degree of stakeholder involvement, they can be categorized as direct stakeholders and indirect stakeholders. Direct stakeholders mainly include project investors, construction agents, contractors, designers, supervisors, and users; while indirect stakeholders mainly include government departments and banks [75]. Furthermore, the interests and demands of stakeholders in engineering projects are more complex and often contradictory [76], leading to potential conflicts in their relationships. Due to the dynamic nature of engineering projects, cost and schedule control tend to lead the involved parties to focus only on their interests [77]. Niederman et al. pointed out that stakeholders, as the core of an organization, interact more as an art form (knowing when and how to provide what kind of information) rather than a science, which is a part that AI finds difficult to replace [78].

Employee Characteristics: High Digital Literacy vs. Low Digital Literacy. Compared to engineering projects, workers involved in the gig economy are often younger, more educated, and more technologically proficient Internet users [79]. However, in the current engineering field, there are more workers with lower levels of education and older ages [80]. In China, workers on engineering projects are mainly with only a junior high school education or below [80]. When using digital platforms and algorithmic management to allocate, monitor, and evaluate work tasks, it is essential to fully consider the transparency needs of construction workers regarding algorithmic management.

Management Aspect

Management Events: Explicit vs. Ambiguous. For the gig economy, management events are relatively standardized and refined, with a high degree of industrial chain division of labor and modularization. However, for engineering projects, there are a large number of uncertain management events, and complex internal and external organizational changes make it difficult to quantify and standardize management events.

Management Operations: Simple and Repetitive vs. Complex and Diverse. The management of the gig economy is mostly based on the simple repetition of single events, while the characteristics displayed at different stages of engineering projects are also different, there is coordination and coherence between different stages, making it necessary for engineering project management to span the entire project life cycle [81].

Management Risk: Small vs. Large. In the gig economy, management event failures often result in relatively minor losses, while due to the unique and permanent nature of engineering projects, project management exhibits significant one-time characteristics [82]. Once errors occur in management, the cost of correction is typically enormous, potentially leading to serious losses for the project.

5.2   HCAM Addressed These Differences and Challenges

By summarizing the differences between engineering projects and the gig economy, further validation has been provided for the reasons why current algorithmic management cannot be applied to traditional organizations. It also listed the solutions that can be applied by human-centered algorithmic management to address these differences and achieve further goals (Table 3).

Table 3. HCAM applied to the gig economy vs. engineering projects

Content		Gig economy	Engineering projects	Goals from HCAM	Solutions from HCAM
Work	Work content	Simple	Complex	Autonomous	Coordinative algorithmic management
	Work mode	Independent work	Coordination and collaboration across multiple job types	Autonomous Collaborative	Coordinative algorithmic management Interactive testing among humans
Personnel Characteristic	Composition of stakeholders	Simple	Complex	Satisfactory	Interactive testing among humans
	Employee characteristics	High digital literacy	Low digital literacy	Interpretable Understandable	Algorithmic specialty position Necessary algorithmic skills training
Management	Management events	Explicit	Ambiguous	Autonomous Collaborative	Coordinative algorithmic management Rating system improvement
	Management operations	Simple and repetitive	Complex and diverse	Autonomous Collaborative	Coordinative algorithmic management Rating system improvement

(continued)

Table 3. (*continued*)

Content		Gig economy	Engineering projects	Goals from HCAM	Solutions from HCAM
	Management risk	Small	Large	Trustworthy	Algorithm auditing Laws & Policies & Standards

6 Conclusions

The core of algorithmic management is human management, because the structure of personnel, work content, and work style in different organizations are extremely different, thus leading to differences in their applicability in different organizations. In addition, current algorithmic management has many human-related challenges, such as ethical issues and restricted employee autonomy and creativity. The human-centered algorithmic management framework better addresses the challenges of current algorithmic management and can be scaled up and applied across different people characteristics and organizational characteristics. The framework not only enables its use in different organizational environments but also helps organizations safeguard employee rights and improve organizational efficiency when using algorithmic management.

The limitations of this study lie in the restricted analysis of organizational forms and the variety of work environments involved, and it does not extend to the practical application within actual algorithmic management. Future research could further explore the difficulties faced when applying algorithmic management to particular traditional organizations, especially in terms of employee characteristics and job content specificities.

Acknowledgments. The authors would like to acknowledge the support from the National Natural Science Foundation of China (72171030), the Chongqing Municipal Federation of Social Sciences (2022YC049), and the 2022 Reform in College Elite Curriculum Research Project of Chongqing University, China (CQU-EIE-2022011).

References

1. Employers Embrace Artificial Intelligence for HR. https://www.shrm.org/topics-tools/news/employers-embrace-artificial-intelligence-hr. Accessed 3 Jan 2024
2. Lee, M.K., Kusbit, D., Metsky, E., Dabbish, L.: Working with machines: the impact of algorithmic and data-driven management on human workers. In: Proceedings of the 33rd Annual ACM Conference on Human Factors in Computing Systems, pp. 1603–1612. Association for Computing Machinery, New York, NY, USA (2015). https://doi.org/10.1145/2702123.2702548

3. Wu, X., Liu, Q., Qu, H., Wang, J.: The effect of algorithmic management and workers' coping behavior: an exploratory qualitative research of Chinese food-delivery platform. Tour. Manage. **96**, 104716 (2023). https://doi.org/10.1016/j.tourman.2022.104716

4. Gagné, M., Parent-Rocheleau, X., Bujold, A., Gaudet, M.-C., Lirio, P.: How algorithmic management influences worker motivation: a self-determination theory perspective. Can. Psychol./Psychologie canadienne. **63**, 247–260 (2022). https://doi.org/10.1037/cap0000324

5. Schultze, U., Orlikowski, W.J.: Metaphors of virtuality: shaping an emergent reality. Inf. Organ. **11**, 45–77 (2001). https://doi.org/10.1016/S1471-7727(00)00003-8

6. Noponen, N., Feshchenko, P., Auvinen, T., Luoma-aho, V., Abrahamsson, P.: Taylorism on steroids or enabling autonomy? A systematic review of algorithmic management. Manag. Rev. Q. (2023). https://doi.org/10.1007/s11301-023-00345-5

7. Lippert, I., Kirchner, K., Wiener, M.: Context matters: the use of algorithmic management mechanisms in platform, hybrid, and traditional work contexts. In: Proceedings of the 56th Hawaii International Conference on System Sciences, pp. 5282–5291 (2023)

8. Cropanzano, R., Keplinger, K., Lambert, B.K., Caza, B., Ashford, S.J.: The organizational psychology of gig work: an integrative conceptual review. J. Appl. Psychol. **108**, 492–519 (2023). https://doi.org/10.1037/apl0001029

9. Duggan, J., Sherman, U., Carbery, R., McDonnell, A.: Algorithmic management and app-work in the gig economy: a research agenda for employment relations and HRM. Hum. Resour. Manag. J. **30**, 114–132 (2020). https://doi.org/10.1111/1748-8583.12258

10. Adams-Prassl, J.: What if your boss was an algorithm? Economic incentives, legal challenges, and the rise of artificial intelligence at work. Comp. Lab. L. Pol'y J. **41**, 123 (2019)

11. Kellogg, K.C., Valentine, M.A., Christin, A.: Algorithms at work: the new contested terrain of control. Annals **14**, 366–410 (2020). https://doi.org/10.5465/annals.2018.0174

12. Jabagi, N., Croteau, A.-M., Audebrand, L.K., Marsan, J.: Gig-workers' motivation: thinking beyond carrots and sticks. J. Manag. Psychol. **34**, 192–213 (2019). https://doi.org/10.1108/JMP-06-2018-0255

13. Lee, M.K.: Understanding perception of algorithmic decisions: fairness, trust, and emotion in response to algorithmic management. Big Data Soc. **5**, 205395171875668 (2018). https://doi.org/10.1177/2053951718756684

14. Galperin, H., Greppi, C.: Geographical discrimination in digital labor platforms. SSRN J. (2017). https://doi.org/10.2139/ssrn.2922874

15. Xu, W., Gao, Z.: Enabling human-centered AI: a methodological perspective (2023). https://doi.org/10.48550/ARXIV.2311.06703

16. Lee, M.K., Kim, J.T., Lizarondo, L.: A human-centered approach to algorithmic services: considerations for fair and motivating smart community service management that allocates donations to non-profit organizations. In: Proceedings of the 2017 CHI Conference on Human Factors in Computing Systems, pp. 3365–3376. ACM, Denver Colorado USA (2017). https://doi.org/10.1145/3025453.3025884

17. Schmidt, A.: Interactive human centered artificial intelligence: a definition and research challenges. In: Proceedings of the International Conference on Advanced Visual Interfaces, pp. 1–4. ACM, Salerno Italy (2020). https://doi.org/10.1145/3399715.3400873

18. Thompson, P., Van Den Broek, D.: Managerial control and workplace regimes: an introduction. Work Employ Soc. **24**, 1–12 (2010). https://doi.org/10.1177/0950017010384546

19. Smith, C.: Continuity and change in labor process analysis forty years after Labor and Monopoly Capital. Labor Stud. J. **40**, 222–242 (2015). https://doi.org/10.1177/0160449X15607154

20. Wood, A.J., Graham, M., Lehdonvirta, V., Hjorth, I.: Good gig, bad gig: autonomy and algorithmic control in the global gig economy. Work Employ Soc. **33**, 56–75 (2019). https://doi.org/10.1177/0950017018785616

21. European Agency for Safety and Health at Work.: Foresight on new and emerging occupational safety and health risks associated with digitalisation by 2025. Publications Office, LU (2018)

22. Deci, E.L., Ryan, R.M.: The "What" and "Why" of goal pursuits: human needs and the self-determination of behavior. Psychol. Inq. **11**, 227–268 (2000). https://doi.org/10.1207/S15327 965PLI1104_01

23. Kinowska, H., Sienkiewicz, ŁJ.: Influence of algorithmic management practices on workplace well-being – evidence from European organisations. ITP **36**, 21–42 (2023). https://doi.org/10.1108/ITP-02-2022-0079

24. Benlian, A., et al.: Algorithmic management: bright and dark sides, practical implications, and research opportunities. Bus. Inf. Syst. Eng. **64**, 825–839 (2022). https://doi.org/10.1007/s12599-022-00764-w

25. Langfred, C.W.: The downside of self-management: a longitudinal study of the effects TF conflict on trust, autonomy, and task interdependence in self-managing teams. AMJ **50**, 885–900 (2007). https://doi.org/10.5465/amj.2007.26279196

26. Won, J., Lee, D., Lee, J.: Understanding experiences of food-delivery-platform workers under algorithmic management using topic modeling. Technol. Forecast. Soc. Chang. **190**, 122369 (2023). https://doi.org/10.1016/j.techfore.2023.122369

27. Meijerink, J., Bondarouk, T.: The duality of algorithmic management: toward a research agenda on HRM algorithms, autonomy and value creation. Hum. Resour. Manag. Rev. **33**, 100876 (2023)

28. Meijerink, J., Boons, M., Keegan, A., Marler, J.: Algorithmic human resource management: synthesizing developments and cross-disciplinary insights on digital HRM. Int. J. Hum. Resource Manage. **32**, 2545–2562 (2021). https://doi.org/10.1080/09585192.2021.1925326

29. Goods, C., Veen, A., Barratt, T.: "Is your gig any good?" Analysing job quality in the Australian platform-based food-delivery sector. J. Ind. Relat. **61**, 502–527 (2019). https://doi.org/10.1177/0022185618817069

30. Barati, M., Ansari, B.: Effects of algorithmic control on power asymmetry and inequality within organizations. J. Manag. Control. **33**, 525–544 (2022). https://doi.org/10.1007/s00187-022-00347-6

31. Gal, U., Jensen, T.B., Stein, M.-K.: Breaking the vicious cycle of algorithmic management: a virtue ethics approach to people analytics. Inf. Organ. **30**, 100301 (2020). https://doi.org/10.1016/j.infoandorg.2020.100301

32. Yam, K.C., Tang, P.M., Jackson, J.C., Su, R., Gray, K.: The rise of robots increases job insecurity and maladaptive workplace behaviors: multimethod evidence (2022)

33. Möhlmann, M., Zalmanson, L., Henfridsson, O., Gregory, R.W.: Algorithmic management of work on online labor platforms: when matching meets control. MIS Quar. **45** (2021)

34. Schulze, L., Cai, Z., Trenz, M., Tan, C.-W.: Algorithmic unfairness on digital labor platforms: how algorithmic management practices disadvantage workers (2022)

35. 2024 Global Talent Trends. https://www.mercer.com/insights/people-strategy/future-of-work/global-talent-trends/. Accessed 3 Jan 2024

36. Duggan, J., Sherman, U., Carbery, R., McDonnell, A.: Boundaryless careers and algorithmic constraints in the gig economy. Int. J. Hum. Resource Manage. **33**, 4468–4498 (2022). https://doi.org/10.1080/09585192.2021.1953565

37. Ashford, S.J., Caza, B.B., Reid, E.M.: From surviving to thriving in the gig economy: a research agenda for individuals in the new world of work. Res. Organ. Behav. **38**, 23–41 (2018)

38. Becker, L., Wurm, B., Hess, T.: Will algorithms replace managers? A systematic literature review on algorithmic management (2023)

39. Cameron, L.: Management Department University of Pennsylvania, USA, Laura Lamers, Behavioural Management and Social Sciences University of Twente, Netherlands, Ulrich

Leicht-Deobald, Trinity Business School Trinity College Dublin, The University of Dublin, Ireland, Christoph Lutz, Department of Communication and Culture BI Norwegian Business School, Norway, Jeroen Meijerink, Behavioural Management and Social Sciences University of Twente, Netherlands, Mareike Möhlmann, Information and Process Management Department Bentley University, USA: Algorithmic Management: Its Implications for Information Systems Research. CAIS, vol. 52, pp. 518–537 (2023). https://doi.org/10.17705/1CAIS.05221

40. Xu, W., Dainoff, M.J., Ge, L., Gao, Z.: Transitioning to human interaction with AI systems: new challenges and opportunities for HCI professionals to enable human-centered AI. Int. J. Hum.-Comput. Interact. **39**, 494–518 (2023). https://doi.org/10.1080/10447318.2022.2041900

41. Andrienko, N., Andrienko, G., Adilova, L., Wrobel, S.: Visual analytics for human-centered machine learning. IEEE Comput. Graphics Appl. **42**, 123–133 (2022). https://doi.org/10.1109/MCG.2021.3130314

42. Ozmen Garibay, O., et al.: Six human-centered artificial intelligence grand challenges. Int. J. Hum.-Comput. Interact. **39**, 391–437 (2023). https://doi.org/10.1080/10447318.2022.2153320

43. Shneiderman, B.: Human-centered AI. Oxford University Press (2022). https://doi.org/10.1093/oso/9780192845290.001.0001

44. Shneiderman, B.: Human-centered artificial intelligence: reliable, safe & trustworthy. Int. J. Hum.-Comput. Interact. **36**, 495–504 (2020). https://doi.org/10.1080/10447318.2020.1741118

45. Longo, F., Nicoletti, L., Padovano, A.: Smart operators in industry 4.0: a human-centered approach to enhance operators' capabilities and competencies within the new smart factory context. Comput. Indust. Eng. **113**, 144–159 (2017). https://doi.org/10.1016/j.cie.2017.09.016

46. Colquitt, J.A., Hill, E.T., De Cremer, D.: Forever focused on fairness: 75 years of organizational justice in Personnel Psychology. Pers. Psychol. **76**, 413–435 (2023). https://doi.org/10.1111/peps.12556

47. Woods, S.A., Ahmed, S., Nikolaou, I., Costa, A.C., Anderson, N.R.: Personnel selection in the digital age: a review of validity and applicant reactions, and future research challenges. Eur. J. Work Organ. Psy. **29**, 64–77 (2020). https://doi.org/10.1080/1359432X.2019.1681401

48. Ahmad, K., Abdelrazek, M., Arora, C., Agrahari Baniya, A., Bano, M., Grundy, J.: Requirements engineering framework for human-centered artificial intelligence software systems. Appl. Soft Comput. **143**, 110455 (2023). https://doi.org/10.1016/j.asoc.2023.110455

49. Herrmann, T., Pfeiffer, S.: Keeping the organization in the loop: a socio-technical extension of human-centered artificial intelligence. AI Soc. **38**, 1523–1542 (2023). https://doi.org/10.1007/s00146-022-01391-5

50. Battistoni, P., Di Gregorio, M., Romano, M., Sebillo, M., Vitiello, G.: Can AI-oriented requirements enhance human-centered design of intelligent interactive systems? results from a workshop with young HCI designers. Multimodal Technol. Interact. **7**, 24 (2023). https://doi.org/10.3390/mti7030024

51. Nazar, M., Alam, M.M., Yafi, E., Su'ud, M.M.: A systematic review of human–computer interaction and explainable artificial intelligence in healthcare with artificial intelligence techniques. IEEE Access **9**, 153316–153348 (2021). https://doi.org/10.1109/ACCESS.2021.3127881

52. Riedl, M.O.: Human-centered artificial intelligence and machine learning. Hum. Behav. Emerg. Technol. **1**, 33–36 (2019). https://doi.org/10.1002/hbe2.117

53. Sacha, D., et al.: What you see is what you can change: human-centered machine learning by interactive visualization. Neurocomputing **268**, 164–175 (2017). https://doi.org/10.1016/j.neucom.2017.01.105

54. Yang, Q., Steinfeld, A., Rosé, C., Zimmerman, J.: Re-examining whether, why, and how human-ai interaction is uniquely difficult to design. In: Proceedings of the 2020 CHI Conference on Human Factors in Computing Systems, pp. 1–13. Association for Computing Machinery, New York, NY, USA (2020). https://doi.org/10.1145/3313831.3376301

55. Witteman, H.O., et al.: User-centered design and the development of patient decision aids: protocol for a systematic review. Syst. Rev. **4**, 11 (2015). https://doi.org/10.1186/2046-4053-4-11

56. Garrett, J.J.: The elements of user experience: user-centered design for the web and beyond. New Riders, Berkeley, Calif (2011)

57. Weidinger, L., et al.: Sociotechnical safety evaluation of generative AI systems. https://arxiv.longhoe.net/abs/2310.11986v2. Accessed 25 May 2024

58. Al-Azzawi, M., Doan, D., Sipola, T., Hautamäki, J., Kokkonen, T.: Artificial intelligence cyberattacks in red teaming: a scoping review. In: Rocha, Á., Adeli, H., Dzemyda, G., Moreira, F., Poniszewska-Marańda, A. (eds.) Good Practices and New Perspectives in Information Systems and Technologies. WorldCIST 2024. LNNS, vol. 985. Springer, Cham (2024). https://doi.org/10.1007/978-3-031-60215-3_13

59. Neylan, J., Biddlestone, M., Roozenbeek, J., Van Der Linden, S.: How to "inoculate" against multimodal misinformation: a conceptual replication of Roozenbeek and van der Linden (2020). Sci. Rep. **13**, 18273 (2023). https://doi.org/10.1038/s41598-023-43885-2

60. Moore, R.C., Hancock, J.T.: A digital media literacy intervention for older adults improves resilience to fake news. Sci. Rep. **12**, 6008 (2022). https://doi.org/10.1038/s41598-022-08437-0

61. Carlos Alvarez De La Vega, J., Cecchinato, E.M., Rooksby, J.: Why lose control?" A Study of Freelancers' Experiences with Gig Economy Platforms. In: Proceedings of the 2021 CHI Conference on Human Factors in Computing Systems, pp. 1–14. ACM, Yokohama Japan (2021). https://doi.org/10.1145/3411764.3445305

62. De Stefano, V.: The rise of the "Just-in-Time Workforce": on-demand work, crowd work and labour protection in the "Gig-Economy." SSRN J. (2015). https://doi.org/10.2139/ssrn.2682602

63. Todolí-Signes, A.: The 'gig economy': employee, self-employed or the need for a special employment regulation? Transf. Eur. Rev. Labour Res. **23**, 193–205 (2017). https://doi.org/10.1177/1024258917701381

64. Stewart, A., Stanford, J.: Regulating work in the gig economy: what are the options? Econ. Labour Relat. Rev. **28**, 420–437 (2017). https://doi.org/10.1177/1035304617722461

65. Möhlmannn, M., Alves de Lima Salge, C., Marabelli, M.: Algorithm sensemaking: how platform workers make sense of algorithmic management. J. Assoc. Inform. Syst. **24**, 35–64 (2023). https://doi.org/10.17705/1jais.00774

66. Möhlmann, M.: Algorithmic nudges don't have to be unethical. Harvard Bus. Rev. **22** (2021)

67. Hu, Y., Chan, A.P.C., Le, Y., Jin, R.: From construction megaproject management to complex project management: bibliographic analysis. J. Manage. Eng. **31**, 04014052 (2015). https://doi.org/10.1061/(ASCE)ME.1943-5479.0000254

68. Khazaeni, G., Khanzadi, M., Afshar, A.: Fuzzy adaptive decision making model for selection balanced risk allocation. Int. J. Project Manage. **30**, 511–522 (2012). https://doi.org/10.1016/j.ijproman.2011.10.003

69. Fellows, R., Liu, A.M.M.: Managing organizational interfaces in engineering construction projects: addressing fragmentation and boundary issues across multiple interfaces. Constr. Manag. Econ. **30**, 653–671 (2012). https://doi.org/10.1080/01446193.2012.668199

70. Rochet, J.-C., Tirole, J.: Platform competition in two-sided markets. J. Eur. Econ. Assoc. **1**, 990–1029 (2003). https://doi.org/10.1162/154247603322493212

71. Frederick, W.C.: Business and society: corporate strategy, public policy, ethics

72. Chen, Y.Q., Zhang, Y.B., Zhang, S.J.: Impacts of different types of owner-contractor conflict on cost performance in construction projects. J. Constr. Eng. Manage. **140**, 04014017 (2014). https://doi.org/10.1061/(ASCE)CO.1943-7862.0000852

73. Iorio, J., Taylor, J.E.: Boundary object efficacy: the mediating role of boundary objects on task conflict in global virtual project networks. Int. J. Project Manage. **32**, 7–17 (2014). https://doi.org/10.1016/j.ijproman.2013.04.001

74. Niederman, F.: Project management: openings for disruption from AI and advanced analytics. ITP. **34**, 1570–1599 (2021). https://doi.org/10.1108/ITP-09-2020-0639

75. Shaw, A., Fiers, F., Hargittai, E.: Participation inequality in the gig economy. Inf. Commun. Soc. **26**, 2250–2267 (2023). https://doi.org/10.1080/1369118X.2022.2085611

76. 刘杨: 2020年农民工监测调查报告_部门政务_中国政府网. https://www.gov.cn/xinwen/2021-04/30/content_5604232.htm#tdsub. Accessed 16 Jan 2024

77. Liao, T.W., Egbelu, P.J., Sarker, B.R., Leu, S.S.: Metaheuristics for project and construction management – a state-of-the-art review. Autom. Constr. **20**, 491–505 (2011). https://doi.org/10.1016/j.autcon.2010.12.006

78. Design and Construction Building in Value. Elsevier professional, Erscheinungsort nicht ermittelbar (2002)

Public Perception of AI: A Review

Aimee Kendall Roundtree[✉] [iD]

Texas State University, San Marcos, TX 78666, USA
akr@txstate.edu

Abstract. This review gives designers deeper insights into public perceptions of artificial intelligence (AI). Ethical complexities surround AI, including privacy concerns, social deployment, and nonhuman decision-making. This project included English-language, peer-reviewed surveys and reviews published within the past five years. It also conducts topic modeling of one year's worth of social media data. Data were gathered from various academic databases and social media platforms and analyzed with topic modeling and sentiment analysis to provide external validation of insights into public sentiment and attitudes towards AI. Surveys and reviews worldwide revealed an understanding of AI concepts and positive sentiment toward AI integration in healthcare. Concerns persisted regarding data privacy, safety, and AI's impact on employment. Individual factors like age and education influence attitudes. Reviews mirrored survey findings with safety concerns about autonomous vehicles and calls for collaboration and regulation in clinical AI implementation. Social media discussions delved into AI's ethical, market, and policy implications, but Quora leaned more positively and Reddit more speculatively. Reviews, surveys, and social media provide insights into global attitudes toward AI, highlighting widespread understanding but persistent concerns. Collaboration, regulation, and ongoing education are essential for responsible AI integration across domains and regions to address privacy, security, and ethical concerns. Designers must prioritize transparency, accountability, and human-centered design to build trust and address public apprehensions.

Keywords: public · perception · attitudes · artificial intelligence · AI · topic modeling · survey · review · social media

1 Introduction

User experience mixed methods offer useful insights on public perceptions of artificial intelligence (AI). More consensus definitions, multidisciplinary analyses, public engagement, and attention are critical [1]. Public opinion reflects the ethical complexities surrounding privacy and social deployment of AI and attitudes about involving nonhuman agents in decision-making and the consequences and human autonomy [2]. To determine public-centered dimensions important to the public pertaining to AI implementations, this project uses three methodological approaches. First, this article summarizes findings from public attitude surveys on AI. Second, it provides an overview of peer-reviewed findings from reviews on public perception of AI. Third, text mining analyzes social media content to build a consensus of attitudes about AI. Finally, the project synthesizes these findings using a people-centered and science of engagement framework to derive recommendations and best practices for improving public trust and understanding of AI.

2 Methods

The article reviews peer-reviewed surveys and reviews about public perceptions of AI. For both surveys and reviews, integrative review methods were deployed. All data were from peer-reviewed journals published in the past five years, given the fast-paced nature of AI developments. Only English-language publications were included. Only peer-reviewed material was included to ensure the highest level of credibility and verification. Information sources included peer-reviewed journals. Theses and non-peer-reviewed articles were eliminated, as were publications older than five years. Any article that did not focus on public perception or attitudes was eliminated. Google Scholar, PubMed, Web of Science, Scopus, ScienceDirect, Elsevier, ERIC, IEEE Xplore, ACM, and JSTOR. Keywords included AI, artificial intelligence, public perception, public attitudes, survey, and questionnaire. Article methods, results, and conclusions sections were reviewed. Key findings from the results sections of included articles were extracted and summarized using close reading. Data analysis included summarizing and grouping summaries pertaining to similar topics.

The article also conducts topic modeling on a year's worth of social media discussions pertaining to AI. Social media posting titles reflect questions, comments, and concerns about various subjects. Natural language processing was completed using Orange Data Mining, with data analysis workflows assembled in a visual programming environment. Steps taken to preprocess the text data before applying topic modeling techniques included stop-word removal, lowercasing, stemming, handling of special characters, numbers, and punctuation, and parsing and removing URLS. The specific topic modeling algorithm used was the Hierarchical Dirichlet process approach, which uses a Dirichlet process for each data group for all groups that share a base distribution. The base distribution itself is based on the Dirichlet process. The specific sentiment analysis approach was Vader, a lexicon- and rule-based sentiment analysis. This method allows groups to share statistical strength by sharing clusters across groups and yields high internal validity. The quality of the generated topics was addressed with a topic coherence score that measures the similarity between high-scoring words in the topic. Sampling included the first postings offered by and permitted scraping by Instant DataScraper from Reddit and Quora. External validity was assessed by comparing two social media sites. Instant DataScraper collected 1546 Quora discussion titles and 2200 Reddit titles randomly selected from the past year. Orange is (an open-source data visualization, machine learning, and data mining toolkit) was used for text mining and natural language processing. Data was organized into meaningful clusters for an overview of domains and text classification.

3   Results

Findings from surveys, reviews, and social media content follow. Overall, factors like job loss, AI efficacy, and socio-economic environments impacted AI acceptance and public perception, as do concerns about data privacy, AI's impact on employment, privacy, personal data use, safety, and differing attitudes towards AI deployment in journalism. Still, there was relatively high awareness and acceptance of AI technologies, with some positive sentiments about its integration in healthcare services. Students viewed AI positively as a partner in improving their fields, emphasizing its potential to revolutionize medicine and dentistry.

Table 1. Survey and Review Inclusion and Exclusion.

	Surveys	Reviews
Total Retrieved	34	54
No access	1	0
Not peer reviewed	1	0
Repeat	7	6
Impertinent	14	42
Thesis	1	0
Language	1	0
Total Included	9	6

3.1   Surveys

The database search yielded 34 articles, only nine meeting inclusion criteria. See Table 1. The peer-reviewed surveys found were mostly from countries other than the United States, and these public surveys reveal mixed feelings about AI. Studies examined attitudes about AI deployment in different settings, from general attitudes to uses in advertising, social media, and journalism. Public, peer-reviewed studies found concern about AI's impact on employment. A study by Vu et al. (2022) examined factors influencing public attitudes across 28 European countries [3]. The perceived threat of job loss and perceived level of efficacy of AI predict acceptance of AI/Robot, with regression coefficients of $\beta = -1.066$ (p < .000) and $\beta = 0.596$ (p < .000), respectively. These variables explain 22.5% of the total variance in the public accepting AI. A country's techno-socio environment (including innovation, government effectiveness, and GDP per capita) significantly predicted individual-level variables. It positively predicted digital technology efficacy ($\beta = 0.183$, p < .000, $R2 = .53$) and negatively predicted the perceived threat of general job loss ($\beta = -0.124$, p < .000, $R2 = .37$), but not acceptance of AI/Robot ($\beta = 0.163$, p = .212, $R2 = .07$).

Another study of the public in Germany examined the public's attitudes about using AI in advertising and again found mixed attitudes. In Kozyreva et al. (2020), 86% of participants were familiar with AI, 58% had heard of computer algorithms, and 42% were familiar with machine learning [4]. Most people find personalization of political advertising (61%) and news sources (57%) unacceptable but accept personalized entertainment (77%), shopping (78%), and search results (63%). Most found unacceptable the collection and use of personal information, especially sensitive information like religious or political views. Most (82%) of respondents were concerned about data privacy.

There are slightly more positive public attitudes about AI used in social media. A survey by Cui and Wu (2021) found that the public in China generally perceives AI as more beneficial than risky [5]. Whether respondents found AI personally relevant positively predicted their risk perception, benefit perception, and policy support (b = 0.53, p < .001). Perceived AI knowledge did not significantly predict risk perception (b = 0.01, p > .05), benefit perception (b = 0.07, p > .05), or policy support (b = 0.06, p > .05). Negative emotions positively predicted risk perception (b = 0.34, p < .001) and negatively predicted benefit perception (b = −0.24, p < .001) and policy support (b = −.021, p < .001). Media use accounted for 3.7% of the variance in benefit perception. Traditional media (newspapers and TV) had significant but contradictory effects on benefit perception. WeChat positively predicted benefit perception (b = 0.12, p < .05), while Weibo had no significant effect.

There were mixed attitudes about AI deployments in journalism. In Sun et al. (2022), most respondents were familiar with AI applications in journalism (mean score of 3.94 out of 5) [6]. Positive emotions towards AI-produced news achieved a mean score of 3.78 out of 5. Negative emotions towards AI-produced news achieved a mean score of 2.13 out of 5. Concerns about AI in journalism achieved a mean score of 3.14 out of 5. A range from 52.1% to 73.7% preferred traditional reporting over AI reporting in various news content categories. About 57% of respondents agreed that AI and traditional modes should complement each other. There was a negative correlation between age and positive emotions toward AI anchors (r = −.059, p < 0.05) and between age and negative emotions toward AI anchors (r = -.070, p < 0.01). There was positive correlation between education and existing knowledge of AI in journalism (r = .236, p < 0.001), positive emotions towards AI anchors (r = .099, p < 0.001), and perceived benefits of AI in journalism (r = .097, p < 0.001), as well as positive correlation between income and existing knowledge of AI in journalism (r = .161, p < 0.001), positive emotions towards AI anchors (r = .110, p < 0.001, and perceived benefits of AI in journalism (r = .147, p < 0.001).

A subset of peer-reviewed surveys on public attitudes found mixed attitudes about AI deployments in medicine and health. Studies generally show that, for the public, the further the deployment is away from actual clinical care and the more it is considered a tool rather than a replacement, the more accepted it is, and, in reverse, the closer the deployment is to clinical care and human replacement, the more concerns emerge. For example, In Guha's (2021) study, fifty Delhi participants aged 18–50 who were health-conscious and proficient in technology usage reported a desire for AI integration in medical services [7]. Most respondents preferred AI integration in various aspects of healthcare services. Specifically, 78% preferred AI for appointment booking, 88% for comprehensive diagnosis and risk factor analysis, 98% for complex surgeries, 92% for COVID-19-related queries, and 94% for general health maintenance.

Public attitudes about AI aiding health and medicine were generally positive. However, the prospect of AI replacing human providers in health and medicine was less accepted. For example, Chen et al. (2020) assessed the public perspectives of 400 respondents on the potential replacement of human doctors by AI in the medical field [8]. Significant differences ($p < 0.01$) in responses were observed among the four groups categorized by occupational status and gender. Cluster analysis revealed two distinct groups: on-job women and on-job men. The survey found that 82.5% of respondents followed AI-related news. The average score for "public attitude towards AI application in the medical field" was 2.828 out of 5, or a negative stance below the neutral threshold (score = 3).

Stai et al. (2020) conducted a survey at the Minnesota State Fair involving 264 participants to measure public perception and comprehension of medical AI and robotic surgery [9]. Overall, there was equal trust in AI and physician diagnoses, but participants were significantly more likely to trust AI for cancer diagnosis than doctors. Although 55% expressed discomfort with robotic surgery, 88% mistakenly believed it was already AI-led. Most participants were willing to pay for AI review of medical imaging, with varying confidence levels for seeking a second opinion. Older participants and participants with higher broadband subscriptions were more uncomfortable with robotic surgery; higher median incomes correlated with greater comfort.

Health- and medical-related studies also compared public attitudes about AI deployments in health and medicine to provider attitudes and found that the public had slightly more concerns. Still, all groups perceived fast adoption of AI in health and medicine. Tamori et al. (2022) investigated the acceptance of AI in medicine among Japanese doctors and the public [10]. Also, 65.4% of respondents believed AI in medicine would be necessary in the future. Yet only 44.7% expressed an intention to use AI-driven medicine. Moreover, 73.1% believed regulatory legislation was necessary, with 73.5% expressing concerns about accountability. Doctors were more likely (mean 3.43, SD 1.00) than the public (mean 3.23, SD 0.92) to express an intention to use AI-driven medicine (P < .001). There was greater optimism among doctors. While many respondents were optimistic about AI's role in medicine, they also expected regulation and accountability of AI deployments. Over 50% of respondents rated the usefulness and necessity of AI in medicine positively. However, only 44.7% expressed intention to use AI-driven medicine. Doctors showed greater knowledge of AI in medicine compared to the public.

Students generally view AI as a partner in improving medicine and dentistry. Bisdas et al. (2021) surveyed 3,133 medical and dental students from 63 countries, and significant statistical findings emerged regarding students' perceptions and attitudes towards AI in medicine and dentistry [11]. Results indicated that most respondents had at least a moderate understanding of AI technologies, with higher agreement associated with being male, tech-savvy, pre-clinical students, and from developed countries. Additionally, students perceived AI as a partner rather than a competitor, with a majority believing it would revolutionize medicine and dentistry. Most students expressed eagerness to incorporate AI into their future practice, with 85.6% agreeing that AI should be part of medical training. Notably, students primarily relied on web-browsing for AI information, which highlighted the need for AI integration into medical and dental school curricula. While most students did not find AI developments frightening, there was some variance in responses regarding fears about AI. A third of respondents selected their university as a source of information on AI. Most students (60.01%) also believe that AI could lead to an optimized medical education highlighting the room for improvement in the current teaching methods. Despite varying levels of fear about AI, students primarily relied on web browsing for AI information, suggesting a need for AI integration into medical and dental school curricula to optimize education.

Surveys show generally high awareness and acceptance of AI across different regions and contexts. Surveys found a widespread understanding of AI. Significant proportions of participants in these peer-reviewed public surveys were familiar with AI-related terms and concepts. There was some positive sentiment about the integration of AI in health-care services. Studies show support among both the public and medical professionals for various AI applications, ranging from appointment booking to complex surgeries, suggesting a recognition of AI's potential to revolutionize healthcare delivery. Medical and dental students held positive attitudes about AI integration into their future practice as potential partners rather than competitors. While there was acceptance of AI in certain areas like entertainment and shopping, there are concerns about its use in sensitive domains such as political advertising. Concerns about AI's impact on employment, privacy, and personal data use persisted across different countries. Studies found mixed attitudes about AI deployment in various sectors and a nuanced public understanding of its potential risks and benefits. Additionally, individual factors such as age, education, economic health, and income influence perceptions of AI. Youth, education level, and economic strength were associated with positive attitudes. Despite recognizing AI's potential benefits, including increased efficiency and innovation, the public remained wary of its potential drawbacks and limitations and expects careful consideration and regulation of AI implementations.

3.2 Reviews

The database search yielded 54 articles, only six meeting inclusion criteria. See Table 1. Reviews of public perception of AI confirmed peer-reviewed survey findings. The public has shared preferences regarding data privacy and desires to control access to their health data. Beets et al. (2023) analyzed data from 11 nationally representative surveys, with sample sizes ranging from 1,001 to 10,260 respondents [12]. In a 2015 survey by the Monmouth University Polling Institute, 70% of Americans had heard of the term "artificial intelligence" or "AI". In a 2020 survey, 83% of Americans reported using smartphones, and 29% reported using smart personal assistants like Alexa and Siri. The survey found that 48% of Americans were unaware of using AI for disease diagnosis. According to the same survey, 34% of respondents believed AI would likely improve health, while 31% thought it was unlikely. A 2021 Pew Research Center survey found that 35% of respondents were concerned about AI diagnosing medical problems. A 2014 Pew Research Center survey revealed that 65% of respondents believed it would be a change for the worse if lifelike robots became primary caregivers for the elderly and sick. In a 2019 Rock Health and the Stanford Center for Digital Health survey, 82% of respondents expressed a desire to control access to their health data. According to a 2018 survey, Americans were most willing to share anonymized health information with personal doctors (61%), followed by family members (41%). In a 2020 Pew Research

Center survey, 52% of respondents found it acceptable for the government to track people who tested positive for COVID-19, while 37% found it acceptable to ensure compliance with social distancing measures.

Safety is important in shaping public perception. Othman (2021) reviewed surveys on public perception of autonomous vehicle (AV) use and found that safety is the primary public concern for potential AV users; 82% of respondents prioritized safety over cost and laws [13]. However, a notable portion (74%) did not trust AVs to perform better than human drivers. They expressed concerns about malfunctions (74%), poor awareness of surroundings (57%), programming issues (52%), and control issues (50%). Moreover, surveys suggested that consumers were reluctant to adopt AVs immediately; 62.5% preferred to wait more than two years before considering a purchase. Lack of trust in the technology (41%) and safety concerns (24%) were primary reasons for this hesitation, overshadowing cost considerations. International surveys corroborated widespread concerns about AV safety across different countries and high levels of apprehension about poor weather conditions, interaction with pedestrians, and general system safety. Analysis of social media data following an AV accident showed a decline in positive sentiment towards AVs, suggesting a loss of trust compared to previously positive sentiments. Extensive media coverage of AV accidents contributed to heightened public fear–the more accidents reported, the more public apprehension. AV manufacturers must prioritize safety and address concerns through transparent communication and robust safety measures. Negative sentiment intensifying following accidents might persist in the long term.

Participants identified multifaceted challenges and emphasized the importance of ongoing collaboration, regulation, and thoughtful implementation strategies for clinical AI. Hogg et al. (2023) conducted a comprehensive review of 4437 articles and identified 111 (2.5%) for inclusion [14]. Health care professionals (HCPs) comprised the largest stakeholder group (70%), followed by patients (11.4%), care providers, and other public members (7.7%), developers (7.5%), and health care managers and leaders (3.4%). These studies covered 23 nations and 25 clinical specialties, focusing mostly on primary care. Analysis revealed five stakeholder groups, each identifying implementation factors for clinical AI, mapped across subdomains, including non-adoption, abandonment, scale-up, spread, and sustainability subdomains. Differences existed in areas like intellectual property and sociocultural attitudes. Developers faced challenges balancing technical and clinical expertise with clinical duties. Usability/accessibility and tool adaptability influenced adoption. HCPs perceived value in using AI for training, task reduction, outcome improvement, and practice expansion, but barriers like time constraints and skepticism were a concern. Healthcare managers and leaders supported implementation, emphasizing careful tool selection, stepwise adoption, and co-design. Patients and care providers expressed concerns about HCP basing changes and substitution on AI decision-making, but they favored patient-facing AI under HCP oversight. Public perception varied, and it was influenced by the media and trust in HCPs. Regulatory oversight and stakeholder collaboration must address legal and policy concerns.

Addressing public concerns is crucial for ensuring ethical and effective AI integration in healthcare. Vo et al. (2023) conducted a systematic review of 105 articles on attitudes towards AI in healthcare published between 2001 and 2021 [15]. Participants' perceptions of AI varied widely. Concerning knowledge and familiarity, patients, the public, and health professionals showed limited understanding of AI (n = 18 publications). Perceived benefits included improved test accuracy, reduced medical errors, and workload reduction (n = 49). Risks such as data privacy and healthcare disparities were highlighted (n = 47). Challenges included delivering empathic care and technical uncertainties (n = 30). Overall, acceptability depended on factors like trust, affordability, and ease of use (n = 59), with most expressing positive attitudes toward AI (n = 28). Some hesitated due to a preference for human interaction or mistrust (n = 8). Health professionals, patients, and the public agreed that AI in healthcare should prioritize validation, transparency, and accountability. They emphasized the importance of AI algorithms being developed and validated within clinical contexts, with clinicians playing a crucial role in validation processes. Furthermore, stakeholders underscored the necessity of education and training for healthcare professionals to effectively utilize AI while maintaining professional autonomy. The human-AI relationship should be one of collaboration, with AI assisting but not replacing human judgment, particularly in clinical decision-making.

The public sees AI as an enhanced practice that is contingent on education, collaboration, and ongoing research, but as an aid for practitioners rather than a replacement. Yang et al. (2023) conducted a scoping review on AI in radiology and identified seven key themes: predicted impact, potential for radiologist replacement, trust in AI, knowledge gaps, education needs, economic factors, and medicolegal implications [16]. Respondents foresaw AI significantly impacting radiology, but they doubted radiologists would be replaced soon. Collaboration between radiologists and AI experts was crucial for improving patient care. Limited AI knowledge, especially among non-computer scientists, necessitates further education. Respondents stressed the importance of research on non-Western perspectives, non-radiologist stakeholders, and addressing economic and medico-legal concerns. Furthermore, Young et al. (2021) conducted a systematic review of 23 studies from 2000 to 2020 on patient and public attitudes toward clinical AI [17]. Of these, 26% assessed existing or imminent AI tools, and 74% evaluated hypothetical AI. Despite positive overall attitudes, participants preferred human involvement. Six themes emerged: AI concept, acceptability, relationship with humans, development and implementation, strengths and benefits, and weaknesses and risks. Methodological quality varied, with frequent selection bias. The review recommended future studies to guide clinical AI's safe, equitable, and patient-centered implementation.

The reviews revealed attitudes and concerns, as the surveys did. The reviews indicate varying awareness and acceptance of AI across different populations. Concerns about data privacy, safety, and the impact on healthcare delivery persist. Safety emerged as a paramount concern, particularly regarding autonomous vehicles. A significant portion of the public distrusted autonomous cars' capabilities. In healthcare, stakeholders emphasized the importance of collaboration, regulation, and transparency in implementing clinical AI. Limited understanding of AI among patients and healthcare professionals underscored the need for education and training. Despite positive attitudes toward AI's potential benefits in healthcare, there was a preference for human involvement in decision-making. Trust, validation, and accountability were key factors influencing acceptability and adoption. Overall, the public saw AI as enhancing healthcare practice but advocated for its role as an aid rather than a replacement for human judgment.

3.3 Social Media

Discussions on social media confirm growing interest and acceptance of AI, with a generally neutral sentiment towards its impact on various aspects of society. Across Quora and Reddit, discussions about AI covered various topics, including its current uses and impact on jobs, creativity, and careers. Topic modeling yielded relatively strong topic coherence (0.79 out of 1.0).

Generally, Quora yielded positive (average = 0.34) and neutral sentiments (average = 0.63). See Table 2. The first Quora topic focused on creativity, particularly questions and statements about poetry, plagiarism, and engineering: *"Can artificial intelligence be more creative than the average person?"* The second Quora topic covered future predictions about public goals, expectations, and reservations about AI: *"Can technology and artificial intelligence contribute to preventing conflicts and fostering peace worldwide?"* The third Quora topic covered AI authenticity and evaluation compared with human intelligence: *"What techniques can be used to make artificial intelligence behave more like a human?"* The fourth Quora topic covered AI conventions in design: *"What are some free benchmarks to test artificial intelligence?"* The fifth Quora topic covered the importance of AI: *"How important is it to embrace artificial intelligence and advocate for the adoption of cutting-edge innovations?"* The sixth Quora topic covered AI deployments in common or everyday settings: *"Is Chat GPT artificial intelligence or anything else?"* The seventh Quora topic covered AI social implications: *"As a techie neanderthal can you explain to me in plain English why human made artificial Intelligence is seen as a potential threat to us?"* The eighth Quora topic covered the benefits of AI: *"If artificial intelligence develops at the current speed will it be in another 10 years Human beings will not have to work and artificial intelligence will work to support us."* The ninth Quora topic covered AI research: *"What types of problems can artificial intelligence solve that human can't solve using pure math?"* Finally, the tenth Quora topic covered AI in medicine: *"What role can artificial intelligence play in enhancing personalized healthcare and medical diagnostics?"* Quora topics span creativity, AI ethics, benchmarks, social impact, benefits, and AI in medicine, aligning with the themes that emerged from the surveys and reviews in subject matter, but generally more positive and neutral than both.

Similarly, Reddit yielded primarily positive (average = 0.35) and neutral (average = 0.50). See Table 3. The first Reddit topic covered AI ethical and philosophical questions: *"If artificial intelligence can understand humans better than humans can understand artificial intelligence why is this the case?"* The second Reddit topic covered AI in the market and economy: *"Can artificial intelligence bring a new tech boom to San Francisco?"* The third Reddit topic covered AI policy and governance: *"What is the role of artificial intelligence in modern society?"* The fourth Reddit topic covered AI invention and innovation: *"Can artificial intelligence really be used to trade legally the markets stocks or whatever with most accuracy?"* The fifth Reddit topic covered AI design and techniques: *"What are some research problems in artificial intelligence that could lead to big breakthroughs in machine learning?"* The sixth Reddit topic covered outcomes of AI: *"Will artificial intelligence eventually surpass human intelligence and what are the potential implications of this?"* The seventh Reddit topic covered the value and philosophy of AI: *"How long is it until artificial intelligence has a consciousness and a free thinking mind?"* The eighth Reddit topic covered AI education: *"Which IIT provides a course in Artificial Intelligence?"* The ninth Reddit topic covered the benefits of AI: *"Will artificial intelligence give more benefits or problems to human?"* Finally, the tenth Reddit topic covered AI politics: *"Is there such a thing as too much artificial intelligence Is there such a thing as not enough artificial intelligence?"* Reddit topics include AI ethics, market impact, policy, invention, design, outcomes, consciousness, education, benefits, and politics.

Table 2. Quora Results.

Topic	Theme	Terms	+	−	neutral	composite
1	creativity	genuine, poetry, gas, develop, advance, engineering, plagiarism	0.32	0.03	0.64	0.49
2	future	poised, able, survival, expect, reservations, years, goals, respond	0.34	0.03	0.63	0.51
3	authenticity	ways, artists, expect, trick, developed, calling, favour, evaluated, synthetic	0.34	0.03	0.63	0.51
4	convention	streaming, pros, box, every day, experiences, superintelligence, accept, replicated, benchmarks, reduce	0.32	0.03	0.65	0.48
5	importance	profess, copies, links, adoption, atheism, matrix, compete, prospects, importance, accountancy	0.33	0.03	0.64	0.51
6	deployment	smartphones, workflows, share, thinks, real, professional, crimes, chatbots, taking, deploying	0.32	0.03	0.64	0.49

(continued)

Table 2. (*continued*)

Topic	Theme	Terms	+	−	neutral	composite
7	social	solution, socialism, progress, activation, customer, plain, finance, innovative, probability, biases	0.29	0.03	0.68	0.46
8	benefits	online, masses, never, today, represent, beneficial, live, nothing, potential, possibilities	0.30	0.03	0.67	0.45
9	research	say, days, tested, phd, cutting, us, newsreaders, implore, solid, developing	0.34	0.03	0.63	0.56
10	medicine	parts, combines, emerging, send, innovations, opinions, dementia, stifle	0.34	0.03	0.63	0.50

Quora and Reddit discussions explore facets of AI that emerged in the surveys and reviews, including ethics, market impact, policy, invention, design, outcomes, consciousness, education, benefits, and politics. They both reflect societal interests and concerns. However, Quora tends to exhibit more positive and neutral sentiments towards AI topics than Reddit. Quora topics often delved into specific questions and scenarios, while Reddit discussions seemed more open-ended and speculative. Both platforms explored the complexities of AI and its impact on society.

Table 3. Reddit Results.

Topic	Theme	Terms	+	−	neutral	composite
1	ethics	planet, drawing, survival, matrix, pets, fall, plagiarism, benefit, growing, centralist	0.33	0.03	**0.64**	**0.50**
2	market	perfect, buy, university, advanced, agree, personnel, create, computing, easy	0.34	0.04	**0.62**	**0.50**

(*continued*)

Table 3. (*continued*)

Topic	Theme	Terms	+	−	neutral	composite
3	policy	regulating, forward, teachers, topics, screening, thoughts, eliminate, far, systems, publish	0.33	0.03	**0.64**	**0.53**
4	invention	persuasive, simulation, developed, machines, rent, invented, humanity, planner	0.33	0.03	**0.64**	**0.50**
5	design	chain, restrict, token, fostering, status, connotations, curve, oracle, achievable	0.32	0.03	**0.65**	**0.52**
6	outcomes	desires, types, obsolete, whats, steps, destroy, goals, awareness, outcome, recommended	0.29	0.04	**0.67**	**0.47**
7	value	equal, harnessed, quantum, plagiarism, myth, nature, advantages, thinking, gone, revolutionizing	0.35	0.02	**0.63**	**0.51**
8	education	categories, eliminated, expect, qualities, rising, chances, age, solve, tutorial	0.32	0.04	**0.64**	**0.47**
9	benefits	visual, machines, protect, pure, token, demand, save, impacts	0.33	0.06	**0.62**	**0.45**
10	politics	levels, everybody, russian, firms, came, rapid, way, dystopian, manner	0.35	0.03	**0.62**	**0.50**

4 Conclusion

Reviews, surveys, and social media offer valuable insights into public perceptions of AI across different regions and contexts. Surveys consistently find widespread understanding of AI concepts, with positive sentiment regarding its integration in healthcare services. Medical professionals and students view AI as a potential partner in healthcare delivery rather than a competitor. However, concerns about AI's impact on employment, privacy, and personal data use persisted globally. Similarly, reviews revealed attitudes and concerns like surveys and emphasized the importance of collaboration, regulation, and transparency in implementing clinical AI. Both surveys and reviews highlight the public's preference for human involvement in decision-making despite recognizing AI's potential benefits. Social media discussions echoed themes from surveys and reviews, covering ethics, market impact, policy, invention, design, outcomes, education, benefits, and politics. While both platforms reflect societal interests and concerns about AI, Quora conveys more positive and neutral sentiments than Reddit. Quora often addressed specific questions. Reddit conversations were more speculative.

The review and analysis revealed that human factors, including expectations, mental models, age, and gender, impact the trust and interpretability of AI. Transparency of data privacy and safety, design, customizability, and perceived company benevolence also play a role, as does media and social network coverage. The context of use, user requirements, and design evaluation also help build trust and understanding. Personality traits such as the propensity to trust other technology and general behavioral tendencies also impact public perception of and trust in AI. Surveys articulate concerns about AI privacy, poor customer service, and misuse in public safety. Age and education impact AI awareness. The public lacks deep knowledge of AI's inner workings. There are high expectations and heightened fears around workplace impact (both potential for positive and negative implications). Surveys show that the public wants safeguards and transparency that AI delivers on its promises without unacceptable risks and in the right context at the right time. Worries exist about AI replacing rather than assisting human employees, as well as regarding deceptive uses such as identity theft, deep fakes, and deceptive content. The public expects policies to help manage and mitigate these issues. Social media content revealed uncertainty about the definition of artificial intelligence, the nature of AI intelligence, and the stage of AI prevalence we are experiencing currently. Philosophies and psychology of trust and trustworthiness serve as a framework for understanding how these perception domains reflect implications for demonstrating respect and social values and minimizing social risk and threat in ways that increase AI trustworthiness.

The public's perceptions of AI across various sectors like healthcare, advertising, social media, journalism, and autonomous vehicles are diverse. Studies show mixed attitudes, influenced by factors such as perceived risks, benefits, familiarity, and socioeconomic context. In healthcare, the public generally supports AI integration for tasks like appointment booking and diagnosis but hesitates about AI replacing human care. Concerns about privacy, data security, and job displacement persist. Medical professionals generally have more optimistic views toward AI's potential benefits but also stress the importance of validation, transparency, and collaboration. Similar concerns and attitudes are observed in radiology, where AI is seen as enhancing practice but not replacing radiologists entirely. Additionally, public perception studies indicate varying levels of trust and awareness regarding AI, with safety being a primary concern, especially in autonomous vehicles. There's also a need for further education and research to address knowledge gaps and ensure responsible AI deployment. Overall, stakeholders emphasize the importance of ongoing collaboration, regulation, and thoughtful implementation strategies to address legal, ethical, and societal concerns surrounding AI integration across different domains.

The results presented in the provided text offer valuable insights into public attitudes toward artificial intelligence (AI) across various domains and regions. However, there are several limitations to consider regarding these studies. The surveys primarily focus on specific countries or regions, such as European countries, China, Germany, and the United States. Surveys in one country may not capture the perspectives of individuals from different cultural backgrounds. They may not represent global attitudes toward AI, and attitudes toward AI vary across cultures and societies. Some studies had relatively small sample sizes or specific participant demographics, which could introduce bias and limit generalizability. Citing peer-reviewed studies might skew toward publishing statistically significant findings or aligning with hypotheses. Negative or inconclusive results might be underrepresented. The surveys span different years, and public attitudes toward AI may have evolved rapidly due to technological advancements, media coverage, and societal changes. Older studies may not accurately reflect current sentiments. Survey respondents may not always provide accurate or truthful responses due to social desirability bias where participants provide answers they perceive as socially acceptable. Different studies used varying measurement scales and methodologies; therefore, direct comparisons were not practicable. Healthcare, journalism, advertising, and social media were covered, but not all domains were represented. Qualitative research methods, such as interviews or focus groups, could offer deeper insights into the underlying reasons behind attitudes. Future studies should address and investigate these limitations.

Despite the limitations of the reviews, surveys, and social media analysis, designers must recognize and address public concerns about AI, including privacy, data security, job displacement, and safety. They must design AI systems with transparent data privacy policies and robust security measures to build trust among users. It is crucial to prioritize human-centered design principles to ensure that AI systems are intuitive, easy to use, and aligned with user expectations and mental models, and to consider factors such as age, gender, and education level in design decisions. AI systems must be as transparent and accountable as possible, with clear explanations of how algorithms work to ensure that users understand the limitations and potential biases. Designers should advocate for collaboration between stakeholders, including designers, developers, regulators, and users, to address legal, ethical, and societal concerns surrounding AI integration and support the development of regulations and policies to govern AI deployment responsibly. Education and training opportunities for users, particularly healthcare professionals, would aid AI engagement and increase user autonomy. Fostering ongoing learning and collaboration between AI experts and domain experts is key. Public attitudes toward AI vary across different domains and regions, so designers should tailor AI systems to specific contexts and user requirements and consider cultural differences and socio-economic factors Mechanisms for evaluation and improvement of AI systems should be based on user feedback and real-world performance data. Iterating design solutions would address emerging challenges and optimize user experiences. Ethical considerations should be integrated into the design process to ensure that AI systems prioritize respect for human values and minimize social risks and threats. AI systems should enhance, rather than replace, human judgment and decision-making. By following these recommendations, designers can contribute to developing ethical, trustworthy, and user-centered AI systems that meet the needs and expectations of diverse stakeholders.

Acknowledgments. Funding from the NEC Foundation supported this project.

References

1. Roundtree, A.K.: AI explainability, interpretability, fairness, and privacy: an integrative review of reviews. In: Degen, H., Ntoa, S. (eds.) Artificial Intelligence in HCI. HCII 2023. LNCS, vol. 14050. Springer, Cham (2023). https://doi.org/10.1007/978-3-031-35891-3_19
2. Roundtree, A.K.: Ethics and facial recognition technology: an integrative review. In: 2021 3rd World Symposium on Artificial Intelligence (WSAI), pp. 10–19. IEEE (2021)
3. Vu, H.T., Lim, J.: Effects of country and individual factors on public acceptance of artificial intelligence and robotics technologies: a multilevel SEM analysis of 28-country survey data. Behav. Inform. Technol. **41**(7), 1515–1528 (2022)
4. Vo, V., Chen, G., Aquino, Y.S.J., Carter, S., Do, Q., Woode, M.E.: Multi-stakeholder preferences for the use of artificial intelligence in healthcare: a systematic review and thematic analysis. Soc. Sci. Med. **116357**, 1–11 (2023)
5. Kozyreva, A., Herzog, S., Lorenz-Spreen, P., Hertwig, R., Lewandowsky, S.: Artificial intelligence in online environments: representative survey of public attitudes in Germany. Max Planck Institute for Human Development and the University of Bristol (2020)
6. Cui, D., Wu, F.: The influence of media use on public perceptions of artificial intelligence in China: evidence from an online survey. Inf. Dev. **37**(1), 45–57 (2021)
7. Sun, M., Hu, W., Wu, Y.: Public perceptions and attitudes towards the application of artificial intelligence in journalism: From a China-based survey. Journalism Practice, pp. 1–23 (2022)
8. Guha, S.: Public perspectives on Healthcare and Artificial Intelligence (AI): a survey study. Int. J. Innov. Educ. Res. **9**(7), 1–8 (2021)
9. Chen, Y.Y., Li, Y., Li, C.J.: Could artificial intelligence make human doctors obsolete? A survey based on public attitudes. Eur. J. Public Health Suppl. **5**, 544 (2020)
10. Stai, B., et al.: Public perceptions of artificial intelligence and robotics in medicine. J. Endourol. **34**(10), 1041–1048 (2020)
11. Tamori, H., Yamashina, H., Mukai, M., Morii, Y., Suzuki, T., Ogasawara, K.: Acceptance of the use of artificial intelligence in medicine among Japan's doctors and the public: a questionnaire survey. JMIR Hum. Factors **9**(1), e24680, pp. 1–10 (2022)
12. Bisdas, S., Topriceanu, C.C., Zakrzewska, Z., Irimia, A.V., Shakallis, L., Subhash, J.: Artificial intelligence in medicine: a multinational multi-center survey on the medical and dental students' perception. Front Public Health, pp. 1–9 (2021)
13. Beets, B., Newman, T.P., Howell, E.L., Bao, L., Yang, S.: Surveying public perceptions of artificial intelligence in health care in the United States: systematic review. J. Med. Internet Res. **25**(e40337), 1–12 (2023)
14. Othman, K.: Public acceptance and perception of autonomous vehicles: a comprehensive review. AI Ethics **1**(3), 355–387 (2021)

15. Hogg, H.D.J., et al.: Stakeholder perspectives of clinical artificial intelligence implementation: systematic review of qualitative evidence. J. Med. Internet Res. **25**, e39742, 1–22 (2023)
16. Yang, L., Ene, I.C., Arabi Belaghi, R., Koff, D., Stein, N., Santaguida, P.: Stakeholders' perspectives on the future of artificial intelligence in radiology: a scoping review. Eur. Radiol. **32**(3), 1477–1495 (2022)
17. Young, A.T., Amara, D., Bhattacharya, A., Wei, M.L.: Patient and general public attitudes towards clinical artificial intelligence: a mixed methods systematic review. Lancet Digital Health **3**(9), E599-e611 (2021)

Towards a Simplified AI Adoption Framework: Success Factors for the Implementation of Artificial Intelligence Information Systems

Emir Kučević[(✉)], Frederik Grünewald, and Niklas Schanz

Universität Hamburg, Hamburg, Germany
emir.kucevic@uni-hamburg.de,
{frederik.gruenewald,niklas.schanz}@studium.uni-hamburg.de

Abstract. Adopting AI within organizations promises various benefits, including enhanced productivity, cost reduction, process automation, and the innovation of services and business models. However, many organizations, particularly small and medium-sized enterprises (SMEs) with limited resources, face challenges in successfully implementing AI, such as lack of expertise or insufficient data quality. Therefore, this study aims to address these challenges by developing a comprehensive framework for identifying and synthesizing success factors for AI adoption. Utilizing a design science research (DSR) approach, the study combines insights from a systematic literature review and expert interviews across different industries. The resulting outcome represents a simplified AI adoption framework designed to support AI adoption by aggregating success factors across several clusters: Strategy and Planning, AI Expertise and Support, Data Considerations, Infrastructure and Resources, Market and Competition, Ethical and Legal, and Implementation and Integration. Each cluster encompasses interrelated factors prioritized based on their frequency in the literature and validation through experts. The framework could serve as a starting point for organizations, particularly for SMEs, to navigate AI adoption effectively. It emphasizes the importance of relevant success factors such as defining an AI strategy, establishing data structures, fostering an innovative corporate culture, and ethical considerations. Organizations can mitigate risks and enhance their AI integration efforts by addressing these factors. The study contributes to the literature by offering a practice-based artifact aggregating existing success factors, providing a valuable entry point for organizations embarking on AI adoption projects.

Keywords: Artificial Intelligence · AI Adoption · AI Implementation · Success Factors · AI Strategy · Data Strategy

1 Introduction

Artificial intelligence (AI) is transforming business landscapes [1,2] and adopted by organizations to leverage their service quality, support coordination efforts,

H. Degen and S. Ntoa (Eds.): HCII 2024, LNCS 15382, pp. 88–106, 2024.
https://doi.org/10.1007/978-3-031-76827-9_6

gain productivity benefits, and reduce costs (e.g., [3,4]). The vast amount of data coupled with improved computing capabilities [5] and recent technological breakthroughs in learning algorithms-especially in the context of large language models such as the GPT models-provides organizations with the opportunity to gain a competitive advantage, as the data contains valuable information [6, 7]. This development accelerates a paradigm shift that led to various AI-based information systems (IS) that mirror and supplement human intelligence (e.g., [8]).

According to [9], tasks that can be associated with human intelligence in the context of AI are "learning" and "problem-solving". Moreover, AI not only empowers organizations with the capabilities to perform tasks such as learning, reasoning, and problem-solving, expanding the scope of pure data analysis (e.g., [10,11]) but enables them to explore innovative opportunities, exploring new use cases and accelerate digital transformation by automating tasks, developing intelligent products and redefining the design of innovative services and business models [12–14].

However, to leverage the benefits and advantages of AI, proper integration into the organization is required [7,15]. Despite this, the successful adoption of AI technologies is still hindered by (organizational and individual) challenges that are crucial to long-term success [16].

In this vein, human-centric phenomena, especially in the context of human-AI collaboration, can pose significant risks to the widespread adoption of AI. In this regard, many employees express concerns, for instance, including algorithmic aversion [17,18] and the 'black box problem' [19–21]. In addition to these risks, [22] has identified various additional factors, referred to as barriers to adopting AI technologies. Further studies related to AI adoption barriers, partly identifying identical barriers and discovering new ones [23–27]. Similar to the barriers, a large number of success factors are researched [28–31]. For example, [28] identified different success factors. By adopting a holistic perspective for addressing success factors at an early stage, challenges that may arise with adopting AI can be avoided.

However, to properly consider the success factors and avoid potential risks, a comprehensive set of success factors could be beneficial. In this regard, previous studies are non-profound, not using systematic approaches to collect success factors from the literature [7]. In addition, the comprehensiveness of existing success factors remains to be considered, as a study conducted by the Boston Consulting Group echoes the calls of [29,32] for more research on success factors, especially based on practical experience. In this context, explanatory knowledge about considering relevant adoption factors for AI, leveraging success factors, and thus lowering risks is essential for the development of an effective AI transformation strategy for organizations [16,33].

The literature indicates that these factors must be understood for the successful adoption of AI (e.g., [34]). Nevertheless, current research lacks a comprehensive understanding of the factors that influence AI adoption, leading to a lack of business impacts and failed adoptions (e.g., [7,16,35]). Therefore, this study addresses the following research question:

"How can success factors be synthesized into a framework to improve organizations' understanding of AI adoption?"

To achieve this goal, we conducted a design science research (DSR) project following [36]. We combined the results of a systematic literature review and expert interviews from different organizations to build an artifact that intends to support AI adoption. The resulting framework includes a structured amalgamation of success factors relevant to AI adoption, as demanded by [7,28,37]. The framework is organized into clusters, based on interrelated factors that were prioritized in a preliminary step according to their frequency of occurrence in the existing literature and the expert interviews. This synthesized framework could serve as a valuable foundation for organizations, especially for small and medium-sized enterprises (SMEs), enabling them to gain greater insight into upcoming AI adoption initiatives.

2   Related Research

2.1   Artificial Intelligence Adoption in Organizations

The adoption of AI in organizations offers various opportunities to increase efficiency and support decision-making. Organizations can utilize AI for data analysis, predictive modeling, automating routine tasks, and improving customer experience. Especially for SMEs, AI can address challenges such as limited data and the lack of expertise by offering scalable and customizable solutions [38]. To adopt AI in an organization, several frameworks have been proposed to guide organizations through the AI adoption process. These frameworks provide, for instance, structured approaches to address the technological, organizational, and environmental factors that can be relevant for successful AI integration. In this regard, the TOE framework [39] has been adopted and extended by various researchers to integrate technological factors such as compatibility, organizational factors like the top management support or culture and structure, as well as environmental factors such as regulations and customer readiness [39–42]. In addition, the acceptance research in the context of technology adoption can be helpful as it can be used to understand and describe the acceptance and intention of individuals to use an AI solution and to identify the factors that significantly influence system (non-)use [43,44]. In this context, researchers have developed various theories and frameworks, such as the Technology Acceptance Model (TAM), the Theory of Planned Behavior (TPB), the Unified Theory of Acceptance and Use of Technology (UTAUT), which aim to explain perceived usefulness and perceived ease of use and thus identify the intention of use in various domains [43,45]. Another evolution of the aforementioned frameworks is the Technology Readiness and Acceptance Model (TRAM) which integrates principles of talent, trust and technology and emphasizes the roles of optimism, innovativeness, insecurity and discomfort in technology adoption [44,46].

In the context of AI adoption, [34] modified the UTAUT, included components for intelligent systems, and demonstrated the applicability and relevance of their modified UTAUT model for AI adoption. Further, the AI Quality Information Framework (AI-QIF) represents an AI adoption framework developed specifically for the healthcare sector and focuses on ensuring high-quality information and implementation of AI through a structured approach [47]. Another example is the Artificial Intelligence Risk Management (AIRM), which provides a roadmap for integrating AI risk management [48].

Although these frameworks provide valuable insights and structured approaches for (AI) technology adoption, their generalizability could have limitations, as they are tailored to specific industries or organizational contexts. In addition, more complex and resource-intensive approaches may not be suitable for smaller organizations to implement AI effectively, as there could be differences in organizational imperatives for successful adoption that need to be addressed [38].

In light of these considerations, it seems that a single framework cannot comprehensively cover all aspects of AI adoption. In this vein, the study's objective was to design a simplified framework incorporating success factors for AI adoption and providing organizations with applicable guidance to serve as a starting point for AI endeavors.

2.2   Success and Risk Factors of Artificial Intelligence Adoption

By recognizing and addressing success and risk factors, organizations could develop robust strategies to overcome obstacles and ensure a smoother integration process. These can be divided into organizational, technological, social, and economic factors [49].

Organizational risks include the lack of qualified personnel with expertise in AI and data science (e.g., [50]). Further, the resistance to change and lack of support from top management can hinder the adoption process, and ineffective change management practices can lead to reduced benefits of AI initiatives (e.g., [24]).

Technical risks include the lack of sufficient high-quality data, which can affect the accuracy and effectiveness of AI models (e.g., [50]). Moreover, the complexity of AI solutions can be overwhelming, especially for SMEs [38]. Security and accuracy concerns are also important [24].

Social risks include fear of the unknown, as employees may fear job loss and AI's complex aspects, resulting in resistance and skepticism [49]. Further, ethical concerns, such as bias and fairness issues, could pose additional challenges [51].

Economic risks include unbalanced economic conditions between different organizations [49]. In addition, the uncertainty regarding AI projects' return on investment (ROI) can incentivize organizations to be reluctant to allocate resources [24].

To counteract these risks, several factors that contribute to the successful adoption of AI, including investing in training and education to build a skilled workforce, focussing on upskilling employees and attracting top talent [52] as well as fostering a supportive corporate culture, could be beneficial [53]. In this regard, the support from the top management and a clear vision can drive successful adoption [24] as well as implementing effective data management practices to ensure the availability and protection of high-quality data, which forms the basis for AI systems [40]. Moreover, considering aspects of responsible AI that emphasize fairness, transparency, privacy, and accountability can increase trust in AI solutions [54].

3 Research Methodology

The main objective of this study is to design a framework that supports the successful adoption of AI-based IS. In order to accomplish this objective and ensure a systematic approach, the DSR paradigm was utilized, adopting the three-cycle perspective outlined by [36]. Our research approach is organized and implemented based on the diagram shown in Fig. 1 and aims to design an adequate artifact. The in-depth descriptions of each step involved in our DSR project are described in the following.

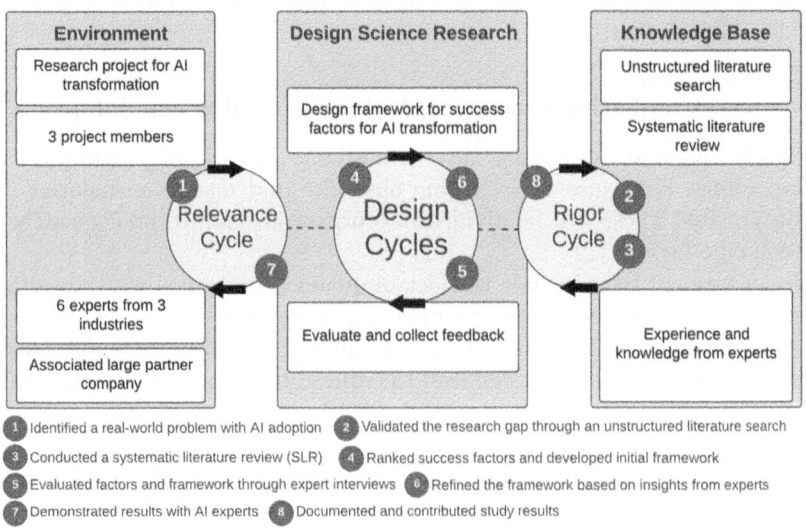

Fig. 1. DSR three cycle view and our research activities, adapted from [36]

The initial step of our DSR project consisted of identifying a relevant real-world problem that requires attention. As AI is becoming more prevalent, many organizations struggle to adopt AI efficiently. The current state of research indicates that there is a lack of profound and systematic approaches to collect success factors from the literature [7] and studies providing sufficiently comprehensive AI adoption factors, including practical perspectives [29, 32]. As a consequence, we address this research gap.

In the second step, we expanded our understanding of the research gap and validated it by conducting an unstructured literature search to address the defined problem appropriately. The literature results analyzed served as the basis for step three, the systematic literature review (SLR).

Consequently, in the third step, we performed an extensive SLR to improve our understanding of AI transformation and the associated AI adoption. This literature review examines the factors contributing to success factors in AI transformation (projects) and the related concepts of adoption without focussing only on the success factors themselves. To conduct the SLR, we based our search on the structure proposed by [55]. The databases used are ProQuest ABI, AISel, JSTOR, ACM DL, and IEEE to ensure a comprehensive examination of the available research. For this study, we searched for the terms 'AI Transformation,' 'AI Strategy,' 'AI Innovation', and 'AI Project' in the databases to obtain a wide range of publications and derive relevant success factors. The used terms can be summarized in the following search string: 'AI Transformation' OR 'AI Strategy' OR 'AI Innovation' OR 'AI Project'. Since each database has its own format for entering search queries, customized search strings were developed when required. In addition, the literature review focussed only on scientific publications. The SLR resulted in 2845 identified sources. According to [56], we defined exclusion criteria for the search results to determine whether a reference should be considered for data extraction and analysis.. In the first screening, articles with a specific focus not addressing AI transformation aspects were removed. Furthermore, in the second screening, the resulting articles were filtered according to their relevance and assessed based on the title, abstract and access to the publication, resulting in 62 publications included in the full-text analysis. These results were then analyzed and reviewed in depth, and articles that did not match our study objective were excluded, resulting in 34 relevant sources. Our main objective during this procedure was to identify items that are pertinent to our study objectives to identify relevant success factors for AI adoption. In addition, five articles were added based on forward and backward search, resulting in a final set of 39 articles.

In step four, the insights obtained from the literature review were used to create the initial ranked factors, forming the framework's basis. Therefore, the articles were thoroughly analyzed for explicit or inferable factors that may influence the outcome of an AI transformation project. The factors were then organized into a database, summarized, and transferred to a comprehensive factor table. This allowed us to create a comprehensive set of success factors; each assigned a rank based on the frequency with which it was mentioned. In addition, these factors were systematically grouped into clusters to describe relevant concepts necessary for our framework's development.

After the initial ranked factors and their related clusters were prepared, an evaluation was carried out in step five. This involved conducting semi-structured expert interviews according to [57] with six representatives from three organizations across various industries and degrees of experience. The experts for this study were chosen based on their proficiency in AI and relevant experience.

Preceding the interviews, a standardized guide was developed to systematically gather relevant information for expanding our framework. In this regard, questions were formulated to facilitate a profound understanding of the perspectives held by the selected experts.

Subsequently to the evaluation, in step six, the proposed structure was modified and expanded. This was done by combining insights obtained from expert interviews to identify similarities and variations in the framework.

During step seven, a demonstration of the results was carried out by interacting with experts who were working in AI transformation projects, utilizing their practical knowledge, enhancing and confirming the strength of the framework.

Finally in step eight, we documented our study results and described them in the following section and thus contribute to the knowledge base.

4   Results

4.1   Success Factors for Artificial Intelligence Adoption

Based on the conducted DSR activities, we identified, aggregated, evaluated and demonstrated success factors for the adoption of AI systems in organizations. We ranked the success factors based on each factor's occurrence in the analyzed scientific studies, and experts assessed their relevance and appropriateness. The set of success factors contains 36 factors analyzed, serving as a foundation for the developed framework structuring these factors into clusters. Overall, the results provide a comprehensive overview of factors for the successful adoption of AI-based IS in organizations. The results are depicted in Fig. 2.

A critical factor for the successful adoption of AI systems in organizations is the **establishment and availability of a robust IT infrastructure** [28]. This factor ensures the effective **integration and operation of AI technologies into the existing infrastructure** and facilitates data processing, storage, and communication (e.g., [28,58–60]). A well-designed IT infrastructure, providing compatibility through suitable interfaces, can optimize computational resources, accelerate model training, and improve overall system performance (e.g., [32]). In addition, it enables the effective handling of large amounts of data, which is crucial for AI algorithms (e.g., [59,60]), and enables AI-driven processes that can support the **scalability of AI solutions** (e.g., [61]).

The results of our study show that one of the most critical factors mentioned for the successful adoption of AI-based IS is **ensuring the necessary AI expertise**. In order to address the challenges of these systems, it is essential to have access to people with the required knowledge, skills, and experience in the field of AI (e.g., [28]). One of the challenges is the complexity of these systems, as AI is a multifaceted field encompassing various subfields like machine learning, natural language processing, computer vision, and robotics. Therefore, managing these systems requires expertise in these areas, and knowledge of algorithms, data structures, and computational techniques (e.g., [62–64]). The (continuous) training of employees and the fostering of AI literacy in organizations poses a further challenge, as (technical) skills need to be built up or improved to exploit

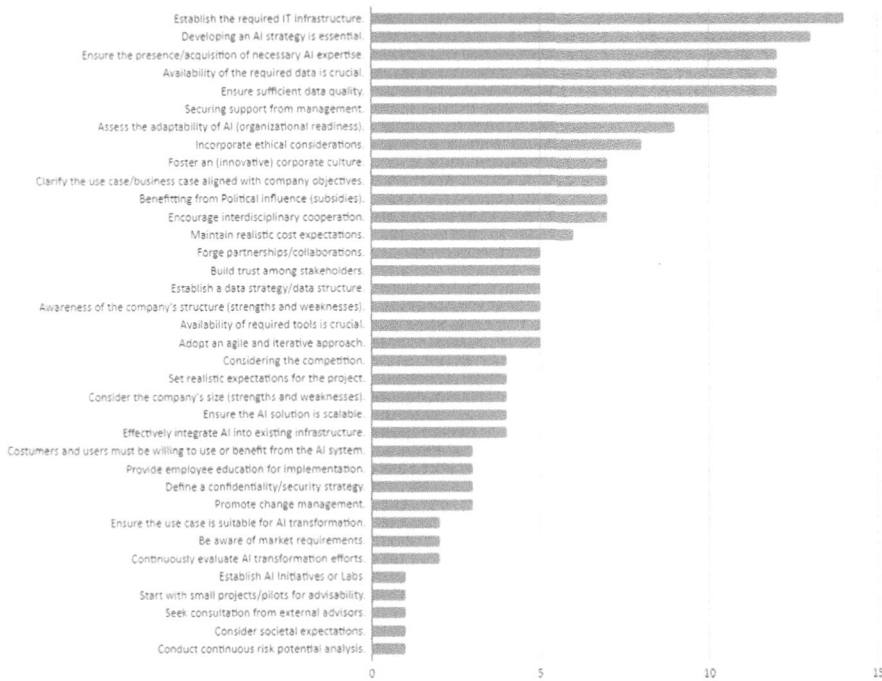

Establish the required IT infrastructure.
Developing an AI strategy is essential.
Ensure the presence/acquisition of necessary AI expertise.
Availability of the required data is crucial.
Ensure sufficient data quality.
Securing support from management.
Assess the adaptability of AI (organizational readiness).
Incorporate ethical considerations.
Foster an (innovative) corporate culture.
Clarify the use case/business case aligned with company objectives.
Benefitting from Political influence (subsidies).
Encourage interdisciplinary cooperation.
Maintain realistic cost expectations.
Forge partnerships/collaborations.
Build trust among stakeholders.
Establish a data strategy/data structure.
Awareness of the company's structure (strengths and weaknesses).
Availability of required tools is crucial.
Adopt an agile and iterative approach.
Considering the competition.
Set realistic expectations for the project.
Consider the company's size (strengths and weaknesses).
Ensure the AI solution is scalable.
Effectively integrate AI into existing infrastructure.
Costumers and users must be willing to use or benefit from the AI system.
Provide employee education for implementation.
Define a confidentiality/security strategy.
Promote change management.
Ensure the use case is suitable for AI transformation.
Be aware of market requirements.
Continuously evaluate AI transformation efforts.
Establish AI Initiatives or Labs.
Start with small projects/pilots for advisability.
Seek consultation from external advisors.
Consider societal expectations.
Conduct continuous risk potential analysis.

Fig. 2. Success factors ranked according to their occurrence in publications

AI applications' full potential (e.g., [65]). Therefore, to provide **employee education for implementation** of AI-based IS is considered a success factor.

Due to these systems' complexity and especially the black-box nature, employees struggle to understand how to use AI or resist adopting it [3,66]. Therefore, the **management's support** is vital, as it helps the organization's AI initiatives and provides the necessary resources, funding, and strategic direction to successfully integrate AI technologies into existing workflows (e.g., [28]).

However, the focus of organizations is still on the technological adoption of AI while neglecting the strategic and business challenges that AI brings [67]. In particular, adopting such disruptive technologies should be comprehensive at the system level and go beyond specific projects to realize the most value [68]. In addition, as AI is polymorphic, multiple instances should be adapted and implemented in different areas of an organization [69]. Therefore, the **existence of a clearly defined AI strategy** is a relevant factor for the successful adoption and utilization of AI, outlining a strategic focus, which not only includes the organizational perspective on AI but also establishes a strategic agenda for its integration and related factors within the organization [10].

Further, **fostering an (innovative) corporate culture** contributes to the success of AI adoption as it encourages employees to embrace AI solutions and adapt to new ways of working, enabling innovation and experimentation and thus reducing resistance or skepticism among employees towards AI adoption [28].

Considering the **availability and quality of data** is also relevant. AI models (usually) require high-quality and large amounts of data for effective training and are considered a prerequisite for the successful learning process of AI [28]. A lack of data availability or quality can, therefore, lead to inaccurate models and incorrect outputs. Thus, sufficient and high-quality data can improve the performance of AI systems and increase users' trust. Additionally, it can be important to understand which systems the data is stored and assess its transferability and compatibility across platforms.

Also, in addition to the technological perspective on AI itself, the related business opportunities and capabilities that can result from the adoption of AI are important for organizations [40,70]. Many organizations struggle to understand the potential that AI could offer them. Therefore, the **business case should be aligned with the organization's objectives** and **be suitable** for AI transformation.

A supportive factor for successful AI adoption is the appropriate **assessment of the adaptability** of organizations and their AI readiness. It is defined as the willingness of organizations to embrace changes through AI applications and technologies [42]. Further, it provides the basis for determining whether the organization is in a suitable state to successfully implement and leverage AI technologies, including the readiness for human, financial, and resources (e.g., [71]). In addition, it enables organizations to **identify potential capability gaps and proactively reduce the uncertainties** associated with AI adoption (e.g., [42,72]).

In this context, exerting political influence contributes to addressing digital and physical threats and political security through regulation [28,73]. Organizations can **benefit from political influence** and receive subsidies from government agencies to minimize security risks and exploit opportunities. In China, for example, tech giants are encouraged by the government to set up AI platforms to promote partnerships and provide access to AI technology at a lower cost [61]. It is also important to **encourage interdisciplinary collaboration** and **forge partnerships** between different stakeholders, for instance, with **external experts**. However, such collaboration or partnerships are often difficult because individuals or organizational entities typically have limited resources or may face communication difficulties. Therefore, it could be beneficial to **start with small pilot projects** to experiment. Nevertheless, an interdisciplinary approach and active involvement of partners in **AI initiatives** support their adoption, as a wide range of roles covers relevant perspectives, such as data, analytics, privacy, legal, compliance, risk, business strategy, HR, and ethics (e.g., [28,74,75].

In particular, the ethical perspective becomes more relevant in AI adoption projects as the use of AI increases and, consequently, the number of **ethical issues** [76]. AI-based IS are at risk for biased learning and unethical outcomes [58]. Organizations need to counteract this shift and consider measures such as establishing ethics committees that employees can consult in case of concerns, policies, regulations, ethical guidance, safety violations, or discrimination in AI outcomes (e.g., [58, 71, 74]).

Establishing realistic cost expectations and **considering social expectations** for AI adoption can be vital to assist organizations in planning budgets effectively and avoiding overruns. Typically, AI adoption involves various expenses, such as data collection, infrastructure setup, (model) development, specialist costs, and ongoing maintenance (e.g. [64, 77]). Unrealistic cost expectations can result in financial burdens, project delays, or even project failure (e.g., [64, 77]). Here, through accurate cost estimation but also **realistic expectations for the project**, organizations can make informed decisions, allocate resources efficiently, and reduce costs so that the value of AI systems outweighs the costs. This enables AI teams to make better decisions and prioritization [64], which could counter market pressures and consequently contribute to competitiveness [78].

Other aspects, such as individual concerns about AI-related risks, can decrease the willingness of users or customers to engage with AI systems [79]. In particular, AI systems that have either visible or invisible capabilities require the **willingness of customers or users to use or benefit from the AI system** in order to be successfully adopted [79]. Without **building trust among stakeholders,** the acceptance of AI-based IS cannot achieve its intended goals [34, 71, 79]. Here, **promoting change management** supports these AI adoption endeavors [42] and can include the design of the interaction between humans and AI, especially in terms of usability, user needs, explainability, transparency, and user acceptance [64].

For AI systems to be integrated appropriately across the entire organization, it is relevant to have a well-considered technological foundation, such as data structures and collecting comprehensive and (up-to-date) data [80]. A common reason why AI adoption projects fail is due to insufficient data governance structures (e.g., [81, 82]). Therefore, a comprehensive **data strategy** is required that focuses on essential data-related factors such as data availability, data quality, data flow, and data access (e.g., [58, 83]) as well as **defining a security strategy**.

The **awareness of the organization's structure (strengths and weaknesses)** helps to align AI adoption strategies with the organization's goals. This ensures that AI initiatives are integrated into existing workflows and support the overall mission and goals of the organization. Large organizations often have more access to resources but conversely have inflexible structures (e.g. [28, 32]). On the other hand, smaller organizations typically tend to have fewer resources available but operate more flexibly and can, thus, utilize their resources efficiently (e.g., [28, 84]. Therefore, **considering the organization's size** can help to analyze the given structure and understand the strengths and weaknesses to enable better resource allocation for AI initiatives. Here, **continuous evaluation** of the transformation efforts can help to prioritize investments where AI can have the greatest impact and avoid wasting resources on initiatives that may not align with the organization's strategic goals [42, 72]. For example, **adopting an agile**

and iterative approach can help ensure that project teams are well-informed about the organization's objectives and aligned with business goals (e.g., [85]) as well as **be aware of market requirements** [86].

Considering the competition for organizations, for example, how competitors use AI, can help them position themselves in the market, which positively impacts the adoption of AI (e.g., [28,86]).

When adopting AI, a common challenge is finding the **right set of tools** to develop or represent the AI technology. Providing access to the necessary tools enables organizations, especially teams, to experiment with different approaches and techniques of AI development. This can foster innovation and collaboration as teams can explore new ideas and methods to solve complex problems more effectively (e.g., [28,64]).

4.2 Simplified Framework for AI Adoption

The developed 'Simplified AI Adoption Framework for Artificial Intelligence Adoption' comprises seven clusters covering key aspects of integrating AI technologies in organizations. These clusters provide a structured overview of relevant factors for AI adoption to systematically support the integration of AI and, particularly, aid the planning phase of adoption projects. Each cluster represents a higher-level aggregation entity of various related success factors of AI adoption, as shown in Fig. 3.

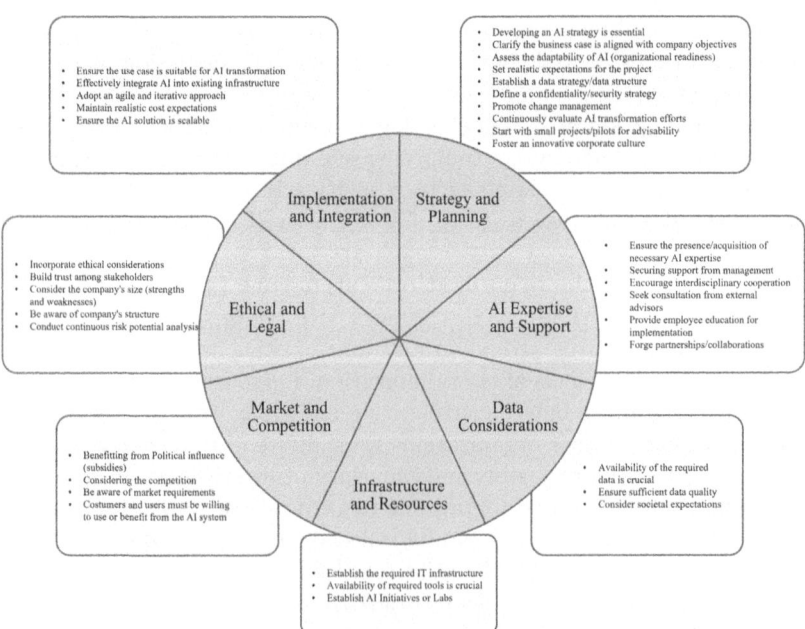

Fig. 3. Simplified AI Adoption Framework

The 'Strategy and Planning' cluster includes success factors that support systematic and methodical planning for adopting AI-based IS, such as developing a comprehensive AI strategy, a profound data strategy and infrastructure, and data protection and security aspects.

The 'AI Expertise and Support' cluster includes factors that focus on ensuring the required expertise and support from management and promoting collaboration.

The 'Data Considerations' cluster encompasses data availability and quality factors. Another factor is access to the required data sources and that data is available in sufficient quantity [28,58].

The 'Infrastructure and Resources' cluster includes technological and organizational prerequisites such as setting up the necessary IT infrastructure [28] and the availability of the necessary tools and the establishing AI initiatives or labs.

The 'Market and Competition' cluster incorporates success factors such as benefitting from policy influences, addressing market requirements, and ensuring customer and user acceptance.

The Ethical and Legal cluster includes factors that address the ongoing monitoring and assessment of potential (technical) risks, ethical, legal and societal aspects, and building trust with stakeholders.

The 'Implementation and Integration' cluster addresses considerations regarding the suitability of selected business use cases and the integration of AI into existing infrastructures, and providing scalable systems.

5   Discussion

Organizations are rushing to adopt AI into their business environments, given its potential to achieve competitive advantage by improving productivity, reducing costs, supporting or automating processes, as well as redefining the design of innovative services and business models (e.g., [3,4,12–14]). However, many organizations are in an early lifecycle stage of AI, and their AI adoption endeavors are failing despite the promising potential benefits (e.g., [7,16,35]).

To support AI adoption in transformation projects, we have developed a framework that includes a comprehensive perspective on success factors relevant in literature and practice. This artifact is intended to help organizations, especially SMEs with limited resources, to have a first starting point to guide them in their AI adoption projects by providing a comprehensive overview of relevant factors for minimizing potential risks. In this context, the successful adoption of AI in organizations demands a structured and prioritized approach. Not all clusters and success factors included in the developed framework need to be addressed. However, each organization should individually determine which cluster and factors are important to implement in different phases and with different priorities.

One possible approach is to start with the 'Data Considerations' cluster to focus on data quality and consider organizations' access to the required data sources to ensure that data is available in sufficient quantity as data are the heart of AI applications.

Following, the 'Strategy and Planning' cluster can be considered relevant in order to develop upon the prior considerations a profound data strategy that provides the backbone of (most) AI initiatives, including a well-designed data infrastructure and a clearly defined concept for data protection and security [58]. In addition, a well-considered (AI) strategy and careful planning could help successfully integrate AI in organizations and serve as a basis for ensuring that AI initiatives can not only be launched but also implemented sustainably and successfully. In this regard, developing a comprehensive AI strategy that serves as a roadmap and defines goals to be achieved in utilizing AI [10] can be vital. This strategy should align with the overarching business goals and strategies and clearly emphasize the business benefits of AI applications so that AI initiatives are not siloed but seen as an integral part [68]. In addition, change management could be considered relevant, as the adoption of AI technologies often entails far-reaching changes that need to be understood and accepted by employees (e.g., [42,64]). In this context, the continuous evaluation of transformation efforts could help as opportunities, but also to perform necessary adjustments can be identified [42,72].

Moreover, the framework cluster 'AI Expertise and Support' could be relevant to ensure that the required specialists are in place, i.e., that organizations have sufficient internal specialists with the technical skills and knowledge to successfully implement AI projects (e.g., [28]). In addition, the involvement of (external) specialists from various disciplines and forging partnerships could be beneficial to enhance innovative approaches to develop AI solutions that meet the organization's diverse requirements and to utilize synergies and gain access to the latest developments and technologies or to promote knowledge transfer and accelerate innovation (e.g., [28,74,75]). Further, through the support, commitment, and understanding of AI for the organization at the top management level, the necessary resources can be allocated (e.g., [28]), for example, to train the employees or foster acceptance.

At the same time, the 'Ethical and Legal' cluster could help to focus on the ethical and legal aspects that need to be considered when adopting AI, ensuring that AI initiatives are not only technically feasible but are also carried out responsibly and do not discriminate or cause other negative impacts [58,71, 74].

In addition, the 'Market and Competition' cluster deals with the external environmental conditions and market forces that influence the adoption of AI and includes considerations on how organizations can benefit from policy influences, address market requirements, and ensure customer and user acceptance.

Once the foundations have been laid, the 'Infrastructure and Resources' cluster could be considered as it focuses on establishing the necessary IT infrastructure that enables AI projects to be realized efficiently and effectively [28].

Finally, the 'Implementation and Integration' cluster may support AI adoption as it deals with practically realizing and embedding AI in an organization's existing structures. It can be important to ensure that the selected use cases are suitable for the AI transformation endeavors since not all business processes and tasks may be equally applicable for use with AI. The effective integration of AI into the existing infrastructure is another critical aspect, which can be addressed through pilot projects, allowing AI solutions to be tested in a controlled environment and gain valuable insights.

By comprehensively categorizing the relevant factors, organizations could make more informed decisions and allocate resources more efficiently. In addition, we contribute to the existing body of knowledge in the field of AI adoption, enriching the literature with valuable theoretical and practical insights and deepening the understanding of AI adoption. Our framework provides a comprehensive entry point for organizations, especially before adopting more complex frameworks. It could help organizations quickly gain an overview of relevant considerations for AI adoption factors.

In particular, leaders, such as IT managers and C-levels, could use the framework to pose vital questions at the beginning of AI adoption projects and thus better assess associated risks. In addition, the clustered success factors in the framework can be valuable for planning and designing a roadmap for AI adoptions.

6   Limitations and Future Research

In our research work, we encountered limitations that are important for interpreting the research results. Unfortunately, we could only conduct interviews with six experts as part of our study, and it would have been desirable to have a larger sample. However, despite this limitation, the interviews were meaningful as the results were consistent and mutually corroborative. Another factor to consider is that we focused primarily on the success factors without analyzing the underlying causes. This focus allowed us to identify specific influencing factors, but future research could focus on exploring the causes of these factors. Here, further research could reduce the large number of success factors, focus on the critical factors, and incorporate them into the lifecycle phases of AI. Moreover, future research could include the relevance of AI and data strategies in organizations, tactics, and best practices and fostering (individuals) AI literacy, for instance, through the implementation of appropriate formats. The literature especially lacks guidelines or options for developing an AI strategy and its characteristics. They need to be developed to guide organizations in their AI endeavors, offering a starting point as well as a communication instrument. Finally, research into the characteristics of AI-compliant data governance could help lay the foundations for the effective adoption of AI-based IS.

References

1. Clarke, S., Whittlestone, J.: A survey of the potential long-term impacts of AI: how AI could lead to long-term changes in science, cooperation, power, epistemics

and values. In: Proceedings of the 2022 AAAI/ACM Conference on AI, Ethics, and Society, pp. 192–202. ACM (2022)

2. Cooper, R.G.: The AI transformation of product innovation. Ind. Mark. Manag. **119**, 62–74 (2024)
3. Davenport, R.R.T.H.: Artificial intelligence for the real world. Harvard Bus. Rev. (2018)
4. Iansiti, M., Lakhani, K.R.: Competing in the age of AI: strategy and leadership when algorithms and networks run the world. Harvard Business Review Press (2020)
5. Rzepka, C., Berger, B.: User interaction with AI-enabled systems: a systematic review of is research. In: 39th International Conference on Information Systems, San Francisco 2018 (2018)
6. Merhi, M.I.: A process model of artificial intelligence implementation leading to proper decision making. In: Dennehy, D., Griva, A., Pouloudi, N., Dwivedi, Y.K., Pappas, I., Mäntymäki, M. (eds.) I3E 2021. LNCS, vol. 12896, pp. 40–46. Springer, Cham (2021). https://doi.org/10.1007/978-3-030-85447-8_4
7. Merhi, M.I.: An evaluation of the critical success factors impacting artificial intelligence implementation. Int. J. Inf. Manag. **69**, 102545 (2023)
8. Wang, W., Chen, L., Xiong, M., Wang, Y.: Accelerating AI adoption with responsible AI signals and employee engagement mechanisms in health care. Inf. Syst. Front. **25**(6), 2239–2256 (2023)
9. Shinde, P.P., Shah, S.: A review of machine learning and deep learning applications. In: 2018 Fourth International Conference on Computing Communication Control and Automation (ICCUBEA), pp. 1–6 (2018)
10. Calp, M.H.: The role of artificial intelligence within the scope of digital transformation in enterprises. In: In Advanced MIS and digital transformation for increased creativity and innovation in business, pp. 122-146. IGI Global. (2020)
11. Dwivedi, Y.K., et al.: Artificial intelligence (AI): multidisciplinary perspectives on emerging challenges, opportunities, and agenda for research, practice and policy. Int. J. Inf. Manag. **57**, 101994 (2021)
12. Vocke, C., Constantinescu, C., Popescu, D.: Application potentials of artificial intelligence for the design of innovation processes. Procedia CIRP **84**, 810–813 (2019)
13. Dogru, A.K., Keskin, B.B.: Ai in operations management: applications, challenges and opportunities. J. Data Inf. Manag. **2**(2), 67–74 (2020)
14. Åström, J., Reim, W., Parida, V.: Value creation and value capture for AI business model innovation: a three-phase process framework. RMS **16**(7), 2111–2133 (2022)
15. Sheikhtaheri, A., Sadoughi, F., Hashemi Dehaghi, Z.: Developing and using expert systems and neural networks in medicine: a review on benefits and challenges. J. Med. Syst. **38**(9), 110 (2014)
16. Venkatesh, V.: Adoption and use of AI tools: a research agenda grounded in UTAUT. Ann. Oper. Res. **308**(1), 641–652 (2022)
17. Dietvorst, B.J., Simmons, J.P., Massey, C.: Algorithm aversion: people erroneously avoid algorithms after seeing them err. J. Experimental Psychol. General (2015)
18. Jussupow, E., Benbasat, I., Heinzl, A.: Why are we averse towards algorithms? A comprehensive literature review on algorithm aversion. In: European Conference on Information Systems (2020)
19. Brasse, J., Broder, H.R., Förster, M., Klier, M., Sigler, I.: Explainable artificial intelligence in information systems: a review of the status quo and future research directions. Electron. Mark. **33**(1), 26 (2023)

20. Berente, N., Bin, G., Recker, J., Santhanam, R.: Managing artificial intelligence. MIS Q. **45**, 1433–1450 (2021)
21. Ca stelvecchi, D.: Can we open the black box of AI? : Nature News. **538**(7623) (2016)
22. Shrivastav, M.: Barriers related to AI implementation in supply chain management. J. Glob. Inf. Manag. **30**, 1–19 (2022)
23. Büttner, K., Antons, O., Arlinghaus, J.: Exploring implementation barriers of machine learning in production planning and control. Procedia CIRP **120**, 1546–1551 (2023)
24. Bérubé, M., Giannelia, T., Vial, G.: Barriers to the implementation of AI in organizations: findings from a Delphi study. In: HICSS 2021 Proceedings (2021)
25. Chomutare, T., et al.: Artificial intelligence implementation in healthcare: a theory-based scoping review of barriers and facilitators. Int. J. Environ. Res. Publ. Health **19** (2022)
26. Bahl, M.: Artificial intelligence in clinical practice: implementation considerations and barriers. J. Breast Imaging **4**(6), 632–639 (2022)
27. Al Alamin, M.A., Uddin, G., Malakar, S., Afroz, S., Haider, T., Iqbal, A.: Developer discussion topics on the adoption and barriers of low code software development platforms. Empir. Softw. Eng. **28** (2022)
28. Hamm, P., Klesel, M.: Success factors for the adoption of artificial intelligence in organizations: a literature review. In: AMCIS 2021 Proceedings (2021)
29. Sangers, T.E., Wakkee, M., Moolenburgh, F.J., Nijsten, T., Lugtenberg, M.: Towards successful implementation of artificial intelligence in skin cancer care: a qualitative study exploring the views of dermatologists and general practitioners. Arch. Dermatol. Res. **315**, 1187–1195 (2023)
30. Wolff, J., Pauling, J., Keck, A., Baumbach, J.: Success factors of artificial intelligence implementation in healthcare. Front. Digit. Health **3** (2021)
31. Bertl, M., Ross, P., Draheim, D.: Systematic AI support for decision-making in the healthcare sector: obstacles and success factors. Health Policy Technol. **12**(3), 100748 (2023)
32. Demlehner, Q., Schoemer, D., Laumer, S.: How can artificial intelligence enhance car manufacturing? A Delphi study-based identification and assessment of general use cases. Int. J. Inf. Manag. **58**, 102317 (2021)
33. Nguyen, Q.N., Sidorova, A., Torres, R.: Artificial intelligence in business: a literature review and research agenda. Commun. Assoc. Inf. Syst. **50**(1), 7 (2022)
34. Wanner, J., Herm, L.-V., Heinrich, K., Janiesch, C.: The effect of transparency and trust on intelligent system acceptance: Evidence from a user-based study. Electron. Mark. **32**(4), 2079–2102 (2022)
35. Nascimento, A., Meirelles, F.: An artificial intelligence adoption intention model (ai2m) inspired by UTAUT : ISLA 2022 Proceedings 21, (2022)
36. Hevner, A.: A three cycle view of design science research. Scand. J. Inf. Syst. **19** (2007)
37. Duan, Y., Edwards, J.S., Dwivedi, Y.K.: Artificial intelligence for decision making in the era of big data - evolution, challenges and research agenda. Int. J. Inf. Manag. **48**, 63–71 (2019)
38. Bettoni, A., Matteri, D., Montini, E., Gadysz, B., Carpanzano, E.: An AI adoption model for SMEs: a conceptual framework. IFAC-PapersOnLine **54**, 702–708 (2021)
39. Tornatzky, L.G., Fleischer, M., Chakrabarti, A.K.: The Processes of Technological Innovation. Lexington Books (1990)

40. Pumplun, L., Tauchert, C., Heidt, M.: A new organizational chassis for artificial intelligence - exploring organizational readiness factors. In: European Conference on Information Systems (2019)
41. Smit, D., Eybers, S., van der Merwe, A., Wies, R.: South African Institute of Computer Scientists and Information Technologists. CCIS, vol. 1878. Springer, Cham (2023). https://doi.org/10.1007/978-3-031-39652-6
42. Alsheibani, S., Cheung, Y., Messom, C.: Artificial intelligence adoption: AI-readiness at firm-level. In: PACIS 2018 Proceedings (2018)
43. Sohn, K., Kwon, O.: Technology acceptance theories and factors influencing artificial intelligence-based intelligent products. Telematics Inform. **47**, 101324 (2020)
44. Lin, C.-H., Shih, H.-Y., Sher, P.J.: Integrating technology readiness into technology acceptance: the tram model. Psychol. Mark. **24**, 641–657 (2007)
45. Davis, F.D., Bagozzi, R.P., Warshaw, P.R.: User acceptance of computer technology: a comparison of two theoretical models. Manag. Sci. **35**(8), 982–1003 (1989)
46. Gal, H.C.B., Tursunbayeva, A.: 3T framework for AI adoption in Human Resource Management: A Strategic Assessment Tool of Talent, Trust, and Technology. In: ITAIS 2022 Proceedings, vol. 28 (2022)
47. Nilsen, P., et al.: A framework to guide implementation of AI in health care: protocol for a cocreation research project. JMIR Res. Protoc. **12**, e50216 (2023)
48. Blolcheva, P., Valchev, E.: Roadmap for risk management integration using AI. J. Risk Control, 13–28 (2022)
49. Arlinghaus, T., Kus, K., Behne, A. Teuteberg, F.: How to overcome the barriers of AI adoption in healthcare: a multi-stakeholder analysis. In: Proceedings of the 26th Pacific Asia Conference on Information Systems (PACIS 2022) (2022)
50. El-Deeb, A.: AI adoption: why the software industry is slow to go past the hype? SIGSOFT Softw. Eng. Notes **47**, 16–17 (2022)
51. Ismail, A., Thakkar, D., Madhiwalla, N., Kumar, N.: Public health calls for/with AI: an ethnographic perspective. Proc. ACM Hum.-Comput. Interact. **7**(CSCW2), 1–26 (2023)
52. Lee, Y.S., Kim, T., Choi, S., Kim, W.: When does AI pay off? AI-adoption intensity, complementary investments, and R&D strategy. Technovation **118**, 102590 (2022)
53. Stecher, P., Pohl, M., Turowski, K.: Enterprise architecture's effects on organizations' ability to adopt artificial intelligence - a resource-based perspective. In: Proceedings of the 28th European Conference on Information Systems (ECIS), An Online AIS Conference (2020)
54. Tjondronegoro, D., Yuwono, E., Richards, B., Green, D., Hatakka, S.: Responsible AI implementation: A human-centered framework for accelerating the innovation process (2022). arXiv preprint arXiv:2209.07076
55. Vom Brocke, J., Simons, A., Niehaves, B., Riemer, K., Plattfaut, R., Cleven, A.: Reconstructing the giant: on the importance of rigour in documenting the literature search process. ECIS. Verona. In: 17th European Conference on Information Systems (ECIS) (2009)
56. Xiao, Yu., Watson, M.: Guidance on conducting a systematic literature review. J. Plan. Educ. Res. **39**(1), 93–112 (2019)
57. Meuser, Nagel, U.: Das Experteninterview konzeptionelle Grundlagen und methodische Anlage, pp. 465–479. VS Verlag für Sozialwissenschaften (2009)
58. Jöhnk, J., Weißert, M., Wyrtki, K.: Ready or not, AI comes-an interview study of organizational AI readiness factors. Bus. Inf. Syst. Eng. **63**(1), 5–20 (2021)

59. Groopman, J.: AI readiness: five areas businesses must prepare for success in artificial intelligence. Kaleido Insights (2018). http://www.kaleidoinsights.com/wpcontent/uploads/2018/08/Report_07.18_rev6sample.pdf. Accessed 17 Feb 2024
60. Intel: The AI readiness model (2018). https://www.intel.com/content/dam/www/public/us/en/documents/white-papers/ai-readiness-model-whitepaper.pdf. Accessed 20 Feb 2024
61. Jacobides, M.G., Brusoni, S., Candelon, F.: The evolutionary dynamics of the artificial intelligence ecosystem. Strateg. Sci. **6**(4), 412–435 (2021)
62. Rana, R., Staron, M., Hansson, J., Nilsson, M., Meding, W.: A framework for adoption of machine learning in industry for software defect prediction. In: 2014 9th International Conference on Software Engineering and Applications (ICSOFT-EA), pp. 383–392 (2014)
63. Kordon, A.: Applied artificial intelligence-based systems as competitive advantage. In: 2020 IEEE 10th International Conference on Intelligent Systems (IS), pp. 6–18 (2020)
64. Yildirim, N., et al.: How experienced designers of enterprise applications engage AI as a design material. In: Proceedings of the 2022 CHI Conference on Human Factors in Computing Systems, CHI '22. Association for Computing Machinery (2022)
65. Schäfer, C., Lemmer, K., Samy Kret, K., Ylinen, M., Mikalef, P., Niehaves, B. Truth or Dare? How can we influence the adoption of artificial intelligence in municipalities?. In: Proceedings of the 54th Hawaii International Conference on System Sciences (2021)
66. Herremans, D.: AIstrom-a roadmap for developing a successful AI strategy. IEEE Access **9**, 155826–155838 (2021)
67. Alsheibani, S.A., Messom, C., Cheung, Y., Alhosni, M.: Reimagining the strategic management of artificial intelligence: five recommendations for business leaders. In: AMCIS 2020 Proceedings (2020)
68. Agrawal, A.G.A., Gans, J.S.: Artificial intelligence adoption and system-wide change. J. Econ. Manag. Strateg. (2023)
69. Wamba-Taguimdje, S.-L., Wamba, S.F., Kamdjoug, J.R.K., Wanko, C.E.T.: Influence of artificial intelligence (AI) on firm performance: the business value of AI-based transformation projects. Bus. Process Manag. J. **26**(7), 1893–1924 (2020)
70. Jürgen Kai-Uwe Brock and Florian von Wangenheim: Demystifying ai: What digital transformation leaders can teach you about realistic artificial intelligence. Calif. Manage. Rev. **61**(4), 110–134 (2019)
71. Lu, X., Wijayaratna, K., Huang, Y., Qiu, A.: Ai-enabled opportunities and transformation challenges for SMEs in the post-pandemic era: a review and research agenda. Front. Publ. Health **10** (2022)
72. Alshawi, M.: Rethinking IT in Construction and Engineering: Organisational Readiness, Taylor & Francis, New York (2007)
73. Sweeney, D., Nair, S., Cormican, K., An exploratory analysis: Scaling AI-based industry 4.0 projects in the medical device industry. Procedia Comput. Sci. **219**, 759–766 (2023)
74. Kelley, S.: Employee perceptions of the effective adoption of AI principles: JBE. J. Bus. Ethics **178**(4), 871–893 (2022)
75. Windl, M., Feger, S.S., Zijlstra, L., Schmidt, A., Wozniak, P.W.: It is not always discovery time: four pragmatic approaches in designing AI systems. CHI '22. Association for Computing Machinery (2022)
76. Kaplan, A., Haenlein, M.: Rulers of the world, unite! the challenges and opportunities of artificial intelligence. Bus. Horiz. **63**(1), 37–50 (2020)

77. Brunnbauer, M., Piller, G., Rothlauf, F.: idea-AI: Developing a Method for the Systematic Identification of AI Use Cases. In: AMCIS (2021)

78. Eitle, V., Buxmann, P.: Cultural differences in machine learning adoption: an international comparison between Germany and the united states. In: European Conference on Information Systems (2020)

79. Carter, L., Liu, D., Cantrell, C.: Exploring the intersection of the digital divide and artificial intelligence: a hermeneutic literature review. AIS Trans. Hum.-Comput. Interact. **12**(4), 253–275 (2020)

80. Chui, C.K., Lin, S.-B., Zhang, B., Zhou, D.-X.: Realization of spatial sparseness by deep ReLU nets with massive data. IEEE Trans. Neural Netw. Learn. Syst. **33**(1), 229–243 (2022)

81. Monah, S.R., et al.: Data governance functions to support responsible data stewardship in pediatric radiology research studies using artificial intelligence. Pediatr. Radiol. **52**(11), 2111–2119 (2022)

82. Janssen, M., Brous, P., Estevez, E., Barbosa, L.S., Janowski, T.: Data governance: organizing data for trustworthy artificial intelligence. Gov. Inf. Q. **37**(3), 101493 (2020)

83. Huang, S., Siddarth, D.: Generative AI and the digital commons. arXiv (2023)

84. Luisa, K., Wunderlich, N., Beck, R.: Artificial Intelligence for the financial services industry: what challenges organizations to succeed. In: Proceedings of the 52nd Hawaii International Conference on System Sciences (2019)

85. Tominc, P., Oreški, D., Rožman, M.: Artificial intelligence and agility-based model for successful project implementation and company competitiveness. Information **14**(6), 337 (2023)

86. Nurski, L.: AI adoption in the public sector: a case study. Technical report, Bruegel (2023)

Realizing the Promise of AI Governance Involving Humans-in-the-Loop

Margaret H. McKay[1,2](✉) 🆔

[1] Digital Technologies , National Research Council of Canada, Ottawa, Canada
margaret.mckay@nrc-cnrc.gc.ca
[2] Osgoode Hall Law School, Toronto, Canada

Abstract. Human-in-the-loop ("HITL") approaches have been proposed as an important element to ensure safety and fairness for higher-risk applications of artificial intelligence ("AI") enabled decision-making. This paper examines the question: To what extent does the current state of knowledge enable the definition of factors and mitigations necessary for the effective implementation of HITL approaches? Previous research examining internal (individual) and external (implementation-related structural and contextual) factors in human decision-making are surveyed and assessed for potential relevance. This analysis highlights factors likely to be of relevance and reveals gaps which hinder the elaboration of factors and mitigations relevant to the effectiveness of HITL approaches.

In order to realize the potential for HITL approaches to enhance safety for those reliant on or subject to AI systems, governance implementation will need to include minimum requirements applicable to both human overseers and to the context in which they work and are assessed. Factors identified as relevant include: complacency, persuasion, workload, conformity, unequal treatment of different kinds of error, and organizational polices and norms which may deter thorough review and human challenge of AI recommendations. There is also a need for further research: to enhance understanding of the practical significance of HITL effectiveness risks factors and their management; to enable the classification of HITL-implementation environments; and, to provide robust measurement methodologies to enable the identification of the most promising human candidates for HITL overseer roles.

Keywords: Human-in-the-Loop · Governance · AI · Automation Bias

1 Introduction

Human-in-the-loop ("HITL") approaches have been proposed as an important element to ensure safety and fairness for higher-risk applications of artificial intelligence ("AI") enabled decision-making processes. This paper examines the extent to which the current state of knowledge enables the definition of factors and mitigations necessary for the effective implementation of HITL approaches.

© The Author(s), under exclusive license to Springer Nature Switzerland AG 2024
H. Degen and S. Ntoa (Eds.): HCII 2024, LNCS 15382, pp. 107–123, 2024.
https://doi.org/10.1007/978-3-031-76827-9_7

1.1   Introduction - Governance

This paper focusses on anticipated challenges to the operational implementation of AI governance through HITL approaches and identifies areas in need of additional examination. The process of implementing high-level policy is known to be fraught [1]. Governance involves an assemblage of interconnected elements. This typically begins with high-level policy and vision, which is translated into statutes and eventually regulations, and then further interpreted in standards and operational policies. Individuals and teams then attempt to understand and apply this guidance within their specific context, norms, and priorities.

Examples of AI Governance Documents – Treatment of Human Oversight. Among the most discussed legislative efforts is the European Artificial Intelligence Act ("EU AIA") [2]. The preamble to the EU AIA proposes that where "high-risk" AI systems are involved, human overseers should have the competence, training, and authority to carry out their role. The EU AIA further requires that high-risk AI systems be "designed and developed in such a way that they can be effectively oversee by natural persons".

Implementing legislation requires the creation and use of more granular materials. Secondary materials may vary in force and approach. For example, the NIST AI Risk Management Framework ("AI RMF") provides comparatively high-level guidance and does not enumerate circumstances requiring human oversight. Nonetheless, it recognizes that such oversight will be needed in some circumstances and it calls for further consideration and research into instances where human oversight may be required [3].

The United Kingdom Information Commissioner's Office's updated "AI and data protection toolkit" ("UK Toolkit") contains both guidance and requirements. This toolkit advises organizations to ensure that human overseers "remain engaged, critical and able to challenge the system's outputs wherever appropriate." [4].

Even where core elements needed for effective human oversight are described, as in the EU AIA and the UK Toolkit, widely adopted implementation-level guidance such as standards and best practices are currently limited. This paper explores the feasibility of bridging this gap.

1.2   Introduction – Role of Human-Computer Interactions in HITL Implementation Governance

There are good reasons to want a human in the loop in relation to some sensitive AI-enabled decisions. AI-enabled tools can have weaknesses, including for example issues with "hallucination," and bias [5, 6]. For example, medical diagnostics systems trained on light-skinned or privileged populations can provide inaccurate or inadequate results when serving patients having darker skin or belonging to a marginalized group [7]. Effective HITL approaches can help offset such risks.

There is a strong history of research into factors which can undercut the effectiveness of human decision-making or human incentives to act on decisions. Despite this, opportunities for knowledge from these areas to be integrated to inform AI governance remain largely unexplored. This gap has the potential to frustrate efforts to effectively implement AI governance requirements.

1.3   Introduction – The Overseer's Context

To be effective, human-in-the-loop ("HITL") approaches to responsible AI require that the human in the loop both exercises and acts upon their own independent judgement. This raises two broad areas for governance attention: factors affecting the willingness or ability of the human overseer to think independently; and, factors affecting their willingness or ability to act in accordance with that thinking.

The human "supervising" an AI is likely to be in a very different situation from the supervisor of a traditional human team. Not only is the AI impervious to threats of consequences from the human overseer; but, in many cases the human and the AI will be subject to parallel and potentially inter-related performance analyses implemented by those outside their immediate group. Companies which have invested in AI tools are seeking to improve efficiency and or (sometimes) the quality of their outputs, at least in part by substituting labor for capital (AI) expenses [8]. In such cases, the human overseer is relatively disempowered compared to someone who supervises humans.

In an HITL situation, both the overseer and their management may consider the AI to be a dominant technical (informational/analytical) expert: the AI tool has presumably been adopted because it can do the job faster and is informed by a greater volume of task-specific data than most human overseers will have experienced. For example, an AI has already out-performed an experienced fighter pilot in a simulator dogfight, and has safely and autonomously flown a real fighter aircraft in a simulated dogfight [9]. Concerns are being raised that AI dominance may eventually lead to deskilling of the humans involved [10]. Structured anecdotal evidence suggests that the introduction of AI tools has in some cases already coincided with a move to employing lower-skill humans to work with the AI. This is despite concerns among those subject to the AI's decisions that the AI tools fail to account for contextual factors and that the lower-skill employees simply defer to the AI [11]. Considerations such as these may impact the way a human overseer approaches their role, as well as their practical ability to be effective in that role.

The UK Toolkit requires organizations relying on HITL to ensure that overseers remain engaged and critical, and also able to challenge AI system outputs. Succeeding in these areas will require managing human behavioral tendencies, human knowledge, organizational context, and features of the AI-enabled system itself. AI system design is an area of active enquiry and largely beyond the scope of this work. This paper focusses on human and contextual factors and also briefly considers the implications of persuasion research to inform defensive strategies to reduce the risk that overseers are influenced by persuasion from the machines they are intended to oversee.

This analysis begins in Part II which provides a review of research relating to human and structural factors likely to impact the exercise and action upon independent human thought in an HITL context. These factors are subdivided into: (i) human tendencies to err due to internal factors related to the human and/or the interaction between the human and aspects of the AI system's design; and, (ii) structural features which create incentives for rational humans to choose to neglect aspects of their HITL role.

Part III provides recommendations for next steps to enable the establishment of initial governance approaches while related research continues. It also provides comments on some key areas where future research is needed to inform effective governance requirements and to enable the measurement and classification necessary for consistent implementation.

2 Factors Impacting Human Judgement and Related Action

The tendency of humans to be influenced by the presence and judgement of others was first studied in relation to human-human interactions. The resultant understanding of human tendencies toward conformity have now been extended into the human-machine context. This also provided information on the tendency toward social loafing, which bears close similarity to findings in the human-machine context.

Research on human-machine interactions began in parallel, initially focused largely on human responses to earlier automated systems. This work has also evolved into the human-AI context, provided deeper understanding of automation bias related topics (discussed here) and also expanding to include human-AI teaming (which, while not immediately applicable to the more rigid HITL context, still holds great research promise to enhance the understanding of underlying human predispositions and behaviors).

The third area considered here derives from behavioral economics and encompasses decision theory and norm theory, which describe the potential for factors within the HITL implementation context to create disincentives for overseers to intervene when they think an AI error is probable. Some readers will suspect the existence of common threads underlying observations in these three areas. Further examination of these deeper threads is beyond the scope of a paper on governance implementation. Recognizing these limitations, this paper focusses on impacts while attempting to respect the vocabulary specific to each research area in its review of past research. As governance is impact driven, factors with different academic histories but similar triggers and impacts are nonetheless grouped together for discussion of possible mitigation considerations in Part 3.

2.1 Conformity

The tendency of individuals to conform to the views of others has been studied since at least the 1950s. Early work by Solomon Asch [12] focused on the tendency of individuals to conform to a publicly stated and clearly erroneous group conclusion on a question of pure fact (comparing the length of a test line to three other reference lines). Over half the test subjects conformed with an erroneous group response at least once. Additionally, over 10% of test subjects chose a "compromise" answer between the obviously correct answer and the majority answer. Results were not significantly affected when subjects were advised that their individual results for each test would be assessed by the research team later.

Although 25% of Asch's subjects maintained their independence throughout the main experiment, the remaining subjects showed varying levels of conformity to the group. In post-experiment interviews, some subjects admitted to having consciously conformed to the majority despite disagreeing privately. Even then, they tended to underestimate how frequently they conformed. Those who were able to retain their independence frequently expressed having experienced doubt and a sense of loneliness as a result. Most subjects reported being concerned when their answer disagreed with the majority answer, as well as having concerns that by voicing disagreement they would reveal a defect in themselves. The independent voices included some very self-confident individuals, as well as those having a profound sense that they owed a duty to provide their own independent conclusions [12].

A lack of confidence, fear of judgement, and the potential for others to know of a disagreement, are all factors which drive a tendency to conformity, or a reluctance to voice disagreement [12, 13]. A role has been proposed for both normative and informational influences in driving the tendency toward human-human conformity [14]. Normative influences have been postulated to reflect a desire to conform to the expectations of others. If correct, this suggests the potential for attenuation of such influence in the human-AI context where the lack of human peer to cast judgment or alienate might attenuate the impulse to norm. On the other hand, informational influences have been postulated to relate to the individual's perception that the opinion offered by the other has evidentiary value. Thus, where the AI is seen as a useful source of information, informational influence may continue to apply, even if normative influence does not. More recent results suggest a human tendency to give greater weight to advice from an algorithm than they give to advice from another human, for both visual estimation and forecasting tasks [15]. These results support the possibility that (at least) informational influence remains a factor driving conformity, even in a human-algorithm context.

Individual Characteristics in Conformity. The transferability of conclusions drawn from human – human conformity studies conducted at a particular moment of time and cultural context has been studied. Subsequent studies have repeated Asch's approach and have identified modest differences in conformity levels related to culture and gender. However, generational impacts have also been observed, with overall levels of conformity decreasing since Asch's time [16]. This complicates comparisons between studies.

In a governance and hiring context, blanket categorizations of individuals based on group membership are unlikely to be desirable. Individual screening for the tendency to conform in a real or simulated human-AI context is likely to align better to organizational needs and to the human rights expectations of HITL candidates. Further research is needed to develop standard methods suitable for routine candidate screening.

2.2 Machine-Specific Studies: Automation Bias, Complacency, and Vulnerability to Persuasion

Automation Bias and Complacency. Automation bias involves the tendency of humans to favor or give excessive weight to suggestions from automated systems. Early studies in this area identified two types of overseer error: Human failure to identify a problem which had not been identified by the automated system; and, human failure to countermand (or disregard) erroneous automated advice despite the availability of reliable contradictory information from other sources [17].

The human failure to identify problems missed by the machine has been linked to the human tendency to minimize cognitive investment also observed in human-human teams ("social loafing") [17, 18]. Factors contributing to this behavior include the potential for evaluation of individual effort, and the perceived meaningfulness of the task [18].

Studies measuring the verification-related activities of individuals tasked with overseeing an automated system revealed that all participants engaged in inadequate verification (complacency) at least some of the time. Merely informing overseers that the system is fallible and requires verification is not fully effective at preventing automation bias. However, when overseers experience and recognize an error by the automated system, this reduces their trust in it, resulting in reduced complacency [17].

Less complacent overseers require more time to complete their verifications. Failures to engage in adequate verification were more frequent in systems when the system was seen as very reliable and where the human was juggling many contemporaneous demands [19]. Thus, workload is one example of a linkage between the context of implementation/oversight and human-specific factors. It demonstrates the importance of establishing minimum requirements and measuring their impact at both the individual and the structural / contextual level.

The early work on complacency and automation bias was focused on systems where the automation in place was generally simpler than modern AI-enabled decision or recommendation systems [20]. However, similar results have been observed in the context of more complex algorithmic systems. For example, improper acceptance of erroneous machine advice has been explicitly linked to excessive trust in automated systems, as well as a belief that the judgement of the automated system was likely to be superior to that of the individual [19]. This bears close similarity to the findings in Asch's human-human conformity experiments and hints at informational influence.

More recently, research on "algorithmic aversion" indicates that humans are likely to give more weight to algorithmic advice than human advice related to objective questions; [15] yet, they are also likely to suffer a greater loss of confidence in an algorithmic adviser than a human one upon seeing each make a similar mistake [21]. This reinforces the ongoing relevance of automation bias and complacency to HITL approaches, while also highlighting the need for further research to illuminate the apparently strong but brittle human – AI trust relationship.

Impacts of Accountability and Experience. A sense of individual accountability appears to reduce complacency [17]. Overseers with extensive experience in the task assigned to the AI also appear to be more willing to substitute their own opinion for that of the AI. A recent study involving radiologists demonstrated that very experienced radiologists were less likely to accept erroneous AI advice. None-the-less, about half the time even very experienced radiologists could be negatively influenced by an incorrect AI recommendation [22].

The tendency to be excessively deferential to AI systems is not limited to those lacking expertise in such systems. Even data scientists and AI experts have been shown to over-trust the ability of AI tools to detect issues [23]. This is consistent with previous findings that theoretical knowledge and risk awareness on their own are insufficient to prevent errors related to excessive trust, particularly for objective questions [24, 25].

The Need For Caution – An Example of Potential Unintended Consequences. When developing and testing potential HITL governance implementation approaches, it will be important to remain alert to the risk of unintended consequences. The impact of proposed mitigation approaches should be assessed not only on the factor to which they are targeted, but also on overall HITL effectiveness. The so-called "white-box paradox" provides an example: "explainability" has been described as a characteristic of trustworthy AI systems [26] represents one element of good overall AI governance [27].

In an HITL context, useable explainability of AI decisions could be helpful to a diligent over-seer who is attempting to assess the quality of an AI-recommendation. However, claims of explainability are also a factor impacting human trust. Preliminary work in this area suggests that the existence of even an insubstantial explanation can cause humans to increase their trust in the algorithmic system, even when it provides erroneous advice [28, 29]. Thus, it is possible that mitigating one factor could aggravate another. Trade-offs between factors to mitigate may be justified; but only once the magnitude of the overall impact has been assessed.

Human Vulnerability to Persuasion Technology. In some non-HITL contexts, the ability of machines to influence humans is a desirable goal. Design factors such as the gender of a robot's voice and its manner of speech (e.g., loud or soft, grammatically correct or imperfect) can be adjusted to make a robot more or less persuasive to individuals [30, 31]. While persuasive robots may be valuable in some applications, persuasion of the HITL by the AI they oversee is something to be resisted. The implications of persuasion research should be considered in the general design and personalized tuning of HITL user interfaces to reduce potential for machine persuasion of overseers.

2.3 Incentive Alignment Factors

Humans who are able to exercise independent judgement may none-the-less be deterred from acting on the fruits of that judgement as a result of structural and contextual factors in their work context.

Decision Theory and Subjective Utility. This section focusses on the potential for irrationality not by the overseer but within the organizational implementation and management of HITL situations. By definition, the HITL is a human. They live in the real world and are subject to a range of pressures and requirements not limited to the specific question assessed by the AI. At a practical level, overseers can be expected to weigh not only the information considered by the AI in reaching its decision, but also other potential impacts.

In formal terms, research on decision theory provides that individuals make decisions with reference to subjective expected utility. The decision-making process involves consideration of a range of factors such as the probability of various outcomes, information quality, interdependence of outcomes, and ambiguity in the question asked [32–35]. This suggests that a rational overseer who is deciding how thoroughly to validate an AI decision and whether to accept a suspicious recommendation will consider their own accountability and performance situation, and not just the risk of harm to others. Issues such as the chance of an error being noticed, and the impact of different kinds of error on the overseer's career can become relevant.

The comparative weight of these considerations may depend on the individual, the workplace policies and processes within which they operate, and broader legal and social norms and factors. These factors may not always be independent. The subjective utility of any particular outcome will depend on the individual's belief with respect to the utility of the outcome and its probability [32].

In highly simplified terms, one can imagine that the subjective utility (S) that an individual assigns to a particular decision to act or not to act would reflect the overall subjective probability (P) and impact (I) of benefit or harm to each stakeholder including the overseer themselves, their organization, the person impacted by the decision (data subject), and the community. For a decision with the potential for multiple outcomes, an idealized utility of the decision would be the sum of the subjective utilities of each possible outcome, each calculated as:

$$S = PI_{overseer} + PI_{organization} + PI_{data\ subject} + PI_{community} \qquad (1)$$

This calculation is based on subjective utility as assessed by the individual making the decision. Consequently, the full scope of factors which impact an individual's preference for various outcomes is relevant. Prior research looking at financial decision-making suggests that individuals do not consistently seek outcomes with the greatest personal benefit. However, issues such as fairness and sharing with a member of a perceived lower social class frequently led individuals to choose less personally remunerative outcomes which preserved their sense of fairness or superiority [36, 37]. Further research is needed to elucidate the potential impact and mitigation options for HITL effectiveness, particularly where data subjects may be from disadvantaged groups.

As an interim measure until research provides a more refined understanding of the relevant factors evolves, workplaces using HITL approaches should ensure that organizational performance measures and internal processes align overseer incentives and risks with objectively determined benefits and risks to data subjects (those subject to the results of the AI-assisted decision) and the community.

Example - Impact of HITL Contextual Factors - Asymmetric Blame. Formal and informal governance structures and processes within the overseer's workplace can be expected to impact the subjective utility they assign to various outcomes, thereby influencing their decisions. Formal structural factors will include the incentive and overseer performance assessment structures of the workplace, and organizational tolerance for different kinds of risks. Informal elements may include local norms with respect to deference to so-called expertise (including machine expertise), as well as the extent to which different kinds of errors are monitored and remembered.

Harm resulting from an individual's inaction is generally assessed as less blameworthy than harm arising from their action [38]. Similarly, deviations from normal practice are assessed as more blameworthy than similar harms arising from perceived-normal conditions [39]. To the extent that AI-enabled systems are intended to serve as expert decision-makers, deviations from AI recommendations could be seen as a deviation from the normal state, and an error of commission rather than omission. Both these factors would be expected to give rise to greater perceived overseer blameworthiness in the event of error.

People also judge actions by humans and machines differently. Where an action is clearly seen as harmful (e.g., discriminatory actions), people tend to blame a human decision-maker more harshly than a machine [40]. In the case of joint human-machine errors, the human will be judged more harshly [41]. Taken together, these factors indicate that it may be quite risky for an overseer to interfere with an AI's decision unless the overseer is very certain not only that the machine is wrong, but also that they themselves are correct and can demonstrate that fact.

Given this, a human overseer who suspects an error in the AI system they supervise must make several calculations in order to assess the subjective utility of potential decision options. While these calculations are unlikely to be conscious and explicit, they are formalized here in a simplified form for demonstration purposes: Consider the case of a human overseer charged with overseeing the decisions of a system which identifies individuals on social assistance who should receive priority for subsidized housing. For the sake of this example, assume that the decision is a binary "yes/no" where the overseer's only choice is between allowing the AI's decision to stand, or reversing it without the opportunity for additional investigation. Focusing on the career interests of an overseer who strongly suspects that the AI is wrong, but cannot be absolutely certain of that, the calculation of the subjective utility of the decision with respect to career impacts on the overseer herself is as follows:

Case A: If the overseer does not over-rule the AI's decision, the value of the magnitude of the negative career consequences (N_n) she risks from non-action depends on:

W: the likelihood that the AI's decision is wrong

C: the likelihood that the overseer's superiors will learn of the error; and,

P: the extent to which the overseer will be seen as blameworthy for failing to reverse the AI's decision (P).

Thus, in the case of non-action,

$$N_n = PCW \tag{2}$$

Case B: If the overseer does engage, the calculation becomes more complex.

The likelihood that the AI's decision is wrong (W), and the likelihood that the error will come to the attention of the overseer's superiors C remain as described in Case A (and are held constant for the purposes of this example).

Given that the overseer disagrees with the AI's decision, the sum of AI error (W) plus overseer error must equal 1. Thus, the likelihood that the overseer is wrong is $(1-W)$.

Once the human chooses to intervene, their blameworthiness will be assessed as active (A). Thus, A replaces P from Case A (non-intervention). Given that active errors are judged as more blameworthy than passive ones (A > P), it is possible to express the blameworthiness associated with an active error as (P+i), where i is the increased blameworthiness attached to an active error as opposed to a passive one.

Thus, in the case of intervention by the human, a conservative estimate of the value of the magnitude of the negative career consequences (N_a) the overseer risks facing from action is:

$$N_a = CA(1 - W) \tag{3}$$

Since A = P+i, then

$$N_a = C(P + i) - WC(P + i) \tag{4}$$

If the overseer assesses the risk that the AI is wrong at 50%, then W = 0.5, giving:

$$N_n = PC/2 \tag{5}$$

$$N_a = PC/2 + (3/2)Ci \qquad (6)$$

Since P, C, and i are always > 0

$$N_n < N_a \qquad (7)$$

Table 1. Summary of HITL Factors Discussed

Factor	Factor Components	Governance Implication Examples
Conformity	*Normative Influencers:* Fear of Judgement Reluctance to Outgroup *Informational Influencers:* Perceived expertise of advisor *Both:* Personal Confidence	**Hiring**: screening for self-confidence, tolerance for disagreement **Training**: build assessment confidence, tolerance for isolation
Automation Bias	Complacency & Social Loafing • Excessive Trust • Heavy Workload • Individual Accountability • Sense of Importance of Work	**Training**: exposure to machine error **Operational**: Limit overseer tasking **Operational**: Verification / human action minimum requirements (by system) **Operational**: Monitoring of actual verification and challenge levels **Training**: exposure to machine error **Training**: risks and harms of errors
Persuasion	Vocal characteristic Communication strategies	**System**: system interfaces should be customizable and tailored to each user to reduce likely persuasive factors **System & and Operational**: counter newly identified persuasion risks
Incentive Alignment	Unequal Perceptions of Error Blameworthiness • Action / Inaction • Human / Machine Performance Measures • Favoring Throughput • Favoring Verification • Favoring action on concerns	**Operational**: treat action / inaction errors the same **Operational**: treat human errors the same regardless of the AI recommendation **Operational**: Limit overseer tasking based on verification rate and time requirements **Operational** Avoid incentives for excess throughput **Operational**: require minimum decision verification % from overseers **Training & Operational**: implement and train on processes to counteract bias against active errors **Operational**: randomly spot-check overall overseer-AI "team" accuracy

This indicates that the overseer will need to be more confident in their own answer than they would be in the AI's before the risk of intervention is warranted in terms of their own career. This creates an inherent disincentive to active oversight.

Of course, humans are not pure statistical machines. Individuals will also assess their own level of confidence in their independent conclusions. Where available, they can also be expected to assess the AI's reported confidence in its recommendation. Additionally, they may have the option of further investigation (at an opportunity cost of time or throughput). Nonetheless, this simple example demonstrates that all else being equal, in the absence of specific mitigation measures, there will be disincentives to effective HITL oversight. Standards organizations, as well as organizations employing HITL approaches should establish requirements to mitigate the impact of the human preference for passive errors over active ones. This will enable more effective oversight. These requirements should mandate performance assessment approaches which treat errors of omission and commission equally and which recognize human and machine errors as equally concerning.

A simplified summary of the major factors considered in this section is provided in Table 1. As AI-enabled systems become increasingly common, research in this area must expand. These developments should be monitored and their lessons integrated into standards and regulations to ensure the effectiveness of HITL approaches.

3   Coming Challenges and Next Steps

AI governance approaches which rely on human-in-the-loop are at risk of reduced effectiveness unless implementation standards, guidelines, and practices demand a high level of rigor in design, training requirements, and deployment. More research is needed to fully elucidate the factors involved, mitigation measures, and, to develop and validate the necessary measurement and classification tools. However, AI deployment will not wait for this work and neither should initial efforts to establish minimum requirements.

3.1   Considerations for Standards and Best Practices

Past experience with privacy legislation such as the EU's *General Data Protection Regulation* ("GDPR") has demonstrated the value of requirements for "appropriate technical and organizational measures" [42] and similar language in defining requirements. Such approaches enable minimum legal requirements to evolve with technology and society's understanding of the issues.

Governance approaches to HITL implementation for the mitigation of AI-related risks should take a similar approach. Organizations relying on HITL to satisfy any part of their responsibility to ensure AI-related safety should be required to take appropriate technical and organizational measures to ensure HITL effectiveness. These requirements should scale based on the complexity and risk involved.

At the level of standards and guidelines, consideration should be given to establishing minimum requirements in each of the areas described in Table 1. There is also an urgent need for research-backed measurement and classification approaches to support effective implementation. For example, it will be necessary to classify the complexity of different kinds of HITL roles to enable proportionality between requirements and risks. Further research is also needed to enhance existing measurement approaches to assess the human factors described within an operational HITL context.

The initial steps described below are proposed for discussion as potential preliminary measures. They are intended to introduce the idea of HITL requirements into the broader AI implementation conversation, and to provide suggestions on mitigation of some already-identifiable risks. Future research results should inform the evolution of such requirements.

Overseer Selection. Candidates for HITL positions should be screened for behaviors associated with HITL risks. While validation in an operational HITL context should be pursued in parallel, existing research results are sufficient to identify some interim factors for initial overseer screening. These may be useful in identifying candidates who are more likely to be effective overseers. This approach should be supplemented by research on methods to teach necessary behaviors and skills to a wider range of individuals. Depending on legal, social, and practical factors impacting the hiring process, candidate screening might involve assessment during mock scenarios calculated to reveal the behaviors and skills of interest.

Conformity: Candidates for overseer positions should be screened for the ability to resist conformity, at least in terms of informational influencers.

Complacency: Candidates should be tested for actual complacency in a mock-up scenario. Approaches informed by the work of Skitka [17] and Bahner [19] may prove useful.

Confidence: Candidates should be screened for generalized confidence. Only those demonstrating the capability to remain confident in the face of adversity should be considered for HITL roles.

Expertise: Candidates should be assessed for expertise in the kind of decisions the AI system is tasked with making. The scope and nature of necessary expertise should be revisited routinely to account for research developments and the potential identification of other desirable skills, such as those favoring appropriate reliance on AI advice [43].

Standardized assessments for tendencies toward conformity and complacency will be needed, as will research-backed training programs to develop and maintain these skills. Best practices establishing minimum levels for each characteristic for different classes of HITL role could then guide employers in their selection of employees.

Overseer Training. Overseers should receive initial and ongoing training in coping strategies to deal with the stress of not conforming and of taking actions seen as out of the normal, even in the absence of certainty. This should also include education on the facts related to human tendencies to treat different types of errors differently as well as a description of the processes their employer has put in place to prevent these issues from negatively affecting the performance assessment of effective overseers.

Initial training of overseers should include experience of AI error in the system they will be using. Furthermore, high-level anonymized overviews of known cases of serious AI errors should be shared among the overseer community for various types of systems on an ongoing basis. In addition to providing case-specific information, this would reinforce the message that these systems are fallible and the job of the overseer is important. Given business confidentiality concerns, legislative action may be needed to establish the requirements and parameters for such sharing, and to establish confidentiality requirements. The intent of this system would be to keep the overseer and AI system operator community informed. Thus, unlike public-facing transparency reporting requirements, this system should require information sharing even where no personal or financial harm resulted from the error.

Organizational Processes. Overseer workloads should be capped based on verified time required for an average overseer to verify a single average output of that system, multiplied by the volume of AI responses the overseer will be responsible for and the percentage of AI responses the organization expects the overseer to verify.

Overseer performance measures should:

- Include measures of complacency (ensuring actual verification activity)
- Explicitly ensure equal performance measurement consequences for passive (inactive) and active (interventionist) errors
- Reflect expectations for diligent verification and action on conclusions
- Establish a minimum percentage of AI responses to be thoroughly verified by each overseer for specific systems.
- Include and monitor overseer action with respect to periodic "test" decisions which would be expected to trigger verification action by a diligent overseer
- Provide no incentive to exceed the maximum throughput possible while respecting target verification rates and thoroughness

3.2   Gaps and Future Research Areas

Implementation of HITL governance represents a sizable challenge. Further research is needed to expand the understanding of the factors discussed and approaches to mitigate them. The real-world effectiveness of the mitigations proposed here need to be assessed, and appropriate modifications proposed. There is also an urgent need for evaluation approaches useful in selecting promising overseer candidates in view of the factors listed in Table 1.

Multidisciplinary research and development will be needed to develop efficient initial and ongoing training approaches for overseers and to define effective organizational policies and performance measurement approaches which support incentives for active oversight and action while also enabling organizational efficiency goals.

Research in decision theory and judgement and decision-making should be expanded to develop experimentally validated guidelines suitable for organizational use to mitigate the unequal treatment of active and passive errors and structural factors which may create disincentives to HITL intervention.

Overall cost-benefit efficiency will require that the extent of HITL-implementation requirements applicable to an AI system is proportional to the risks associated with HITL oversight failure. This will require a systematic approach to classifying the complexity and risk associated with different HITL roles and potential failures. All of these elements should be grounded in reproducible research results.

4 Conclusions

The current state of knowledge enables the definition of some factors and mitigations needed to make HITL-enabled approaches to AI safety effective. However, many gaps remain and current findings represent only a first step. AI adoption is increasing rapidly. Delaying the definition of operational HITL governance implementation requirements increases the risk of frequent but ineffective efforts to implement HITL approaches to AI safety. This could result in HITL failures, permitting harm to individuals and organizations, and leading to higher costs when requirements are imposed remedially.

The suggestions here are a possible beginning. The end is many years away. More research is needed, not only within the specific fields discussed but also across them and others. Many of the practical and urgent requirements identified, such as those for real-world routine screening and measurement protocols, training strategies, and organizational processes can only be satisfied by combined insights and knowledge from different disciplines.

AI-enabled systems have a huge potential for good. To the extent that the realization of that promise depends on the effective implementation of HILT approaches, it is incumbent on researchers and governance professionals to act quickly. Nearly a century of research on human decision-making is reflected in the modest list of proposed preliminary mitigation approaches discussed here. It is quite likely that the next decade will need to see that much research again, combined with strong governance analysis and documentation in order to ensure HITL effectiveness in the medium term.

5 Appendix: Methods

5.1 Approach

A modified legal research approach was taken. This reflects the breadth of disciplines and materials involved in addressing the core research question ("To what extent are HITL-reliant governance approaches to AI safety sufficiently enabled by available research results?"). A general qualitative analysis approach was employed [44].

The foundational propositions (qualitative hypotheses) were focused on the general theme of whether HITL-reliant approaches to AI safety seen in current AI governance are currently enabled by a sufficient body of research. Proposition #1 was: Current governance approaches requiring HITL to ensure AI safety are inadequate because they fail to specify the human and contextual factors which must be managed to enable effectiveness. Proposition #2 was: Areas of uncertainty remain in relation to the factors and requirements needed to enable the effectiveness of governance approach which relay on HITL to enable AI safety.

Classification-related propositions (the categories examined and used to structure the analysis and findings) were updated to reflect early findings. The initial classification proposition was that three categories of factors existed for analysis: compliance behavior, automation bias, and structural factors reflecting uneven treatment of different kinds of errors in the context of decision theory. As the literature review advanced, an additional category was added to enable recognition of the potential of machine persuasion related factors to undercut HITL effectiveness.

It will be understood that this paper reflects an early effort to identify and comment upon factors of likely significance for the effectiveness of HITL governance approaches. The scope of the challenge, and the diversity of the fields involved preclude any claim to exhaustiveness. The author sincerely hopes that this work will stimulate others to further explore and expand the understanding of these and other factors and their implications for effective HITL implementation.

Acknowledgments. The author wishes to thank Terrence C. Stewart, Alana M. Gin, and all anonymous reviewers for providing valuable comments which significantly improved this paper.

Disclosure of Interests. The author has no competing interests to declare that are relevant to the content of this article.

References

1. Hudson, B., Hunter, D., Peckham, S.: Policy failure and the policy-implementation gap: can policy support programs help? Policy Des. Pract. **2**(1), 1–14 (2019). https://doi.org/10.1080/25741292.2018.1540378
2. Regulation of the European Parliament and of the Council laying down harmonised rules on artificial intelligence and amending Regulations (EC) No 300/2008, (EU) No 167/2013,(EU) No 168/2013, (EU) 2018/858, (EU) 2018/1139 and (EU) 2019/2144 and Directives 2014/90/EU, (EU) 2016/797 and (EU) 2020/1828 (Artificial Intelligence Act) Ch. III, Sec.2, Art. 14 c.1. Accessed 21 May 2024
3. National Institute of Standards and Technology, U.S. Department of Commerce. Artific. Intell. Risk Manage. Framework (AI RMF 1.0) **23**, 40 (2023) https://doi.org/10.6028/NIST.AI.100-1
4. Information Commissioner's Office (UK) Guidance on AI and data protection, vol. 98 (2023)
5. Draude, C., Klumbyte, G., Lucking, P.: Situated algorithms: a sociotechnical systemic approach to bias. Online Inf. Rev. **44**(2), 325–342 (2020). https://doi.org/10.1108/OIR-10-2018-0332
6. Yan, Z.L.D., et al.: ChatGPT on guidelines: providing contextual knowledge to GPT allows it to provide advice on appropriate colonoscopy intervals. J. Gastro. Hepatol. **39**(1), 81–106 (2024)
7. Saint, J.A.Y.: Making decisions: bias in artificial intelligence and data-driven diagnostic tools. Aust. J. Gen. Pract. **52**(7), 439–442 (2023)
8. Holman, J., Smialek, J.: Will A.I. boost productivity? Companies Sure Hope So. New York Times 1 April 2024
9. D'Urso, S.: AI Flew X-62 VISTA During Simulated Dogfight Against Armed F-16 The Aviationist 18 April 2024. https://theaviationist.com/2024/04/18/ai-flew-x-62-vista-during-dogfight/
10. Sutton, S.G., Arnold, V., Holt, M.: How much automation is too much? Keeping the human relevant in knowledge work. J. Emerg. Tech. Accounting **15**(2), 15–25 (2018)
11. Koreff, J., Baudot, L., Sutton, S.G.: Exploring the impact of technology dominance on audit professionalism through data analytic-driven healthcare audits. J. Info. Sys. **37**(3), 59–80 (2023). https://doi.org/10.2308/ISYS-2022-023
12. Asch, S.E.: Studies of independence and conformity: a minority of one against a unanimous majority. Psychol. Monogr. Gen. Appl. **70**(6), 1–70 (1956)
13. Lee, H.E.: A Markov chain model for Asch-type experiments. J. Math. Sociol. **2**, 131–142 (1972)

14. Deutsch, M., Gerard, H.B.: A study of normative and informational social influences upon individual judgment. J. Abnorm. Soc. Psychol. **51**(3), 629–636 (1955). https://doi.org/10.1037/h0046408
15. Logg, J.M., Minson, J.A., Moore, D.A.: Algorithmic appreciation: people Prefer Algorithmic to Human Judgement. Org. Behav. Hum. Dec. Proces. **151**, 90–103 (2019). https://doi.org/10.1016/j.obhdp.2018.12.005
16. Bond, R., Smith, P.B.: Culture and conformity: a meta-analysis of studies using Asch's (1952b, 1956) line judgement task. Psychol. Bull. **119**(1), 111–137 (1996)
17. Skitka, L.J.: Accountability and automation bias. Int. J. Hum. Comput. Stud. **52**, 701–717 (2000). https://doi.org/10.1006/ijhc.1999.0349
18. Karau, S.J., Williams, K.D.: Social loafing: a meta-analytic review and theoretical integration. J. Personal Soc. Psychol. **65**(4), 681–706 (1993)
19. Bahner, J.E., Huper, A.-K., Manzey, D.: Misuse of automated decision aids: complacency, automation bias and the impact of training experience. Int. J. Hum. Comput. Stud. **66**, 688–699 (2008)
20. D. Wickens, C.D., Hollands, J.G., Banbury, S., Parasuraman R.: Engineering psychology and human performance 4th edn., pp. 388–393. Int. Pearson Education, Inc. Upper Saddle River N.J. (2013)
21. Dietvorst, B.J., Simmons, J.P., Massey, C.: Algorithm aversion: People erroneously avoid algorithms after seeing them err. J. Exp. Psychol. Gen. **144**(1), 114–126 (2015). https://doi.org/10.1037/xge0000033
22. Dratsch, T., et al.: Automation bias in mammography: the impact of artificial intelligence BI-RADS suggestions of reader performance. Radiology **307**(4) e222176 (2023). https://doi.org/10.1148/radiol.222176
23. Kaur, H., Nori, H., Jenkins, S., Caruana, R., Wallach, H., Wortman Vaughan, J.: Interpreting interpretability: understanding data scientists' use of interpretability tools for machine learning. In: Proceedings of the 2020 CHI Conference on Human Factors in Computing Systems (CHI 2020), pp. 1–14. Association for Computing Machinery, New York (2020) https://doi.org/10.1145/3313831.3376219
24. Riva, P., Aureli, N., Silvestrini, F.: Social influences in the digital era: When do people conform more to a human being or an artificial intelligence? Acta Physiol. (Oxf) **229**, 103681 (2022). https://doi.org/10.1016/j.actpsy.2022.103681
25. Hawkins, G.E., Cooper, G., Cavallaro, J.-P.: The standard relationship between choice frequency and choice time is violated in multi-attribute preference choice. J. Math. Psychol. **115**, 102775 (2023). https://doi.org/10.1016/j.jmp.2023.102775
26. Phillips, P.J., A. Hahn, C.A., Fontana, P.C., Yates, A.N., Greene, K.: Four principles of explainable artificial intelligence national institute of standards and technology (U.S.A.), vol. 1 (2021) https://doi.org/10.6028/NIST.IR.8312
27. Chamola, V., Hassija, V., Sulthana, A.R., Ghosh, D., Dhingra, D., Sikdar, B.: A review of trustworthy and explainable artificial intelligence (XAI). IEEE Access (2023). https://doi.org/10.1109/ACCESS.2023.3294569
28. Eiband, M., Buschek, D., Kremer, A., Hussmann, H.: The impact of placebic explanations on trust in intelligent systems. In: CHI Ea 2019 Extended Abstracts: Extended Abstracts of the 2019 CHI Conference on Human Factors in Computing Systems (2019)
29. Ghassemi, M., Oakden-Rayner, L., Beam, A.L.: The false hope of current approaches to explainable artificial intelligence in health care. Lancet Digital Health **3**(11), e745–e750 (2012). https://doi.org/10.1016/S2589-7500(21)00208-9
30. Liu, B., Tetteroo, D., Markopoulos, P.: A systematic review of experimental work on persuasive social robots. Int. J. Soc. Robot. **14**, 1339–1378 (2022). https://doi.org/10.1007/s12369-022-00870-5

31. Siegel, M., Breazeal, C., Norton, M.I.: Persuasive robotics: the influence of robot gender on human behaviour. In: Proceedings: 2009 IEEE/RSJ International Conference on Intelligent Robots and Systems, pp. 2563–2568. St. Louis, MO, USA (2009)
32. Savage, L.J.: Foundations of statistics, 2nd edn. Dover Publications, Mineola (1972)
33. Ellsberg, D.: Risk, ambiguity, and the savage axioms. Quart. J. Econ. **75**(4), 643–669 (1961)
34. Gilboa, I., Schmeidler, D.: Maxmin expected utility with non-unique prior. J. Math. Economics **18**, 141–153 (1989)
35. Hey, J.D., Lotito, G., Maffioletti, A.: The descriptive and predictive adequacy of theories of decision making under uncertainty/ambiguity. J. Risk Uncertain. **41**, 81–111 (2010). https://doi.org/10.1007/s11166-010-9102-0
36. Bazerman, M.H., Sezer, O.: Bounded awareness: implications for ethical decision-making. Organ. Behav. Hum. Decis. Process. **136**, 95–105 (2016)
37. Garcia, S.M., Tor, A., Bazerman, M., Miller, D.T.: Profit maximization versus disadvantageous inequality: the impact of self-categorization. J. Behav. Dec. Mak. **18**, 187–198 (2005)
38. Jamison, J., Yay, T., Feldman, G.: Action-inaction asymmetries in moral scenarios: replication of the omission bias examining morality and blame with extensions linking to causality, intent, and regret. J. Exp. Soc. Psychol. **89**, 103977 (2020). https://doi.org/10.1016/j.jesp.2020.103977
39. Feldman, G., Kutscher, L., Yay, T.: Omission and commission in judgment and decision making: understanding and linking action-inaction effects using the concept of normality. Soc. Pers. Psychol. Compass **14**, 1–15 (2020)
40. Hidalgo, C., Orghian, D., Albo-Canals, J., De Almeida, F., Martin, N.: How humans judge machines, pp. 130–131. The MIT Press, Cambridge (2021)
41. Zhai, S., Gao, S., Wang, L., Liu, P.: When both human and machine drivers make mistakes: whom to blame? Transport. Res. Part A: Policy Pract. **170**, 103637 (2023). https://doi.org/10.1016/j.tra.2023.103637
42. European Commission, Article 32 Consolidated text: Regulation (EU) 2016/679 of the European Parliament and of the Council of 27 April 2016 on the protection of natural persons with regard to the processing of personal data and on the free movement of such data, and repealing Directive 95/46/EC (General Data Protection Regulation, "GDPR")
43. Schemmer, M., Hemmer, P., Kuhl, N., Benz, C., Satzger, G.: Should I follow AI-based advice? measuring appropriate reliance on human-AI decision-making. In: Proceedings of the CHI 2022 TRAIT (2022). arXiv:2204.06916 [cs.HC]
44. Bingham, A.J.: From data management to actionable findings: a five-phase process of qualitative data analysis. Int. J. Qualitat. Methods **22**, 1–11 (2023)

Integrating HCI Datasets in Project-Based Machine Learning Courses: A College-Level Review and Case Study

Xiaodong Qu[✉], Matthew Key, Eric Luo, and Chuhui Qiu

The George Washington University, Washington, DC 20052, USA
{x.qu,matthewlkey,qluo,chqiu}@gwu.edu

Abstract. This study explores the integration of real-world machine learning (ML) projects using human-computer interfaces (HCI) datasets in college-level courses to enhance both teaching and learning experiences. Employing a comprehensive literature review, course websites analysis, and a detailed case study, the research identifies best practices for incorporating HCI datasets into project-based ML education. Key findings demonstrate increased student engagement, motivation, and skill development through hands-on projects, while instructors benefit from effective tools for teaching complex concepts. The study also addresses challenges such as data complexity and resource allocation, offering recommendations for future improvements. These insights provide a valuable framework for educators aiming to bridge the gap between theoretical knowledge and practical application in ML education.

Keywords: Machine Learning education · Human-Computer Interfaces (HCI) · Real-World Datasets · Project-based learning · Flexible education · Applied Machine Learning

1 Introduction

1.1 Motivation

The rapid advancement of Machine Learning (ML) and Artificial Intelligence (AI) technologies has created a pressing demand for skilled professionals capable of leveraging these tools across various industries [2,18,29,37,49]. In response, higher education institutions worldwide have expanded their ML curricula to include a diverse range of courses aimed at imparting AI literacy and problem-solving skills to students [6,17,26,28]. These courses cater to a broad audience, from undergraduates beginning their academic journey to working professionals seeking to enhance their technical expertise.

Despite the proliferation of ML courses, significant discrepancies exist in how these courses are designed and delivered. In particular, project-based ML

H. Degen and S. Ntoa (Eds.): HCII 2024, LNCS 15382, pp. 124–143, 2024.
https://doi.org/10.1007/978-3-031-76827-9_8

courses, which emphasize hands-on experience and the practical application of theoretical concepts, exhibit considerable variation in their structure and content. This variability often leads to differing expectations among instructors and students, creating challenges in achieving consistent educational outcomes.

One critical aspect of project-based ML courses is the integration of datasets, which serve as the foundation for practical exercises and projects. Human-Computer Interaction (HCI) datasets, in particular, offer rich and diverse opportunities for students to apply ML techniques in real-world scenarios. However, the effective use of such datasets requires careful consideration of best practices in course design and delivery.

Recognizing the need for clarity and consistency in the delivery of project-based ML courses, this paper seeks to address several key issues. By conducting a comprehensive literature review, analyzing related course websites, and performing a detailed case study, this research aims to identify best practices and provide actionable insights for educators. The primary audience for this study includes computer science professors, referred to herein as instructors, and students categorized into three groups: undergraduates, graduates, and working professionals. The focus on both learners' engagement and instructors' perspectives aims to bridge the gap between theoretical knowledge and practical application, ultimately enhancing the effectiveness of ML education in preparing students for the demands of the AI-driven job market.

1.2 Research Questions

The following research questions guide this study and form the basis for its analysis and conclusions:

- **What best practices can be identified from a review of academic papers related to project-based ML course delivery, particularly those incorporating HCI datasets?**
- **What trends in course design, including the integration of math and statistics, and dataset usage emerge from an analysis of in-person ML courses at colleges and universities?**
- **What insights can be gained from a detailed case study of teaching ML courses with specific HCI datasets over the past three years, considering both learner engagement and instructor perspectives?**

By addressing these questions, this paper aims to bridge the gap between theoretical knowledge and practical application in ML education. The findings are intended to guide educators in enhancing the design and delivery of project-based ML courses, ultimately improving student learning outcomes and better preparing them for the demands of the AI-driven job market.

2 Related Works

2.1 Overview

Historically, higher education in technical fields has relied on a blend of lectures, exercises, and practical labs to foster both theoretical understanding and hands-on proficiency with field-relevant methods [1]. In the domain of computer science, it is crucial for graduates to acquire practical skills that align with industrial demands, ensuring they are well-prepared for the workforce [5,35]. Institutions such as universities of applied sciences emphasize this alignment through curricula designed to bridge academic knowledge and practical application.

Despite these efforts, challenges persist when graduates encounter large, complex real-world projects or when they lack essential teamwork skills [5,35]. These challenges underscore the growing importance of project-based learning (PBL), which involves industrial topics and aims to better prepare students for professional environments [10,11,41]. PBL provides students with opportunities to engage in collaborative, hands-on projects that simulate real-world scenarios, thereby enhancing their problem-solving abilities and teamwork competencies.

2.2 Project-Based Learning in ML Education

In rapidly evolving fields such as deep learning, a subset of Machine Learning (ML), there is a continuous emergence of new trends in algorithms, datasets, and pedagogical approaches [7,14,27,42]. Project-based learning (PBL) has been recognized as an effective pedagogical strategy in these contexts. It facilitates active learning by immersing students in real-world problems and encouraging them to apply theoretical concepts to practical challenges.

Several studies have highlighted the benefits of integrating PBL into ML education. For instance, Huang et al. (2019) emphasize the importance of incorporating contemporary datasets and real-world applications to keep the curriculum relevant and engaging [14]. Miller et al. (2019) discuss how PBL can promote deeper understanding and retention of complex ML concepts by enabling students to work on projects that mirror industrial applications [27]. Brungel et al. (2020) and Wong et al. (2020) further elaborate on how PBL fosters critical thinking and problem-solving skills, which are essential for success in the fast-paced field of ML [7,42].

2.3 K-12 ML Education

The burgeoning interest in K-12 Machine Learning education has prompted a synthesis of existing research to better understand how ML can be effectively integrated into early education. Several studies have explored resources for ML education at the K-12 level, its integration into existing curricula, and innovative pedagogical strategies [25,32–34,39].

Sanusi et al. (2020) and Marques et al. (2020) investigate various pedagogical approaches that can make ML concepts accessible to younger students, emphasizing the importance of foundational understanding and engagement [25,33]. Reddi et al. (2021) highlight the need for curriculum development that not only introduces ML concepts but also integrates them seamlessly into subjects already being taught, thereby enriching the overall educational experience [32]. Sanusi (2023) and Van (2023) provide systematic reviews and emerging trends in K-12

ML education, offering insights into the most effective practices and resources for educators [34,39].

These studies collectively underscore the critical role of early ML education in fostering future generations of tech-savvy individuals who are well-prepared for advanced studies and careers in AI and ML.

3   Methods

This study employed a comprehensive review of academic papers on ML-related courses, supplemented by an extensive survey of relevant course websites. Additionally, a reflective analysis of teaching experiences over the past three years was presented as a case study.

3.1   Keywords

Utilizing the Preferred Reporting Items for Systematic Reviews and Meta-Analyses (PRISMA) approach, pertinent papers were systematically identified over a two-month period, from August to October 2023. The databases explored included Google Scholar, IEEE Xplore, ACM Digital Library, arXiv, and ERIC. The keyword search comprised: ('Machine Learning' OR 'Deep Learning' OR 'ML' OR 'DL') AND ('project-based' OR 'project-based learning' OR 'PBL') AND ('Survey' OR 'Review' OR 'Case Study').

Additionally, the search strings used were: "project-based learning in machine learning", "applied machine learning course design", "teaching strategies for machine learning", "HCI datasets in project-based learning", "challenges in project-based machine learning instruction", "student engagement in project-based machine learning courses".

This strategy aimed to pinpoint papers aligning with the research questions. Table 1 and Fig. 1 visualize the search trajectory, showcasing the number of papers identified and excluded based on set criteria. To cater to the target audience's time constraints, a concise list of papers encapsulating the prevailing trends in the domain was curated.

Table 1. Progression of Paper Search Steps: S1 represents initial search results, S2 indicates potentially relevant findings, S3 highlights confirmed relevant results, and S4 enumerates those results after removing duplicates.

Paper Source (Steps)	S1	S2	S3	S4
Google Scholar	312	230	112	112
ACM DIgital Library	120	90	45	40
IEEE Xplore	66	51	37	35
ERIC	31	21	15	12
arXiv	15	7	5	5
subtotal	544	399	214	204

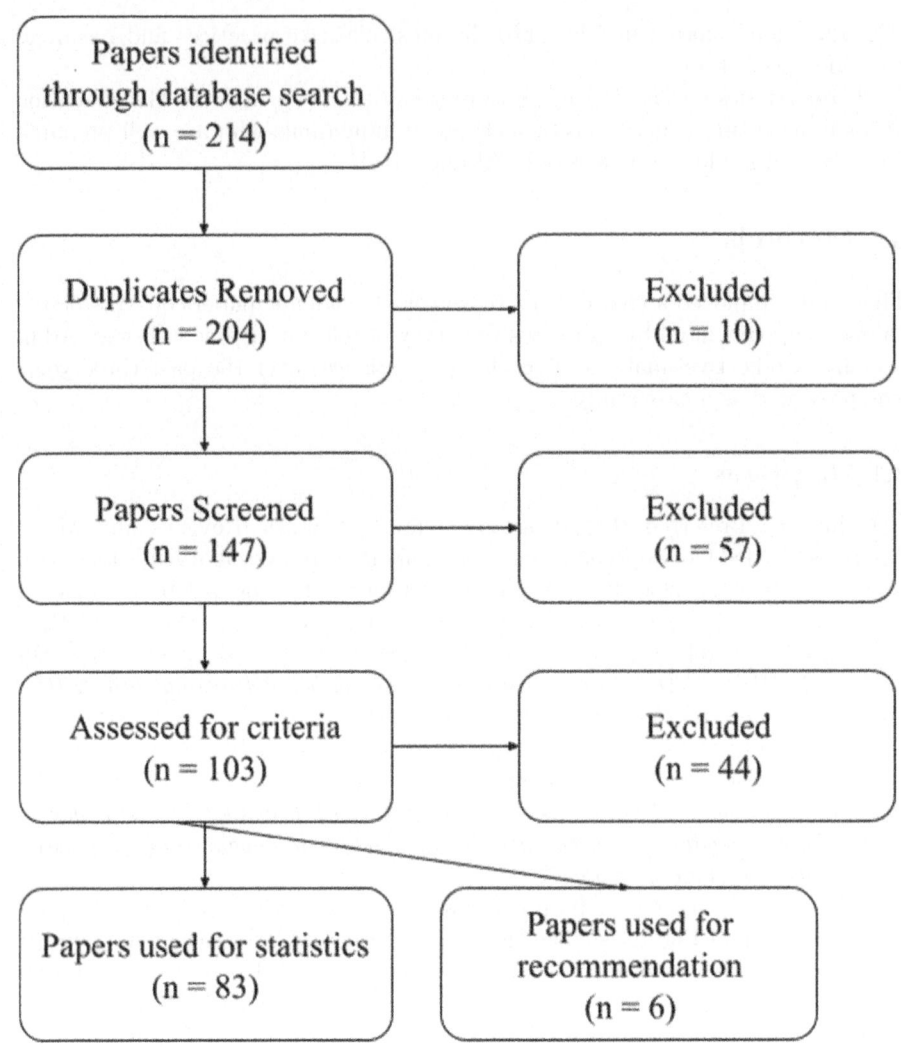

Fig. 1. Selection process for the papers

3.2 Selection Criteria

To ensure the relevance and quality of the review's content, the following criteria were applied:

- **Project-based:** Papers and courses must emphasize project-based machine learning, detailing their design and execution. This focus ensures that the content is practically relevant and applicable to real-world ML problems.
- **Publication Time Frame:** Papers published from 2017 onwards and courses updated after 2020 were included. This time frame ensures that the review encompasses the most recent advancements and trends in ML education.

– **Machine Learning Focus:** Preference was given to content primarily addressing project-based Machine Learning or Deep Learning. This focus aligns with the goal of enhancing practical ML education for professionals.
– **Target Audience:** Papers and courses should cater to computer science (CS) professors, students, or non-CS majors enrolled in such courses. This criterion ensures that the content is relevant to educators and learners who are directly involved in ML education, as well as those from diverse academic backgrounds seeking to gain practical ML skills.

3.3 Case Study

Over the past three years (2022 to 2024), four project-based machine learning courses were delivered by an assistant professor in computer science at two different institutions. In 2021 and 2022, undergraduate students at Swarthmore College, PA, participated in these courses. In 2023, graduate students at George Washington University, DC, were enrolled in similar project-based machine learning courses.

The case study aimed to evaluate the effectiveness of project-based learning in enhancing students' practical machine learning skills and their ability to apply theoretical knowledge to real-world problems. Detailed course outlines, project descriptions, and instructional methodologies were documented and analyzed. These materials are available on the faculty page of the instructor[1].

The study involved a mixed-methods approach to gather comprehensive feedback from students. Thirty-five students were interviewed after completing the courses, providing qualitative data on their learning experiences, challenges faced, and perceived benefits of the project-based approach. Additionally, anonymous course feedback forms were collected and analyzed for each course, offering quantitative insights into student satisfaction and the effectiveness of the instructional strategies employed.

The feedback from students highlighted several key aspects of the courses:

– **Engagement and Motivation:** Students reported high levels of engagement and motivation, attributing this to the hands-on nature of the projects, which allowed them to see the practical applications of machine learning concepts.
– **Skill Development:** Many students noted significant improvements in their technical skills, particularly in areas such as data preprocessing, model development, and evaluation. The projects provided opportunities to work with real-world datasets, enhancing their problem-solving abilities.
– **Collaboration and Teamwork:** The project-based format encouraged collaboration among students, fostering a collaborative learning environment. Students learned to work effectively in teams, an essential skill in professional settings.
– **Challenges and Areas for Improvement:** Some students mentioned challenges related to the complexity of the projects and the steep learning

---

[1] https://faculty.cs.gwu.edu/xiaodongqu/.

curve associated with advanced machine learning techniques. Suggestions for improvement included providing more scaffolding and support during the initial stages of the projects.

The analysis of course feedback revealed that the project-based learning approach was generally well-received, with students appreciating the opportunity to apply theoretical knowledge in practical settings. The insights gained from this case study inform recommendations for enhancing project-based machine learning courses, making them more effective and accessible for students at various academic levels.

This case study underscores the importance of integrating practical, hands-on projects in machine learning education. It provides valuable insights for educators seeking to design and deliver courses that not only impart theoretical knowledge but also equip students with the practical skills necessary for success in the rapidly evolving field of machine learning.

4   Results

4.1   Literature Review

The literature review focused on identifying best practices in Machine Learning (ML) education, particularly in in-person courses offered by colleges and universities. The findings were categorized into several key topics, highlighting common best practices across various studies. Table 2 summarizes these findings.

1. Machine Learning:

– **Comprehensive Curriculum:** Effective ML courses typically offer a well-rounded curriculum that covers fundamental concepts, advanced techniques, and practical applications. This ensures that learners acquire a broad understanding of ML and can apply their knowledge to real-world problems.

Table 2. Paper Results Key: U denotes undergrad-only studies, G for graduate-only, and UG for both levels. R signifies review papers, C indicates case studies, and Best P stands for best practices.

Paper	Level	Type	Best P
[1,2,4,7,15,19,20]	U	R	1,2,3
[5,9,12,14,17,25]	U	C	2,3,4
[3, 6, 11, 18, 21]	UG	R	3,5
[22, 23,26, 28,31]	UG	C	2,6
[16, 24, 29, 33]	G	R	1,2,3,5
[8, 10, 13, 16, 34]	G	C	1, 3, 4

Instructors benefit from a structured curriculum that provides a clear roadmap for teaching complex topics.

- **Integration of Math and Statistics:** A solid foundation in mathematics and statistics is crucial for understanding ML algorithms and their applications. Effective ML courses incorporate relevant math and stats topics, such as linear algebra, calculus, probability, and statistical inference, to equip students with the necessary analytical skills.
- **Hands-On Projects:** Incorporating hands-on projects is crucial in ML education. Studies indicate that projects involving real-world datasets and practical problems significantly enhance learning outcomes by providing learners with practical experience and reinforcing theoretical knowledge. For instructors, these projects offer a means to assess student understanding and application of ML concepts.

2. Project-Based Teaching and Learning:

- **Engagement and Motivation:** Project-based learning (PBL) has been shown to increase student engagement and motivation. By working on relevant and challenging projects, learners are more likely to stay motivated and invested in their studies. Instructors observe higher levels of participation and enthusiasm, which can lead to more dynamic and interactive classrooms.
- **Collaborative Learning:** Many successful PBL courses encourage collaboration among students. Group projects and peer feedback are effective in promoting deeper understanding and developing teamwork skills. Instructors find that collaborative learning environments facilitate peer-to-peer learning and reduce the instructional burden.
- **Practical Application:** PBL emphasizes the application of theoretical knowledge to real-world problems. This approach helps students develop critical thinking and problem-solving skills that are directly applicable to their future careers.

3. Exam-Based Teaching:

- **Assessment of Knowledge:** Exam-based teaching primarily assesses students' understanding of theoretical concepts through written exams and quizzes. This method can effectively measure students' retention of knowledge and their ability to recall and apply information in a controlled setting.
- **Standardization:** Exams provide a standardized way to evaluate all students consistently, making it easier to compare performance across a cohort. This can be particularly useful for large classes where individual assessment of projects may be impractical.
- **Focus on Individual Performance:** Exam-based assessments often focus on individual performance, encouraging students to develop strong independent study habits. However, this approach may not fully capture collaborative and practical skills that are essential in the professional world.

- **Preparation for Certification:** Exams can prepare students for professional certification tests, which often follow a similar format. This can be beneficial for students seeking to obtain credentials that require passing standardized exams.

4. Formal Course Structure:

- **Structured Schedules:** In-person ML courses often benefit from structured schedules that ensure consistent progress and regular engagement. These schedules help students balance their academic responsibilities and maintain steady progress. Instructors can design courses with regular milestones and assessments to keep students on track.
- **Support and Resources:** Providing ample support and resources is critical for in-person course settings. This includes access to office hours, tutoring, instructional videos, and supplemental materials that help learners overcome obstacles. For instructors, it means developing comprehensive resources that can guide students through their learning journey and provide additional support as needed.

5. Students' Feedback:

- **Positive Impact of Structured Learning:** Students frequently highlight the benefits of the structured schedule offered by in-person courses. This structure allows them to balance their studies with other academic and personal commitments effectively. Instructors receive positive feedback on course accessibility and organization, which can enhance course ratings and attract more students.
- **Need for Interactive Elements:** Feedback often suggests that incorporating interactive elements, such as quizzes, labs, and real-time feedback, can enhance the learning experience in in-person courses. Instructors can leverage this feedback to design more engaging and interactive course content, improving student satisfaction and outcomes.

6. Professors' Feedback:

- **Importance of Course Design:** Professors emphasize the significance of well-structured course design in in-person learning environments. Clear learning objectives, organized content, and regular assessments are essential for maintaining student engagement and ensuring successful learning outcomes. Effective course design helps instructors manage course delivery more efficiently and ensures that learning goals are met.
- **Challenges in Providing Support:** While in-person courses offer structure, professors note the challenges in providing timely support and feedback to students. Implementing systems and leveraging technology can help address these challenges. Instructors can use tools such as automated grading systems, learning management systems (LMS), and discussion forums to provide timely support.

By addressing both the learners' and instructors' perspectives and comparing project-based teaching with exam-based teaching, this section provides a comprehensive view of the best practices in ML education within in-person college and university settings. It highlights the benefits and challenges of both teaching methods, offering insights that can inform the design and implementation of effective ML courses.

4.2 Course Websites Analysis

Table 3 showcases the findings from the analysis of existing course websites. This analysis aimed to identify common elements and best practices in Machine Learning (ML) courses offered in-person at colleges and universities. Several key topics were explored to understand how these courses are structured and what resources they provide to both learners and instructors.

7. Course Structure:

- **Modular Structure:** Many analyzed courses feature a modular structure, allowing for systematic progression through the material. This structure is beneficial for organizing the curriculum in a way that builds upon foundational concepts before advancing to more complex topics. For instructors, it provides a clear framework for delivering content effectively.
- **Integration of Math and Statistics:** Effective ML courses integrate essential mathematics and statistics topics, such as linear algebra, calculus, probability, and statistical inference. This integration is crucial for students to understand the theoretical underpinnings of ML algorithms. Instructors can use this foundation to explain complex concepts and ensure students are well-prepared for practical applications.

Table 3. Analysis of Course Websites: U represents undergrad-only courses, G for graduate-only, and UG for both. Best P signifies courses emphasizing best practices.

Course	Level	Institution	Best P
[41, 42]	U	Williams	7,8
[43]	U	Amherst	8
[44,45]	U	Swarthmore	7,9,11,12
[46, 47,48]	U	Pomona	7,8,9,10
[49, 50]	UG	Harvard	7,8,9,11
[50, 51]	UG	Upenn	7, 10, 11,12
[52, 53, 54]	UG	Stanford	7,8,9,10,11,12
[55, 56]	UG	MIT	8,9,10,11
[57,58,59]	UG	CMU	8, 9,11
[60,61,62]	UG	UC B	7,8,9,10, 11

8. Progress Tracking:

- **Tools for Tracking Progress:** Effective courses often include tools for tracking progress, such as dashboards that display completed modules and upcoming tasks. These tools help learners stay organized and motivated. For instructors, progress tracking tools provide insights into student performance and areas that may require additional attention.

9. Project-Based Teaching and Learning:

- **Hands-On Projects:** A significant number of courses incorporate project-based learning, where students work on real-world projects to apply the concepts they have learned. These projects often involve datasets from industry or research, providing practical experience. For instructors, hands-on projects offer a practical way to assess students' application of theoretical knowledge.
- **Peer Collaboration:** Some courses facilitate peer collaboration through discussion forums or group projects, allowing learners to share insights and provide mutual support. This collaboration helps build teamwork skills, which are valuable in professional settings. Instructors benefit from the collaborative learning environment as it can enhance student engagement and reduce the instructional burden.

10. Sample Code:

- **Code Repositories:** Many courses provide access to code repositories, such as GitHub, where learners can find sample code and scripts used in the course. This is particularly useful for understanding practical implementation details. Instructors can use these repositories to demonstrate coding practices and provide students with resources for independent study.
- **Code Walkthroughs:** Courses that include detailed code walkthroughs, either in written form or through video demonstrations, help learners understand the step-by-step process of developing ML models. For instructors, code walkthroughs are an effective teaching tool to illustrate coding techniques and problem-solving strategies.

11. Lecture Slides:

- **Comprehensive Lecture Slides:** High-quality courses offer comprehensive lecture slides that summarize key concepts and provide visual aids to enhance understanding. These slides are often available for download, allowing learners to review them at their own pace. Instructors can use these slides to structure their lectures and provide students with a consistent reference material.

– **Supplemental Materials:** In addition to slides, some courses provide supplemental materials such as cheat sheets, reference guides, and additional readings to deepen learners' understanding. These materials support instructors in offering a richer educational experience and cater to diverse learning needs.

12. Course Videos:

– **Engaging Video Lectures:** Video lectures are a staple of in-person ML courses, often used to supplement classroom teaching. The best courses feature engaging, well-produced videos that clearly explain complex concepts. These videos often include demonstrations, animations, and real-world examples to illustrate key points. Instructors can leverage these videos to reinforce classroom teaching and provide students with additional learning resources.
– **Interactive Elements:** Some courses incorporate interactive elements within videos, such as embedded quizzes or coding challenges, to reinforce learning and keep learners engaged. These elements provide immediate feedback to students and help instructors gauge understanding in real-time.

By addressing both the learners' and instructors' perspectives, this section provides a comprehensive view of the best practices in ML education within in-person college and university settings. It highlights the importance of integrating foundational math and statistics, hands-on projects, and collaborative learning, offering insights that can inform the design and implementation of effective ML courses.

4.3   Case Study

The case study examines the implementation of project-based learning in Machine Learning (ML) courses over the past three years (2022 to 2024) at two institutions: Swarthmore College, PA, and George Washington University, DC. These courses were designed to provide students with hands-on experience in applying ML techniques to real-world problems, with a specific focus on using a brain-computer interfaces (BCI) dataset.

Course Context and Structure:
The courses were structured to include a combination of lectures, hands-on projects, and collaborative learning activities. The primary goal was to bridge the gap between theoretical knowledge and practical application, ensuring that students not only understood ML concepts but could also apply them to solve complex problems.

– **Instructors' Perspective:** The courses were designed by an assistant professor in computer science, who aimed to create a learning environment that was both challenging and supportive. The inclusion of a BCI dataset provided a unique opportunity to explore advanced applications of ML in Human-Computer Interaction (HCI), aligning with the conference's focus.

- **Learners' Perspective:** Students were undergraduate and graduate learners with varying levels of prior knowledge in ML. The project-based approach allowed them to engage deeply with the material and develop practical skills that are highly valued in the industry.

Implementation of the BCI Dataset:
The BCI dataset [16] used in these courses consisted of EEG recordings from subjects engaged in various tasks. This dataset was chosen due to its complexity and relevance to cutting-edge research in HCI.

- **Project Design:** Students were tasked with developing ML models to classify different mental states based on the EEG data. This involved preprocessing the data, extracting features, and training and evaluating ML models.
- **Instructors' Role:** Instructors provided guidance on the technical aspects of the project, including data preprocessing techniques, feature extraction methods, and model selection. They also facilitated group discussions and provided feedback on students' progress.
- **Learners' Experience:** Students reported high levels of engagement and motivation, as the project allowed them to apply ML techniques to a real-world problem. The complexity of the BCI data provided a valuable learning experience, challenging them to think critically and develop innovative solutions.

Outcomes and Feedback:
The outcomes of the courses were evaluated through a combination of student feedback, project assessments, and instructor observations.

- **Engagement and Motivation:** Students demonstrated increased engagement and motivation, with many expressing a deeper interest in HCI and ML applications. The project-based approach, combined with the use of a challenging dataset, was cited as a key factor in maintaining their interest.
- **Skill Development:** Both instructors and students noted significant improvements in technical skills, particularly in data preprocessing, feature extraction, and model development. The hands-on experience with the BCI dataset helped students gain confidence in their ability to tackle complex ML problems.
- **Collaboration and Teamwork:** The courses facilitated collaborative learning, with students working in teams to solve problems and share insights. This not only enhanced their understanding of ML concepts but also developed their teamwork and communication skills.
- **Instructor Insights:** Instructors found that the project-based approach, while resource-intensive, was highly effective in promoting deep learning and practical skill acquisition. The use of a BCI dataset added an additional layer of complexity that enriched the learning experience.

Challenges and Recommendations:
Despite the successes, several challenges were encountered during the implementation of these courses.

- **Data Complexity:** The complexity of the BCI dataset posed significant challenges for students, particularly those with limited prior experience in ML. To address this, instructors provided additional support and resources, such as tutorials on EEG data processing and feature extraction.
- **Time Management:** Balancing the project workload with other course requirements was a challenge for many students. Instructors recommended clearer guidelines and more structured timelines to help students manage their time effectively.
- **Resource Allocation:** The resource-intensive nature of project-based learning required significant instructor time and effort. Future iterations of the course could benefit from additional teaching assistants or automated tools to help manage the workload.

In conclusion, the case study highlights the effectiveness of project-based learning in ML education, particularly when using complex datasets such as those from BCI research. Both learners and instructors benefited from the hands-on, collaborative approach, which facilitated deep learning and practical skill development. The insights gained from this case study provide valuable guidance for educators seeking to implement similar approaches in their courses.

5   Discussion

5.1   Real-World Machine Learning Projects with HCI Datasets

A significant finding from this study is the crucial role of real-world machine learning projects with HCI datasets in enhancing both teaching and learning experiences. These projects provide learners with hands-on experience and practical application of the concepts they have learned. Instructors also benefit from these projects as they provide a rich context for teaching complex ML topics and assessing student understanding. Here is a subset of the experiments that learners and instructors have explored and practiced so far [3,4,8,9,12,13,15,19–24,28,30,31,36,38,40,43,44,44–48].

The projects discussed in this study involved various HCI datasets, including brain-computer interfaces (BCI), eye-tracking, and gesture recognition data. These datasets were chosen for their relevance to cutting-edge research in HCI and their ability to challenge students to apply ML techniques to real-world problems.

Learners' Perspective. For learners, working with HCI datasets offers several benefits:

- **Engagement and Motivation:** Real-world projects involving HCI datasets significantly increase student engagement and motivation. The opportunity to work on projects that have tangible applications in the field of HCI helps students see the relevance of their studies and stay invested in their learning.
- **Skill Development:** Students develop critical technical skills through these projects, including data preprocessing, feature extraction, and model development. The hands-on experience with complex datasets like those from BCI studies enhances their ability to tackle real-world ML problems.
- **Critical Thinking and Problem-Solving:** Projects involving HCI datasets require students to think critically and develop innovative solutions to complex problems. This process helps them build strong problem-solving skills that are essential for their future careers.
- **Collaboration and Teamwork:** Collaborative projects foster teamwork and communication skills. Students learn to work effectively in teams, share insights, and support each other in overcoming challenges.

Feedback from a student highlighted several challenges and learning experiences faced during the course. The student noted that applied ML courses often felt like multiple courses packed into one, each demanding self-guided learning in areas such as problem selection, literature review, proposing novel methods, and technical implementation. This comprehensive approach, while challenging, significantly contributed to their skill development and understanding of the research process.

Instructors' Perspective. For instructors, incorporating real-world projects with HCI datasets into their courses provides several advantages:

- **Effective Teaching Tool:** HCI datasets offer a rich context for teaching complex ML concepts. Instructors can use these datasets to illustrate practical applications of theoretical knowledge, making abstract concepts more concrete and understandable for students.
- **Assessment of Student Understanding:** Real-world projects provide a practical means of assessing student understanding and application of ML concepts. Instructors can evaluate students' ability to preprocess data, extract features, develop models, and interpret results.
- **Enhanced Engagement and Interaction:** Projects involving HCI datasets can lead to more dynamic and interactive classroom environments. Instructors observe higher levels of participation and enthusiasm, which contribute to a more engaging learning experience for all students.
- **Resource for Research and Development:** The projects undertaken by students can contribute to ongoing research and development efforts. Instructors can leverage student projects to explore new ideas, validate hypotheses, and advance their research agendas.

Examples of HCI Projects. Here are a subset of the projects mentioned in this study that learners and instructors explored and practiced, demonstrating the application of ML techniques to HCI datasets:

- Brain-Computer Interfaces (BCI): Developing models to classify different mental states based on EEG signals.
- Eye-Tracking Data: Predicting user intent and analyzing gaze patterns to improve user interface design.
- Gesture Recognition: Creating ML models to recognize and interpret human gestures for controlling devices.

These projects provided valuable insights into the practical application of ML in HCI, offering both students and instructors a deeper understanding of the potential and challenges of these technologies.

Challenges and Recommendations. Despite the successes, several challenges were encountered, and recommendations for future improvements include:

- **Data Complexity:** The complexity of HCI datasets can be overwhelming for students, especially those with limited ML experience. To mitigate this, instructors should provide comprehensive tutorials and support materials on data processing and feature extraction.
- **Time Management:** Balancing project work with other course requirements can be challenging. Instructors should provide clear guidelines and structured timelines to help students manage their workload effectively.
- **Resource Allocation:** Project-based learning requires significant time and resources from instructors. Future courses could benefit from additional teaching assistants or automated tools to help manage the workload and provide timely feedback to students.

5.2   Future Work

Looking ahead, there are several areas where future work can build on the findings of this study:

- **Expanding Dataset Variety:** Future courses could incorporate a wider variety of HCI datasets, including those related to speech recognition, natural language processing, and virtual reality interactions. This would provide students with broader exposure to different types of data and applications.
- **Enhancing Support for Novice Researchers:** Developing structured support systems for students with little or no prior research experience could help them navigate the challenges of self-guided learning. This might include mentorship programs, detailed research guides, and workshops on research methodologies.

- **Leveraging Technology for Support:** Utilizing advanced technologies such as AI-driven tutoring systems and automated feedback tools can help instructors provide timely and personalized support to students, particularly in large classes.
- **Longitudinal Studies on Learning Outcomes:** Conducting longitudinal studies to track the long-term impact of project-based learning on students' careers and research outputs would provide valuable insights into the effectiveness of these educational approaches.
- **Integrating Interdisciplinary Approaches:** Encouraging interdisciplinary projects that combine ML with fields such as psychology, neuroscience, and engineering can enrich the learning experience and lead to innovative solutions to complex problems.

In conclusion, the integration of real-world ML projects with HCI datasets in educational settings significantly enhances both teaching and learning experiences. These projects provide students with practical skills and critical thinking abilities, while offering instructors effective tools for teaching complex concepts and assessing student understanding. The insights gained from this study provide valuable guidance for educators seeking to implement similar approaches in their courses.

6 Conclusion

This study highlights the effectiveness of integrating real-world machine learning (ML) projects with human-computer interfaces (HCI) datasets in enhancing both teaching and learning experiences. By providing hands-on experience and practical application opportunities, these projects significantly increase student engagement, motivation, and skill development. From the instructors' perspective, they offer valuable tools for teaching complex concepts and assessing student understanding. Despite the challenges of data complexity and resource allocation, the benefits of project-based learning are evident. Future work should focus on expanding dataset variety, enhancing support for novice researchers, leveraging technology for support, and conducting longitudinal studies on learning outcomes. The insights gained from this study provide a robust framework for educators seeking to implement similar approaches, ultimately bridging the gap between theoretical knowledge and practical application in ML education.

References

1. Abood, H.G.: E-learning applications in engineering and the project-based learning vs problem-based learning styles: a critical & comparative study. Eng. Technol. J. **37**(4), 391–396 (2019)
2. Alfredo, R., et al.: Human-centred learning analytics and AI in education: a systematic literature review. Comput. Educ. Artif. Intell. 100215 (2024)

3. An, S., Bhat, G., Gumussoy, S., Ogras, U.: Transfer learning for human activity recognition using representational analysis of neural networks. ACM Trans. Comput. Healthc. **4**(1), 1–21 (2023)
4. An, S., Tuncel, Y., Basaklar, T., Ogras, U.Y.: A survey of embedded machine learning for smart and sustainable healthcare applications. In: Pasricha, S., Shafique, M. (eds.) Embedded Machine Learning for Cyber-Physical, IoT, and Edge Computing, pp. 127–150. Springer, Cham (2023). https://doi.org/10.1007/978-3-031-40677-5_6
5. Beckman, K., Coulter, N., Khajenoori, S., Mead, N.R.: Collaborations: closing the industry-academia gap. IEEE Softw. **14**(6), 49–57 (1997)
6. Bennett, B.T.: Teaching artificial intelligence in a multidisciplinary computing environment. J. Comput. Sci. Coll. **33**(2), 222–228 (2017)
7. Brüngel, R., Rückert, J., Friedrich, C.M.: Project-based learning in a machine learning course with differentiated industrial projects for various computer science master programs. In: 2020 IEEE 32nd Conference on Software Engineering Education and Training (CSEE&T), pp. 1–5. IEEE (2020)
8. Chen, P., Ding, H., Araki, J., Huang, R.: Explicitly capturing relations between entity mentions via graph neural networks for domain-specific named entity recognition. In: Proceedings of the 59th Annual Meeting of the Association for Computational Linguistics and the 11th International Joint Conference on Natural Language Processing (Volume 2: Short Papers), pp. 735–742 (2021)
9. Chen, P., et al.: Hytrel: hypergraph-enhanced tabular data representation learning. In: Advances in Neural Information Processing Systems, vol. 36 (2024)
10. Daun, M., Salmon, A., Tenbergen, B., Weyer, T., Pohl, K.: Industrial case studies in graduate requirements engineering courses: The impact on student motivation. In: 2014 IEEE 27th Conference on Software Engineering Education and Training (CSEE&T), pp. 3–12. IEEE (2014)
11. Daun, M., Salmon, A., Weyer, T., Pohl, K., Tenbergen, B.: Project-based learning with examples from industry in university courses: an experience report from an undergraduate requirements engineering course. In: 2016 IEEE 29th International Conference on Software Engineering Education and Training (CSEET), pp. 184–193. IEEE (2016)
12. Dou, G., Zhou, Z., Qu, X.: Time majority voting, a PC-based EEG classifier for non-expert users. In: Kurosu, M., et al. (eds.) HCII 2022. LNCS, vol. 13519, pp. 415–428. Springer, Cham (2022). https://doi.org/10.1007/978-3-031-17618-0_29
13. Gui, S., Song, S., Qin, R., Tang, Y.: Remote sensing object detection in the deep learning era - a review. Remote Sens. **16**(2), 327 (2024)
14. Huang, L.: Integrating machine learning to undergraduate engineering curricula through project-based learning. In: 2019 IEEE Frontiers in Education Conference (FIE), pp. 1–4. IEEE (2019)
15. Jiang, C., Hui, B., Liu, B., Yan, D.: Successfully applying lottery ticket hypothesis to diffusion model. arXiv preprint arXiv:2310.18823 (2023)
16. Kastrati, A., et al.: Eegeyenet: a simultaneous electroencephalography and eye-tracking dataset and benchmark for eye movement prediction. arXiv preprint arXiv:2111.05100 (2021)
17. Kwan, P.: A college freshman's guide to machine learning: short and sweet way to introduce machine learning to college freshman. J. Comput. Sci. Coll. **30**(1), 36–37 (2014)
18. Lao, N.: Reorienting machine learning education towards tinkerers and ML-engaged citizens. Ph.D. thesis, Massachusetts Institute of Technology Cambridge, MA, USA (2020)

19. Li, H., et al.: Spherehead: stable 3D full-head synthesis with spherical tri-plane representation. arXiv preprint arXiv:2404.05680 (2024)
20. Lu, Y., Chen, T., Hao, N., Van Rechem, C., Chen, J., Fu, T.: Uncertainty quantification and interpretability for clinical trial approval prediction. Health Data Sci. **4**, 0126 (2024)
21. Lu, Y., Sato, K., Wang, J.: Deep learning based multi-label image classification of protest activities. arXiv preprint arXiv:2301.04212 (2023)
22. Lu, Y., Shen, M., Wang, H., Wang, X., van Rechem, C., Wei, W.: Machine learning for synthetic data generation: a review. arXiv preprint arXiv:2302.04062 (2023)
23. Ma, X.: Traffic performance evaluation using statistical and machine learning methods. Ph.D. thesis, The University of Arizona (2022)
24. Ma, X., Karimpour, A., Wu, Y.J.: Data-driven transfer learning framework for estimating on-ramp and off-ramp traffic flows. J. Intell. Transp. Syst. 1–14 (2024)
25. Marques, L.S., Gresse von Wangenheim, C., Hauck, J.C.: Teaching machine learning in school: a systematic mapping of the state of the art. Inform. Educ. **19**(2), 283–321 (2020)
26. Martins, R.M., Gresse Von Wangenheim, C.: Findings on teaching machine learning in high school: a ten-year systematic literature review. Inform. Educ. **22**(3), 421–440 (2023)
27. Miller, E.C., Krajcik, J.S.: Promoting deep learning through project-based learning: a design problem. Disc. Interdisc. Sci. Educ. Res. **1**(1), 1–10 (2019)
28. Murungi, N.K., Pham, M.V., Dai, X.C., Qu, X.: Empowering computer science students in electroencephalography (EEG) analysis: a review of machine learning algorithms for EEG datasets. In: The 29th ACM SIGKDD Conference on Knowledge Discovery and Data Mining (KDD) (2023)
29. Ng, D.T.K., Lee, M., Tan, R.J.Y., Hu, X., Downie, J.S., Chu, S.K.W.: A review of AI teaching and learning from 2000 to 2020. Educ. Inf. Technol. **28**(7), 8445–8501 (2023)
30. Qu, X., Liu, P., Li, Z., Hickey, T.: Multi-class time continuity voting for EEG classification. In: Frasson, C., Bamidis, P., Vlamos, P. (eds.) BFAL 2020. LNCS (LNAI), vol. 12462, pp. 24–33. Springer, Cham (2020). https://doi.org/10.1007/978-3-030-60735-7_3
31. Qu, X., Mei, Q., Liu, P., Hickey, T.: Using EEG to distinguish between writing and typing for the same cognitive task. In: Frasson, C., Bamidis, P., Vlamos, P. (eds.) BFAL 2020. LNCS (LNAI), vol. 12462, pp. 66–74. Springer, Cham (2020). https://doi.org/10.1007/978-3-030-60735-7_7
32. Reddi, V.J., et al.: Widening access to applied machine learning with tinyML. arXiv preprint arXiv:2106.04008 (2021)
33. Sanusi, I.T., Oyelere, S.S.: Pedagogies of machine learning in k-12 context. In: 2020 IEEE Frontiers in Education Conference (FIE), pp. 1–8. IEEE (2020)
34. Sanusi, I.T., Oyelere, S.S., Vartiainen, H., Suhonen, J., Tukiainen, M.: A systematic review of teaching and learning machine learning in k-12 education. Educ. Inf. Technol. **28**(5), 5967–5997 (2023)
35. Shaw, M., Herbsleb, J., Ozkaya, I.: Deciding what to design: closing a gap in software engineering education. In: Proceedings of the 27th International Conference on Software Engineering, pp. 607–608 (2005)
36. Tan, J., Zhang, X., Wu, S., Wang, Y.: State-space model based inverse reinforcement learning for reward function estimation in brain-machine interfaces. In: 2023 45th Annual International Conference of the IEEE Engineering in Medicine and Biology Society (EMBC), pp. 1–4. IEEE (2023)

37. Tan, M., Lee, H., Wang, D., Subramonyam, H.: Is a seat at the table enough? Engaging teachers and students in dataset specification for ml in education. Proc. ACM Hum.-Comput. Interact. **8**(CSCW1), 1–32 (2024)

38. Tang, Y., Song, S., Gui, S., Chao, W., Cheng, C., Qin, R.: Active and low-cost hyperspectral imaging for the spectral analysis of a low-light environment. Sensors **23**(3), 1437 (2023)

39. Van Mechelen, M., et al.: Emerging technologies in k-12 education: a future HCI research agenda. ACM Trans. Comput.-Hum. Interact. **30**(3), 1–40 (2023)

40. Wang, J., Chang, R., Zhao, Z., Pahwa, R.S.: Robust detection, segmentation, and metrology of high bandwidth memory 3D scans using an improved semi-supervised deep learning approach. Sensors **23**(12), 5470 (2023)

41. Winzker, M.: Semester structure with time slots for self-learning and project-based learning. In: Proceedings of the 2012 IEEE Global Engineering Education Conference (EDUCON), pp. 1–8. IEEE (2012)

42. Wong, K., Tomov, S., Dongarra, J.: Project-based research and training in high performance data sciences, data analytics, and machine learning. J. Comput. Sci. Educ. **11**(1) (2020)

43. Yi, L., Qu, X.: Attention-based CNN capturing EEG recording's average voltage and local change. In: Degen, H., Ntoa, S. (eds.) HCII 2022. LNCS, vol. 13336, pp. 448–459. Springer, Cham (2022). https://doi.org/10.1007/978-3-031-05643-7_29

44. Yunoki, I., Berreby, G., D'Andrea, N., Lu, Y., Qu, X.: Exploring AI music generation: a review of deep learning algorithms and datasets for undergraduate researchers. In: Stephanidis, C., Antona, M., Ntoa, S., Salvendy, G. (eds.) HCII 2023. LNCS, vol. 1958, pp. 102–116. Springer, Cham (2023). https://doi.org/10.1007/978-3-031-49215-0_13

45. Zhang, Z., Tian, R., Ding, Z.: Trep: transformer-based evidential prediction for pedestrian intention with uncertainty. In: Proceedings of the AAAI Conference on Artificial Intelligence, vol. 37, pp. 3534–3542 (2023)

46. Zhang, Z., Tian, R., Sherony, R., Domeyer, J., Ding, Z.: Attention-based interrelation modeling for explainable automated driving. IEEE Trans. Intell. Veh. **8**(2), 1564–1573 (2022)

47. Zhao, S., et al.: Deep learning based CETSA feature prediction cross multiple cell lines with latent space representation. Sci. Rep. **14**(1), 1878 (2024)

48. Zhao, Z., Zhou, F., Xu, K., Zeng, Z., Guan, C., Zhou, S.K.: Le-UDA: label-efficient unsupervised domain adaptation for medical image segmentation. IEEE Trans. Med. Imaging **42**(3), 633–646 (2022)

49. Zheng, C., et al.: Charting the future of AI in project-based learning: a co-design exploration with students. In: Proceedings of the CHI Conference on Human Factors in Computing Systems, pp. 1–19 (2024)

Human Centered Approaches and Taxonomies for Explainable Artificial Intelligence

Helen Sheridan(✉) ⓘ, Emma Murphy ⓘ, and Dympna O'Sullivan ⓘ

School of Computer Science, TU Dublin, Grangegorman, Dublin, Ireland
{helen.sheridan,emma.x.murphy,dympna.osullivan}@tudublin.ie

Abstract. Recent interest within the research community related to explainable artificial intelligence (XAI) has led to a profuse amount of literature on the subject. Those who wish to tackle the domain from an HCI focus may be presented with overwhelming material, most of which does not pertain to human aspects of XAI. Taxonomies can serve to categorize a subject into topic areas and distill content into an overview of the field. This late breaking work intends to help those within the HCI community with a focus on XAI to understand relevant aspects of human centered XAI. We also present a taxonomy which can be used when categorizing real world XAI to identify gaps in XAI methods and predict future areas of research. Lastly, we introduce a novel aspect, practical XAI evaluation methods from a human centered perspective allowing for more effective evaluation of the AI – human interaction.

Keywords: Explainable Artificial Intelligence · Taxonomies · Human Centered Explainable Artificial Intelligence

1 Introduction

The breadth of recent work to demystify and explain the often-opaque nature of complex AI systems has witnessed an immense undertaking. This involves the research, categorization, and assessment of explainable artificial intelligence (XAI) methods. As AI systems become ever more sophisticated and accurate, often trading accuracy for interpretability [1] and with advancements in AI making life changing decisions for society the need for ethical, human centered AI systems has become a pressing issue [2]. Legislation such as the EU's AI act calls for explanations for AI systems considered high risk in domains such as employment, medicine, criminal justice, and education [3]. However, explaining the outputs of complex AI systems such as deep neural networks (DNNs), whose inner workings are difficult to comprehend and thus explain, has been a great challenge for those who develop and deploy these systems [4]. Research into XAI has played a vital role in rectifying the lack of understanding and opaque nature of AI systems' reasoning and decisions by presenting human comprehensible representations of how these systems compute outputs [4]. Most of the current XAI methods are designed to cater for AI practitioners and domain experts and don't adequately consider the needs or requirements of lay or novice users [5]. For those tasked with research and

H. Degen and S. Ntoa (Eds.): HCII 2024, LNCS 15382, pp. 144–163, 2024.
https://doi.org/10.1007/978-3-031-76827-9_9

development in XAI navigating the vast quantity of literature charting XAI topics, new developments and trends can seem daunting. For this reason, taxonomies can serve as a useful tool to act as a means of categorizing and charting the landscape of XAI [6]. However, one succinct taxonomy which covers this broad topic would not be practical or realistic and as such, taxonomies with a focus or emphasis serve a more useful purpose [6].

In our prior work we investigated users' mental models of AI systems and XAI methods and utilized XAI taxonomies to map results to real world XAI [61]. This work highlighted a gap in the literature for a practical, human centered XAI taxonomy which includes XAI evaluation methods with a focus on end user evaluations. Our human centered taxonomy bridges this gap and serves as a useful survey and framework for those researching, designing, or developing explanations for AI systems. Not only did this previous research and mapping exercise identify where users' mental models aligned with existing explanation methods but also identified gaps and areas for future development where XAI methods might require novel approaches and designs to bridge those gaps [61].

To respond to the challenges related to research within human-centered XAI we propose a taxonomy with a focus on human-centered XAI classification and a framework which emphasizes the evaluation of XAI for different users (AI practitioners, auditors/regulatory agents, domain experts and lay users/customers).

Our contribution to HCI literature with this late breaking work is threefold: First we survey recent XAI research and present a unified taxonomy with a human-centered focus and second, our taxonomy can be used when categorizing real world XAI to identify gaps in XAI methods and predict future areas of research. Lastly, we include a novel aspect, XAI evaluation methods both quantitative and qualitative which are a crucial stage in the development of human comprehensible explanations for AI systems.

2   Related Work

2.1   Human-Centered XAI

With the far-reaching use context for AI which includes users such as AI practitioners, auditors/regulators, domain experts and lay users the role of explainability is crucial in providing information beyond just the output or decision of the system. Research has revealed that the current explainability approaches do not sufficiently consider a key factor: Who are these explanations aimed at? [7]. Predominantly XAI methods are generated to explain to AI practitioners as a means of inspecting the AI system rather than for other end-users who may have different explainabillity needs [8]. One consideration is the inclusion of teachings from social sciences and human computer interaction (HCI) alongside AI to create explanations which are more human-like or explain in a way humans can understand [9]. Since users anticipate that AI systems will present an explanation in a human-like fashion and since AI systems do not function like human thought processes including HCI theories and practice in the design and development of XAI should yield more human comprehensible explanations and enhance human-AI interaction [10].

2.2 Taxonomies for XAI

A taxonomy of any subject can be best described as a list of terms arranged in a hierarchy which are used to describe and classify content [11]. Approaches for constructing taxonomies for XAI include functioning-based, result-based, conceptual, and mixed approaches with mixed approaches considered the best method for those new to XAI [6]. Glass & Vassey maintain that *"without an organizing framework, researchers and practitioners find it hard to generalize, communicate, and apply research findings"* [12] and that taxonomies can fulfil this role. Taxonomies work by systematically describing and interpreting areas of most relevance within a subject but can also serve to make predictions about future development areas [12]. Take the periodic table as an example which made predictions about elements before they were even discovered. Many taxonomies for XAI are broad in focus [1, 4, 6, 13–15] and although useful the need for a more defined scope, such as taxonomies for those researching in human-centered XAI might help in distilling the most pertinent aspects of the domain of XAI for those researching from a human-centered perspective.

3 Our Approach

To present an overview of current research in XAI we reviewed 45 papers which referenced or presented taxonomies of explanations for AI systems or which presented aspects of XAI which would be useful for those researching XAI from a human-centered perspective. While we don't claim to present a systematic literature review of the topic our aim is to present a succinct analysis of aspects of human centered XAI from the literature in a digestible form for those tasked with navigating the extensive landscape of XAI. We grouped prior literature by category or area of focus with six main areas represented, three of which are sub divided to represent more specific categorization. Categories include: Input data, output format, explanation method (global, local, cohort, simplification, feature relevance, by example and contrastive), user type (auditors/regulatory agents, domain experts, lay users/customers and AI practitioners), model type (opaque, interpretable) and evaluation method (human centered methods including XAI measurement scales, XAI evaluation methods and non XAI methods including measurement scales and evaluation methods). These categories serve as an initial basis and areas of focus for our final human-centered taxonomy which expands on these categories giving a more detailed view of XAI from a human-centered perspective. Examining the literature and amalgamating categories in this way facilitated us in the design of our human centered XAI taxonomy diagram and framework showing the interrelationship between elements which contribute to the design and development of explanations for AI systems for different users.

3.1 Research Methods

Our search and selection method consisted of two main criteria, papers or articles which described or presented taxonomies for XAI and a broader search for XAI and AI articles. Exclusion criteria included:

- Articles, papers, or research which were not peer reviewed.
- Articles, papers, or research which were published in a language other than English.

A search of the following databases ACM and Scopus and a Google scholar search was carried out using the following terms and combinations of these terms, *"explainable artificial intelligence"*, *"XAI"*, *"explainable machine learning"*, *"taxonomy"* and *"guide"*. Over 500 articles were scanned by title and promising articles by abstract to further narrow our search to terms within the broader areas of XAI and taxonomies which included; Input data, output format, explanation method, user type, model type and evaluation method. This informed our categorization as described above. Of several hundred research articles 45 were considered for review with five specifically presenting taxonomies for XAI and 40 presenting relevant aspects of XAI.

4   Results

To choose a suitable XAI method for particular use cases it is imperative that those tasked with designing XAI methods understand the scope of XAI. For example, this should include explanation method (What to explain?), output format (How to explain?), input data, user type (Who to explain to?), model type and XAI evaluation methods. Navigating the vast landscape of XAI can be challenging for those tasked with researching XAI from a human centered focus.

We designed an XAI Taxonomy diagram, Appendix 1 Fig. 18 as a visual tool which will aid XAI developers in the design, development, and implementation of XAI. This diagram gives a succinct overview of six areas of focus for our work as well as assisting XAI developers who wish to gain insight into human centered aspects of XAI. We also discuss each area of focus in more detail as an overview of aspects of human centered XAI and include a concise diagram for each section.

4.1   Explanation Method (What?)

Explanation method examines the What? of XAI. What level of explanation is required and what methods will be used to explain the AI system's decision to an end user. Considerations should be focused on locality which includes global, local and cohort explanations [16–18]. Following this, consideration should concentrate on explanation methods including explanation by simplification, feature relevance, by example and using contrastive methods. An overview of these aspects can be viewed in Fig. 1.

- **Global Explanation:** Explains all predictions and/or the model prediction process [1, 16].
- **Local Explanation:** Explains a single prediction [17].
- **Cohort Explanation:** Explains a subset of predictions [18].

  Along with locality, XAI methods include:

- **Simplification:** explanation by simplification is a technique where a system is developed which represents a simplified and optimized version of the original AI system. They are designed to reduce complexity whilst maintaining a similar performance [4].

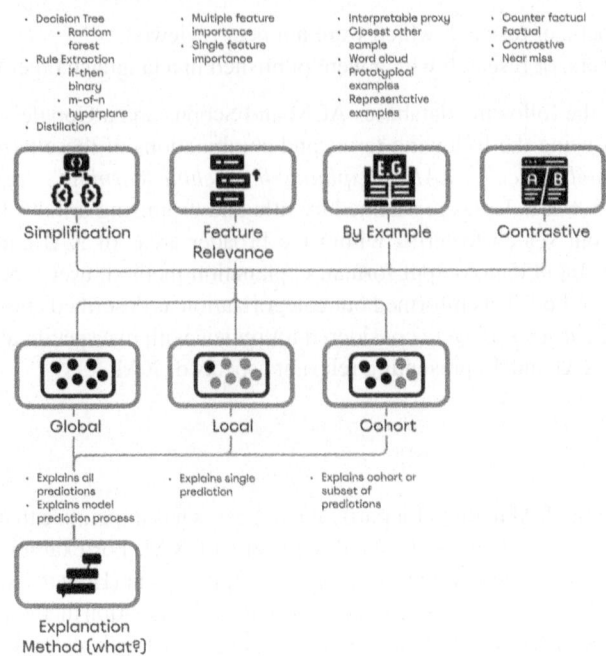

Fig. 1. Explanation Method (What?)

Examples include but are not limited to decision trees (random forest) [19, 20], rule extraction (if-then binary) [21]), (m-of-n) [22, 23], (hyperplane) [24] and distillation [25]. Examples of decision tree and if-then binary explanations are shown in Figs. 2 and 3.

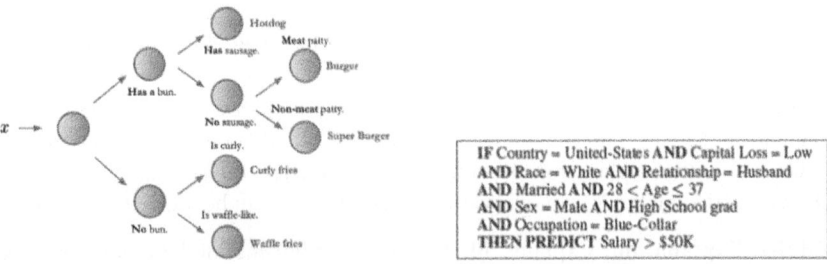

Fig. 2. Decision tree [66]   **Fig. 3.** If-then binary explanation [65]

- **Feature Relevance:** Explanation using feature relevance can be described as a method of simplifying the inner workings of AI systems through calculating a score for each variable which influences the output. Used for post-hoc explanations, the score assigned to variables corelates to the sensitivity that feature has on the model's output. Each score reflects the importance that variable has on the final output and as such feature relevance can indirectly explain those decisions [4]. These can be represented as multiple feature importance or single feature importance such as with SHAP (Shapley Additive Explanations) for global post-hoc approach [26]. SHAP provides explanations specifically for tree-based models and, using a game theory approach, presents an explanation of the system's decision across all instances. See Fig. 4. LIME (Local Interpretable Model Agnostic Explanations), as an alternative can be employed for a local post-hoc approach [17]. Whereas SHAP is suitable for specific types of models LIME can be used for explaining any model or AI system and generates local explanations, meaning that it explains a system's decision for a specific instance or observation. See Fig. 5.

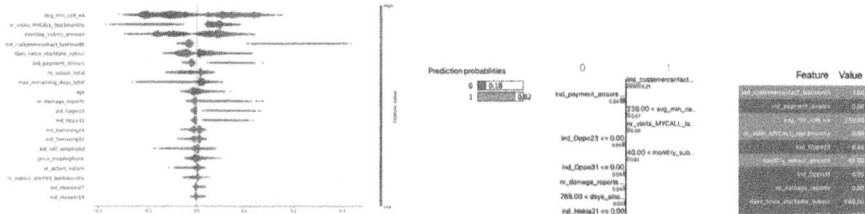

Fig. 4. SHAP values impact on model output [64]

Fig. 5. LIME explanation for local feature relevance [64]

- **By Example:** XAI by example helps users understand the output of AI systems by showing representations of similar cases with similar correlations to the output produced. The use of examples sheds some light on the innerworkings of the AI system as they mimic how humans understand decisions. Examples could include interpretable proxy such as LIME (Local Interpretable Model Agnostic Explanations) [27], closest other sample [28, 31], word cloud [29], prototypical examples and representative examples [21, 30]. See Figs. 6 and 7 for examples.

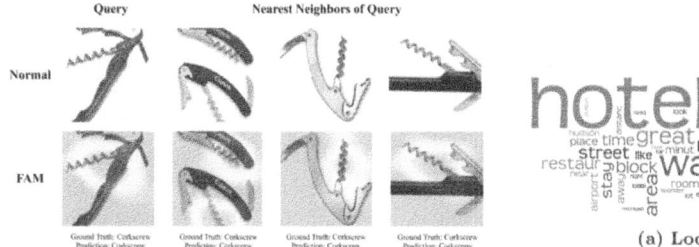

(a) Location

Fig. 6. Closest other sample. Correct classification of an image of a corkscrew with closest image to the test image shown. Most important features also highlighted. [28]

Fig. 7. Word cloud for online review data showing topic distribution for the aspect of location. [29]

- **Contrastive:** Contrastive explanations can be considered a subsection of example-based explanations since they often utilize examples in their function [32]. However, for our taxonomy we will classify contrastive explanations as a method of explanation which is distinct from example based. Contrastive explanations compare different outputs or predictions of AI systems for different inputs. Included in contrastive explanations are factual and counterfactual explanations [33, 34] which can be further broken down into pertinent positives and pertinent negatives [32] and near miss [35]. In essence contrastive explanations explain a system's output based on "Why this output (the fact) as opposed to the other (the foil)?". Pertinent positives refer to what needs to be minimally present to justify a classification and pertinent negatives refer to what should be minimally absent. A visual representation can be viewed in Fig. 8. What makes contrastive explanations particularly useful for users is the representation of explanations which advise on what a user might change or improve to gain a different outcome [34].

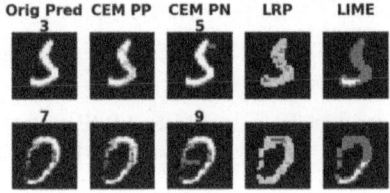

Fig. 8. Contrastive explanations including pertinent positives and pertinent negatives. [32]

4.2   Output Format (How?)

Another area which requires consideration and inclusion in any taxonomy of XAI is output format. Format refers to the How? of XAI. How should the explanation be represented to the end user? Different criteria and situations require different output formats for explainability and include, numerical, rules, textual, visual, mixed [6, 14]. An overview of output formats can be viewed in Fig. 9.

- **Numerical:** Mostly used to represent global explanations these have been shown to be the least suitable method for lay users [6, 36]. Numerical explanations can be represented as graphs such as bar charts.
- **Rules:** An intuitive form of explanation which mimics human reasoning and logic using If....Then statements or and/or operators. They are a useful format to explain input features' effect on the final output. An example for a loan request would be "e = hr = {age $\leq$ 25, job = clerk, income $\leq$ 900} $\rightarrow$ deny" [34] and expressed as a decision tree in Fig. 10 [34].
- **Textual:** Natural language formats which mimic human speech styles have been utilised to explain AI outputs. Written in an intuitive style an example would be "This is an image of a tree sparrow because this bird has a brown crown, brown primaries, and a brown belly" [14, 37].

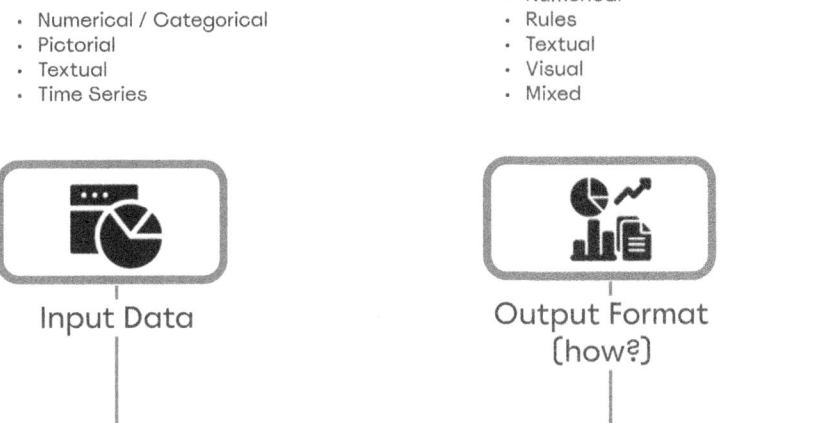

- Numerical / Categorical
- Pictorial
- Textual
- Time Series

- Numerical
- Rules
- Textual
- Visual
- Mixed

Input Data

Output Format
(how?)

Fig. 9. Input data & Output format

- **Visual:** This output format is one which is most used in XAI and can include heat maps applied to both images and text, graphs and diagrams [13, 17]. Colour coding has also been used to indicate which class words or parts of images contribute to the model's output [17, 38].
- **Mixed:** Explanations which are represented using a combination of numerical, visual, rules, textual and/or visuals incorporate the strengths of combined formats for example in Fig. 11 [39] the use of visual heat mapping in combination with text explanations. In combination both visual and textual explanations show which parts of each image contribute to the final decision.

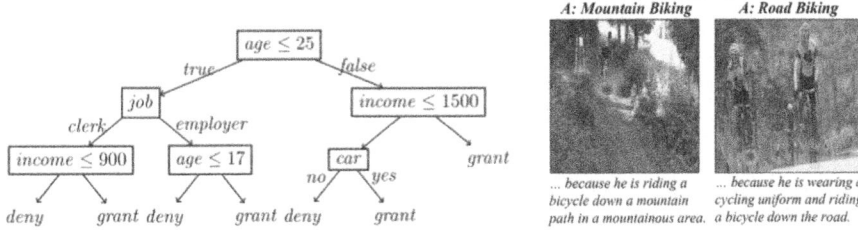

Fig. 10. Decision tree mimicking the local behavior of a black box [34].

Fig. 11. Mixed explanations combining visual and textual [39].

4.3   Input Data

Methods used to explain a model's output are often determined by the type of input data such as numerical, pictorial, textual or time based. Like output format, input data can influence suitability or choice of XAI method used [14]. See Fig. 9.

4.4 User Type

User type is a crucial factor in any consideration related to human centered XAI and for our purposes we categorize XAI end users as auditors/regulatory agents, domain experts, lay users/customers and AI practitioners [14]. One aspect of our research is considerations related to end user, what methods, and formats of XAI are most effective for lay users or customers engaging with an AI system? User type also plays an important role in human centered evaluation methods as user type often determines which evaluation scales and methods might be most effective. See Figs. 12 and 13. Evaluation methods related to functionality and application are represented on our diagram but not expanded upon as our focus is on human centered evaluation methods.

4.5 Model Type

AI models, as a basic form of categorization, can be broken down into opaque (black-box) or interpretable (white-box).

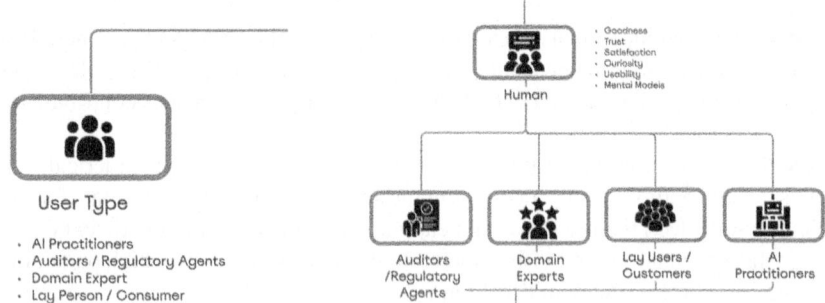

Fig. 12. User Type

Fig. 13. The user as a consideration for evaluation methods

- **Opaque AI**: These forms of AI are not readily understandable to humans as their inner workings are complex and do not function in a manner comparable to human thought or decision making [40, 41]. These forms of AI require a post-hoc explanation method which acts as a surrogate model which is interpretable [42] and therefore functions as an explanation for users. Opaque models include deep neural networks (DNNs), tree ensembles, reinforcement learners and agents [43] and large language models [44]. Some XAI methods are also model agnostic in that they can be applied to any type of model (LIME, SHAP, Example based explanations) or model specific in that they can only be applied to specific model types (LRP, CAM, Grad-CAM, Decision trees) [43].

LRP (Layer-wise relevance propagation) is an XAI technique which can be applied to neural networks where a set of formulas calculates relevance scores producing an output which represents which input features are most relevant in the decision. See Fig. 14. CAM (Class Activation Mapping) and more recent advances in Grad-CAM (Gradient weighted class activation mapping) are XAI methods which can be applied to

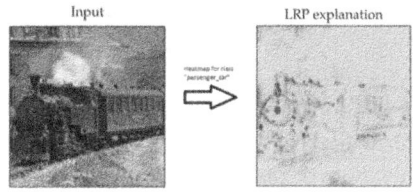
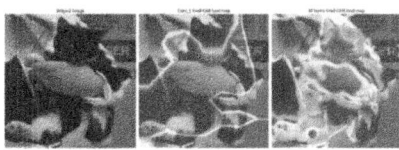

Fig. 14. LRP explanation showing prediction as passenger car. Red areas contribute positively to the prediction and blue areas negatively [67].

Fig. 15. Grad-Cam heat map showing original input, final layer in model and all model layers identifying Cat.

convolutional neural networks, where a heat map is produced which highlights which areas of the output are important to the final prediction. See Fig. 15 for example of Grad-CAM heat map.

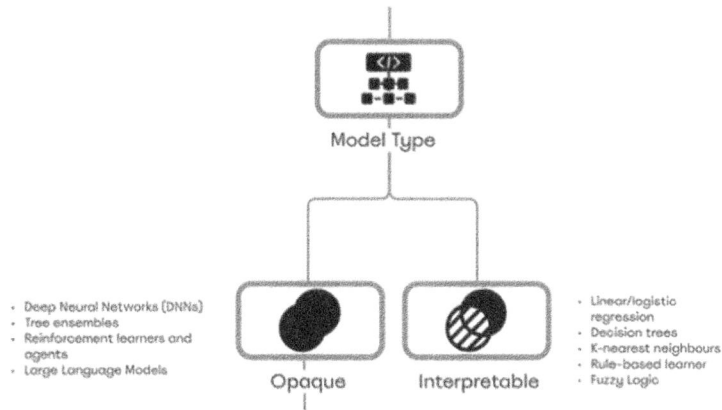

Fig. 16. Model Type

- **Interpretable/Transparent AI:** These forms of AI are ones which are understandable by humans and don't need a post-hoc explanation [43] such as decision trees, rule-based learner and fuzzy logic [45]. However, even with transparent AI, explanation format and method should be considered especially when we consider user types and what constitutes an understandable XAI especially for lay users. It should be noted that transparency and interpretability are not the same as explainable AI. Explainable AI is an interface which communicates between users and AI systems, both opaque and transparent, to make the AI model more understandable to humans [4]. See Fig. 16.

4.6   Evaluation Methods

An integral aspect of our human centered XAI research is in evaluating XAI methods and formats, including the evaluation of XAI solutions with AI and HCI experts, and the evaluation of newly designed XAI interfaces with AI and HCI experts and lay users. This research centers around human based evaluations as opposed to evaluation of XAI functionality and application. Evaluations should be designed with the user type in mind with some evaluation methods and scales being specifically designed for AI practitioners such as the goodness check [46, 47] and AI practitioners and other users such as shadowbox and shadowbox-lite [49].

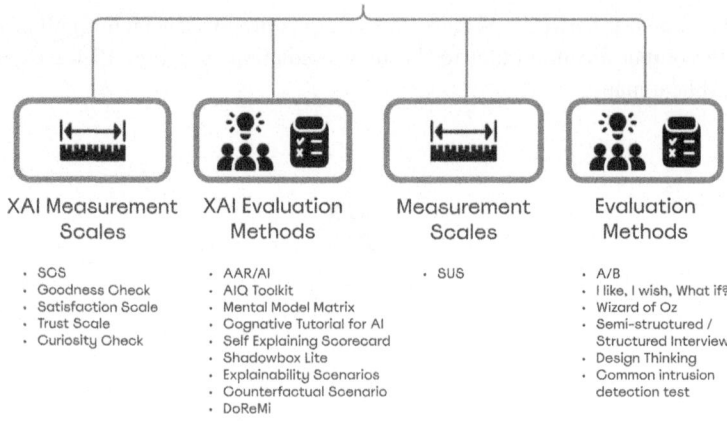

Fig. 17. Human Centered Evaluation Methods for XAI

This literature describes evaluation scales, those designed to evaluate XAI (SCS, goodness check, satisfaction scale, trust scale and curiosity check) [47, 48, 50] and those designed to evaluate web and software applications (SUS) [51] but which have been used in the evaluation of XAI. Also included is an overview of evaluation methods specifically designed for XAI: AAR/AI, AIQ toolkit, Mental Model Matrix, Cognitive tutorial for AI, Self-Explaining Scorecard, Shadowbox Lite, Explainability Scenario, Counterfactual Scenario, DoReMi [49, 52–56, 63]. Those designed for other human centered forms of evaluation but which have been used to evaluate XAI include: A/B, I like, I wish, What if?, Wizard of Oz, Semi-structured / Structured Interview, Design Thinking and Common Intrusion Detection Test [57–62]. See Fig. 17. These methods can be combined when qualitative and quantitative evaluations are required.

4.7 Measurement Scales

Measurement scales or rating scales can be best described as a quantitative means of measuring how people engage with a product or service often used to evaluate both the emotional and cognitive effects of this engagement [68]. In recent years with the proliferation of AI and now the growing requirement for XAI, scales specifically tailored for the evaluation of AI and/or XAI are being developed and validated within the research community. We give a short overview of each to facilitate our evaluation of XAI with users but also for other HCI researchers who wish to examine scales that might suit their own needs.

XAI Measurement Scales

- **SCS:** The SCS scale, developed by [50] is specifically tailored for those wishing to evaluate the quality of explanations given by XAI. The SCS measures the XAI in terms of usefulness and how usable the explanation interface is. Comprised of a 10-point scale with each point having 5 response options, like a Likert rating between 1 and 5 (strongly agree to strongly disagree). The scale has been used and validated in clinical settings using the Farmingham Risk Tool [50] and in the evaluation of explanations for an AI powered web-based tool for Oral Tongue Cancer Prognostication [70].
- **Satisfaction scale, trust scale and curiosity check:** Three scales developed as part of the AIQ (Artificial Intelligence Quotient) toolkit sponsored by DARPA comprising their larger XAI program, the satisfaction scale, trust scale and curiosity check are designed to measure users' engagement with AI explanations. Following a Goodness check with an AI system's designer an assessment for satisfaction of an explanation from a user perspective is employed. Satisfaction can be best described as the level to which the user can understand the AI system or process that the XAI is explaining. The test of satisfaction is also presented as a scale with 7 points rated using a Likert scale but, in this instance, it is used to evaluate participants' judgements after they have interacted with an XAI solution and seen the benefits of its use [50]. What follows in the AIQ toolkit are a series of scales to assess users' comprehension of the XAI solution including scales to evaluate their curiosity and trust in the system. The curiosity check asks users the question *"Why have you asked for an explanation?"* with 6 possible reasons users check all that apply [50]. The trust scale presents 7 points rated using a 5 point Likert scale (strongly agree to strongly disagree) and specifically measures end users' trust in AI generated explanations [50].

XAI Measurement Scale Designed for AI Practitioners

- **Goodness Check:** Preceding the satisfaction scale, trust scale and curiosity check a test for goodness is completed from the perspective of an AI system's designer whereby a 7-point checklist is marked as either yes or no to 7 questions related to an XAI. This would be completed by a researcher who is not the developer or designer of the XAI system being evaluated. This is the first check or evaluation employed before assessing satisfaction of an explanation from a user perspective [50].

Non-XAI Measurement Scale

- **SUS:** Scales not specifically designed for the evaluation of XAI such as SUS have been used to evaluate XAI with successful outcomes [70]. Most notably in clinical settings such as Alabi et al. use of SUS along with SCS to evaluate the usability and quality of explanations generated by a web-based prognostic tool for tongue cancer [70]. It must be noted that in this use case, both SUS and SCS scales were used. It is not clear had SUS been used without the use of SCS would the outcomes have been as successful.

XAI Evaluation Methods

- **AAR/AI:** After Action Review for AI (AAR/AI) which is heavily designed around the AAR for military operations but with an AI emphasis. A process adapted from the US military usually for domain experts designed as a series of steps for a human participant to evaluate an AI agent and the explanation it provides. The 7 steps include: define the rules, explain the AI's objectives, review what was supposed to happen, identify what happened, examine why it happened, formalise learning, formalise learning holistically [71].
- **AIQ Toolkit:** Included in this toolkit, along with the scales described above, are a range of XAI methods to evaluate users' mental models of AI and XAI systems. The authors' AIQ strategy begins with a mental model matrix (MMM) [63] designed to help users gain a better mental model of the AI system they are using. Designed as a quadrant, each section asks the users to consider the AI system under different criteria. How the system works?, How the system might fail?, How to make the system work? And How users get confused? The mental model matrix was used as an initial step in the calibration of tools in the AIQ toolkit [63]. The Cognitive Tutorial for AI (CTAI) which is also part of the AIQ toolkit, can be used to help AI systems users, both novice and more experienced, better understand how AI systems work but also how they might falter [49]. The self explaining scorecard works by presenting examples of how an AI system works but also instances of when it breaks with diagnoses of why the system may have broken down. This method is aimed at AI and XAI systems developers and uses a 7-point categorization system which ranks a system's level of explainability from null, where no explainability is provided to level 7, interactive adaptation where actionable feedback is provided. The scorecard can be used to classify existing XAI methods, identify alternative methods to present information, consider methods to enrich explanations and can be implemented in the system development stages or system evaluation stages of XAI design and development [50, 53]. Shadow box lite can be used to evaluate the understanding of non-expert / lay users whereby they give a rationale for the AI systems decisions which is compared to the understanding of an AI practitioner [49].

- **Explainability scenarios and counterfactual scenarios:** These are narrative descriptions of how a persona (user) might interact with a system. These are designed to facilitate participants in considering what types of explanation users might need while using that AI system. Scenarios can be used in many UX processes such as with design thinking [54, 61]. A counterfactual scenario describes where participants are presented with a scenario which includes an explanation, an input and output and are tasked with describing what would need to change to change the model's output to a more desirable result [55].
- **DoReMi:** Describes a three-step method which the authors call DoReMi. Domain analysis, requirements analysis and multi-modal interaction design. This method can be used by AI practitioners throughout the lifecycle of an AI system design, development and deployment to evaluate requirements for all users [56].

Non-XAI Evaluation Methods. Evaluation methods more familiar in the UX (user experience) domain have been used for the evaluation of AI systems and XAI. A/B testing, where participants compare two or more versions of an experience to evaluate which performs the best relative to some objective measure has been used in the evaluation of XAI for a clinical decision support tool [69]. Our research has utilized design thinking, semi-structured, and structured interviews [61] and more recently I like, I wish, What if? techniques to evaluate users' mental models of AI systems as a stage in the development of more human centered XAI [61]. The common intrusion detection test, a form of forward simulation and accident/error analysis where participants describe what seems wrong in an explanation has been used in the detection of intruder words in an unsupervised text analysis tool. Participants are tasked with finding the difference between the AI system's true output and some corrupted output. This will determine the participants' understanding of the true output [62]. This is by no means an exhaustive list of non-XAI evaluation methods which can or have been applied to the evaluation of AI or XAI but a short overview of different methods which might be useful dependent on the context of use. These evaluation methods should be adapted to suit the objectives of the researcher and the requirements of those participating in the evaluation. Further research should be undertaken to apply and validate these and other non-XAI evaluation methods to XAI.

5 Discussion

Our human centered XAI taxonomy has facilitated work in the organization and indexing of information related to human centered XAI so that we can find relevant information on the subject more easily. Our taxonomy can also be used as a means of classifying and describing content specifically related to human centered XAI. For our research this has served two purposes. Firstly, during early exploratory investigations of users' mental models of AI systems we classified results using taxonomies for XAI but identified a gap in that generic XAI taxonomies were too broad for our specific, human centered approach. For this reason, our taxonomy can be used when human centered classification is needed.

And secondly, we used our taxonomy to classify already existing explanations for AI systems. This has facilitated in identifying explanations in-the-wild and in research literature and categorizing them according to factors such as user type, explanation method and/or output format. Our inclusion of a unique aspect, human centered evaluation methods for XAI, will be instrumental during our own evaluations of existing and newly designed explanations allowing us to determine the most suitable evaluation methods for each user type and context. We also envisage our taxonomy facilitating the design of an information architecture for future work in presenting new XAI designs.

6 Conclusion

Advances and research in AI are rising and the impact of these advancements upon society are far reaching. While explanations for AI system's decisions for AI practitioners have been extensively researched and developed, explanations for other types of users, especially lay or non-technical users have been given less attention. One aspect of this research is the evaluation of users' interactions with AI systems from a human-centered perspective. To facilitate categorizing aspects of XAI for those investigating the domain from an HCI focus, we designed a human-entered taxonomy for XAI with a novel aspect, evaluation methods which consider the human in the loop of XAI. The taxonomy presented by Schwalbe & Finzel [13] does include human-grounded metrics such as interpretability, effectiveness, or degree of understanding but doesn't detail how a researcher might go about measuring these factors.

Our taxonomy includes quantitative and qualitative methods which have been used to evaluate XAI from a human perspective including scales which evaluate quality, goodness, trust and curiosity and evaluation methods which evaluate users' mental models, understanding and interactions with AI systems. We also include those evaluation methods not necessarily designed specifically for the evaluation of XAI, but which have been used with success. Our proposed taxonomy allows for (a) researchers in HCI with a focus on XAI to gain an understanding of the most pertinent aspects of the domain in an easily accessible form; (b) researchers to identify gaps in XAI methods and predict future development areas; and (c) researchers to identify suitable human-centered evaluation methods, including scales and other HCI methods. We envisage this human-centered taxonomy as an organic framework. As the AI and XAI landscape changes so too will human-centered requirements and our taxonomy will be adapted, expanded, and updated as necessary. We anticipate the use of this taxonomy as an ongoing area of our research.

Appendix 1

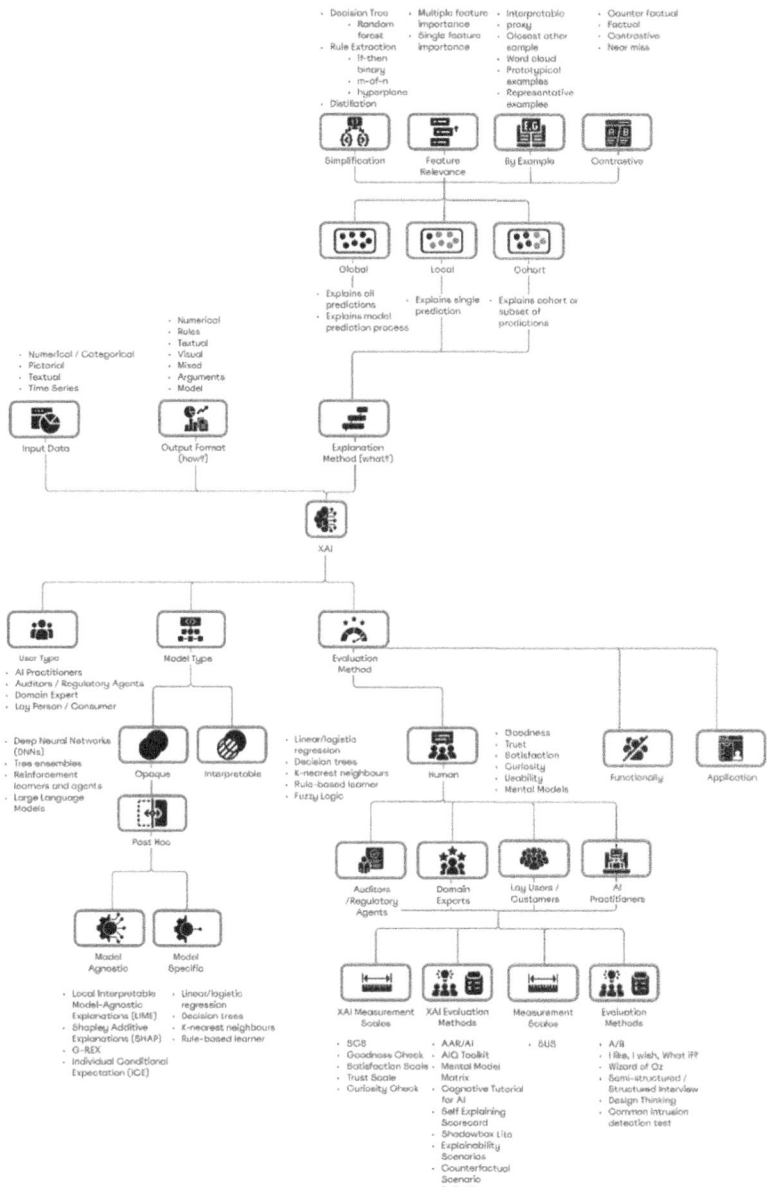

Fig. 18. Human Centered Taxonomy Diagram

References

1. Guidotti, R., Monreale, A., Ruggieri, S., Turini, F., Giannotti, F., Pedreschi, D.: A survey of methods for explaining black box models. ACM Comput. Surv. **51**(5), 1–42 (2018)
2. Liao, Q.V., Varshney, K.R.: Human-centered explainable ai (xai): from algorithms to user experiences. arXiv preprint arXiv:2110.10790 (2021)

3. Madiega, T.: Artificial intelligence act. European Parliament: European Parliamentary Research Service (2021)
4. Arrieta, A.B., et al.: Explainable Artificial Intelligence (XAI): concepts, taxonomies, opportunities and challenges toward responsible AI. Inform. Fusion **58**, 82–115 (2020)
5. Miller, T.: Explanation in artificial intelligence: insights from the social sciences. Artif. Intell. **267**, 1–38 (2019)
6. Speith, T.: A review of taxonomies of explainable artificial intelligence (XAI) methods. In: Proceedings of the 2022 ACM Conference on Fairness, Accountability, and Transparency, pp. 2239–2250 (2022)
7. Ribera, M., Lapedriza García, À.: Can we do better explanations? A proposal of user-centered explainable AI. In: CEUR Workshop Proceedings (2019)
8. Kim, S.S., Watkins, E.A., Russakovsky, O., Fong, R., Monroy-Hernández, A.: Help me help the AI: understanding how explainability can support human-AI interaction. In: Proceedings of the 2023 CHI Conference on Human Factors in Computing Systems, pp. 1–170 (2023)
9. Miller, T., Howe, P., Sonenberg, L.: Explainable AI: Beware of inmates running the asylum or: How I learnt to stop worrying and love the social and behavioural sciences. arXiv preprint arXiv:1712.00547 (2017)
10. Bertrand, A., Viard, T., Belloum, R., Eagan, J.R., Maxwell, W.: On selective, mutable and dialogic XAI: a review of what users say about different types of interactive explanations. In: Proceedings of the 2023 CHI Conference on Human Factors in Computing Systems, pp. 1–21 (2023)
11. Laubheimer. Taxonomy 101: definition, best practices, and how it complements other IA work (2022). https://www.nngroup.com/articles/taxonomy-101/. Accessed 09 Jan 2024
12. Glass, R.L., Vessey, I.: Contemporary application-domain taxonomies. IEEE Softw. **12**(4), 63–76 (1995)
13. Gesina, S., Finzel, B.: A comprehensive taxonomy for explainable artificial intelligence: a systematic survey of surveys on methods and concepts. Data Min. Knowl. Discov. 1–59 (2023)
14. Vilone, G., Longo, L.: Classification of explainable artificial intelligence methods through their output formats. Mach. Learn. Knowl. Extract. **3**(3), 615–661 (2021)
15. Emamirad, E., Omran, P.G., Haller, A., Gregor, S.: A system's approach taxonomy for user-centred XAI: a survey. arXiv preprint arXiv:2303.02810 (2023)
16. Setzu, M., Guidotti, R., Monreale, A., Turini, F., Pedreschi, D., Giannotti, F.: Glocalx-from local to global explanations of black box AI models. Artif. Intell. **294**, 103457 (2021)
17. Ribeiro, M.T., Singh, S., Guestrin, C.: Why should I trust you?" Explaining the predictions of any classifier. In: Proceedings of the 22nd ACM SIGKDD International Conference on Knowledge Discovery and Data Mining, pp. 1135–1144 (2016)
18. Patel, H.: What is Global, Cohort and Local Explainability? | Censius AI Observability Blog (2023). https://censius.ai/blogs/global-local-cohort-explainability. Accessed 17 Oct 2023
19. Mahbooba, B., Timilsina, M., Sahal, R., Serrano, M.: Explainable artificial intelligence (XAI) to enhance trust management in intrusion detection systems using decision tree model. Complexity **2021**, 1–11 (2021)
20. Izza, Y., Marques-Silva, J.: On explaining random forests with SAT. arXiv preprint arXiv: 2105.10278 (2021)
21. Macha, D., Kozielski, M., Wróbel, Ł, Sikora, M.: RuleXAI—a package for rule-based explanations of machine learning model. SoftwareX **20**, 101209 (2022)
22. Towell, G.G., Shavlik, J.W.: Extracting refined rules from knowledge-based neural networks. Mach. Learn. **13**, 71–101 (1993)
23. Setiono, R., Leow, W.K.: FERNN: an algorithm for fast extraction of rules from neural networks. Appl. Intell. **12**, 15–25 (2000)
24. Saad, E.W., Wunsch, D.C., II.: Neural network explanation using inversion. Neural Netw. **20**(1), 78–93 (2007)

25. Termritthikun, C., Umer, A., Suwanwimolkul, S., Xia, F., Lee, I.: Explainable knowledge distillation for on-device chest x-ray classification. IEEE/ACM Trans. Comput. Biol. Bioinform. (2023)
26. Lundberg, S.M., Lee, S.I.: A unified approach to interpreting model predictions. Adv. Neural Inform. Process. Syst. **30** (2017)
27. Nguyen, H.T.T., Cao, H.Q., Nguyen, K.V.T., Pham, N.D.K.: Evaluation of explainable artificial intelligence: shap, lime, and cam. In: Proceedings of the FPT AI Conference, pp. 1–6 (2021)
28. Kenny, E.M., Keane, M.T.: Explaining Deep Learning using examples: optimal feature weighting methods for twin systems using post-hoc, explanation-by-example in XAI. Knowl.-Based Syst. **233**, 107530 (2021)
29. Wu, Y.,Ester, M.:, February. Flame: a probabilistic model combining aspect based opinion mining and collaborative filtering. In: Proceedings of the eighth ACM International Conference on Web Search and Data Mining, pp. 199–208 (2015)
30. Hesse, L.S., Namburete, A.I.: INSightR-Net: interpretable neural network for regression using similarity-based comparisons to prototypical examples. In: Wang, L., Dou, Q., Fletcher, P.T., Speidel, S., Li, S. (eds.) Medical Image Computing and Computer Assisted Intervention – MICCAI 2022. MICCAI 2022. LNCS, vol. 13433. Springer, Cham (2022). https://doi.org/10.1007/978-3-031-16437-8_48
31. Papernot, N., McDaniel, P.: Deep k-nearest neighbors: towards confident, interpretable and robust deep learning. arXiv preprint arXiv:1803.04765. conference on computer vision and pattern recognition pp. 8779–8788 (2018)
32. Dhurandhar, A., et al.: Explanations based on the missing: Towards contrastive explanations with pertinent negatives. Adv. Neural Inform. Process. Syst. **31** (2018)
33. Mittelstadt, B., Russell, C., Wachter, S.: Explaining explanations in AI. In: Proceedings of the Conference on Fairness, Accountability, and Transparency, pp. 279–288 (2019)
34. Guidotti, R., Monreale, A., Giannotti, F., Pedreschi, D., Ruggieri, S., Turini, F.: Factual and counterfactual explanations for black box decision making. IEEE Intell. Syst. **34**(6), 14–23 (2019)
35. Herchenbach, M., Müller, D., Scheele, S., Schmid, U.: Explaining image classifications with near misses, near hits and prototypes: supporting domain experts in understanding decision boundaries. In International Conference on Pattern Recognition and Artificial Intelligence, pp. 419–430. Springer International Publishing, Cham (Cham)
36. Colley, A., Väänänen, K., Häkkilä, J.: November. tangible explainable AI-an initial conceptual framework. In: Proceedings of the 21st International Conference on Mobile and Ubiquitous Multimedia, pp. 22–27 (2022)
37. Barratt, S.: Interpnet: Neural introspection for interpretable deep learning. arXiv preprint arXiv:1710.09511 (2017)
38. Strobelt, H., Gehrmann, S., Pfister, H., Rush, A.M.: Lstmvis: a tool for visual analysis of hidden state dynamics in recurrent neural networks. IEEE Trans. Visual Comput. Graphics **24**(1), 667–676 (2017)
39. Park, D.H., et al.: Multimodal explanations: Justifying decisions and pointing to the evidence. In: Proceedings of the IEEE (2018)
40. Fainman, A.A.: Opaque AI. Fourth Industrial Revolution, p. 44 (2020)
41. Mostowy, W.A.: Explaining opaque AI decisions, vol. 35, p. 1291. Legally. Berkeley Tech. LJ (2020)
42. Prince, S.: Explainability I: local post-hoc explanations - Borealis AI (2022). https://www.borealisai.com/research-blogs/explainability-i-local-post-hoc-explanations/#Taxonomy_of_XAI_approaches. Accessed 08 May 2023

43. Kurdziolek, M.: Explaining the unexplainable: explainable AI (XAI) for UX. User Experience Magazine (2022). https://uxpamagazine.org/explaining-the-unexplainable-explainable-ai-xai-for-ux/. Accessed 13 April 2023
44. Ramlochan, S.: The black box problem: opaque inner workings of large language models (2023). https://promptengineering.org/the-black-box-problem-opaque-inner-workings-of-large-language-models. Accessed 29 Oct 2023
45. Liu, H., Cocea, M.: Fuzzy rule based systems for interpretable sentiment analysis. In: 2017 Ninth International Conference on Advanced Computational Intelligence (ICACI), pp. 129–136. IEEE (2017)
46. Hoffman, R.R., Mueller, S.T., Klein, G., Litman, J.: Metrics for explainable AI: challenges and prospects. arXiv preprint arXiv:1812.04608 (2018)
47. Hoffman, R.R., Mueller, S.T., Klein, G., Litman, J.: Measures for explainable AI: explanation goodness, user satisfaction, mental models, curiosity, trust, and human-AI performance. Front. Comput. Sci. **5**, 1096257 (2023)
48. Hoffman, R.R., Jalaeian, M., Tate, C., Klein, G., Mueller, S.T.: Evaluating machine-generated explanations: a "Scorecard" method for XAI measurement science. Front. Comput. Sci. **5**, 1114806 (2023)
49. Mueller, S., Tan, Y.Y., Linja, A., Klein, G., Hoffman, R.: Authoring guide for cognitive tutorials for artificial intelligence: purposes and methods (2021)
50. Holzinger, A., Carrington, A., Müller, H.: Measuring the quality of explanations: the system causability scale (SCS) comparing human and machine explanations. KI-Künstliche Intelligenz **34**(2), 193–198 (2020)
51. Brooke, J.: Sus: a "quick and dirty' usability. Usabil. Eval. Indust. **189**(3), 189–194 (1996)
52. Khanna, R., et al.: Finding AI's faults with AAR/AI: an empirical study. ACM Trans. Interact. Intell. Syst. **12**(1), 1–33 (2022)
53. Klein, G.: AIQ (Artificial Intelligence Quotient): Helping People Get Smart about the Smart Machines They Are Using (2023). https://medium.com/about-work/helping-people-get-smart-about-smart-machines-they-are-using-f9e0095846fe. Accessed 29 Oct 2023
54. Wolf, C.T.: Explainability scenarios: towards scenario-based XAI design. In: Proceedings of the 24th International Conference on Intelligent User Interfaces, pp. 252–257 (2019)
55. Doshi-Velez, F., Kim, B.: Towards a rigorous science of interpretable machine learning. arXiv preprint arXiv:1702.08608. (2017)
56. Schoonderwoerd, T.A., Jorritsma, W., Neerincx, M.A., Van Den Bosch, K.: Human-centered XAI: developing design patterns for explanations of clinical decision support systems. Int. J. Hum Comput Stud. **154**, 102684 (2021)
57. King, R., Churchill, E.F., Tan, C.: Designing with data: Improving the user experience with A/B testing. O'Reilly Media, Inc. (2017)
58. Rekonen, S.: Unlocking the potential of interdisciplinary teams. In: Passion-Based Co-creation pp. 90–101. Aalto University (2017)
59. Kelley, J.F.: An iterative design methodology for user-friendly natural language office information applications. ACM Trans. Inform. Syst. **2**(1), 26–41 (1984)
60. Ngo, T., Kunkel, J., Ziegler, J.: Exploring mental models for transparent and controllable recommender systems: a qualitative study. In: Proceedings of the 28th ACM Conference on User Modeling, Adaptation and Personalization, pp. 183–191 (2020)
61. Sheridan, H., Murphy, E., O'Sullivan, D.: Exploring mental models for explainable artificial intelligence: engaging cross-disciplinary teams using a design thinking approach. In: Degen, H., Ntoa, S. (eds.) Artificial Intelligence in HCI. HCII 2023. LNCS, vol. 14050. Springer, Cham (2023). https://doi.org/10.1007/978-3-031-35891-3_21
62. Chang, J., Gerrish, S., Wang, C., Boyd-Graber, J., Blei, D.: Reading tea leaves: How humans interpret topic models. Adv. Neural Inform. Process. Syst. **22** (2009)

63. Borders, J.: Introducing the Mental Model Matrix (2021). https://www.shadowboxtraining. com/news/2021/02/25/introducing-the-mental-model-matrix/. Accessed 29 Oct 2023

64. Heuvel, T.: Opening the Black Box of Machine Learning Models: SHAP vs LIME for Model Explanation | by Thomas ten Heuvel | Cmotions | Medium (2023). https://medium.com/cmotions/opening-the-black-box-of-machine-learning-models-shap-vs-lime-for-model-explanation-d7bf545ce15f. Accessed: 29/04/2024

65. Ribeiro, M.T., Singh, S., Guestrin, C.: Anchors: High-precision model-agnostic explanations. In: Proceedings of the AAAI Conference on Artificial Intelligence, vol. 32, no. 1 (2018)

66. Wan, A.: Making Decision Trees Accurate Again: Explaining What Explainable AI Did Not. https://bair.berkeley.edu/blog/2020/04/23/decisions/. Accessed 29 April 2024

67. Kumar, P.: Overview of Explainable AI and Layer wise relevance propagation (LRP) | by Praveen | Medium (2021). https://praveenkumar2909.medium.com/overview-of-explainable-ai-and-layer-wise-relevance-propagation-lrp-cb2d008fec57. Accessed 29 April 2024

68. Rosala, M.: Rating scales in UX research: likert or semantic differential? (2020). https://www. nngroup.com/articles/rating-scales/. Accessed 29 Oct 2023

69. Oliveira, E., Braga, C., Sampaio, A., Oliveira, T., Soares, F., Rosado, L.: Designing XAI-based computer-aided diagnostic systems: operationalising user research methods (2023)

70. Alabi, R.O., Almangush, A., Elmusrati, M., Leivo, I., Mäkitie, A.: Measuring the usability and quality of explanations of a machine learning web-based tool for Oral Tongue Cancer Prognostication. Int. J. Environ. Res. Public Health 19(14), 8366 (2022)

71. Mai, T., et al.: Keeping it" organized and logical" after-action review for AI (AAR/AI). In: Proceedings of the 25th International Conference on Intelligent User Interfaces, pp. 465–476 (2020)

Enhancing Explainability in Medical AI: Developing Human-Centered Participatory Design Cards

Tianyue Zhang and Xin He[✉]

School of Mechanical Science and Engineering of Huazhong University of Science
and Technology, Wuhan, Hubei, China
{zhangtianyue,xinh}@hust.edu.cn

Abstract. Explainable artificial intelligence (XAI) aims to develop AI systems
that are easy for humans to understand and explain the decision-making process
clearly. Especially in high-risk fields such as medical, the explainability of AI
systems is particularly crucial. However, designers face significant challenges
in implementing explainable AI design activities in the medical domain. This
research aims to provide systematic guidance for designers on medical XAI design
methods, addressing the challenges faced by designers and users in designing
explainable medical AI. Through comprehensive literature review and thematic
analysis based on the PRISMA process, we developed medical XAI Design cards
from a human-centered perspective to assist designers in exploring solutions. Combining qualitative and quantitative research, we collected feedback from designers
and users, validating the effectiveness of the Design Cards and aiding in maintaining a focus on medical explainability during the design process. This research
fills the gap in enabling designers to engage in medical XAI design activities,
enhancing the explainability of XAI systems in the medical field.

Keywords: Explainable Artificial Intelligence · Medical · User Experience
Design · Participatory Design · Human-Centered Design

1 Introduction

In recent years, AI has shown great potential in diagnosis, treatment, and medical
decision-making in the healthcare domain [3, 50, 58]. Consequently, there has been
an increasing demand for the explainability of algorithms. The importance of Explainable AI (XAI) is rising [40, 60, 65, 88]. In high-risk fields involving human life and
health, such as medical care, highly reliable and explainable decisions are required,
and the explainability of medical AI algorithms are increasingly important. Systems are
responsible for providing explanations to end users, as stipulated by Articles 13 and 14
of the EU General Data Protection Regulation (GDPR), granting data subjects the right
to receive "meaningful information about the logic involved" [49]. End users also need
algorithms to provide explanations to ensure reliable decisions [65, 82]. If AI medical
products fail to provide explanations to end users, several issues may arise, such as: 1)

Lack of trust in diagnostic results [48]; 2) Unfair outcomes [10, 22, 97]; 3) Legal and ethical issues [66]. Therefore, there is an urgent need for explanations in the AI medical field [78, 110].

In previous research, our team developed an XAI Needs library for end users in the healthcare domain [46], empirically validating its effectiveness. However, when user needs were handed over to designers, significant challenges were encountered: designers often struggled to implement design practices after collecting user needs due to a lack of relevant knowledge, consistent with previous studies [113–115].

In response to the above problems, we developed an design tool for designers in the field of medical XAI, to bridge the gap in designers' understanding of XAI, so that they can effectively participate in the design, and then improve the explainability in the medical field to a certain extent.The specific process of this research is as follows: conducting a comprehensive literature review, the research constructs a systematic medical XAI design method from a human-centered perspective, emphasizing the design of medical AI explainable interface accessible to users from a human-centered perspective. The final outcome, presented in the form of popular Design Cards, are named "Medical XAI Design Cards" (referred to as "Design Cards"). These cards cover five dimensions from macro to micro, from theory to practice: "Design Principles - Presentation Forms - Presentation Modalities - Design Methods - Practical Cases," with a total of 15 sub-content items, which were validated through workshops.

Our contributions focus on the following aspects:

1) For practitioners looking to engage in medical XAI design activities, there is a lack of systematic design method guidance and related tools. This research aims to fill this gap by reviewing and summarizing existing non-algorithmic AI model explanation methods from the perspectives of medical AI explainability and design. Based on this, we developed Design Cards for designers to supplement knowledge, inspire creativity, and provide solutions; 2) This tool supports collaboration among stakeholders from different professional backgrounds, enabling them to participate collectively in AI healthcare design to enhance explainability and transparency. The Design Cards not only serve as practical tools but also facilitate knowledge sharing and transfer, providing an effective communication medium for designers and end users, promoting collaboration. Through these Design Cards, designers and users can collaboratively engage in the design and development of medical XAI systems, thereby enhancing the human-centered explainbility of these systems; 3) We summarize insights, experiences, and lessons learned during the research process, outlining future research directions to promote the development of transparent AI in the medical field. This research aims to provide tools and references for improving explainability in the medical AI field.

2   Literature Review

2.1   Explainable Artificial Intelligence Interface Design

Explainable Artificial Intelligence (XAI) refers to AI technologies and methods that aim to make AI systems' decision-making processes transparent and easy to understand. XAI helps users comprehend, trust, and effectively use AI systems by providing explanations of model behavior and decision logic [2, 34, 79]. Its goal is to ensure that AI systems can clearly demonstrate the reasons and rationale behind their decisions. Currently, there are two main ways to obtain AI explainable information. One is to enhance explainability by developing explainable models such as Grad-CAM [91], and the other is to obtain explanation through explainable interface (XUI) [96]. XUI refers to the sum of the outputs of XAI systems that the user can interact with [26]. The core objective of XUI is to transparently and intuitively display the AI system's decision-making process and logic, enabling users to understand and trust these systems. It acts as a bridge between users and XAI systems [1] and is the foundation of human-centered AI, aiming to "amplify and augment human performance" [87].

In the medical field, XAI interface design is particularly significant, as doctors and other medical professionals rely on these systems for critical diagnostic and treatment decisions [2]. End users obtain explanations of medical decisions and results through explainable interfaces. Schoonderwoerd developed human-centered design patterns and designed explainable clinical decision support systems based on these patterns to assist doctors in decision-making [84]. Barda created a human-centered explanation display framework and developed machine learning-based clinical prediction tools for clinicians based on this framework [11]. Müller proposed an interactive visual explanation method and developed explainable interfaces for clinical decision support systems [70]. Despite these studies applying explainable design to the medical field, they did not consider the knowledge differences among designers during practical operations in the medical XAI field. There is a gap in research that enables designers to effectively integrate design for medical AI explainability from a human-centric perspective.

2.2 Application of Participatory Design in Medical

Participatory Design (PD) is a design methodology that aims to ensure design outcomes better meet user needs by actively involving end users and other stakeholders in the design process [52, 69]. Originating in Scandinavia in the 1970s to improve worker conditions [17], PD's core principles include co-creation, equitable dialogue, and iterative processes, emphasizing the importance of users' expertise and experience in the design process [101]. Research has shown that PD can significantly enhance user satisfaction and the practicality of design outcomes [23]. Over time, PD methods have been widely applied in healthcare [42], including public health interventions, emergency medical services [57], medical education [16], and various clinical fields [77]. These applications include patient and public involvement [38] and patient- and family-centered care [30, 80]. PD has been used for various diseases, such as breast and lung cancer services [100], cardiovascular diseases [15, 76], and mental health [43, 105]. PD ensures user involvement at all stages of medical product and service design, valuing the experiences and knowledge of different stakeholders [37] and stimulating creativity within design teams [83].

2.3 Current Status of Design Tools in the AI Field

To effectively implement participatory design, tools can be provided to aid in presentation and design, making the design process comprehensible, reducing friction, and lowering time costs [59], and fostering innovative thinking [55]. Design tools can integrate and optimize specialized knowledge, skills, and experience in the medical field [12]. Design tools come in various forms; Card-Based Design tools are particularly effective in participatory design. They provide structured, easy-to-use Design Cards that help users and designers brainstorm and evaluate solutions during the design process [29, 81]. Currently, design tools in the AI field are still primarily focused on AI technical systems [14, 85], with relatively few supporting designers in AI design. The existing design field has produced several human-centered AI design guides: including Microsoft's "Guidelines for Human-AI Interactions" which provides guidance from a user interaction perspective, covering interactions throughout the user's lifecycle [4]; Google's "People + AI Guidebook" [36] which focuses on user experience design; and Apple's "Human Interface Guidelines" which emphasize user interface design norms [6]. There are also other formal and informal recommendations such as the "Human-AI Guidelines Cheat-sheet" [51] and "Deloitte Insights" [28]. While these design guides have made significant contributions in providing theoretical frameworks and principles, more practical tools and methods are still needed to further support the practical application of AI design. Especially, tools and techniques that can promote interdisciplinary participation, integrate specialized knowledge, and offer specific operational guidance are necessary. These will help designers and users communicate and collaborate more effectively, driving more innovative and efficient AI system designs.

In summary, there is a lack of practical tools available for designers in the medical AI field to guide design practice. Therefore, this research aims to develop a card-based design tool to guide explainable AI design practice in healthcare and stimulate creativity.

3 Design Cards

We conducted a systematic literature review of relevant scholarly articles. The literature review followed the systematic review and PRISMA guidelines [5] (Fig. 1).

3.1 Search Strategy

Recent years have witnessed an explosive growth in the number of publications related to Explainable Artificial Intelligence (XAI). To capture this surge, we conducted a comprehensive literature search using the Web of Science (WOS) and ACM databases, focusing on the past five years up to the end of 2023. Our search keywords included "XAI," "explainable Artificial intelligence" and "design". Our search yielded a total of 2241 papers. After applying inclusion/exclusion criteria, starting with abstract reviews and then full-text reviews, we conducted snowball sampling and utilized the Triangle method [67] to obtain an additional two papers. Ultimately, 57 articles were included in our review (see table), showcasing the entire screening process (Tables 1, 2 and 3).

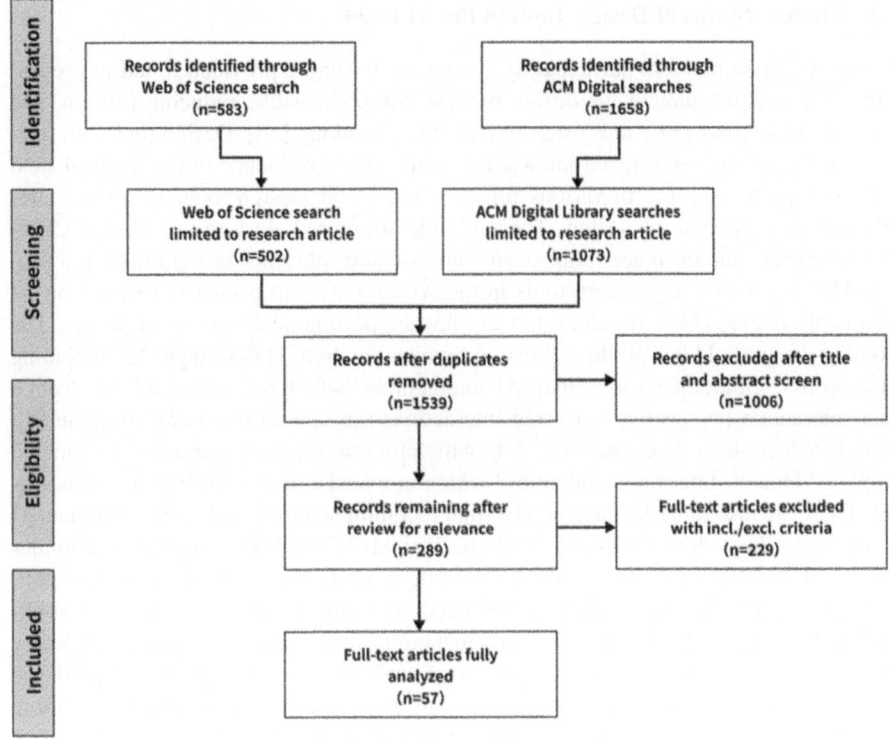

Fig. 1. PRISMA flow diagram.

Table 1. Contains the search terminology

Key Concepts	Explainable Artificial Intelligence	Design
Search terminology	Explainable Artificial Intelligence	Design
	XAI	Graphic Design
	Explainable AI	Interface Design
	Interpretable artificial intelligence	Interaction Design
	Interpretable AI	Information Design
		Service Design
		Web Design

Table 2. Inclusion/exclusion criteria.

Inclusion criteria	Exclusion criteria
It is a research article	It is not a research article (e.g., it is a commentary, editorial, abstract, workshop summary)
Related to explainable artificial intelligence	Duplicate (not detected by bibliography software)
Design related methods/guidelines/strategies/recommendations are proposed	Unable to gain access to online version of full article
Design related XAI cases are presented	Studies only focus on technical aspects (e.g., algorithms/models design)
	Not relevant to medical or design fields
	Nothing to do with explainable AI

Table 3. Articles included in the review

No.	References	No.	References	No.	References	No.	References	No.	References
01	[87]	13	[47]	25	[59]	37	[93]	49	[33]
02	[41]	14	[56]	26	[92]	38	[103]	50	[95]
03	[111]	15	[112]	27	[63]	39	[104]	51	[7]
04	[18]	16	[72]	28	[74]	40	[65]	52	[27]
05	[45]	17	[84]	29	[73]	41	[8]	53	[61]
06	[64]	18	[26]	30	[9]	42	[2]	54	[32]
07	[106]	19	[24]	31	[98]	43	[94]	55	[35]
08	[90]	20	[109]	32	[46]	44	[68]	56	[20]
09	[25]	21	[54]	33	[62]	45	[75]	57	[13]
10	[21]	22	[66]	34	[96]	46	[71]		
11	[99]	23	[44]	35	[108]	47	[89]		
12	[107]	24	[39]	36	[102]	48	[53]		

3.2 Identifying and Classifying Design Methods

The classification of Design Cards was determined collaboratively through manual reading. Initially, we read through 57 papers, coding the explanatory design content mentioned in each. We then performed triangulation, reviewing disputed content until consensus was reached. These 57 selected papers were coded using NVIVO to extract 5 key design dimensions: "Presentation Format," "Presentation Mode" "Design Principle" "Design Method" and "Design Case". However, we noted the absence of a specific classification framework for explanatory design content. Eiband (2018) proposed a stage-based participatory design process, which aligns with our coded content, guiding the specification of product needs—what to explain—and iterative solution design—how to explain [31]. We further added "why provide this explanation?" and "UI cases," aligning with scholars advocating general principles and UI cases for explainability [59].

Through joint discussions, we finalized the content for each Design Card into four parts: 1) description of the problem(what); 2) explanation of the solution(how); 3) rationale for the solution(why); 4) UI examples(case). The authors then mapped all coded content into these four sections. The results were compared by two authors, who discussed and redefined categories as needed. After confirming the content of each card, we dimensified these cards and clustered existing papers explaining design types. We then invited two medical XAI designers to review, finalizing five dimensions from macro to micro, theory to practice: "Design Principle- Presentation Format-Presentation Mode" "Design Methods- Design Case" with 15 sub-concepts. "Practice cases" serve as both specific content presentation for each explanatory type and provide practical, actionable guidance for designers.

3.3   Design Cards Toolkit Composition

Based on the above steps, we developed an XAI design tool for designers. The toolkit features: 1) Focus on explainable design in medical AI; 2) Applicability in participatory design workshops to stimulate creative solutions; 3) Accessibility for non-AI expert.

We finalized a set of 19 cards across five dimensions. Four title cards introduce key concepts: 1) **"Presentation Format" includes three cards:** "Textual Explanation," "Visual Explanation," and "Mixed Explanation."; **2) "Presentation Mode" includes three cards:** "Static Explanation," "Interactive explanation," and "Dialogue Explanation." 3) **"Design Principles" includes three cards:** "Contextual Explanation", "Personalized Explanation" and "Progressive Disclosure"; **4) "Design Methods" includes six cards:** "Global Explanation" "Local Explanation", "Counterfactual Explanation," "Feature-based Explanation," "Example-based Explanation," and "Contrastive Explanation." Each card includes examples of XAI interfaces. We conducted in-depth interviews with five senior designers to gather iterative feedback, resulting in the final version of the Design Cards.

3.4   Detailed Introduction to the Design Cards Content

This section provides a detailed introduction to the content and sources of the cards, outlining the five dimensions of the toolkit (Figs. 2, 3, 4, 5, 6 and Tables 4, 5, 6, 7, 8):

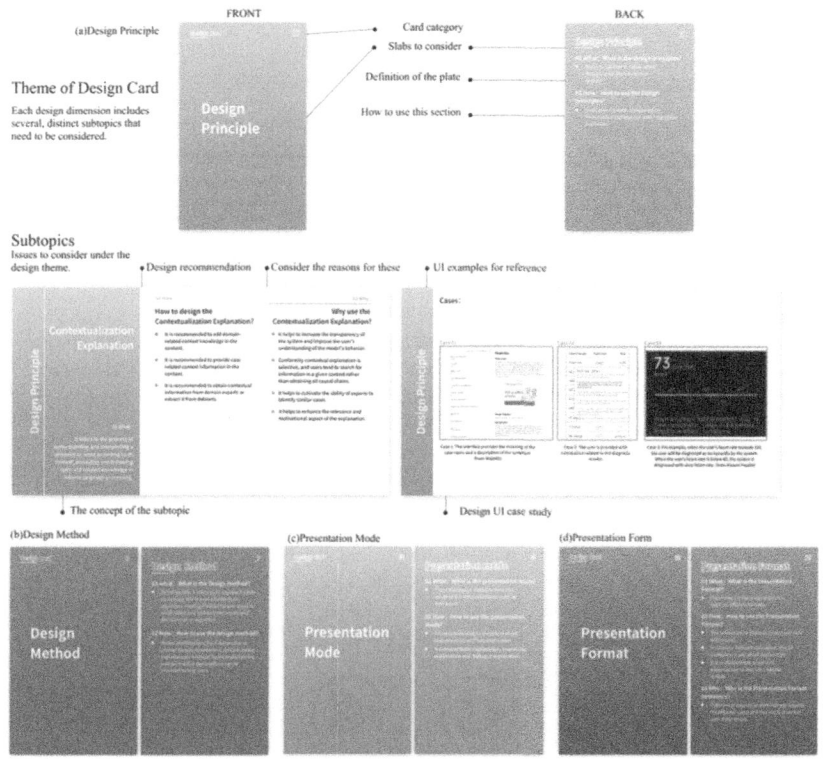

Fig. 2. Design Cards' structure

Table 4. Design Cards' 5 dimensions

	Concepts (what)	How to design (How)
Presentation Format	Presenting the same explanation to users in different formats (14,25,26,29,31,36,4,49,52)	• The presentation depends on the user and the context. (29,52) • It contains Textual Explanation (02,14,18,22,23, 28,31,41,53), Visual Explanation and Mixed Explanation. (07,14,18,21,23,28,31) • It is recommended to present explanations to users in a simple format. (14)
Presentation Mode	The presentation modality indicates whether the explanation is static or interactive. (57)	• It is recommended to provide multiple explanation methods and modes. (18) • It contains Static explanation (18,25,46,52, 56,57), Interactive explanation (01,02,04,08,09,11,13,14,18,25,26,50,52,56,57) and Dialogue explanation. (11,18,20,32)

(continued)

Table 4. (*continued*)

	Concepts (what)	How to design (How)
Design Principle	Some guidelines to follow when designing for the XAI medical domain	It contains Contextual explanation (04,11,16,26,47), Personalized explanation (03,11,16,18,19,23,24,30, 56), and Progressive disclosure. (18,23,37,43,56)
Design Method	In this toolkit, it refers to an approach taken to increase the interpretability of an algorithm, making it easier for end users to understand and interpret the results and decisions of an algorithm	Global explanations (02,04,19,23,32), local explanations (07,13,23,27,31,34,48,49,52), counterfactual explanations (01,10,16,25,26,31,32,35,38,45,46,52), feature-based explanations (04,07,11,32), example-based explanations (06,07,10,11,16,23,25,27, 28,32, 33,46), and contrastive explanations (03,10,11,20, 03,10,11,20,36,40,47) can be provided to end users
Design Case	Corresponding to the medical AI explainable UI examples for reference in each part of the explanation content. (01,09,11,18,30,31,32,35,39)	

Table 5. Presentation Format

Textual explanation	What	Textual explanation is the presentation format that describes a model or reasoning in the form of words, phrases, or natural language. (22,23,28,41,53)
	How	• It is recommended to combine textual explanation with visual cues. (18,23,31) • It is recommended to use textual explanation in static recommendation environments. (14,31)
	Why	• In line with the intuitive characteristics of text interpretation, text interpretation can better reflect the mapping of the underlying system. (02) • It helps to understand the operation mechanism of the system, thereby improving their trust and satisfaction, (02,14,18)
Visual explanation	What	Visual explanation involves presenting the principles behind a model using visual elements. (12,15,21,22,23,26,28,41,53)
	How	• It is recommended to convert the data into visual images or elements and consider human visual habits. (07,21) • It is recommended to combine visual elements with other presentation formats or design methods. (18,28,31) • It is recommended to provide different levels of visual explanation based on the cognitive abilities of users. (31)

(*continued*)

Table 5. (*continued*)

	Why	• Visual explanation, characterized by their compact and engaging format, effectively convey a wealth of information. (39) • It helps to produce recommendations with higher precision, making recommendations easier to accept and understand. (02,12,28) • It helps to enhance the influence of the user's control perception on the system, improve user trust, and improve user satisfaction with the system. (02,19)
Mixed explanation	What	Mixed explanations present explanations in multiple styles. (14,31)
	How	• It is recommended to use a maximum of three or four explanation styles. (14) • It is recommended to combine visual explanations with textual explanations of different levels of complexity according to user requirements. (31)
	Why	• Mixed explanation, characterized by their comprehensiveness, can meet the requirements of different users and application domains. (31) • It helps to reduce understanding errors caused by differences in knowledge levels between users. (18,31) • It helps to improve the explainability and reduce the time to understand the explanation. (22,31)

3.5 Using the Design Cards

The Design Cards can be combined in various ways:

a. "Design Method", "Presentation Format", and "Presentation Mode" can be combined randomly. For example, choosing "Example-based Explanation" from "Design Method","Visual Explanation" from "Presentation Format" and "Static Explanation" from "Presentation Mode" results in a "static visual example-based explanation." Different combinations yield multiple design solutions.

b. "Design Principle" should guide designers to continuously consider aspects such as personalization, contextual explanations, and progressive disclosure based on user characteristics.

FRONT   BACK

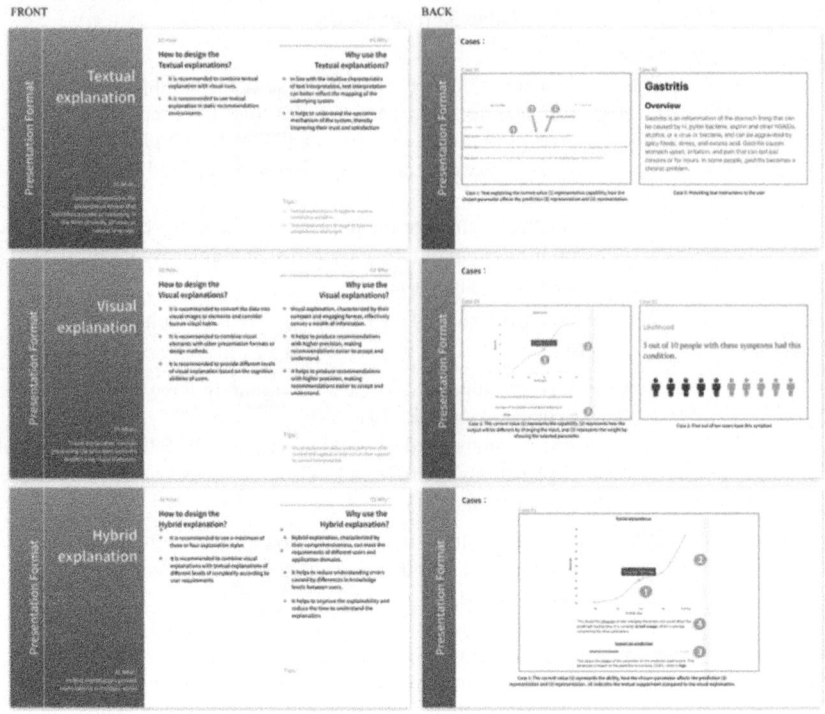

Fig. 3. "Presentation Format" cards display.

Table 6. Presentation Mode

Static explanation	What	Static explanation refers to explanations that do not change as a result of user feedback. (18,52,57)
	How	It is recommended to use in the early stages of system usage (e.g., explaining input and output data). (25)
	Why	• It helps to make sense of the available information • It helps to provide new information about the system. (25)
Interactive Explanation	What	Interactive explanation is driven by both human and machine, with the system providing different types of explanations for users according to the context. (18,52,57)

(continued)

Table 6. (*continued*)

	How	• It is recommended to provide information based on individual user characteristics (experience, background, needs, preferences, feedback, cognitive effort and process). (08,18) • Users are able to customize the explanations they receive to meet their needs. (01,04,08,09,18,46,50) 1) It is recommended to provide users with the ability to freely explore for follow-up questions and drill down. (04,09,18,50) 2) It is recommended to allow users to adjust or change specific parameters or configurators to generate different explanation instances. (46) 3) It is recommended to enable feedback schemes for users to monitor progress and enhance user intuition. (08) 4) It is recommended to allow users to adjust the information granularity and interaction to adjust the explanation. (08) 5) It is recommended that the user can control the process of explanation and the order of explanation content. (01,08,46) 6) It is recommended to provide hierarchical or iterative features that allows the follow-up of initial explanations. (18)
	Why	• Conforming to the interactive explanation is characterized by social, and the process of seeking explanations is interactive. (08,11,13,25,26) • Allowing exploration of explanations can help users build better mental models. (04,18) • Controllable interfaces are more appealing. (14) • It helps to increase the user's control perception of the system and improve satisfaction. (02,09,18,25,50)
Dialogue Explanation	What	Dialogue explanation is an interactive concept that involves the exchange of question and answer ideas between users and the system, much like what occurs in human conversation. (18,20,56)
	How	• It is recommended to lower the threshold of abilities required by users through natural dialogue and gradually build mental models. (18) • It is recommended that enhancing the design through anthropomorphic image helps to boosting user trust. (11) • It is recommended to enable users to explore information in the form of question-and-answer between users and the system. (18)

(*continued*)

Table 6. (*continued*)

	Why	• Conforming to the characteristics of dialogue explanations, design with flexibility, helps to meet the needs of different users. (11,44) • Conforming to the dialogue explanation is characterized by sociality, and it transmits knowledge through dialogue or interaction. (20) • It conforms to user (dialogue) habits and helps to improve system usability. (11, 20, 50)

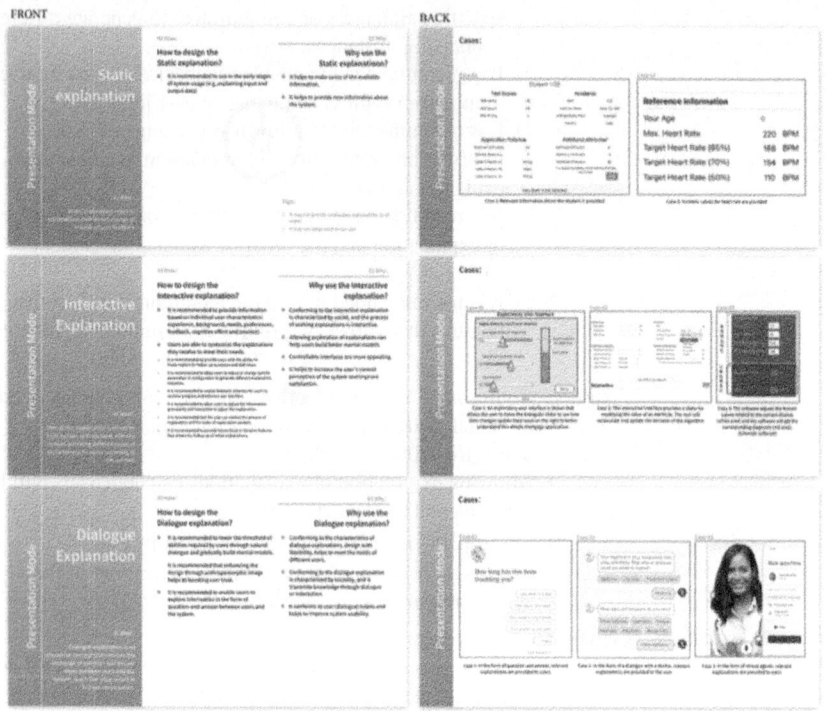

Fig. 4. "Presentation mode" cards display.

Table 7. Design principles

Contextualization Explanation	What	It refers to the process of understanding and interpreting a sentence or word according to its context, preceding and following texts and related knowledge in natural language processing. (04,06)
	How	• It is recommended to add domain-related context knowledge in the content. (04,06,47) • It is recommended to provide case related context information in the content. (04) • It is recommended to obtain contextual information from domain experts or extract it from datasets. (04)
	Why	• It helps to increase the transparency of the system and improve the user's understanding of the model's behavior. (04, 47) • Conformity contextual explanation is selective, and users tend to search for information in a given context rather than obtaining all causal chains. (11, 16, 26) • It helps to cultivate the ability of experts to identify similar cases. (47) • It helps to enhance the relevance and motivational aspect of the explanation. (47)
Personalized explanation	What	Personalized explanation is an explanation tailored for users, which includes user-driven personalized explanation and system-driven personalized explanation. (14,19,24)

	How	• It is recommended to provide user-driven personalized explanations. (03,04,11,14,19,23,24,46)
		  1) It is recommended that users choose whether to provide explanations or not. (14,24)
		  2) It is recommended that users can adjust the order, type, content and format of the explanation by themselves. (03,11,23,46)
		  3) It is recommended that users can control the amount of interface information by themselves. (03,04)
		• It is recommended that from the source, context information can be provided by domain experts or extracted from datasets. (01,03,04,08,09,10,11,14,16,19,23,24,25,29,31,46,54)
		  1) It is recommended that the proposal system customizes the explanation style, scope, format, level of detail, etc. according to the user goals, personal characteristics, level of professionalism, preferences and situation. (01,03,04,08,09,10,11,14,16,19,23,24,25,29,31,46,54)
		  2) It is recommended that the system combines and ranks explanations based on user goals, personal characteristics, degree of professionalism, preferences, and situations. (23)

(continued)

Table 7. (*continued*)

	Why	• It helps to reduce the user's perceived cognitive effort, thereby increasing the accessibility of the system. (23) • It helps users to weigh the validity and usability of explanations. (16) • It helps to meet the preferences and needs of different users and increases the satisfaction of users. (18,19,23,24) • It helps to trust the alignment goal and makes the interface output more suitable for the user's experience and reasoning process. (46)
Progressive Disclosure	What	Progressive disclosure refers to presenting explanatory information in layers based on user needs. (37,43)

	How	• It is recommended to consider (from a content perspective) when designing progressive disclosur. (01,03,07,12,13,18,19,24,37,43,46,50,55)
		  1) It is recommended to present information hierarchically from simple to complex and allow the user to follow up on the initial explanation. (01,03,18,19,37,43)
		  2) It is recommended to layer pages according to different information granularity. (03,12,55)
		  3) It is recommended to present in categories at an abstract level. (03,07,12,13,19,24,46,50)
		• It is recommended to design based on context and provided information (to better meet user needs) (19,43)
		• It is recommended to consider (from the user's point of view) the user's needs, preferences, cognitive level, background, etc. (03,13,14,19,21,22,24,37,43,18)

	Why	• It helps to avoid cognitive overload caused by information overload. (07,16,37,46) • Providing decisions at different levels of abstraction helps users to browse information efficiently. (46) • Consistent with users' preference for gradually increasing system transparency. (37) • Consistent with the characteristic that explanations have contingency and are provided only when needed. (37)

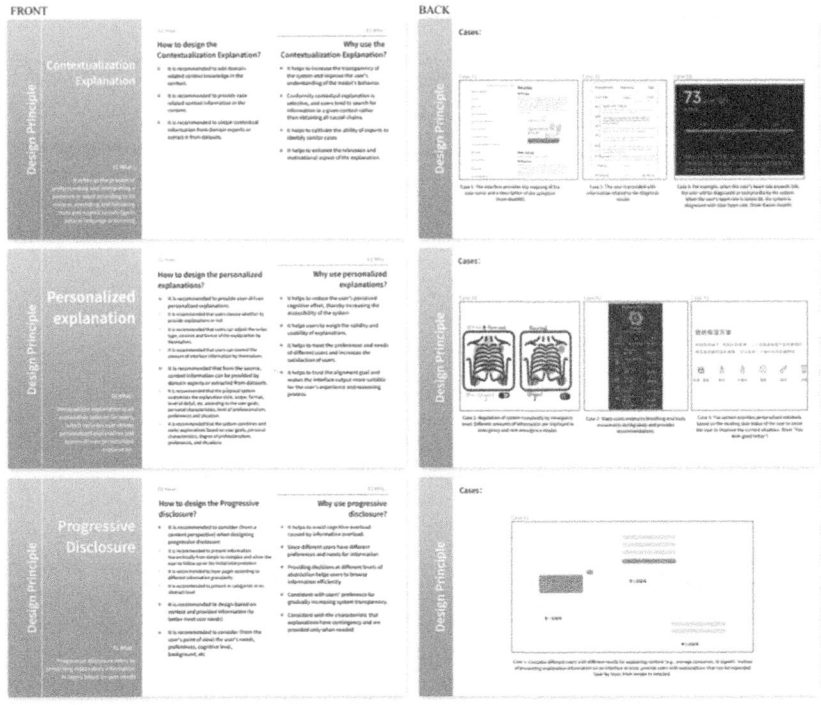

Fig. 5. "Presentation Principle" cards display.

Table 8. Design Method

Global Explanation	What	Global explanation is explanation that provides information relevant to the overall model. (04,06,13,16,22,23,27,28,31,34,42,46,48,49,51)
	How	• It is recommended to provide technical information related to the overall model, such as system logic, system training data, etc. (23) • It is recommended to provide performance metrics of the overall model, such as model confidence, etc. (16,18,23,28,46)
	Why	• It helps users understand the internal logic of the model. (04,23) • It helps make the overall decision-making process of the model transparent. (23) • It helps users fully understand the relevant information of the model. (04,19)

(continued)

Table 8. (*continued*)

Local Explanation	What	Describe the rationale behind a particular prediction. (04,13,27,31,34,48,49,51)
	How	• It is recommended to display decision-relevant data, such as historical or supplementary data. (07,23) • It is recommended to provide input options with adjustable parameters. (23) • It is recommended to provide what-if scenarios for users to simulate. (23) • It is recommended to provide the user with the influence of the features on the output instance results of the model. (23)
	Why	• It helps to reduce the cognitive effort of the user and increase the amount of perceived information and credibility. (06) • Consistent with the user's interest, understanding the rationale behind a particular prediction is fitting. (04)
Counterfactual Explanation	What	The counterfactual explanation quantifies the situation in which the AI changes its recommendations, i.e., how would the outcome change if a certain feature or event were changed. (10,16,17,25,31,38,46,52)
	How	• It is recommended to present the proposal as an interactive interface. (38) • It is recommended to consider domain and rule constraints before making hypothetical scenarios. (16) • It is recommended to capture user preferences. (38)
	Why	• It helps to trigger reasoning for human causal explanations and improve user understanding. (16,27,38) • It helps to mitigate the anchoring bias. (16) • Consistent with the characteristic of contrast, conformity interpretation involves informing users about the contrast with the predicted result. (25,26,45,52)
Feature-based Explanation	What	Describe the impact of a feature on the model as a whole (global features) or on the outcome of an instance of the model output (local features). (04,25)

(continued)

Table 8. (*continued*)

	How	• Provide global features, i.e. describe the impact of each feature on the model as a whole. (25)
		• Provide local features, that is, describe the impact of each feature on the outcome of the model output instanc:
		  1) It is recommended to supplement information from three levels: ML system, ML application domain, and external factors. (04)
		  2) It is recommended to show the importance of features or the positive
		or negative impact on the model. (07)
		  3) It is recommended to show an example of a feature value change that predicts the change. (04)

	Why	• Reasons for using local features:
		  1) It helps to improve the transparency of diagnosis, avoid cognitive bias, and understand the reasons related to decisions. (06,07,11)
		  2) It helps users make more efficient and accurate judgments. (27)
		  3) It helps to improve the user's trust in the diagnosis. (11)
		  4) It helps to make up for the lack of user domain information and improve the user experience. (04,07,11)

Example-based Explanation	What	• By providing representative cases, demonstrate to users the workings of the model and the rationality of its decisions. (11,16,17,25,27,28,33,46)
	How	• It is recommended to provide similar, same or different examples depending on the features. (04,11,16) • It is recommended to provide functionality for exploring cases. (06) • It is recommended to highlight similar or different examples. (07)
	Why	• It helps to promote users 'learning of knowledge and help users make better medical decisions. (11) • Consistent with the user's preference to explore relevant examples. (07,10,25) • Compared with no explanation, global explanation and local explanation, it has higher user perception and understandability. (16)

(*continued*)

Table 8. (*continued*)

Contrastive Explanation	What	• Explanations are contrastive, and people compare a certain phenomenon with similar ones. (10,11,20,36,40)
	How	• It is recommended to arrange the comparative content in a parallel manner. (47) • It is recommended to make comparisons across time or across patients. (03) • It is recommended to conduct group comparisons based on differences. (03)
	Why	• It helps to distinguish between typical features and features of diagnostic significance. (47) • Consistent with users' habit of comparative analysis, the method of comparison is easier for users to accept and learn. (07,11,26,47) • It helps users understand AI results and reduces cognitive load. (03,40) • It helps to draw the user's attention to the need to check for even significant abnormal events. (47)

4 Participatory Design Workshop for Human-Centered Medical XAI Systems

This section presents a case research of a participatory design workshop to explore the effectiveness of Design Cards and user-generated satisfaction with design healthcare AI design content. We employed a mixed-methods approach, combining qualitative and quantitative research.

4.1 Participants

Since medical applications usually target young people, we mainly selected young participants for this workshop. Therefore, the target participants were recruited in universities and asked participants to: 1) participants had used applications related to medical AI diagnosis; 2) Designer participants must have more than two years of design experience and be able to self-assess based on their design experience; 3) We made it clear before recruitment that we would conduct anonymous questionnaire survey and user interview with them in the process of the participatory workshop, and obtain information of the users during the sequence of sessions. During the workshop, we would take photos and audio recordings, and the participants agreed to obtain and use the above information. After receiving applications from potential participants who met the above criteria, we screened the participants. After the pre-review, a total of 40 participants were recruited. The participants of this workshop were divided into 8 groups, each group included 2 users and 3 designers, of which 4 groups were the control group, that is, no Design Cards were used. Group 4 was the experimental group, that is, the Design Cards was used. All groups can use the Needs Card to obtain user requirements. Null hypothesis

Fig. 6. "Design Method" cards display.

(H0) There is no difference between designers using the Design Cards and not using Design Cards when designing medical XAI; Alternative Hypothesis (H1): It is more effective for designers to use the Design Cards when designing medical XAI than not to apply the Design Cards.

4.2 Method

In past research, we created a Needs library that summarizes and formalizes all the explainable needs that end users may have in the AI domain [46], iterating it into Needs cards. In the design practice described in this research, we used Needs card in the early stage of finding requirements.

The workshop first introduced the theme workshop and toolkit titled Then we introduced the detailed process of the workshop. The workshop was divided into four stages:

Phase 1: Get the needs. We provided all the participants with the same medical AI application "Pocket Medical Treasure" on the market for experience. Users proposed their own explanation needs according to the experience of the APP users, and recorded the number of explanations needs. Then the Needs card is used. After using the Needs card, the user puts forward all the explanation needs he wants to know, and records the number of explanation requirements. The moderator counted and ranked the requirements of all users, and clustered out the 11 explanation needs with the largest number of proposals (Fig. 7).

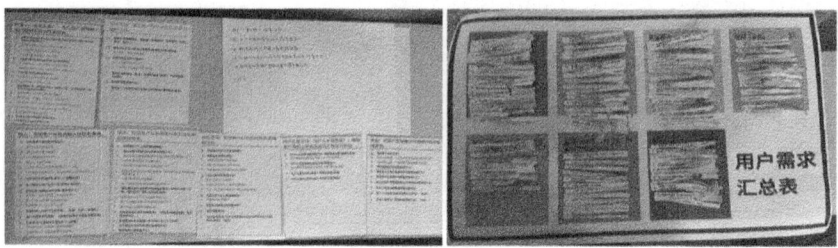

Fig. 7. Collects and summarizes user needs.

Phase 2: Design phase. Using these needs as design goals for each group, users work with designers to complete the design. The control group can not use the Design Cards during the design process, and the experimental group can use the Design Cards during the design process. In order to minimize the factors affected in the control experiment, we require that all groups should not use electronic products and social media to obtain resources during the design process, and communication between each group is prohibited (Fig. 8).

Phase 3: Delivery phase. After designing the low-fidelity prototype of each group, the scheme was presented, and all the schemes were scored by the user through the 5-point Hoffman explanation satisfaction scale (1 = disagree, 3 = neutral, 5 = agree). In order to ensure the fairness of the scores, each design is anonymous, and users in each group

Fig. 8. The participatory design processes.

cannot rate the designs in their own group. Hoffman's explanatory satisfaction scale contains 5 questions. The problems are as follows: (1) The explanation is satisfactory. (2) The explanation is useful for the target. (3) The explanation gave me confidence in the tool. (4) The explanation is clear. (5) The explanation is practical. After the scoring, a semi-structured interview was conducted with all participants (Fig. 9).

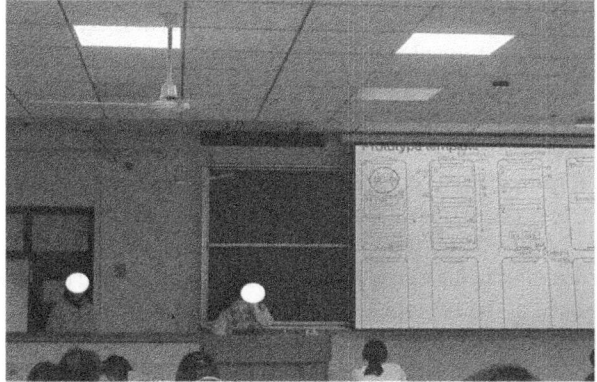

Fig. 9. Low-fidelity prototype presentation process.

Phase 4: Evaluation phase. In the fourth stage, three professional designers were invited to conduct two stages of analysis on the low-fidelity model samples of eight designs from four groups in the workshop, the eight low-fidelity design proposals were not annotated with any information from the participants in research. **Step 1:** After the workshop, 3 professional designers will receive including Needs cards and the Design Cards and 11 selected in Stage 1 as design target user requirements in order to fully understand the design background and card kit. **Step 2:** three designers discussed, explored and analyzed the Design Cards step by step. In terms of evaluation strategy, participants first judged whether each group of solutions solved the needs (completion of solving the requirements), how many needs were solved (number of solved needs), and how the needs were solved (number of explanation methods used) to evaluate.

5 Result

In this section, we show how participants evaluated the two card sets in different human-centered design activities. The first is a quantitative survey of program and card satisfaction evaluation and a qualitative analysis of organizing focus groups for discussion. Then a quantitative versus qualitative analysis after completing the evaluation program workshop, and finally we discuss informal observations of the moderator.

5.1 Design Cards Produce Better Design Results While Improving User Satisfaction

According to the statistics of users' scores on all design schemes, the score of the design scheme in the experimental groups (using the Design Cards) were significantly higher than that in the control groups (not using the Design Cards) (the full score was 5). The specific results are as follows: In the experimental group, the average score of satisfaction was 3.75, the average score of explanation clarity was 4.92, and the average score of practicality was 3.875, while the score of each dimension in the non-card group was lower than 3.5. This indicates that the feedback obtained in the user evaluation for the scheme of designing using the Design Cards were positive, thus verifying that the Design Cards are an effective tool to solve user needs and produce medical AI explainability, so H1 holds.

In the process of semi-structured interviews, users generally indicated that the reason why they gave lower scores to some control group design schemes was that these design schemes deviated from their needs, while the design scheme of the experimental group was more in line with user expectations. The analysis of the design scheme of the low-fidelity prototype of the control group by the professional designers in the fourth stage showed that the design scheme of the control group was more like an iterative design of the APP experienced at the beginning of the workshop, which failed to fully consider the explanation needs of the users. In contrast, the design scheme of the experimental group responded to the design goal.

In the interview, the designers in the experimental group said that "we have no knowledge about AI explainable design, and we can only rely on our own design experience in the design process." While the designers in the control group stated that "the Design Cards are very helpful for the design process, it systematically organized the design methods in medical AI explainable, and I learned a lot about AI explainable design in the process." "I think this is very suitable for the explainable design of medical AI. When designing the design goal, you can consider which design method or presentation method is more appropriate. According to the reference case provided at the back of the card, some new presentation methods will be developed."

5.2 Design Cards can Help Inspire Design Ideas and Optimize Design Solutions

Design cards can help designers produce better design solutions. The designers said that during the design process, they can make random combinations of Design Cards and discuss with users about better solutions. One designer pointed out that "It is conventional (based on experience), (the card) will give some new inspiration, and the design will be improved and optimized compared to the previous design." "You can look at the card and the problem, and then look at the case and come up with new ways of presenting it." This approach not only stimulates the designer's design inspiration, but also improves the user's satisfaction with the explanation.

In the workshop, the designers in the control group usually designed independently based on their own experience and knowledge, and then gave the design scheme to the user for evaluation, and iterated repeatedly according to the user's suggestions. After determining the needs of users, the designers in the experimental group arranged and combined with the users according to the dimensions of the Design Cards, and then combined with the existing cases provided by the Design Cards to produce a variety of design schemes, and discussed and agreed on the optimal design scheme with the users. This iterative process helps them continuously optimize the design and improve the quality of the design.

5.3 Design Cards can Facilitate User Involvement in the Design Process

Design Cards show obvious advantages in promoting users to participate in the design process. By providing a common communication language and design examples, they can effectively overcome communication barriers during the design process and help users to better integrate into the participatory design process.

The user participants in the experimental group expressed in the interview that during the participatory design process with the designer, they were confused about the field of XAI and the professional terminology used by the designer, which hindered the communication between them and the designer, and felt that they were difficult to integrate into the design process quickly. Designers played a leading role in the design. The users of the Design Card groups said that the cards were the communication medium in their design process, and the content in the cards enabled them to understand the relevant knowledge of the design field, especially the design examples in the Design Cards, which became the key to overcome their communication barriers. For example, one user said that "during the design process, I discussed with the designer the explanation of presenting progressive disclosure, which was more understandable to me, and then the designer adopted my suggestion, and the whole process was harmonious". Before participatory design begins, the designer collaborates with the user to create a vision of the product's environment, and in the process of co-participating in the design, there is continuous communication, feedback, and iteration.

6 Discussion

In addition, based on the process of this participatory design workshop, we make the following suggestions for reference:

1. It can decompose the design elements sorted out by theme analysis, and allow designers to arrange and combine freely to stimulate design inspiration. Through the decomposition and reorganization of design elements, designers can find new combinations between different elements, stimulate more creativity and inspiration, and avoid falling into conventional design thinking. This modular design tool can help designers quickly produce a large number of design solutions in a short workshop, significantly improving design efficiency and quality [86]. In addition, our research also found differences in the impact of the toolkit on idea generation at different design stages. In the early stages, designers are more inclined to explore a wide range of possibilities, while in the later stages, the toolkit helps them focus on more feasible and refined design solutions. This indicates that modular tools are not only effective in the idea generation phase, but also have an important role in the idea screening and optimization phase. Our research further highlights the multidimensional nature of design element decomposition, particularly in defining element function and meaning. It should be noted that the effect of the toolkit is heavily dependent on the experience and proficiency of the designer.

2. Participants can be provided with knowledge and tools for interdisciplinary **collaboration in a user-friendly way to promote interdisciplinary collaboration and communication.** In the participatory design process, the effectiveness of interdisciplinary participatory design is significantly related to the user's mastery of domain knowledge and the influence of collaborative tools [19]. Users can reduce communication barriers between disciplines through collaborative tools, improve collaboration efficiency and innovation of results [29]. We found that the toolkit had different effects when applied to teams with different disciplinary backgrounds. For user participants with no design knowledge, the toolkit helps them better understand and apply design thinking. For designers with design knowledge, the toolkit promotes their breakthrough and innovation in design solutions. This shows the adaptability and diversity of the toolkit in different disciplinary contexts.

7 Conclusion

For practitioners who want to carry out medical XAI design activities, there is a lack of systematic combing of design methods and related tools, and this research aims to bridge this gap. Design cards are not only a practical tool, but also promote the sharing and transmission of knowledge, providing an effective communication medium for designers and end users to promote their communication and collaboration. Through these Design Cards, designers and users can participate in the design and development of medical XAI systems together, thereby enhancing the human-centered explainability of the system. This research aims to provide tools and references for the development of medical artificial intelligence in improving transparency and explainability.

References

1. Abdul, A., et al.: Trends and trajectories for explainable, accountable and intelligible systems: an HCI research agenda. In: Proceedings of the 2018 CHI Conference on Human Factors in Computing Systems (2018)
2. Adadi, A., Berrada, M.: Peeking inside the black-box: a survey on explainable artificial intelligence (XAI). IEEE Access **6**, 52138–52160 (2018)
3. Amato, F., et al.: Artificial neural networks in medical diagnosis. J. Appl. Biomed. **11.2**, 47–58 (2013)
4. Amershi, S., et al.: Guidelines for human-AI interaction. In: Proceedings of the 2019 Chi Conference on Human Factors in Computing Systems (2019)
5. Tricco, A.C., Lillie, E., Zarin, W., et al.: PRISMA Extension for Scoping Reviews (PRISMA-ScR): checklist and explanation. Ann Intern Med, **169**, 467–473 (2018). [Epub 4 September 2018]. https://doi.org/10.7326/M18-0850
6. Apple: Human Interface Guidelines. https://developer.apple.com/design/human-interface-guidelines/. Accessed 30 Dec 2010
7. Arya, V., et al.: One explanation does not fit all: A toolkit and taxonomy of ai explainability techniques. arXiv preprint arXiv:1909.03012 (2019)
8. Arrieta, A.B., et al.: Explainable Artificial Intelligence (XAI): Concepts, taxonomies, opportunities and challenges toward responsible AI. Inform. Fusion **58**, 82–115 (2020)
9. Baldauf, M., Peter, F., Rainer, E.: Trust me, I'm a doctor–user perceptions of AI-driven apps for mobile health diagnosis. In: Proceedings of the 19th International Conference on Mobile and Ubiquitous Multimedia (2020)
10. Band, S.S., et al.: Application of explainable artificial intelligence in medical health: a systematic review of interpretability methods. Informatics in Medicine Unlocked 101286 (2023)
11. Barda, A.J., Horvat, C.M., Hochheiser, H.: A qualitative research framework for the design of user-centered displays of explanations for machine learning model predictions in healthcare. BMC Med. Inform. Decis. Mak. **20**, 1–16 (2020)
12. Barac, R., et al.: Scoping review of toolkits as a knowledge translation strategy in health. BMC Med. Inform. Dec. Mak. **14**, 1–9 (2014)
13. Bellucci, M., et al.: Towards a terminology for a fully contextualized XAI. Procedia Comput. Sci. **192**, 241–250 (2021)
14. Blaschke, T., et al.: REINVENT 2.0: an AI tool for de novo drug design. J. Chem. Inform. Model. **60.12**, 5918–5922 (2020)
15. Brewer, L.C., et al.: Promoting cardiovascular health and wellness among African-Americans: community participatory approach to design an innovative mobile-health intervention. PloS one **14.8**, e0218724 (2019)
16. Brand, G., et al.: Whose knowledge is of value? Co-designing healthcare education research with people with lived experience. Nurse Educ. Today **120**, 105616 (2023)
17. Bødker, S., Pekkola, S.: Introduction the debate section: a short review to the past and present of participatory design. Scand. J. Inf. Syst. **22**(1), 4 (2010)
18. Bove, C., et al.: Contextualization and exploration of local feature importance explanations to improve understanding and satisfaction of non-expert users. In: 27th International Conference on Intelligent User Interfaces (2022)
19. Brown, T.: Change by design: how design thinking creates new alternatives for business and society. Collins Business (2009)
20. Buschek, D., Eiband, M., Hussmann, H.: How to support users in understanding intelligent systems? an analysis and conceptual framework of user questions considering user mindsets, involvement, and knowledge outcomes. ACM Trans. Interact. Intell. Syst. **12**(4), 1–27 (2022)

21. Cabour, G., et al.: An explanation space to align user studies with the technical development of Explainable AI. AI Soc. **38.2**, 869–887 (2023)
22. Caruana, R., et al.: Intelligible models for healthcare: Predicting pneumonia risk and hospital 30-day readmission. In: Proceedings of the 21th ACM SIGKDD International Conference on Knowledge Discovery and Data Mining (2015)
23. Colonius, I., Sandra, B., Roberta, A.: Participatory design for challenging user groups: a case study. In: Proceedings of the 28th Annual European Conference on Cognitive Ergonomics (2010)
24. Chatti, M.A., et al.: Is more always better? The effects of personal characteristics and level of detail on the perception of explanations in a recommender system. In: Proceedings of the 30th ACM Conference on User Modeling, Adaptation and Personalization (2022)
25. Cheng, H.-F., et al.: Explaining decision-making algorithms through UI: Strategies to help non-expert stakeholders. In: Proceedings of the 2019 Chi Conference on Human Factors in Computing Systems (2019)
26. Chromik, M., Andreas, B.: Human-XAI interaction: a review and design principles for explanation user interfaces. In: Human-Computer Interaction–INTERACT 2021: 18th IFIP TC 13 International Conference, Bari, Italy, August 30–September 3, 2021, Proceedings, Part II 18. Springer International Publishing (2021)
27. Crupi, R., et al.: Counterfactual explanations as interventions in latent space. Data Min. Knowl. Discov. 1–37 (2022)
28. Deloitte AI. Deloitte Insights (2019). https://www2.deloitte.com/us/en/insights/deloitte-ins ights-magazine.html
29. Deng, Y., Antle, A.N., Neustaedter, C.: Tango cards: a card-based design tool for informing the design of tangible learning games. In: Proceedings of the 2014 Conference on Designing Interactive Systems (2014)
30. Donetto, S., Tsianakas, V., Robert, G.: Using Experience-based Co-design (EBCD) to improve the quality of healthcare: mapping where we are now and establishing future directions, pp. 5–7. King's College London, London (2014)
31. Eiband, M., et al. "Bringing transparency design into practice. In: 23rd International Conference on Intelligent User Interfaces (2018)
32. Gehrmann, S., et al.: Visual interaction with deep learning models through collaborative semantic inference. IEEE Trans. Visual. Comput. Graph. **26.1**, 884–894 (2019)
33. Ghajargar, M., et al.: Graspable AI: Physical forms as explanation modality for explainable AI. In: Proceedings of the Sixteenth International Conference on Tangible, Embedded, and Embodied Interaction (2022)
34. Gilpin, L.H., et al.: Explaining explanations: An overview of interpretability of machine learning. In: 2018 IEEE 5th International Conference on data science and advanced analytics (DSAA). IEEE (2018)
35. Gobbo, B., et al.: xai-primer. com—a visual ideation space of interactive explainers. In: CHI Conference on Human Factors in Computing Systems Extended Abstracts (2022)
36. Google PAIR. 2019. People + AI Guidebook. pair.withgoogle.com/guidebook
37. Greenhalgh, T., et al.: Achieving research impact through co-creation in community-based health services: literature review and case study. Milbank Quart. **94.2**, 392–429 (2016)
38. Greenhalgh, T., et al.: Frameworks for supporting patient and public involvement in research: systematic review and co-design pilot. Health Expect. **22.4**, 785–801 (2019)
39. Guesmi, M., et al.: On-demand personalized explanation for transparent recommendation. In: Adjunct Proceedings of the 29th ACM Conference on User Modeling, Adaptation and Personalization (2021)
40. Guidotti, R., et al.: A survey of methods for explaining black box models. ACM Comput. Surv. **51.5**, 1–42 (2018)

41. Guo, L., et al.: Building trust in interactive machine learning via user contributed interpretable rules. In: 27th International Conference on Intelligent User Interfaces (2022)
42. Gustavsson, S.M.K., Andersson, T.: Patient involvement 2.0: experience-based co-design supported by action research. Action Res. **17.4**, 469–491 (2019)
43. Hagen, P., et al.: Participatory design of evidence-based online youth mental health promotion, intervention and treatment (2012)
44. Herm, L.-V., et al.: A nascent design theory for explainable intelligent systems. Electron. Mark. **32.4**, 2185–2205 (2022)
45. Hernandez-Bocanegra, D.C., Ziegler, J.: Conversational review-based explanations for recommender systems: exploring users' query behavior. In: Proceedings of the 3rd Conference on Conversational User Interfaces (2021)
46. He, X., et al.: What are the users' needs? Design of a user-centered explainable artificial intelligence diagnostic system. Int. J. Hum. Comput. Interact. **39.7**, 1519–1542 (2023)
47. Hohman, F., et al.: Gamut: a design probe to understand how data scientists understand machine learning models. In: Proceedings of the 2019 CHI Conference on Human Factors in Computing Systems (2019)
48. Holzinger, A., et al.: Causability and explainability of artificial intelligence in medicine. Wiley Interdiscipl. Rev. Data Min. Knowl. Discov. **9.4**, e1312 (2019)
49. Hoofnagle, C.J., Van Der Sloot, B., Borgesius, F.Z.: The European Union general data protection regulation: what it is and what it means. Inform. Commun. Technol. Law **28.1**, 65–98 (2019)
50. Johnson, K.W., et al.: Artificial intelligence in cardiology. J. Am. College Cardiol. **71.23**, 2668–2679 (2018)
51. Josh, L.: Human-centered AI Cheat-sheet (2019). https://uxdesign.cc/human-centered-ai-cheat-sheet-1da130ba1bab
52. Kensing, F., Blomberg, J.: Participatory design: issues and concerns. Comput. Support. Cooperat. Work **7**, 167–185 (1998)
53. Kim, C., et al.: Learn, generate, rank, explain: a case study of visual explanation by generative machine learning. ACM Trans. Interact. Intell. Syst. **11.3–4**, 1–34 (2021)
54. Kim, M.-Y., et al.: A multi-component framework for the analysis and design of explainable artificial intelligence. Mach. Learn. Knowl. Extract. **3.4**, 900–921 (2021)
55. Kvan, T.: Collaborative design: what is it? Autom. Constr. **9**(4), 409–415 (2000)
56. Kouki, P., et al.: Generating and understanding personalized explanations in hybrid recommender systems. ACM Trans. Interact. Intell. Syst. **10.4**, 1–40 (2020)
57. Leask, C.F., et al.: Framework, principles and recommendations for utilising participatory methodologies in the co-creation and evaluation of public health interventions. Res. Involve. Engage. **5**, 1–16 (2019)
58. Lei, L., Li, J., Li, W.: Assessing the role of artificial intelligence in the mental healthcare of teachers and students. Soft Comput. 1–11 (2023)
59. Liao, Q.V., Gruen, D., Miller, S.: Questioning the AI: informing design practices for explainable AI user experiences. In: Proceedings of the 2020 CHI Conference on Human Factors in Computing Systems (2020)
60. Lipton, Z.C.: The mythos of model interpretability: in machine learning, the concept of interpretability is both important and slippery. Queue **16**(3), 31–57 (2018)
61. Liu, J., et al.: Increasing user trust in optimisation through feedback and interaction. ACM Trans. Comput.-Hum. Interact. **29.5**, 1–34 (2023)
62. Lopes, P., et al.: XAI systems evaluation: A review of human and computer-centred methods. Appl. Sci. **12.19**, 9423 (2022)
63. Markus, A.F., Kors, J.A., Rijnbeek, P.R.: The role of explainability in creating trustworthy artificial intelligence for health care: a comprehensive survey of the terminology, design choices, and evaluation strategies. J. Biomed. Inform. **113**, 103655 (2021)

64. Meske, C., Bunde, E.: Design principles for user interfaces in AI-Based decision support systems: The case of explainable hate speech detection. Inf. Syst. Front. **25**(2), 743–773 (2023)
65. Miller, T.: Explanation in artificial intelligence: insights from the social sciences. Artif. Intell. **267**, 1–38 (2019)
66. Mohseni, S., Zarei, N., Ragan, E.D.: A multidisciplinary survey and framework for design and evaluation of explainable AI systems. ACM Trans. Interact. Intell. Syst. **11**(3–4), 1–45 (2021)
67. Morse, J.M., et al.: Verification strategies for establishing reliability and validity in qualitative research. Int. J. Qual. Meth. **1.2**, 13–22 (2002)
68. Mucha, H., et al.: Interfaces for explanations in human-AI interaction: proposing a design evaluation approach. In: Extended Abstracts of the 2021 CHI Conference on Human Factors in Computing Systems (2021)
69. Muller, M.J., Kuhn, S.: Participatory design. Commun. ACM **36**(6), 24–28 (1993)
70. Müller, J., et al.: A visual approach to explainable computerized clinical decision support. Comput. Graph. **91**, 1–11 (2020)
71. Naiseh, M., et al.: Explainable recommendation: when design meets trust calibration. World Wide Web **24.5**, 1857–1884 (2021)
72. Naiseh, M., et al.: How the different explanation classes impact trust calibration: the case of clinical decision support systems. Int. J. Hum. Comput. Stud. **169**, 102941 (2023)
73. Nakao, Y., et al.: Toward involving end-users in interactive human-in-the-loop AI fairness. ACM Trans. Interact. Intell. Syst. **12.3**, 1–30 (2022)
74. Nazar, M., et al.: A systematic review of human–computer interaction and explainable artificial intelligence in healthcare with artificial intelligence techniques. IEEE Access **9**, 153316–153348 (2021)
75. Neerincx, M.A., et al.: Using perceptual and cognitive explanations for enhanced human-agent team performance. In: Harris, D. (eds.) Engineering Psychology and Cognitive Ergonomics. EPCE 2018. LNCS, vol. 10906. Springer, Cham (2018). https://doi.org/10.1007/978-3-319-91122-9_18
76. Partogi, M., et al.: Sociotechnical intervention for improved delivery of preventive cardiovascular care to rural communities: participatory design approach. J. Med. Internet Res. **24.8**, e27333 (2022)
77. Pollack, A.H., et al.: PD-atricians: leveraging physicians and participatory design to develop novel clinical information tools. In: AMIA Annual Symposium Proceedings, vol. 2016. American Medical Informatics Association (2016)
78. Rajkomar, A., Dean, J., Kohane, I.: Machine learning in medicine. N. Engl. J. Med. **380**(14), 1347–1358 (2019)
79. Ribeiro, M.T., Sameer, S., Guestrin, C.: Why should i trust you? Explaining the predictions of any classifier. In: Proceedings of the 22nd ACM SIGKDD International Conference on Knowledge Discovery and Data Mining (2016)
80. Robert, G., et al.: Patients and staff as codesigners of healthcare services. Bmj 350 (2015)
81. Roy, R., Warren, J.P.: Card-based design tools: a review and analysis of 155 card decks for designers and designing. Des. Stud. **63**, 125–154 (2019)
82. Rudin, C.: Stop explaining black box machine learning models for high stakes decisions and use interpretable models instead. Nat. Mach. Intell. **1**(5), 206–215 (2019)
83. Sanders, E.B.-N., Stappers, P.J.: Co-creation and the new landscapes of design. Co-design **4.1**, 5–18 (2008)
84. Schoonderwoerd, T.A.J., et al.: Human-centered XAI: developing design patterns for explanations of clinical decision support systems. Int. J. Hum.-Comput. Stud. **154**, 102684 (2021)

85. Sekiguchi, K., Hori, K.: Organic and dynamic tool for use with knowledge base of AI ethics for promoting engineers' practice of ethical AI design. AI Soc. **35**(1), 51–71 (2020)
86. Shneiderman, B.: Creativity support tools: accelerating discovery and innovation. Commun. ACM **50**(12), 20–32 (2007)
87. Shneiderman, B.: Bridging the gap between ethics and practice: guidelines for reliable, safe, and trustworthy human-centered AI systems. ACM Trans. Interact. Intell. Syst. **10**(4), 1–31 (2020)
88. Shneiderman, B.: Human-centered artificial intelligence: reliable, safe & trustworthy. Int. J. Hum.-Comput. Interact. **36**(6), 495–504 (2020)
89. Simkute, A., et al.: XAI for learning: Narrowing down the digital divide between "new" and "old" experts. In: Adjunct Proceedings of the 2022 Nordic Human-Computer Interaction Conference (2022)
90. Sokol, K., Flach, P.: Explainability fact sheets: a framework for systematic assessment of explainable approaches. In: Proceedings of the 2020 Conference on Fairness, Accountability, and Transparency (2020)
91. Song, D., et al.: A new xAI framework with feature explainability for tumors decision-making in Ultrasound data: comparing with Grad-CAM. Comput. Meth. Programs Biomed. **235**, 107527 (2023)
92. Speith, T.: A review of taxonomies of explainable artificial intelligence (XAI) methods. In: Proceedings of the 2022 ACM Conference on Fairness, Accountability, and Transparency (2022)
93. Springer, A., Whittaker, S.: Progressive disclosure: empirically motivated approaches to designing effective transparency. In: Proceedings of the 24th International Conference on Intelligent User Interfaces (2019)
94. Springer, A., Whittaker, S.: Progressive disclosure: when, why, and how do users want algorithmic transparency information? ACM Trans. Interact. Intell. Syst. **10**(4), 1–32 (2020)
95. Sun, L., et al.: Capturing the trends, applications, issues, and potential strategies of designing transparent AI agents. In: Extended Abstracts of the 2021 CHI Conference on Human Factors in Computing Systems (2021)
96. Sun, J., et al.: Investigating explainability of generative AI for code through scenario-based design. In: 27th International Conference on Intelligent User Interfaces (2022)
97. Sun, T.Q., Medaglia, R.: Mapping the challenges of Artificial Intelligence in the public sector: Evidence from public healthcare. Govern. Inform. Quart. **36.2**, 368–383 (2019)
98. Szymanski, M., Millecamp, M., Verbert, K.: Visual, textual or hybrid: the effect of user expertise on different explanations. In: 26th International Conference on Intelligent User Interfaces (2021)
99. Tsai, C.-H., et al.: Exploring and promoting diagnostic transparency and explainability in online symptom checkers. In: Proceedings of the 2021 CHI Conference on Human Factors in Computing Systems (2021)
100. Tsianakas, V., et al.: Implementing patient-centred cancer care: using experience-based co-design to improve patient experience in breast and lung cancer services. Support. Care Cancer **20**, 2639–2647 (2012)
101. Van der Velden, M., Mörtberg, C.: Participatory design and design for values. Handbook of Ethics, Values, and Technological Design: Sources, Theory, Values and Application Domains, pp. 41–66 (2015)
102. van der Waa, J., et al.: Evaluating XAI: a comparison of rule-based and example-based explanations. Artific. Intell. **291**, 103404 (2021)
103. Verma, S., Dickerson, J., Hines, K.: Counterfactual explanations for machine learning: a review. arXiv preprint arXiv:2010.105962 (2020)
104. Vilone, G., Longo, L.: Classification of explainable artificial intelligence methods through their output formats. Mach. Learn. Knowl. Extract. **3**(3), 615–661 (2021)

105. Wadley, G., et al.: Participatory design of an online therapy for youth mental health. In: Proceedings of the 25th Australian Computer-Human Interaction Conference: Augmentation, Application, Innovation, Collaboration (2013)
106. Wang, D., et al.: Designing theory-driven user-centric explainable AI. In: Proceedings of the 2019 CHI Conference on Human Factors in Computing Systems (2019)
107. Wang, Q., et al.: Extending the nested model for user-centric XAI: a design study on GNN-based drug repurposing. IEEE Trans. Visual. Comput. Graph. **29.1**, 1266–1276 (2022)
108. Wang, X., Yin, M.: Are explanations helpful? a comparative study of the effects of explanations in AI-assisted decision-making. In: 26th International Conference on Intelligent User Interfaces (2021)
109. Weitz, K., et al.: "Let me explain!": exploring the potential of virtual agents in explainable AI interaction design. J. Multimodal User Interf. **15.2**, 87–98 (2021)
110. Wiens, J., et al.: Do no harm: a roadmap for responsible machine learning for health care. Nat. Med. **25.9**, 1337–1340 (2019)
111. Xie, Y., et al.: CheXplain: enabling physicians to explore and understand data-driven, AI-enabled medical imaging analysis. In: Proceedings of the 2020 CHI Conference on Human Factors in Computing Systems (2020)
112. Yang, F., et al.: How do visual explanations foster end users' appropriate trust in machine learning? In: Proceedings of the 25th International Conference on Intelligent User Interfaces (2020)
113. Yang, Q.: Machine learning as a UX design material: how can we imagine beyond automation, recommenders, and reminders? AAAI Spring Symp. **1**(2), 1 (2018)
114. Yildirim, N., et al.: How experienced designers of enterprise applications engage AI as a design material. In: Proceedings of the 2022 CHI Conference on Human Factors in Computing Systems (2022)
115. Zhang, A., et al.: Stakeholder-centered AI design: co-designing worker tools with gig workers through data probes. In: Proceedings of the 2023 CHI Conference on Human Factors in Computing Systems (2023)

AI for Decision Making and Sentiment Analysis

SenticNet 8: Fusing Emotion AI and Commonsense AI for Interpretable, Trustworthy, and Explainable Affective Computing

Erik Cambria[1]([✉])[iD], Xulang Zhang[1][iD], Rui Mao[1][iD], Melvin Chen[1][iD], and Kenneth Kwok[2][iD]

[1] College of Computing and Data Science, Nanyang Technological University, Singapore, Singapore
{cambria,rui.mao,xulang.zhang,melvinchen}@ntu.edu.sg
[2] Institute of High Performance Computing, Agency for Science, Technology and Research (A*STAR), Singapore, Singapore
kenkwok@ihpc.a-star.edu.sg

Abstract. ChatGPT has stunned the world with its ability to generate detailed, original, and accurate responses to prompts. While it unlocked solutions to problems that were previously considered unsolvable, however, it also introduced new ones. One of such problems is the phenomenon known as hallucination, the generation of content that is nonsensical or unfaithful to the provided source content. In this work, we propose SenticNet 8, a neurosymbolic AI framework leveraging an ensemble of commonsense knowledge representation and hierarchical attention networks, which aims to mitigate some of these issues in the context of affective computing. In particular, we focus on the tasks of sentiment analysis, personality prediction, and suicidal ideation detection. Results show that SenticNet 8 presents superior accuracy with respect to all four baselines, namely: bag-of-words, word2vec, RoBERTa, and ChatGPT. Unlike these baselines, moreover, SenticNet 8 is also fully interpretable, trustworthy, and explainable.

Keywords: Explainable AI · Affective Computing · Sentiment Analysis

1 Introduction

Generative pretrained transformer (GPT) models enabled humanity to finally design an algorithm able to pass the famous machine intelligence test devised by Alan Turing some seventy years ago [6]. With approximately 1 trillion parameters, ChatGPT has revolutionized the world of natural language processing (NLP) thanks to the high accuracy it can obtain on several information retrieval tasks [38,43]. However, it still presents several issues that limit its widespread adoption, especially in contexts such as medical, ethical, or fail-safe applications [2,48].

© The Author(s), under exclusive license to Springer Nature Switzerland AG 2024
H. Degen and S. Ntoa (Eds.): HCII 2024, LNCS 15382, pp. 197–216, 2024.
https://doi.org/10.1007/978-3-031-76827-9_11

Some researchers defined large language models (LLMs) like ChatGPT as 'stochastic parrots' [4], i.e., systems that haphazardly stitch together sequences of linguistic forms it has observed in its vast training data, according to probabilistic information about how they combine, but without any reference to meaning. LLMs, in fact, are trained (mostly in a self-supervised manner) on 'broad' data, which leads to homogenization (i.e., using same model for fine-tuning and training for different downstream tasks) and emergence (i.e., LLMs can solve tasks they were not originally trained upon). This poses several risks [10], including 'hallucination' [28], which can lead to several ChatGPT failures, including reasoning, factual errors, math, coding, and bias [11]. ChatGPT, moreover, is not interpretable (because we do not get to see its true inner workings, e.g., how cause and effect are associated); it is not trustworthy (because it is only as good as its training data and it often lacks the commonsense knowledge required for disambiguation); and it is not explainable (because we do not get any explanation about the decision-making processes that produce its final results).

In this work, we aim to mitigate these issues in the context of affective computing. We propose SenticNet 8, a neurosymbolic AI framework leveraging an ensemble of commonsense knowledge representation and hierarchical attention networks, which automatically extracts important affective information (such as sentiment polarity, emotion labels, opinion targets, emotion-cause pairs, polarity intensity, personality traits, etc.) from both formal and informal natural language text with state-of-the-art accuracy. This is enabled by an approach to NLP that is both top-down and bottom-up: top-down for the fact that SenticNet 8 leverages symbolic models (namely, conceptual dependency theory and a semantic network of affective commonsense knowledge) to encode meaning; bottom-up because we use sub-symbolic paradigms (namely, hierarchical attention networks and LLMs) to infer syntactic patterns from data. We compare SenticNet 8 with ChatGPT, a robust language model (RoBERTa), pretrained embeddings (word2vec), and the bag-of-words (BoW) model. Results show that SenticNet 8 generally presents superior accuracy with respect to all four models. Unlike these baselines, moreover, SenticNet 8 is also interpretable, trustworthy, and explainable. The remainder of the paper is organized as follows: Sect. 2 lists recent related works; Sect. 3 describes the proposed framework; Sect. 4 presents experimental results; Sect. 5 discusses insights gained; finally, Sect. 6 provides concluding remarks.

2   Related Work

Since Ancient Greece, it has been widely acknowledged that humans seek explanations in an attempt to understand the world [33]. This ubiquitous search for answers and explanations is inherent to human nature and fundamental to integrate technology into everyday lives. As technology advances and human-computer interaction (HCI) becomes more prevalent, in fact, the need for understanding and explaining the decision-making processes of affective computing models has become paramount [18,32].

Various studies have focused on developing machine learning models for emotion recognition from different modalities, such as facial expressions, speech, text, and physiological signals [22]. Traditional approaches include feature engineering and classical machine learning techniques. More recently, deep learning methods, especially transformers, have demonstrated remarkable performance in this domain [56]. However, the black-box nature of deep learning models has raised concerns about their interpretability, motivating researchers to delve into explainable machine learning techniques. Explainable artificial intelligence (XAI) offers methodologies to 'open the black box' of machine learning models and make their decision-making processes understandable to humans [7,12,14,25]. Interpretability techniques, such as saliency maps, feature visualization, and activation maximization, have been applied to emotion recognition systems to highlight the regions in input data that are influential in driving the model's predictions [20,34].

Explainable affective computing represents an ongoing and significant area of research that seeks to bridge the gap between the powerful predictive capabilities of AI systems and the need for human-understandable decision-making processes [3,24,29]. By drawing from various fields, including XAI, HCI, and ethics, researchers aim to create emotionally intelligent systems that are transparent, trustworthy, and capable of enhancing human-computer interfaces in a more natural and empathetic manner [21,37]. Many recent works are using neurosymbolic AI to leverage both the robust pattern recognition capabilities of neural networks and the structured reasoning strengths of symbolic AI [52–54,57,58,60]. As the field continues to evolve, it is expected that advances in explainability will lead to more responsible and ethically-aware affective computing applications in various domains, including healthcare, education, and human-robot interaction [15,30].

3   Proposed Framework

SenticNet 8 aims to mitigate one important issue with current AI models: the symbol grounding problem. Solving this problem is crucial for achieving XAI because it addresses the foundational challenge of connecting abstract symbols or representations to concrete real-world entities and experiences. By establishing a clear and meaningful connection between symbols and their referents, XAI systems can provide more understandable and interpretable explanations for their actions and decisions. This is done through a three-step normalization process (Fig. 1). Firstly, a "syntactic normalization" step leverages a graph-based approach [16] to replace inflections like `bought`, `purchasing`, and `pays for` with their lemmas, e.g., `buy`, `purchase`, and `pay_for`, respectively. Secondly, "semantic normalization" (explained in detail later) leverages conceptual dependency theory [27,41,46,47,51] and a commonsense knowledge graph [49] to replace resulting lemmas like `purchase` and `pay_for`, with their corresponding conceptual primitive, e.g., $BUY(x)$, where x is the direct object indicating the thing acted upon by the primitive.

Finally, the "pragmatic normalization" step draws lessons from the field of semiotics to ground the meaning of resulting conceptual primitives into language-agnostic representations that can better explain the current state of affairs of

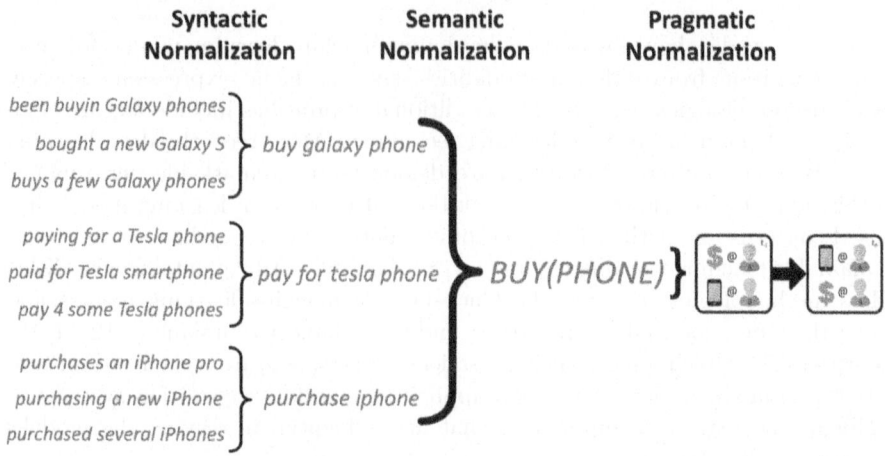

Fig. 1. SenticNet's three-step normalization process

an operating environment. For example, the word buy is nothing more than a three-letter word with some statistical properties for a LLM but in SenticNet $BUY(x)$ is represented as a double transfer of ownership where, at time t_{-1}, agent A owns \$ (a certain amount of money) and agent B owns x while, at time t_0, agent A owns x and agent B owns \$. This sort of universal symbolism is useful for several reasons. Firstly, it represents an interesting attempt to recreate language-agnostic representations to refer to concepts in a universal way, the same way as mathematical symbols or musical notes allow anyone to perform mathematical operations or read and write music, no matter what language they speak. Secondly, it uses more grounded representations that, unlike words or word embeddings, can better replicate or visualize the current state of affairs of an operating environment on the fly, as narratives unfold (this is currently done in terms of 2D symbols but, in the future, it could be implemented by generating 3D representations in a virtual world).

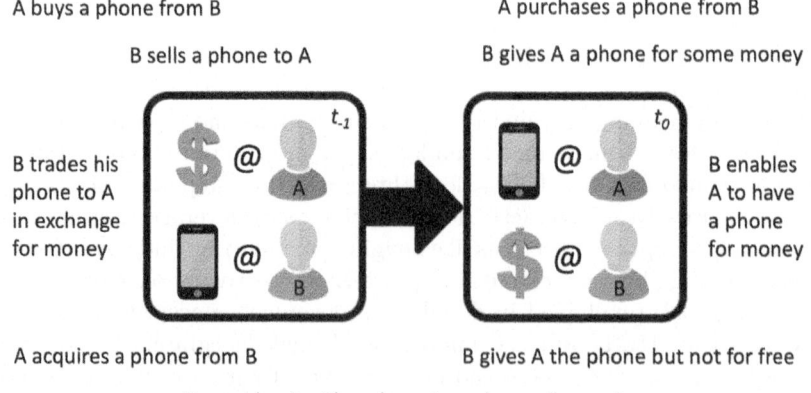

Fig. 2. A universal symbolism can aid in generalization and disambiguation tasks.

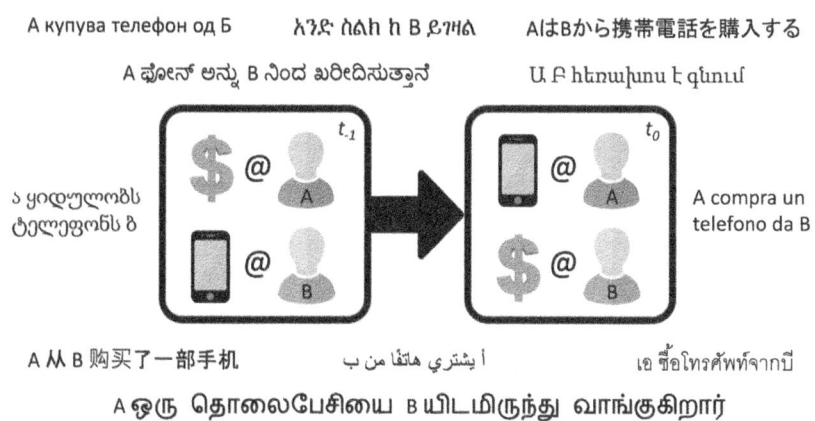

А купува телефон од Б   ኣንድ ስልh h B ይገዛል   AはBから携帯電話を購入する

A ಫೋನ್ ಅನ್ನು B ನಿಂದ ಖರೀದಿಸುತ್ತಾನೆ   U. Բ հեռախոս է գնում

ა ყიდულობს ტელეფონს ბ   A compra un telefono da B

A 从 B 购买了一部手机   أ يشتري هاتفا من ب   เอ ซื้อโทรศัพท์จากบี

A ஒரு தொலைபேசியை B யிடமிருந்து வாங்குகிறார்

Fig. 3. A universal symbolism can aid in machine translation and multimodal tasks.

Additionally, this symbolism can help handle both richness and ambiguity of natural language by having a unique simplified representation for the potentially infinite ways one can express the same concept in natural language (Fig. 2). Similarly, it can aid machine translation efforts by having a common or shared representation for the same concept, which is then referred to by different languages using their own encodings, e.g., sequence of letters versus sequence of characters, left to right versus right to left, text versus speech, etc. (Fig. 3). Lastly, an important novelty introduced by this symbolism is the use of the time dimension for knowledge representation, which is mostly absent from past frameworks but which is very important to better model cause and effect [59], especially in the context of affective computing. Although most emotions only take place in the present (t_0), in fact, many also involve the past (t_{-1}), e.g., regret, nostalgia, remorse, and resignation. Some other involve the future (t_{+1}), e.g., anticipation, hope, anxiety, and relief. Finally, there are also emotions like gratitude, which can span across past (appreciation for past favors), present (current kindnesses), and future (hopeful expectations for future support or kindness).

Another key novelty introduced by this paper is the design of the second step in the above-mentioned normalization process, i.e., the semantic normalization component (Fig. 4). Such component comprises of two main modules, namely polarity detection and lexical substitution (explained later). Given an input sentence $w = (w_1, w_2, \ldots, w_L)$, we first aim to identify the target word t that should be replaced by a primitive for the downstream prediction from w. We extract K primitives from SenticNet 7 [13] as candidates $c = (c_1, \ldots, c_K)$, forming the input (s) as

$$s = <s>, w_1, w_2, \ldots, t, \ldots, w_L, </s>,$$
$$c_1, </s>, c_2, </s>, \ldots, c_K, </s>. \tag{1}$$

$<s>$ and $</s>$ are special tokens that were defined by the employed pretrained language model. The lexical substitution module identifies the best candidate from c as the substitute $\hat{c}$ which retains the original meaning of t in the context by using contrast learning.

Thus, $\hat{c}$ is the symbolic representation of t in context w. Then, the substitute input $w^f = (w_1, \ldots, \hat{c}, \ldots, w_L)$ is fed into a neural network classifier to predict a sentiment label. The objective is that the substitute input w^f increases the probability of correct sentiment prediction. First, through steps (1) and (2) in Fig. 4, the original input is fed into the encoder and the interpretable attention module to obtain the top I tokens with the highest attention weights, which contribute the most to sentiment prediction. In step (3), the sense diversity of each token is computed as the average distance of the token's hidden state to those of its substitution candidates, i.e., the most relevant primitive. Then, through step (4), the top J tokens that are most likely to be replaced by a primitive are selected as targets, because these target tokens may be associated to different primitives in different contexts.

Subsequently, the pre-trained lexical substitution module provides the best substitution to replace each target token, as shown in steps (5) and (6)a. The new input sentence is passed onto the polarity detection module for final prediction through steps (7)a and (8)a, which is used for the sentiment module backpropagation in step (9)a. In order to fine-tune the lexical substitution module and, hence, provide better primitive substitutions that improve the accuracy of sentiment analysis, we implement a dynamic rewarding mechanism (explained later). As shown in steps (5) and (6)b, for each target word, the top N candidates are selected. Each of them is seen as a substitute candidate to calculate the probability of correct sentiment prediction after the replacement in steps (7)b and (8)b. Then, each probability is used to dynamically compute the loss weight when the corresponding primitive candidate is learned by the lexical substitution module as a ground truth as shown in (9)b and (10)b.

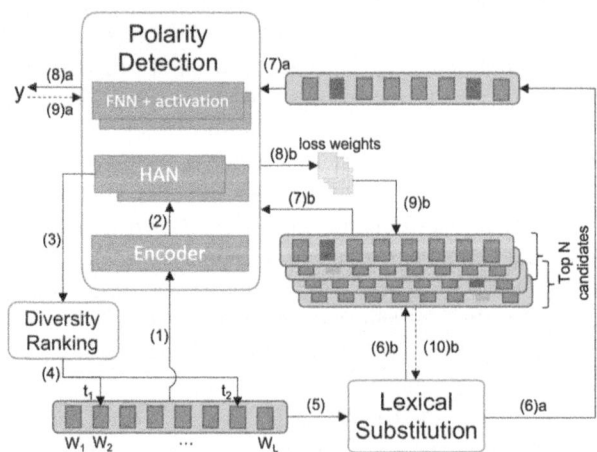

Fig. 4. Semantic normalization component. Dotted lines represent backpropagation. Green blocks indicate the original word being replaced by a word provided by the lexical substitution module. The darker the green, the higher probability it is assigned to by the model. (Color figure online)

If the replacement by a candidate leads to a higher chance of predicting the right sentiment, the candidate is more likely given a higher rank assigned by the lexical substitution module. Otherwise, the module would be less likely to select the candidate as the best replacement. The detailed training process can be seen in Algorithm 1.

Algorithm 1: Semantic normalization.

1 Initialize polarity detection module as Φ, pre-trained lexical substitution module as Ψ;

2 Initialize hyperparameters β, I,J, N;

3 **while** *not done* **do**

4   Sample a sentence $w = w_1, w_2, \ldots, w_L$;

5   **for** *l=1:L* **do**

6   Compute the attention weight a_l of token w_l;

7   **end**

8      $w^{att} \leftarrow$ Top I of w ordered by attention weights $a = a_1, a_2, \ldots, a_L$;

9   **for** *i=1:I* **do**

10          $c \leftarrow$ all possible primitive candidates with the same part-of-speech type as w_i^{att} from SenticNet 7;

11   Compute the average Eulidean distance d_i between the hidden states of w_i^{att} and c, produced by the encoder in Φ;

12   **end**

13      $t = (t_1, t_2, \ldots, t_J) \leftarrow$ Top J of w^{att} ordered by $d = d_1, d_2, \ldots, d_I$;

14      $w^f \leftarrow w$;

15   **for** *j=1:J* **do**

16   Input t_j into Ψ to produce top N candidates $\hat{c} = (\hat{c}_1, \ldots, \hat{c}_N)$, ordered by probability;

17   Replace t_j in w^f with $\hat{c}_1$;

18          $s \leftarrow (<s>, w_1, \ldots, t_i, \ldots, w_L, </s>,$

19          $\hat{c}_1, </s>, \ldots, \hat{c}_N, </s>)$;

20   **for** *n=1:N* **do**

21              $w^s \leftarrow$ Replace t_j in w with $\hat{c}_n$;

22   Input w^s into Φ to obtain the probability of correct sentiment prediction $P(\hat{y} = \tilde{y})$;

23              $\theta_{j,n} \leftarrow \beta P(\hat{y} = \tilde{y})^2$;

24   Compute $\mathcal{L}_{j,n}^{(ls)}$ by feeding s with $\hat{c}_n$ labeled as true substitute into Ψ ;

25              $\mathcal{L}_{j,n}^{(ls)} \leftarrow \theta_{j,n} \mathcal{L}_{j,n}^{(ls)}$;

26   **end**

27   **end**

28      $\mathcal{L}^{(ls)} \leftarrow \mathcal{L}_{1,1}^{(ls)} + \cdots + \mathcal{L}_{1,N}^{(ls)} + \mathcal{L}_{J,1}^{(ls)} + \cdots + \mathcal{L}_{J,N}^{(ls)}$;

29   Compute sentiment analysis loss $\mathcal{L}^{(sa)}$ using w^f as input;

30      $L \leftarrow \mathcal{L}^{(sa)} + \mathcal{L}^{(ls)}$;

31 **end**

3.1 Sentiment Analysis with Interpretability

Given input sentence $w = (w_1, \ldots, w_L)$, the goal is to predict the correct sentiment label $\tilde{y}$. The input is first fed into a pre-trained encoder:

$$V = Encoder(w), \tag{2}$$

where V is hidden states.

Next, we aim to find the tokens that contribute the most to sentiment inference. We adopt an interpretable attention module called hierarchical attention network (HAN), which effectively encodes hidden states with multiple non-linear projections and ranks the most influential tokens based on attention [55]. We stack two blocks of HAN to form our attention module.

$$q, a = HAN(HAN(V)), \tag{3}$$

where vector q is the yielded hidden state and a is the attention weights, indicating the contribution of each token to the final sentiment prediction. To obtain the sentiment prediction, q is passed on to two layers of feedforward neural networks (FNN) to obtain the probability distribution of sentiment prediction, with the first one being activated by ReLU [1], and the second by softmax.

$$h = ReLU(FNN_1(q)) \tag{4}$$

$$\hat{y} = softmax(FNN_2(h)) \tag{5}$$

We denote the prediction of the sentiment analysis module as $\hat{y}^f$ when the input is w^f, which denotes a substitute w where all selected target tokens are replaced by relevant primitives. Thus, the sentiment analysis loss is computed as:

$$\mathcal{L}^{(sa)} = CrossEntropy(\hat{y}^f, \tilde{y}) \tag{6}$$

3.2 Generalization by Lexical Substitution

For the lexical substitution module, we employ a novel pre-training paradigm, termed anomalous language modeling (ALM), which was pre-trained to detect anomalous substituted words from a sequence and retrieve the original words from a set of candidates that contains a positive sample (appropriate primitive of the original word according to the context) and multiple hard negative samples (other primitives associated with the original word) via contrastive learning.

We use the candidates from SenticNet 7 to formulate our input s as in Formula 1. The candidate with the highest score is set as the ground truth substitution $\tilde{c}$. Given the input s, the model encodes it as:

$$U, R = ALM(s), \tag{7}$$

where $U = [u_1, \ldots, u_L]$ is the hidden states of the input sentence, and $R = [r_1, \ldots, r_K]$ is the hidden states of the candidates. We denote the representation of the target word as u_t ($t \in \{1, \ldots, L\}$).

Our training objective is to a) close the distance between the representation of the ground truth candidate r_k, ($k \in \{1, \ldots, K\}$) with u_t, and b) push away incorrect candidates representations r_j ($j \in \{1, \ldots, K | j \neq k\}$) from u_t. Namely, (r_k, u_t) will be regarded as a positive pair, while (r_j, u_t) will be regarded as a negative pair. We follow the InfoNCE loss [42] to achieve these goals, which can be formulated as :

$$\mathcal{L}^{(tune)} = -\sum_i \log \frac{exp(d(u_t, r_k)/\tau)}{\sum_j exp(d(u_t, r_i)/\tau)}, \tag{8}$$

where $i \in \{1, \ldots, K\}$, τ is a temperature hyper-parameter, and $d(\cdot)$ is Euclidean distance. During the inference stage, we choose the candidate $\hat{c}$ whose corresponding hidden state r_k is the most similar to u_t, measured by Euclidean distance:

$$\hat{c} = \arg\min(d(u_t, r_k)) \tag{9}$$

We then use the resulting lexical substitution module to find primitive replacements for the selected target words in sentiment analysis input. To determine which words are selected as primitive targets, we select the top I words in the input with the highest a produced by Eq. 3, forming the set w^{att}. We denote their corresponding representations as $V^{att} = \{v_1^{att}, \ldots, v_I^{att}\}$. For each v_i^{att}, we compute its average Euclidean distance to all of its candidates' hidden states. The candidates consist of relevant primitives from SenticNet 7 under the same part-of-speech type, which are transformed into hidden states $G = \{g_1, \ldots, g_M\}$ using Eq. 2. M represents the number of primitive candidates from SenticNet 7. The top J words in w^{att} with the largest corresponding average distance are considered to be the ones with the most diverse word meanings, and thus are more likely to be replaced. Hence, target words $t = (t_1, \ldots, t_J)$ are selected by finding each corresponding v_j^{att}:

$$v_j^{att} = \arg\max_i (\frac{1}{M} \sum_M d(v_i^{att}, g_m)). \tag{10}$$

3.3 Dynamic Rewarding Mechanism

To fine-tune the lexical substitution module on the downstream task of sentiment analysis, we utilize the top N candidates $\hat{c}_j = \{\hat{c}_{j,1}, \ldots, \hat{c}_{j,n}, \ldots, \hat{c}_{j,N}\}$ produced by the lexical substitution module, for each target word t_j.

The new input resulting from t_j being replaced by candidate $\hat{c}_{j,n}$ is denoted as $w^{j,n}$. Same with Eq. 5, the probability distribution of a sentiment prediction from $w^{j,n}$ is:

$$P(\hat{y})_{j,n} = softmax(FNN_2(h^{j,n})), \tag{11}$$

where $h^{j,n}$ are the hidden states of $w^{j,n}$ produced by Eq. 4 in the sentiment analysis module.

To adjust the model in such a way that a more accurate sentiment prediction results in a higher reward for the corresponding substitution output, we compute the loss weight for $\hat{c}_{j,n}$ being the correct substitution prediction as:

$$\theta_{j,n} = \beta P(\hat{y} = \tilde{y})_{j,n}^2, \tag{12}$$

where β is a hyperparameter for balancing the sentiment analysis and lexical substitution losses, $\tilde{y}$ is the ground truth sentiment label as defined above. We formulate the input s^j to lexical substitution module with sentence w and candidates $\hat{c}_j$, using Formula 1.

Similar to Eq. 8, the loss $(\mathcal{L}_{j,n}^{(ls)})$ of the lexical substitution module when $\hat{c}_{j,n}$ is considered as gold standard is computed as follows:

$$\mathcal{L}_{j,n}^{(ls)} = -\sum_i \log \frac{exp(d(u_t, \hat{c}_{j,n})/\tau)}{\sum_j exp(d(u_t, \hat{c}_j)/\tau)}. \tag{13}$$

Finally, the total loss is computed as:

$$\mathcal{L} = \mathcal{L}^{(sa)} + \theta_{1,1}\mathcal{L}_{1,1}^{(ls)} + \cdots + \theta_{J,N}\mathcal{L}_{J,N}^{(ls)}. \tag{14}$$

The algorithm also works well with emoticons and emojis, which are very important sentiment indicators in social media text. These are aptly replaced with their corresponding primitive, which in most cases is an emotion primitive. In particular, we use the Hourglass of Emotions [50] as emotion categorization model for both verbal and nonverbal content (Fig. 5).

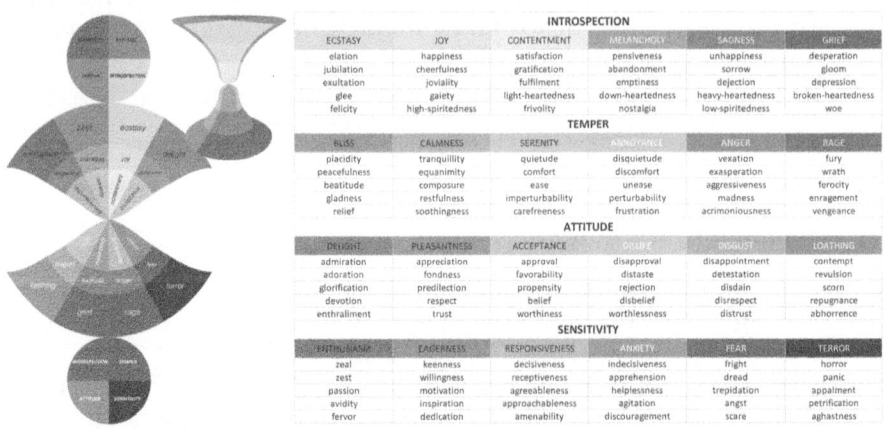

Fig. 5. The Hourglass of Emotions. Unlike other emotion categorization models, the Hourglass represents antithetic emotions very efficiently. Its mirroring capability, in fact, enables the easy handling of negations and other variations of language that can change the sentiment of words otherwise taken in isolation.

4   Evaluation

We test SenticNet 8 against ChatGPT and three more NLP models on three different affective computing datasets. In the following three sections, we describe in detail baselines adopted, datasets used, and results obtained, respectively.

4.1   Baselines

In order to compare the performance of SenticNet 8 on the different tasks, we need to use baselines and train them on the Train portion (while validating on the Dev portion). Besides ChatGPT, we employ three more baselines, which serve as the specialized models specifically tailored for the corresponding downstream task: a robust language model (RoBERTa) trained on a large amount of text; a baseline which uses a word model by employing pretrained word2vec (W2V) embeddings; and a simple Bag-of-Words (BoW) model that utilizes a linear classifier. The hyperparameters of all models are optimized by selecting the hyperparameters yielding the best performance on the Dev portion. Such hyperparameters are tuned using the SMAC toolkit [35], which is based on Bayesian Optimization. The selected hyperparameters are listed in Table 1. Figure 6 illustrates the pipelines of all methods.

Bag of Words. BoW is a simple model that uses only in-domain data for training and no other data for either up- or downstreaming. We utilize the classical technique term frequency – inverse document frequency (TF-IDF), which tokenizes the sentences into words, then, a sentence is represented by a vector of the counts of the words it contains. The vector is then normalized by the term frequency across the entire Train set of the corresponding dataset. We tune the learning rate η of SGD using SMAC.

Word2vec Embeddings. The baseline word2vec [39,40] makes use of pretrained word embeddings, which are trained on a large amounts of text from Google News. The model operates by tokenizing a given text into words, each word is assigned an embedding from the pretrained embeddings. The embeddings are then averaged for all words to give a static feature vector of size 300 for the entire string. An SVM model [8] is then used to predict the given task.

RoBERTa Language Model. The baseline RoBERTa [36] is a pretrained BERT model, which has a transformer architecture. [36] trained two instances of RoBERTa; we use the smaller one, namely *RoBERTa-base*, consisting of 110 million parameters. The model starts by tokenizing a text using subword encoding, which is a hybrid representation between character-based and word-based encodings. The tokens are then fed to RoBERTa to obtain a sequence of embeddings.

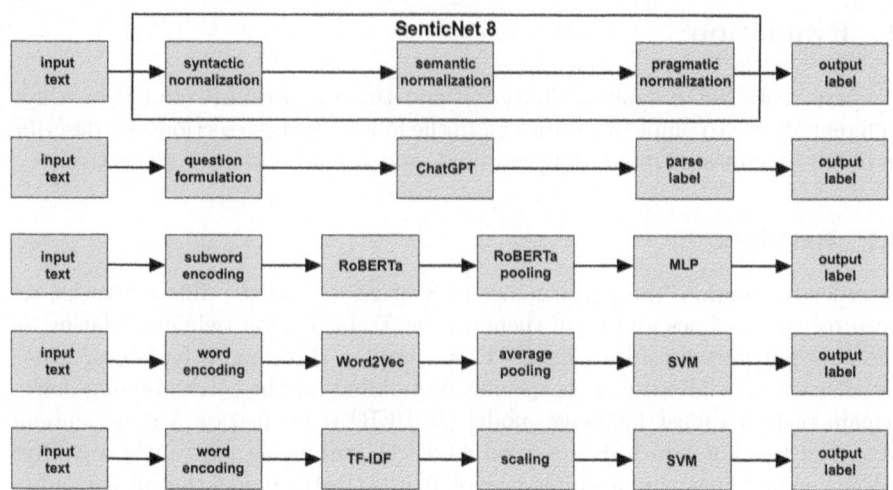

Fig. 6. Evaluation pipelines of SenticNet 8, ChatGPT, RoBERTa, word2vec, and BoW (from top to bottom).

ChatGPT. We introduce the stages of querying ChatGPT as shown in Fig. 6. The general mechanism for collecting answers for each NLP task is as follows:

1. Reformat all the texts of the Test portion of the dataset, by using a format that asks ChatGPT what is their guess about the label of the text.
2. Chunk the examples into 25 examples per chunk.
3. For each chunk, open a new ChatGPT Conversation.
4. Ask ChatGPT (manually) the reformatted question for each example, one-by-one, and collect the answers.
5. Repeat the steps 3–4 until the predictions for the whole Test set are finished.
6. Postprocess the results in case they need some cleanup.

Table 1. Hyperparameters of the different baselines. N is the number of hidden layers, U is the number of neurons in the first hidden layer (which is halved for each subsequent layers), and α is the learning rate. Adam optimizer always yields the best results as compared to SGD. C is the SVM parameter for word2vec. η is the learning rate of the SGD in the BoW model.

	RoBERTa			W2V	BoW
	N	U	α	C	η
Polarity	3	420	2.97×10^{-5}	0.0144	5.25×10^{-6}
O		2	498	5.66×10^{-4}	0.0378	2.47×10^{-3}
C				0.0472	3.09×10^{-6}
E				0.0069	1.09×10^{-5}
A				0.0218	4.65×10^{-4}
N				0.0657	2.21×10^{-6}
Suicide	3	497	8.04×10^{-4}	10.00	4.71×10^{-6}

The formats used for the three NLP tasks are shown in the following snippets. The {*text*} part needs to be replaced with the sample text. Please note that quotation marks need to be kept since it specifies to ChatGPT that this a placeholder used by the question being asked. The formulations for the three NLP tasks are as follows:

1. For sentiment analysis, we formulated the question:
   "What is your guess for the sentiment of the text "{text}"", answer positive, neutral, or negative? it does not have to be correct. Do not show any warning after."
2. For the Big-five personality traits, we asked:
   "What is your guess for the big-five personality traits of someone who said "{text}"", answer low or high with bullet points for the five traits? It does not have to be fully correct. You do not need to explain the traits. Do not show any warning after."
3. For the suicidal ideation detection, we asked:
   "What is your guess if a person is saying "{text}"" has a suicide tendency or not, answer yes or no? it does not have to be correct. Do not show any warning after."

The formulation of the question is of crucial importance to the answers Chat-GPT generates. For anyone who would like to carry out similar investigations in the future, we report four important lessons learnt:

1. Asking the question directly without requesting ChatGPT to guess made it often answer that there is little information provided to answer the question, and it cannot answer it exactly.
2. It is important to ask *what* the guess is and not *"Can you guess"*, because this can generate a response similar to 1., where ChatGPT responds with an answer that starts with *"No, I cannot accurately answer whether..."*. Therefore, the question needs to be assertive and specific.
3. The questions for the suicide assessment task may trigger warnings in the responses of ChatGPT due to its sensitive content.
4. We need to specify the exact output format, because ChatGPT can get creative about the formatting of the answer, which can make it hard to collect answers for our experiment.

The responses of ChatGPT need to be parsed, since ChatGPT can give arbitrary formats for a given answer, even when the content is the same. This is predominant in the personality traits, since there are five traits. Sometimes the answers are listed as bullet points, other times they are all in one comma-separated line. Also, it used different delimiters or order, e.g., "Openness: Low", or "Low in Openness", and "Low: Openness". Additionally, in all problems, it sometimes gives an introduction for the answer, for example, "Here is my guess for ..", or "Based on the statement". We solve this issue by using regular expressions to find and edit such responses.

Table 2. Statistics of the three datasets used for evaluation.

Dataset	Train	Dev	Test	Pos	Neg
Polarity	1,440,144	159,856	359	182	177
O	6,000	2,000	509	333	176
C				286	223
E				214	295
A				340	169
N				274	235
Suicide	138,479	6,270	496	165	331

4.2 Datasets

In this section, we briefly introduce the three datasets we used. A summary of their statistics is presented in Table 2. We utilize publicly available datasets for reproducibility.

Polarity Dataset. We adopt the Sentiment140 dataset [23] for the sentiment analysis task. The dataset is collected from Twitter, which makes the text very noisy and can pose a challenge against many models (especially word models). The dataset consists of tweets and the corresponding sentiment labels (positive or negative).

Personality Dataset. We utilize the First Impressions dataset [44] for the personality task. Personality is represented by the Big-five personality traits (OCEAN), namely, *Openness (to experience), Conscientiousness, Extraversion, Agreeableness,* and *Neuroticism.* The dataset consists of 15 s videos with one speaker, whose personality was manually labelled.

Suicide and Depression Dataset. The Suicide and Depression dataset [19] is collected from the Reddit platform, under different subreddits categories, namely "SuicideWatch", "depression", and "teenagers". The texts of the posts from the "teenagers" category are labelled as negative, while the texts from the other two categories are labelled as positive.

4.3 Results

In this section, we review the results of our experiments. In summary, we evaluated the performance of SenticNet 8 (our commonsense knowledge base of 400,000 concepts, available for download at https://sentic.net/downloads) against four baselines (namely, ChatGPT, RoBERTa, word2vec, and BoW) on three downstream tasks (namely, sentiment analysis, personality recognition, and suicidal ideation detection). Results are shown in Table 3. We use classification accuracy and unweighted average recall (UAR) as performance measures.

UAR has an advantage of exposing if a model is performing very well on a class on the expense of the other class, especially in imbalanced datasets. As also demonstrated by other recent works [26,45], ChatGPT turned out to be jack of all trades but master of none [31] also in the context of affective computing: while the performance of ChatGPT is acceptable on many different NLP tasks, specialized models like SenticNet 8 (and even RoBERTa in most cases) still outperform it on specific tasks. Unlike all baselines used in this work, moreover, SenticNet 8 is also interpretable (because the process that generalizes input words and multiword expressions into their corresponding primitives is fully transparent), trustworthy (because classification outputs always come with a confidence score), and explainable (because classification outputs are explicitly linked to emotions and the input concepts that convey these).

Table 3. Classification accuracy and unweighted average recall (in %) of SenticNet 8 against four baselines (CGPT: ChatGPT; rBERT: RoBERTa; W2V: word2vec; BoW: Bag of Words) on three different NLP tasks (Polarity: sentiment analysis; OCEAN: personality prediction; Suicide: suicidal ideation detection). Bold values show the best method for a combination of specific performance metric and prediction target.

[%]	Accuracy					Unweighted Average Recall				
	SenticNet	CGPT	rBERT	W2V	BoW	SenticNet	CGPT	rBERT	W2V	BoW
Polarity	**88.80**	85.51	85.07	79.41	82.54	**88.67**	85.57	85.02	79.40	82.41
O	**67.91**	46.62	66.03	65.28	59.71	**78.27**	50.12	50.94	50.72	55.61
C	**65.97**	57.40	63.72	62.70	55.60	**79.92**	57.70	60.81	60.09	56.30
E	63.19	55.23	**66.09**	59.92	55.24	**72.76**	54.09	62.30	55.56	53.74
A	**67.86**	44.86	67.42	67.21	58.53	**79.93**	48.45	51.93	51.02	55.75
N	**64.53**	47.29	62.17	56.84	56.09	**77.54**	49.16	61.25	54.64	55.88
Suicide	**99.34**	92.71	97.43	92.16	92.78	**99.35**	91.26	97.40	91.23	90.97

5   Discussion

Intuitively, even if real parrots or stochastic ones (LLMs) produce the appropriate linguistic response relative to the task-related prompts for the three above-mentioned datasets, we would not deem their linguistic behavior trustworthy unless they possess the relevant natural language understanding. Meaning involves a relation between the linguistic form of data and an extralinguistic reality that is distinct from language. Where M denotes meaning, E denotes the form of natural language expressions, and I denotes communicative intent, this relation may be formally represented as $M \subseteq E \times I$ [5]. M contains ordered pairs (e, i) of natural language expressions (e) and communicative intents (i).

Understanding may be interpreted as the process of retrieving i, given e. Since LLMs are pretrained on large datasets and meaning cannot be learnt from linguistic form (e) alone, however impressive their transformer and artificial neural network architecture might be, LLMs will necessarily lack the relevant intentionality.

We do not claim that SenticNet 8 possesses either human-level or the requisite level of natural language understanding. However, as SenticNet 8 relies on commonsense knowledge representation as part of its ensemble, it is better able than ChatGPT to track the extralinguistic reality that is distinct from language. For affective computing tasks, SenticNet 8 is ahead of ChatGPT, as its responses are more firmly grounded in an extralinguistic reality through its reliance on commonsense knowledge representation. SenticNet 8 leverages symbolic models (namely, conceptual dependency theory and a semantic network of commonsense knowledge) to encode meaning in a top-down fashion. Finally, this work does not aim to disdain ChatGPT: we hope future versions of ChatGPT will overcome some of the reported limitations. Given the non-interpretability of its constitutive models, however, it may not happen so soon. As shown in a recent study [17], in fact, ChatGPT seems prone to the "short blanket dilemma": while trying to improve its accuracy on some tasks, OpenAI researchers inadvertently made ChatGPT worse for tasks which it previously excelled at.

6   Conclusion

In this paper, we presented SenticNet 8, a neurosymbolic AI framework leveraging an ensemble of commonsense knowledge representation and hierarchical attention networks, which aims to mitigate the symbol grounding problem. We compared SenticNet 8 against ChatGPT and three more baselines on three downstream tasks. Results show that SenticNet 8's performance is generally superior to all baselines on all tasks. Unlike the other baselines, moreover, SenticNet 8 is interpretable, trustworthy, and explainable. We also propose the idea of a universal symbolism that leverages language-agnostic representations, which can better emulate the current state of affairs of an operating environment on the fly, as narratives unfold.

7   Limitations

A crucial limitation of the presented results is the small amount of data for evaluation (497, 362, and 509 examples for the three tasks), since ChatGPT is only available for manual entries by the consumers and not for automated large-scale testing. Additionally, it only responds to approximately 25–35 requests per hour, in order to reduce the computational cost and avoid brute forcing. Another issue that may limit future experiments is parsing the responses. In our experiments, ChatGPT responded with arbitrary formatting despite specifying the desired format explicitly in the question prompt.

One final limitation of the proposed approach is that pragmatic representations are currently defined manually. However, this is not an issue for our current investigation considering that: (a) these representations need to be created only for conceptual primitives (which are automatically discovered using deep learning); (b) these representations only need to be created once (as conceptual primitives are not subject to concept drift); and (c) in this work we merely consider polar conceptual primitives, i.e., only primitives that can be associated with certain emotions and a positive or negative polarity. In order to apply this approach to more general NLP tasks, a generative AI mechanism for automatically creating such representations should be implemented. Alternatively, this could be done by first establishing a universal set of natural language symbols, e.g., emojis, ISO icons, or blissymbolics [9], and then devising methods for automatically translating different languages into such symbols, similar to how music notation rendering transforms audio into written music scores. We leave this to future work.

Acknowledgments. This research/project is supported by the Ministry of Education, Singapore under its MOE Academic Research Fund Tier 2 (STEM RIE2025 Award MOE-T2EP20123-0005). We would like to thank OpenAI for the usage of ChatGPT. We followed the policy of ChatGPT. Our use of ChatGPT is purely for research purposes to assess emerging capabilities of foundation models, and does not promote the use of ChatGPT in any way that violates its usage policy. In particular, with regards to the subject of self-harm, note that some of the examples in the datasets we used triggered a related warning by ChatGPT.

References

1. Agarap, A.F.: Deep learning using rectified linear units (ReLU). arXiv preprint arXiv:1803.08375 (2018)
2. Amin, M., Cambria, E., Schuller, B.: Can ChatGPT's responses boost traditional natural language processing? IEEE Intell. Syst. **38**(5), 5–11 (2023)
3. Amin, M., Cambria, E., Schuller, B.: Will affective computing emerge from foundation models and general AI? A first evaluation on ChatGPT. IEEE Intell. Syst. **38**(2), 15–23 (2023)
4. Bender, E.M., Gebru, T., McMillan-Major, A., Shmitchell, S.: On the dangers of stochastic parrots: Can language models be too big? In: ACM Conference on Fairness, Accountability, and Transparency, pp. 610–623 (2021)
5. Bender, E.M., Koller, A.: Climbing towards NLU: on meaning, form, & understanding in the age of data. In: ACL, pp. 5185–5198 (2020)
6. Biever, C.: ChatGPT broke the turing test – the race is on for new ways to assess AI. Nature **619**, 686–689 (2023)
7. Biran, O., Cotton, C.: Explanation and justification in machine learning: a survey. In: IJCAI-17 Workshop on Explainable AI (XAI) (2017)
8. Bishop, C.M.: Pattern Recognition and Machine Learning. Springer, New York City, NY, USA (2006)
9. Bliss, C.K.: Semantography (Blissymbolics): A Logical Writing for an Illogical World. Semantography (Blissymbolic) Publications (1949)

10. Bommasani, R., et al.: On the Opportunities and Risks of Foundation Models. arXiv preprint arXiv:2108.07258 (2021)
11. Borji, A.: A Categorical Archive of ChatGPT Failures. arXiv preprint arXiv:2302.03494 (2023)
12. Burkart, N., Huber, M.F.: A survey on the explainability of supervised machine learning. J. Artif. Intell. Res. **70**, 245–317 (2021)
13. Cambria, E., Liu, Q., Decherchi, S., Xing, F., Kwok, K.: SenticNet 7: a commonsense-based neurosymbolic AI framework for explainable sentiment analysis. In: LREC, pp. 3829–3839 (2022)
14. Cambria, E., Malandri, L., Mercorio, F., Mezzanzanica, M., Nobani, N.: A survey on XAI and natural language explanations. Inf. Process. Manag. **60**, 103111 (2023)
15. Cambria, E., Mao, R., Chen, M., Wang, Z., Ho, S.-B.: Seven pillars for the future of artificial intelligence. IEEE Intell. Syst. **38**(6), 62–69 (2023)
16. Cambria, E., Mao, R., Han, S., Liu, Q.: Sentic parser: a graph-based approach to concept extraction for sentiment analysis. In: Proceedings of ICDM Workshops, pp. 413–420 (2022)
17. Chen, L., Zaharia, M., Zou, J.: How is ChatGPT's behavior changing over time? arXiv preprint arXiv:2307.09009 (2023)
18. Cortiñas-Lorenzo, K., Lacey, G.: Toward explainable affective computing: a review. IEEE Trans. Neural Netw. Learn. Syst. (2023)
19. Desu, V., Komati, N., Lingamaneni, S., Shaik, F.: Suicide and depression detection in social media forums. In: Smart Intelligent Computing and Applications. Volume 2, pp. 263–270. Springer Nature, Singapore (2022)
20. Diwali, A., Saeedi, K., Dashtipour, K., Gogate, M., Cambria, E., Hussain, A.: Sentiment analysis meets explainable artificial intelligence: a survey on explainable sentiment analysis. IEEE Trans. Affect. Comput. **15**(3), 837–846 (2024)
21. Fan, C., Lin, J., Mao, R., Cambria, E.: Fusing pairwise modalities for emotion recognition in conversations. Inf. Fusion **106**, 102306 (2024)
22. Gandhi, A., Adhvaryu, K., Poria, S., Cambria, E., Hussain, A.: Multimodal sentiment analysis: a systematic review of history, datasets, multimodal fusion methods, applications, challenges and future directions. Inf. Fusion **91**, 424–444 (2023)
23. Go, A., Bhayani, R., Huang, L.: Twitter sentiment classification using distant supervision. CS224N project report, Stanford **1**(12), 2009 (2009)
24. Górriz, J., et al.: Computational approaches to explainable artificial intelligence: advances in theory, applications and trends. Inf. Fusion **100**, 101945 (2023)
25. Guidotti, R., Monreale, A., Ruggieri, S., Turini, F., Giannotti, F., Pedreschi, D.: A survey of methods for explaining black box models. ACM Comput. Surv. **51**(5), 1–42 (2018)
26. Hendy, A., et al.: How good are GPT models at machine translation? A comprehensive evaluation. arXiv preprint arXiv:2302.09210 (2023)
27. Jackendoff, R.: Toward an explanatory semantic representation. Linguist. Inquiry **7**(1), 89–150 (1976)
28. Ji, Z., et al.: Survey of hallucination in natural language generation. ACM Comput. Surv. **55**(12), 1–38 (2023)
29. Johnson, D., Hakobyan, O., Drimalla, H.: Towards interpretability in audio and visual affective machine learning: a review. arXiv preprint arXiv:2306.08933 (2023)
30. Kazienko, P., Cambria, E.: Towards responsible recommender systems. IEEE Intell. Syst. **39**(3), 5–12 (2024)
31. Kocoń, J., et al.: ChatGPT: jack of all trades, master of none. Inf. Fusion **99**, 101861 (2023)

32. Kumar, M., Aijaz, A., Chattar, O., Shukla, J., Mutharaju, R.: Opacity, transparency, and the ethics of affective computing. IEEE Trans. Affect. Comput. **15**, 4–17 (2024)
33. Lear, J.: Aristotle: The Desire to Understand. Cambridge University Press (1988)
34. Lian, Z., et al.: Explainable multimodal emotion reasoning. arXiv preprint arXiv:1803.08375 (2023)
35. Lindauer, M., et al.: SMAC3: a versatile Bayesian optimization package for hyperparameter optimization. J. Mach. Learn. Res. **23**, 1–9 (2022)
36. Liu, Y., et al.: RoBERTa: a robustly optimized BERT pretraining approach. In: Proceedings of the 20th Chinese National Conference on Computational Linguistics, pp. 1218–1227 (2021)
37. Ma, Y., Nguyen, K.L., Xing, F., Cambria, E.: A survey on empathetic dialogue systems. Inf. Fusion **64**, 50–70 (2020)
38. Mao, R., Chen, G., Zhang, X., Guerin, F., Cambria, E.: GPTEval: a survey on assessments of ChatGPT and GPT-4. In: LREC-COLING, pp. 7844–7866 (2024)
39. Mikolov, T., Chen, K., Corrado, G., Dean, J.: Efficient Estimation of Word Representations in Vector Space. arXiv preprint arXiv:1301.3781 (2013)
40. Mikolov, T., Sutskever, I., Chen, K., Corrado, G.S., Dean, J.: distributed representations of words and phrases and their compositionality. In: Burges, C.J., Bottou, L., Welling, M., Ghahramani, Z., Weinberger, K.Q., (eds.) Advances in Neural Information Processing Systems (2013)
41. Minsky, M.: A framework for representing knowledge. In: Winston, P. (ed.) The psychology of computer vision. McGraw-Hill, New York (1975)
42. Oord, A.V., Li, Y., Vinyals, O.: Representation learning with contrastive predictive coding. arXiv preprint arXiv:1807.03748 (2018)
43. Ouyang, L., et al.: Training language models to follow instructions with human feedback. arXiv preprint arXiv:2203.02155 (2022)
44. Ponce-López, V., et al.: Chalearn lap 2016: first round challenge on first impressions - dataset and results. In: ECCV, pp. 400–418 (2016)
45. Qin, C., Zhang, A., Zhang, Z., Chen, J., Yasunaga, M., Yang D.: Is ChatGPT a General-Purpose Natural Language Processing Task Solver? arXiv preprint arXiv:2302.06476 (2023)
46. Rumelhart, D., Ortony, A.: The representation of knowledge in memory. In: Anderson, C., Spiro, R., Montague, W., (eds.) Schooling and the acquisition of knowledge. Erlbaum (1977)
47. Schank, R.: Conceptual dependency: a theory of natural language understanding. Cogn. Psychol. **3**, 552–631 (1972)
48. Shen, Y., et al.: ChatGPT & other large language models are double-edged swords. *Radiology*, 307(2):e230163, 2023
49. Speer, R., Chin, J., Havasi, C.: ConceptNet 5.5: an open multilingual graph of general knowledge. In: AAAI, pp. 4444–4451 (2017)
50. Susanto, Y., Livingstone, A., Ng, B.C., Cambria, E.: The Hourglass Model revisited. IEEE Intell. Syst. **35**(5), 96–102 (2020)
51. Wierzbicka, A.: Semantics: Primes and Universals. Oxford University Press (1996)
52. Wu, X., Li, Y.L., Sun, J., Lu, C.: Symbol-LLM: leverage language models for symbolic system in visual human activity reasoning. In: Proceedings of NeurIPS (2023)
53. Xing, F., Chaturvedi, I., Cambria, E., Hussain, A., Schuller, B.: Guest editorial: neurosymbolic AI for sentiment analysis. IEEE Trans. Affect. Comput. **14**(4), 1711–1715 (2023)

54. Xu, F., et al.: Symbol-LLM: towards foundational symbol-centric interface for large language models. arXiv preprint arXiv:2311.09278 (2023)
55. Yang, Z., Yang, D., Dyer, C., He, X., Smola, A., Hovy, E.: Hierarchical attention networks for document classification. In: North American Chapter of the Association for Computational Linguistics (NAACL), pp. 1480–1489 (2016)
56. Yue, T., Mao, R., Wang, H., Zonghai, H., Cambria, E.: KnowleNet: knowledge fusion network for multimodal sarcasm detection. Inf. Fusion **100**, 101921 (2023)
57. Zhang, X., Mao, R., Cambria, E.: SenticVec: toward robust and human-centric neurosymbolic sentiment analysis. In: Proceedings of ACL, pp. 4851–4863 (2024)
58. Zhang, X., Mao, R., He, K., Cambria, E.: Neurosymbolic sentiment analysis with dynamic word sense disambiguation. In: Proceedings of EMNLP, pp. 8772–8783 (2023)
59. Zhong, X., Jin, C., An, M., Cambria, E.: XTime: a general rule-based method for time expression recognition and normalization. Knowl.-Based Syst. **297**, 111921 (2024)
60. Zhu, L., Mao, R., Cambria, E., Jansen, B.J.: Neurosymbolic AI for personalized sentiment analysis. In: Proceedings of the 26th International Conference on Human-Computer Interaction (HCII), Washington DC (2024)

Text Characteristics Vector: Rethinking Human-Centered Sentiment Analysis with Emotion-Related Text Characteristics

Cheng Guo[1(✉)], Yanfu Liu[2], Yue Yuan[2], Wuhao Zhang[3], and Sourojit Ghosh[2]

[1] University of California, San Diego, USA
c5guo@ucsd.edu
[2] University of Washington, Seattle, USA
[3] University of Minnesota, Minneapolis, USA

Abstract. To evaluate how emotional expression is related to valence, we built a sentimental classifier based only on quantitative information of the count of eight text characteristics on a dataset of fanfiction reviews. We also integrated the adjusted character count into the counting. To evaluate our text characteristics vector (TCV) model, we compared it with a model built based on the same data through a TF-IDF vectorizer. Our TCV model performed equally to the TF-IDF model with both F1 scores around 0.90. Our research is critical since it shows how emotional expression can be deterministic on the valence of text. Our result reveals the importance of a human-centered approach to NLP. The result is generalizable to all reviews on any social media. We release data and code in our research for reproducing purposes.

Keywords: human-centered natural language processing · natural language processing · sentiment analysis · qualitative coding

1 Introduction

Due to the expedited growth of social media, people have increased their involvement in sharing their opinion and checking out reviews on social media regarding buying certain products [19], planning travels [4], and choosing restaurants [35]. As researchers study those reviews, they concluded that most reviews have emotional input, which is often correlated with *valence* i.e. the 'goodness' or 'badness' of text [11]. While the correlation is asserted [20,30], it is still unclear how strong the correlation between emotion and valence is or whether we can approach sentiment analysis with emotions in text. Moreover, there is still more research required on identifying emotions from texts.

In this paper, we demonstrate a novel method of identifying the valence of a given text based on the emotional expression within it, which we establish to be

H. Degen and S. Ntoa (Eds.): HCII 2024, LNCS 15382, pp. 217–231, 2024.
https://doi.org/10.1007/978-3-031-76827-9_12

a function of the following eight characteristics: emoticons/emojis, exclamation marks, capitalizations, repetitions, action verbs, intentional misspellings, keyboard smashing, and text length. We adopt as our dataset a publicly-available trove of online fanfiction reviews [33], which are known to be rife with emotional expression as reviewers tend to express strong emotions in reaction to stories about their favorite characters [10]. Operating on a ground-truth dataset which we manually code with a taxonomy of emotions from [14], we design two machine learning models: one that uses a standard TF-IDF vectorizer used for this purpose by [13] and another one that predicts the valence based on the aforementioned characteristics (hereafter referred to as 'the TCV model', abbreviated from Text Characteristics Vector Model). We examine whether the TCV model can match the performance of the previous one, as we compare results produced by the two both manually and through computational metrics. Through our work, we make two novel contributions:

(1) We present novel insights into the process of detecting the nature and degrees of emotional expression within short texts. We adopt a slate of eight characteristics of texts – emoticons/emojis, exclamation marks, capitalizations, repetitions, action verbs, intentional misspellings, keyboard smashing, – initially proposed by [13], to which we add an eighth: text length, as a metric of identifying the valence of a short form text. Based on these characteristics, we design a machine learning model for the task of predicting the valence of short-form text (e.g. tweets, social media comments, etc.). We demonstrate that this approach produces comparable results to models that employ TF-IDF vectorizers, the commonly-adopted procedure for this purpose. Our approach proceeds by processing an input dataset of short texts into the counts and frequencies of the aforementioned characteristics, and then applying the counts to classify the texts into Positive, Neutral or Negative valences. This approach demonstrates a significant speedup at the classification stage over TF-IDF vectorizers, as it only operates on the counts and frequencies rather than the words and contents within the text. Upon comparison of results from TF-IDF vectorizers and our model over 100,000 texts, we observed that our model produces 91% similar results to the former. Upon examination of differences, we observe that only 1844 valid disagreements, since the remaining 7606 are not in English and our training data was only in English texts. Manual examination of a random sample of 50 English texts for which the models disagree reveals that although we do agree more overall with the TF-IDF vectorizer's classification of reviews over the TCV model's, we do agree more with the TCV model's classification of Positive Valences. While this approach does not yet represent an improvement upon TF-IDF vectorizers, we believe that it shows promising results and is encouraging as a direction of future work in the field of sentiment analysis.

(2) We contribute towards the growing field of human-centered machine learning [8] by adopting a human-centered approach to designing a sentiment classifier. We extend the work of [13], which covers degrees of positive emotions present within short texts but produces statedly underwhelming results, by establishing how our human-centered approach of building our ground-truth

dataset from manually coding data ourselves led to the aforementioned observation and the emergence of the pattern between texts and the eight characteristics. We hope that our work adds to the literature in the field which seeks to motivate researchers to adopt more human-centered methods in their ML/NLP tasks, by presenting a successful case study.

2   Related Work

2.1   Emotion Classification in Text

The study of emotions and valence within texts has long since been the subject of attention of scholars from a wide range of fields [11]. That people express emotions in text is unsurprising and, over the past few decades, there has been substantial work in analyzing emotions within texts.

Within the field of NLP, researchers have attempted to classify emotions in movie reviews [29], speech [5,7], and tweets [22], to name a few. [29] and [7] used as their method of classification part-of-speech (POS) tagging, which builds vectors based on the modality and syntax of each word in a sentence and joining them together to identify an overall emotion within the sentence [31]. When classifying emotion in tweets, [22] focused on emotion-related hashtags like #joy and developed binary classifiers, like classifying whether a tweet has joy emotion or not, which ends up with a better classifier for positive emotions since more positive tweets were collected. Researchers have also applied Pointwise Mutual Information (PMI) [22,29], a metric that determines the possibility of two different words occurring in the same sentence, to calculate the semantic orientation and the emotion in a sentence. Researchers have also attempted the machine learning approach for emotion classification, such as KNN or neural networks [26].

Recently, deep-learning approaches have been widely studied and applied to solving NLP tasks. Regarding emotion classification, researchers have used a convolutional neural network (CNN) on short texts and achieved better accuracy than SVM and other deep-learning methods, including LSTM and RNN [32]. Deep-learning approaches embed words into feature vectors that can collect information like semantic relevance that is hard to capture from traditional techniques. When classifying emotions of text on the Microblog of China, researchers have found that CNN could obtain an accuracy of about 7.0% better than other approaches [32]. Beyond emotion classification, deep-learning techniques like CNN have proved to perform better in classifying tobacco and health-related datasets [18] since they can extract more information from texts and study them in sequential or hierarchal structures.

2.2   Sentiment Analysis

Since [24] first coined the term 'sentiment analysis', it has risen to become synonymous with the process of computationally determining emotions within the text and is one of the most recognized NLP tasks [21]. [24] defined it as the identification of sentiment expressions, including their polarity and strengths, and their relations to the subject of the text. It generally proceeds by training ML models on a ground-truth dataset of sentiment-labeled texts, and then executing the model on a dataset of unlabeled texts to produce sentiment labels. This type of modeling is called supervised learning and is the most common, though semi-supervised and unsupervised versions are also in common usage for sentiment analysis tasks.

Over the years, researchers have applied various techniques to extract sentiment from various texts, mostly on Twitter [16,17,25] and movie reviews [3,27,28] texts. The researchers started with preprocessing text data, including lemmatization [17,27], removing special characters [16,17,27], and correcting misspelled words [17,25]. Some of them removed slang words [16], but others replaced them with words in the dictionary to maintain the emotional contribution of those words [25]. For the processing stage, they created vectors by feature extraction, including part-of-speech (POS) tagging [17,25] and assigning weights to words [16,25]. Then, they would apply ML models, mostly Naïve Bayes or SVM or both [3,16,17,25,27,28]. For Twitter text, they ended with that while Naïve Bayes and SVM result in models with similar accuracy [17,25], the decision trees method performs better [17]. For movie reviews text, some of them concluded Naïve Bayes is better [3,27], while others claim SVM is better [28].

2.3 Human-Centered Sentiment Analysis

Over the past few years, the emerging field of human-centered machine learning [8] has led to the birth of a human-centered approach towards sentiment analysis [e.g. 2,13,23]. This approach towards sentiment analysis asks to go beyond simply treating texts as data to classify, but rather to consider the emotions and thoughts of the humans who produced such texts. [14] demonstrate how, in classifying the same dataset of online fanfiction reviews as we did, the importance of understanding the subjective differences between different degrees of positive emotions as a function of the ways in which emotional content is expressed, arguing that if a reviewer made a conscious choice of using capitalization (e.g. 'I LOVE THIS' over 'I love this'), then that choice must be respected in understanding the degree of positive emotion expressed. In this vein, they later [13] designed a human-centered machine learning model that attempted to distinguish between different degrees of emotions. We extend their work, which produced underwhelming results, by examining how patterns within the contents of reviews can be used to determine their valence.

2.4 Fanfiction and NLP

As a field with an abundant amount of text, fanfiction attracted lots of NLP researchers to analyze and classify texts. Researchers from Carnegie Mellon University formulated a fully structured pipeline for analyzing fanfiction texts [34].

They introduced SpanBERT-based language models and built a dataset with features like character coherence and quote attribution [34]. They evaluated their pipeline and compared it with pipelines like BookNLP and CoreNLP, hoping that their structured analysis could be generalized to domains other than fanfiction [34]. Researchers have also evaluated various traditional and novel approaches to NLP tasks on fanfiction to see which performs the best. The researchers tested traditional approaches by combining TF-IDF with Naïve Bayes and SVM, and they compared them with deep-learning approaches combined with Word2Vec [9]. In conclusion, they discovered that SVM achieved better accuracy than deep learning approaches and TF-IDF with Naïve Bayes is the best approach, specifically for classification tasks related to fanfiction [9].

3   Methods

3.1   Online Fanfiction Reviews

We use for this study a publicly-available dataset of online fanfiction reviews collected by [33]. The full dataset[1] contains metadata from 6,807,100 stories by 1,516,335 unique authors in 44 different languages, as well as over 176 million reviews across all the stories. In the world of online fanfiction, a 'review' is a comment left on a story by a user. Prior research into these reviews [6,10,14, e.g.] has demonstrated that such reviews are rife with emotional expression, especially expressing extremely positive or extremely negative sentiments clearly and often. Therefore, for our stated goals of detecting valence of short-form texts, this dataset is appropriate.

We began with a random sample of 10000 reviews to qualitatively code (explained in Sect. 3.2) and used the labeled data to train our model. For testing, we extracted another random sample of 100,000 reviews from [33]'s dataset.

3.2   The Eight Text Characteristics

The purpose of this study was to examine whether the text characteristics of Positive emotions proposed by [13] could indeed be used to predict the valence of short form texts. We began this study by qualitatively coding the aforementioned dataset of 10000 fanfiction reviews with a taxonomy of 11 emotions proposed by [14], which are further divided into three categories of Positive, Negative, and Unclassified emotions (full slate of emotions shown in Table 2). Four researchers individually coded 9364 reviews (dataset shortened after removing non-English reviews to avoid errors in translation similarly as [14]), with a specific attention towards the three Positive emotions: Like, Joy/Happiness, and Anticipation/Hope. During the coding process, we had detailed discussion on *why* each researcher coded a review with a Positive emotion, paying close attention to the role played by one of [13]'s characteristics of Positive reviews. In doing so, we examined whether we could find patterns between the emotion chosen and the

---

[1] http://research.fru1t.me/.

text characteristics, specifically whether the presence of one of the characteristics was a stronger indication of a particular emotion over the other. Through tabulations of agreements/disagreements and observations of the presence of the characteristics as determining factors, we adopt the slate of seven characteristics proposed by [13] – emoticons/emojis, exclamation marks, capitalizations, repetitions, action verbs, intentional misspellings, and keyboard smashing– for our work. We further identify an eighth characteristic that played a role in our determining different emotions: text length. We reasoned that longer reviews are indicative of a stronger degree of user investment and might contain a clearer expression of emotions, and therefore adopted it into our slate of characteristics.

3.3   Qualitative Coding

To build the model, we first need qualitatively coded data. To determine the ground truth of the sentiments in fanfiction reviews, a team of four independently coded a random sample of 1000 reviews (different than the ones referred to above) each over five weeks between February and March 2023. For each review, each coder determined its valence by selecting one of the four: positive, neutral, negative, or unknown. Since there are many more positive reviews than all the other three categories combined [10], we decided to put all three other categories into one, named "not positive," coded with 0 in the coded dataset, and positive reviews are coded with 1. By combining four persons' codes, we determined the final valence for each of the 1000 reviews on a majority vote scheme, while if two people coded 0 and two coded 1, we invited a fifth person as a tie-breaker. Now we have 1000 reviews, each with its coded valence in 1 or 0.

3.4   Quantitative Modeling

After we have the qualitative data, we started building the model. We first extracted the count of the following text characteristics: emoticons/emojis, exclamation marks, capitalizations, repetitions, action verbs, intentional misspellings, and keyboard smashing on each review as quantitative measures, then we also take the length of each review as another measure. These eight text characteristics are proved to have correlated with the emotion expressed in the review, especially positive emotions like joy, hope, and like [13]. For counting the capitalization and total length of the text, we incorporated Adjusted Character Count (ACC) since capitalization can embed strong emotions in the text [14]. If in the text, more than three characters except for whitespace are next to each other on the QWERTY keyboard, we would count that as one keyboard smashing. For repetition, we take the number of the character on the keyboard that is typed the most in the sentence. For intentional misspelling, currently we counted every word in the review that is misspelled. These eight quantitative measures are combined as one text characteristics vector (TCV). Based on the TCV, we build a quantitative model to predict a reviews valence in the above two categories: positive or not positive. We chose Linear SVC since it tends to result in a higher accuracy compared to other machine-learning models [1,15,18]. We also build a second model based on TF-IDF statistics and Linear SVC with the 1000 reviews and our code, since TF-IDF is a well-known algorithm in NLP [12]. We compared the two models through their F1 scores because we want to minimize both false positives and false negatives.

3.5 Manual Examination

Beyond building models on 1000 reviews and comparing their performance, we applied the two models to 100,000 fanfiction reviews and retrieved the predictions through both models. We extracted all the English reviews that are classified differently. Then we randomly selected a sample of 50 reviews and compared the results to see which model's result we agree with.

4 Findings

4.1 Model Performances

We have built two ML models, one is a Linear SVC model on the vector of eight text characteristics for each review (TCV model), and the other one is also a Linear SVC model built on tokenizing reviews with the TF-IDF vectorizer. Both models have an F1 score of around 0.90 when classifying reviews as positive or not positive. Specifically, the TCV model has an F1 score of about 0.9130, and the model with TF-IDF vectorizer reached an F1 score of 0.9043. Based solely on the F1 scores, we can say that the model on text characteristics has achieved an acceptable F1 score as with the model with the TF-IDF vectorizer. However, further consideration is required to examine specific reviews and their predicted results from the two models to validate the models" performance (Table 1).

4.2 Manual Examination

Among the 100,000 reviews, 9450 are classified differently. Among the 9450 reviews, there are 1834 in English, 7606 non-English reviews, and 10 reviews consisting of only emoticons. We randomly selected 50 reviews from the 1834 English reviews that are classified differently and compared the results to see which model's result we agree with. Among the 50 reviews we selected, there are 32 reviews in which we agree with the model built on TF-IDF vectorizers, and 18 we agree with the model from the text characteristics method. Among the 32 reviews we agree with the TF-IDF model, three of them we both agree to be positive reviews and 29 of them we both agree to be non-positive. Among the 18 reviews we agree with the model from the text characteristics method, 16 of them we both agree to be positive, and two of them we both agree to be non-positive.

There are five reviews where the TF-IDF model characterizes it to be positive, while the text characteristics model predicts it is not positive. Among these five, four of them contain almost exclusively capital letters. Three of these four we

Table 1. Examples from Manual Examination

Text	TF-IDF Model	TCV Model	Manual Examination
HEY, I DIDN'T REVIEW TIL THE END, IT'S GROOVY! I LOVE HIGH SCHOOL FICS...EVEN GOT ONE OF MY OWN...WELL HURRY UP WITH THE NEXT CHAPTER PLEASE, THIS STORY IS GREAT!	Positive	Not Positive	Positive
Well my prediction was right. And I'm SO SAD! I almost cried! AW WHY VICTORIA? Poor Albus! Why could'nt a[nother] bad guy die? *weep* Oh, and isn't the Griffin supposed to be a Hippogriff? :S I hate u for that death chapter.	Not Positive	Positive	Not Positive
I'm happy to see that this story is being updated again - I love it! Poor Relena, though. :(	Not Positive	Positive	Positive
Anna and kokoro nonoko and yuu sumire and monchu otonashi and kitsuneme those are what I think the parings should be... with Natsume and Mikan, Ruka and Hotaru of course	Positive	Not Positive	Not Positive

agree with the TF-IDF model as positive reviews. Those three reviews contain words like "funny" or "groovy" and encouragement to the author to update soon.

The TF-IDF model characterizes the other 45 reviews as not positive, and we agree with it on 29 reviews. Although we agree that these 29 reviews are not positive, they are neither negative. Those reviews discuss the plot of the fanfiction while the reviewer did not express like or dislike for the fanfiction itself. Those reviews generally used more capitalization, exclamation marks, and emoticons compared to the other 16 reviews, where we agree with the text characteristics model regarding their positivity. Those 16 reviews did not contain many special text characteristics, but there is more encouragement for updating from the author.

5 Discussion

5.1 New Framework for Sentiment Analysis

In the previous approach to sentiment analysis, researchers first preprocess the data through steps like lemmatization [17,27] and removing special characters [16,17,27]. For the process stage, they would extract vectors from text, like part-of-speech (POS) [17,25] or TF-IDF vector [12], then apply machine learning algorithms like Naïve Bayes or SVM [3,16,17,25,27,28]. However, in our approach, we skipped the preprocessing stage since we want to analyze text characteristics beyond their stem form, so we directly extract a vector composed of the count of eight text characteristics and apply Linear SVC to it. Thus, we eliminated the preprocessing stage.

5.2 Manual Examination

During the manual examination, we observed three shortcomings that may hinder model performance.

Counting Emoticons. Since we only considered the count of the eight text characteristics, the model did not include what those text characteristics entail, especially for emoticons. For emoticons, :) implies happy emotions, and :(entails sad emotions. In our code, both of them are counted as one emoticon, so did not consider the different emotions of those emoticons.

Counting Repetitions. We take the count of the most-typed character in the sentence. If in a sentence, there is the usage of a lot of certain English characters, but the reviewer did not repeat it on purpose, that count in the vector represents wrong information of the text.

Identifying Keyboard Smashing. If more than three characters except for whitespace in the text are next to each other on the QWERTY keyboard, we would count that as one occurrence of keyboard smashing. If the reviewer is using keyboards other than the QWERTY keyboard, like T9 or Dvorak keyboards, we cannot identify if they used keyboard smashing.

5.3 Run Time of Building Models

When building a model, it is crucial to consider the Run Time. While we expect the two models we built to cost roughly the same amount of time, this is not true. There are two stages in building the TCV model, the first one is the processing stage, in which we extract the count of those eight features, and the second stage is the classification stage, which is building the model based solely on the eight counts. If we only consider building the model, then the text characteristics method has less time cost since there is no need to vectorize all reviews. However, this model takes a significant amount of time in the processing stage when extracting the count of the text characteristics. In specific, when counting the misspelled words of a review, our code takes the most amount of time, which is about 6 min on 1000 reviews, and the total time required for all features is about 10 min on 1000 reviews. When classifying the 100,000 reviews, since we did not remove non-English reviews, the time usage varies due to our code recognizing every non-English word as misspelled. The total time for building the model with the TF-IDF vectorizer with 1000 reviews is around 5 min and building the model of text characteristics vector takes at least 10 min.

5.4   Implications

The new Text Characteristics Vector model we proposed has the following implications.

Capitalization. People usually express strong emotions through capitalization, but the following review is a counterexample: *I AM GONNA KILL U! HOW COULD U JUST LEAVE IT THERE AND THEN PICK UP THE SEQUEL 7 YEARS LATER! AND Y'D U HAV 2 MAKE THEM BREAK UP! U BETTER FIX IT IN UR SEQUEL CUZ THEY'RE SUPPOSED TO B 2GETHER AND IF THE SEQUELS SEVEN YEARS LATER THAT WOULD BE LIKE NEITHER OF THEM FELTR GUILTY! POST THE SEQUL SOON PLZ CUZ THAT WAS SUCH A HORIBLE ENDING!* Even though the reviewer used most exclusively capitalized letters, we think the reviewer did not express a positive attitude since they asked the author to fix the relationships of two characters in the fanfiction. We agree on the TCV model in this review is not positive. The TF-IDF method would turn words into lower cases and remove all the exclamation marks, and we do not agree with the results from the TF-IDF model.

Emoticon in Text. While we discussed emoticons can entail different emotions, sometimes people use emoticons not with the emotion it implies. Consider the following review: *:(why did ya stop posting? i'm heartbroken...post more please! its my birthday!* Although the reviewer used a sad emoticon :(at the beginning of the review, they encourage the author to post more of this fanfiction as they are reading it in their birthday, and we agree with the TCV model to categorize this review as positive. The TF-IDF method will remove the emoticons before processing, and the TF-IDF model categorizes it as not a positive review.

Generalization of the TCV Model. The results from our model could be applied to all short-formed text in social media like Twitter, Reddit, or movie reviews since people express strong emotions in texts through the eight characteristics. Examples can be this tweet from Donald Trump on January 8, 2021: *The 75,000,000 great American Patriots who voted for me, AMERICA FIRST, and MAKE AMERICA GREAT AGAIN, will have a GIANT VOICE long into the future. They will not be disrespected or treated unfairly in any way, shape or form!!!* There are some capitalizations and exclamation marks, so it can be categorized as a positive tweet through the text characteristics vector, but people who did not vote for Trump may categorize this tweet not as a positive one.

Human-Centered Machine Learning. Researchers who attempted Human-Centered Machine Learning have encouraged future designers to manually code the data [13] and in our research, four coders have coded 1000 reviews independently. We also have a fifth coder for tie-breaking. Our process proves that the human-centered machine-learning approach can be applied to sentiment analysis and result in a model with an F1 score over 0.90. We focused on text characteristics that would normally be removed during the preprocessing stage and created new possibilities for future NLP researchers to extract information from texts beyond the stem form.

6 Future Plan

We would like to improve the Text Characteristics Vector in the following ways.

Table 2. The taxonomy of emotion codes, along with definitions, examples and type of emotion (Positive, Negative, Unclassified) from [14]

Emotion Code	Definition	Example	Emotion Type
Like	The reviewer expresses generic or slightly positive emotions, without going into too much depth.	Wow, I really like this chapter	Positive
Joy/Happiness	The reviewer has more than just a slightly positive reaction to the story and has taken time to adequately express this.	I LOVE this story! Excellent work!	Positive
Anticipation/Hope	The reviewer is expressing their hope of seeing upcoming work.	Good job I'll be waiting for more	Positive
Surprise	The reviewer is surprised, either pleasantly or otherwise.	Whoa I did not see that coming	Positive
Dislike	The reviewer expresses generic or slightly negative emotions, without going into too much depth.	I was a little disappointed	Negative
Disturbed/Disgust	The reviewer expresses discomfort with the content of the story, either with some specific parts or the general tone.	Ugh Snape makes me want to crawl out of my skin	Negative
Anger/Frustration	The reviewer expresses an extreme negative reaction either to the story or the lack of updates.	This is absolutely garbage	Negative
Sadness	The reviewer expresses sadness, either mildly or through tears	Broke my heart :,(I cried a bit	Negative
Confused	The reviewer expresses confusion, as most often indicated by one or more questions.	Why would Harry do that??	Negative
Unknown	The text is either indecipherable or is in a language other than English.	me encanta!	Unclassified
No emotion	Any emotion cannot be reliably assigned to the text.	Im a Boy	Unclassified

Emoticon. For the future version of the vector, we would like to categorize emoticons based on the emotion it entails, for example :) and :> for happy, :(and :< for sad. Then we would count different categories separately so that the model will consider emoticons based on the emotion it implies.

Repetition. In the current algorithm, we just counted the English character that appeared the most times as the number for repetition. However, in the future version, we hope to count the repetition that is intended, like e in yeees, or h in ahhhh. Thus, we need a more precise way to count repetitions in the future version.

Intentional Misspelling. Currently we are counting all the words that are not in English, but sometimes people have unintentional typos. We hope to examine whether the misspelling is intentional or not based on the content of the text in a future version of the vector.

Keyboard Smashing. While the current algorithm for counting keyboard smashing is acceptable, we would like to develop a more rigorous version of it in the future version of the vector so that it can identify a keyboard smash in a convincing way.

Deep Learning. As discussed in the Related Work section, researchers have incorporated deep-learning approaches to classify emotions in text resulting in higher accuracy. We hope to explore the potential of applying the text character-istics vector in deep learning as a neuron in the network to improve performance and make the research more comprehensive and human-centered.

7   Conclusion

We have approached sentiment analysis in a human-centered way by building an ML model based solely on the count of eight text characteristics, including emoticons/emojis, exclamation marks, capitalizations, repetitions, action verbs, intentional misspellings, keyboard smashing, and text length, and compared it with a model with TF-IDF vectorizers. Both models achieved equally well results. Through analyzing the reviews that are categorized differently between the two models, we found that we are more inclined to agree with the TCV model when it predicts a review to be positive, while more likely to agree with the TF-IDF model when it predicts a review to be negative. We provided evidence for encouraging the human-centered approach in sentiment analysis on short texts from social media in that it can substitute the TF-IDF vectorizing process and result in an equally-better model.

References

1. Ahmed, H., Awan, M., Khan, N., Yasin, A., Faisal Shehzad, H.: Sentiment analysis of online food reviews using big data analytics. İlköğretim Online **20**, 827–836 (2021). https://doi.org/10.17051/ilkonline.2021.02.93
2. Ali, K., Dong, H., Bouguettaya, A., Erradi, A., Hadjidj, R.: Sentiment analysis as a service: a social media based sentiment analysis framework. In: 2017 IEEE International Conference on Web Services (ICWS), pp. 660–667. IEEE (2017)
3. Baid, P., Gupta, A., Chaplot, N.: Sentiment analysis of movie reviews using machine learning techniques. Int. J. Comput. Appl. **179**, 45–49 (2017). https://doi.org/10.5120/ijca2017916005
4. Baka, V.: The becoming of user-generated reviews: looking at the past to understand the future of managing reputation in the travel sector. Tour. Manage. **53**, 148–162 (2016). https://www.sciencedirect.com/science/article/pii/S0261517715300091
5. Borchert, M., Dusterhoft, A.: Emotions in speech - experiments with prosody and quality features in speech for use in categorical and dimensional emotion recognition environments. In: 2005 International Conference on Natural Language Processing and Knowledge Engineering, pp. 147–151 (2005). https://doi.org/10.1109/NLPKE.2005.1598724
6. Campbell, J., Aragon, C., Davis, K., Evans, S., Evans, A., Randall, D.: Thousands of positive reviews: distributed mentoring in online fan communities. In: Proceedings of the 19th ACM Conference on Computer-Supported Cooperative Work & Social Computing, p. 691–704. CSCW 2016, Association for Computing Machinery, New York, NY, USA (2016). https://doi.org/10.1145/2818048.2819934, https://doi.org/10.1145/2818048.2819934
7. Caschera, M.C., Grifoni, P., Ferri, F.: Emotion classification from speech and text in videos using a multimodal approach. Multimodal Technol. Interact. **6**(4) (2022). https://doi.org/10.3390/mti6040028, https://www.mdpi.com/2414-4088/6/4/28
8. Chancellor, S.: Toward practices for human-centered machine learning. Commun. ACM **66**(3), 78–85 (2023)
9. Donaldson, C., Pope, J.: Data collection and analysis of print and fan fiction classification. In: International Conference on Pattern Recognition Applications and Methods (2022). https://api.semanticscholar.org/CorpusID:246948382
10. Frens, J., Davis, R., Lee, J., Zhang, D., Aragon, C.: Reviews matter: how distributed mentoring predicts lexical diversity on fanfiction. net. arXiv preprint arXiv:1809.10268 (2018)
11. Frijda, N.H., et al.: The Emotions. Cambridge University Press (1986)
12. Gebre, B.G., Zampieri, M., Wittenburg, P., Heskes, T.: Improving native language identification with TF-IDF weighting. In: Proceedings of the Eighth Workshop on Innovative Use of NLP for Building Educational Applications, pp. 216–223. Association for Computational Linguistics, Atlanta, Georgia (2013). https://aclanthology.org/W13-1728
13. Ghosh, S., et al.: do we like this, or do we like like this? : reflections on a human-centered machine learning approach to sentiment analysis. In: Proceedings of the 4th International Conference on Artificial Intelligence in HCI in the context of the 25th International Conference on Human-Computer Interaction (HCI International), pp. 63–82. Springer (2023)

14. Ghosh, S., Froelich, N., Aragon, C.: i love you, my dear friend: analyzing the role of emotions in the building of friendships in online fanfiction communities. In: Proceedings of the 15th International Conference on Social Computing and Social Media in the context of the 25th International Conference on Human-Computer Interaction (HCI International), pp. 466–485. Springer (2023)
15. Gulati, K., Saravana Kumar, S., Sarath Kumar Boddu, R., Sarvakar, K., Kumar Sharma, D., Nomani, M.: Comparative analysis of machine learning-based classification models using sentiment classification of tweets related to COVID-19 pandemic. Mater. Today Proc. **51**, 38–41 (2022). https://doi.org/10.1016/j.matpr.2021.04.364, https://www.sciencedirect.com/science/article/pii/S2214785321032843, cMAE'21
16. Hasan, A., Moin, S., Karim, A., Shamshirband, S.: Machine learning-based sentiment analysis for twitter accounts. Math. Comput. Appl. **23**(1) (2018). https://doi.org/10.3390/mca23010011, https://www.mdpi.com/2297-8747/23/1/11
17. Jain, A.P., Dandannavar, P.: Application of machine learning techniques to sentiment analysis. In: 2016 2nd International Conference on Applied and Theoretical Computing and Communication Technology (iCATccT), pp. 628–632 (2016). https://doi.org/10.1109/ICATCCT.2016.7912076
18. Kamath, C.N., Bukhari, S.S., Dengel, A.: Comparative study between traditional machine learning and deep learning approaches for text classification. In: Proceedings of the ACM Symposium on Document Engineering 2018. DocEng 2018, Association for Computing Machinery, New York, NY, USA (2018). https://doi.org/10.1145/3209280.3209526, https://doi.org/10.1145/3209280.3209526
19. Kwahk, K.Y., Ge, X.: The effects of social media on e-commerce: a perspective of social impact theory. In: 2012 45th Hawaii International Conference on System Sciences, pp. 1814–1823 (2012). https://doi.org/10.1109/HICSS.2012.564
20. Lelieveld, G.J., Hendriks, H.: The interpersonal effects of distinct emotions in online reviews. Cogn. Emot. **35**(7), 1257–1280 (2021). https://doi.org/10.1080/02699931.2021.1947199, pMID: 34187323
21. Liu, B.: Introduction, pp. 1–17. Studies in Natural Language Processing, Cambridge University Press, 2 edn. (2020). https://doi.org/10.1017/9781108639286.002
22. Mohammad, S.: #emotional tweets. In: *SEM 2012: The First Joint Conference on Lexical and Computational Semantics – Volume 1: Proceedings of the main conference and the shared task, and Volume 2: Proceedings of the Sixth International Workshop on Semantic Evaluation (SemEval 2012), pp. 246–255. Association for Computational Linguistics, Montréal, Canada (7-8 Jun 2012). https://aclanthology.org/S12-1033
23. Nalis, I., Neidhardt, J.: Not facial expression, nor fingerprint–acknowledging complexity and context in emotion research for human-centered personalization and adaptation. In: Adjunct Proceedings of the 31st ACM Conference on User Modeling, Adaptation and Personalization, pp. 325–330 (2023)
24. Nasukawa, T., Yi, J.: Sentiment analysis: capturing favorability using natural language processing. In: Proceedings of the 2nd International Conference on Knowledge Capture, pp. 70–77. K-CAP 2003, Association for Computing Machinery, New York, NY, USA (2003). https://doi.org/10.1145/945645.945658, https://doi.org/10.1145/945645.945658
25. Neethu, M.S., Rajasree, R.: Sentiment analysis in twitter using machine learning techniques. In: 2013 Fourth International Conference on Computing, Communications and Networking Technologies (ICCCNT), pp. 1–5 (2013). https://doi.org/10.1109/ICCCNT.2013.6726818

26. Petrushin, V.: Emotion in speech: recognition and application to call centers. In: Proceedings of Artificial Neural Networks in Engineering, vol. 710, p. 22 (2000)
27. Rahman, A., Hossen, M.S.: Sentiment analysis on movie review data using machine learning approach. In: 2019 International Conference on Bangla Speech and Language Processing (ICBSLP), pp. 1–4 (2019). https://doi.org/10.1109/ICBSLP47725.2019.201470
28. Samal, B., Behera, A.K., Panda, M.: Performance analysis of supervised machine learning techniques for sentiment analysis. In: 2017 Third International Conference on Sensing, Signal Processing and Security (ICSSS), pp. 128–133 (2017). https://doi.org/10.1109/SSPS.2017.8071579
29. Turney, P.D.: Thumbs up or thumbs down? Semantic orientation applied to unsupervised classification of reviews. In: Proceedings of the 40th Annual Meeting on Association for Computational Linguistics, p. 417–424. ACL 2002, Association for Computational Linguistics, USA (2002). https://doi.org/10.3115/1073083.1073153, https://doi.org/10.3115/1073083.1073153
30. Ullah, R., Amblee, N., Kim, W., Lee, H.: From valence to emotions: exploring the distribution of emotions in online product reviews. Decis. Support Syst. **81**, 41–53 (2016). 10.1016/j.dss.2015.10.007, https://www.sciencedirect.com/science/article/pii/S0167923615002018
31. Voutilainen, A.: Part-of-Speech Tagging. The Oxford handbook of computational linguistics, pp. 219–232 (2003)
32. Xu, D., Tian, Z., Lai, R., Kong, X., Tan, Z., Shi, W.: Deep learning based emotion analysis of microblog texts. Inf. Fusion **64**, 1–11 (2020). 10.1016/j.inffus.2020.06.002, https://www.sciencedirect.com/science/article/pii/S156625352030302X
33. Yin, K., Aragon, C., Evans, S., Davis, K.: Where no one has gone before: a meta-dataset of the world's largest fanfiction repository. In: Proceedings of the 2017 CHI Conference on Human Factors in Computing Systems, pp. 6106–6110 (2017)
34. Yoder, M., et al.: FanfictionNLP: a text processing pipeline for fanfiction. In: Akoury, N., Brahman, F., Chaturvedi, S., Clark, E., Iyyer, M., Martin, L.J. (eds.) Proceedings of the Third Workshop on Narrative Understanding, pp. 13–23. Association for Computational Linguistics, Virtual (2021). https://doi.org/10.18653/v1/2021.nuse-1.2, https://aclanthology.org/2021.nuse-1.2
35. Zhang, Z., Ye, Q., Law, R., Li, Y.: The impact of e-word-of-mouth on the online popularity of restaurants: a comparison of consumer reviews and editor reviews. Int. J. Hosp. Manag. **29**(4), 694–700 (2010). 10.1016/j.ijhm.2010.02.002, https://www.sciencedirect.com/science/article/pii/S0278431910000198

Unbiased Recommender Learning
for Enhanced Relevance and Coverage

Tatsuki Takahashi[✉] and Hiroko Shoji

Chuo University Graduate School, 1-13-27 Kasuga, Bunkyo Ward, Tokyo, Japan
a23.kb3g@g.chuo-u.ac.jp, hiroko@kc.chuo-u.ac.jp

Abstract. In recent years, the effect of cognitive bias on recommender systems has become a major concern. These biases are commonly found in data collected through the feedback loop. Ignoring them may cause problems such as homogenization among users and increasing disparity among items. Therefore, it is necessary to address these biases for sustainable and effective operation of the recommender system. To address exposure bias, a method has been proposed that maximizes the relevance of recommendations by integrating matrix factorization (MF) with an inverse propensity score (IPS) estimator in the pointwise loss function. Although MF achieves a high recommendation accuracy, it tends to bias interactions, for instance, by limiting exposure opportunities for certain items. In this study, we demonstrate that incorporating factorization machines (FM), which can handle various features, into the IPS estimator can improve both the relevance and coverage of recommendations— attributes that typically have a trade-off relationship—using biased data. Experimental results from semi-synthetic data indicate that our approach can significantly enhance item coverage while maintaining the high relevance of recommendations, particularly in a large-scale data environment. This advancement allows many users to discover relevant content from biased data and increases exposure opportunities for a broader range of content.

Keywords: Recommender System · Counterfactual Machine Learning · Exposure Bias · Inverse Propensity Score · Factorization Machines

1   Introduction

This study is based on the recognition that addressing data bias is essential for operating a sustainable and effective recommender system. In recent years, several Web-based companies have developed recommender systems to assist users in making decisions based on a large array of choices [1–3]. The influence of cognitive biases on these systems has garnered significant attention [4]. These biases stemming from the feedback loop are influenced by factors such as past recommendation policies, frequency of item exposure, and display position. Ignoring

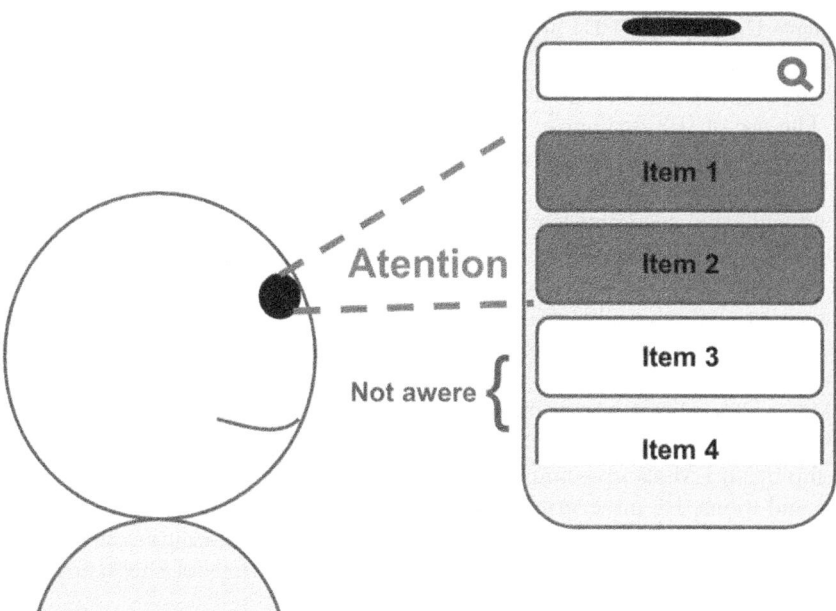

Fig. 1. User Attention on the Web [5]. The top of the screen tends to draw more attention.

these biases can lead to the homogenization of user preferences and disparities among items, often resulting in a system that predominantly recommends popular items [6]. Therefore, a system that accurately reflects the preferences of individual users must be developed.

The objective of this study was to develop a recommender system that simultaneously enhances the relevance of recommendations and the likelihood of item exposure, even when using observational data with exposure bias. To achieve this goal, we propose a novel method that integrates factorization machines (FM) [7] with an inverse propensity score (IPS) estimator of the ideal pointwise loss function [8]. Realizing this objective will foster opportunities for meaningful interactions between all users and content, ensuring that every participant on the platform can fully enjoy the benefits of their engagement.

To address the exposure bias shown in Fig. 1, we can effectively correct the distribution and learn the parameters using the exposure probability as a propensity score and applying inverse weighting to the click data. [8,9] developed an ideal objective function and introduced unbiased estimators that utilized only observed data to enhance the relevance of recommendations. These approaches address the following two primary challenges: First, the "Missing-Not-At-Random" (MNAR) problem occurs when the absence of data depends on the item's exposure label, indicating non-random missing data. Second, the

"Positive-Unlabeled" (PU) problem arises when a user's lack of interaction with an item does not necessarily reflect a negative preference. This ambiguity makes determining whether a non-click signifies disinterest or mere oversight challenging. The use of IPS estimators effectively addresses these issues.

Previous studies on unbiased recommender learning [8,9] predominantly utilized matrix factorization (MF) [10] as the underlying algorithm. MF has a high recommendation accuracy, leading to biased user interactions and widening item disparities [6]. Focusing solely on relevance may reduce the visibility of less popular items and disadvantage content providers, who miss exposure opportunities. Because satisfying both users and suppliers is the key to maximizing a platform's long-term profitability, balancing the accuracy and fairness of recommendations is essential [3].

MF, which relies solely on click data, often overlooks user and item characteristics, resulting in a limited range of recommendations. To address this problem, we employ an FM as a recommendation algorithm that considers the features of users and items. By integrating the FM with the IPS estimator of the pointwise loss function, we demonstrated improved recommendation accuracy and broader item coverage using semi-synthetic data. The contributions of this study are as follows.

- We maximize the relevance of the recommendation list while simultaneously using biased data and improving the coverage rate.
- Similar to conventional MF, FM is integrated into the IPS estimator of the pointwise loss, ensuring the estimator's effectiveness.

2   Related Work

Machine Learning Applications to Recommender Systems. The role of a recommender system is to support users in making decisions based on a large number of choices. As the number of item choices and users increase, it becomes increasingly difficult to deliver preferred items manually to each user. Therefore, efforts to automate decision-making using algorithms such as machine learning have been widely implemented. Applications such as YouTube and Amazon are designed to provide various content options for individual users. This task is known as the Top-N Recommendation, which evaluates the performance of machine learning not only by directly optimizing loss values, such as root mean squared error (RMSE) but also by optimizing aggregate measures, such as Recall and Precision, or ordinal measures, such as discounted cumulative gain (DCG) [11,12].

Data Bias Problem. The vast amount of data observed in an application is known to be biased and not representative of the population [4]. The offline metrics (such as Recall and DCG) and online metrics (such as click and conversion rates) of models trained with such data are inconsistent [13]. This problem leads to unintended consequences, such as recommending only popular items that we would like to recommend items that are relevant to the user.

The main causes of data bias can be attributed to past policies and user behavior. For those caused by past policies, the data reflect the algorithm's tendencies. For example, similar items are recommended if the collaborative filtering continues [6]. The biases caused by user behavior are mainly reflected in explicit and implicit feedback. In the example of explicit feedback, users tend to rate items with higher ratings [14]. That is, they did not assign ratings to all items consumed. This is called selection bias. In an implicit feedback example, users tend to click on items because they are easily visible on the screen [5]. In other words, it cannot be assumed that a user dislikes an item that does not generate a click simply because they are unaware of it. This is called exposure bias. These biases accumulate in a feedback loop to create popularity bias.

Counterfactual Machine Learning. To address bias in the observed data, a technique called counterfactual machine learning, which integrates causal inference and machine learning, was used. By weighting the observed probabilities of the data as a propensity score, the parameters were learned while correcting for deviations in the distribution. To evaluate the deviation of the distribution, it is necessary to develop an estimator that can reduce both the bias and variance of an ideal objective function using the unobservable ground truth as the training data.

Recommendation systems have three main applications. One approach is to address selection bias. There is a learning method that calculates scores based on user rating tendencies by weighting the squared error with inverse probability [15]. The second application was learning-to-rank. The goal is to optimize the order of items for each query or user based on click data. However, because click data contain exposure bias, various loss functions such as pointwise loss [8], pairwise loss [9], and listwise loss [16] weighted by exposure tendency scores based on click models, have been proposed. The third application is learning and evaluating decision-making. There are often situations in which one wants to measure the effectiveness of strategies, such as changing algorithms in recommender systems from A to B, and using observational data to enhance sales. However, the collected data may reflect trends from past policies and may not accurately represent the entire population. Therefore, various estimation methods that use the propensity scores of item selection probabilities from past policies have been proposed. From basic methods such as direct method (DM), IPS, and doubly robust (DR) estimators [17] to advanced estimators that consider action contexts [18] or are suitable for ranking multiple actions in a selection format, a variety of estimation methods have been proposed [19].

3   Problem Formulation

3.1   Click Model

In this study, we assumed that only the click data were observable, as shown in Fig. 2. The occurrence of clicks is then modeled as in [8] and is expressed as follows:

Recommendation Position	Relevance: R (unobservable)	Recognition: O (unobservable)	Click: Y ┌─ ─(observable)─ ─┐
1	R = 1	O = 1	Y = 1
2	R = 0	O = 1	Y = 0
3	R = 0	O = 0	Y = 0
...	...	...	...
10	R = 1	O = 0	Y = 0

Fig. 2. Relationship between relevance (R), recognition (O), and click (Y) in the recommender system [8].

$$Y_{u,i} = R_{u,i} \cdot O_{u,i} \tag{1}$$
$$\mathbb{P}(Y_{u,i} = 1) = \mathbb{P}(R_{u,i} = 1) \cdot \mathbb{P}(O_{u,i} = 1) \tag{2}$$
$$= \gamma_{u,i} \cdot \theta_{u,i} \tag{3}$$

where relevance $R_{u,i} \in \{0,1\}$ is a binary random variable indicating that user u prefers item i, and recognition $O_{u,i} \in \{0,1\}$ is a binary random variable indicating that user u is aware of item i. In other words, a click occurs only if the user likes an item and recognizes it, as shown in Fig. 2.

3.2   Objective Function

The pointwise loss function to be solved ideally is defined as follows:

$$\mathcal{L}_{ideal}(\hat{R}) = -\frac{1}{|\mathcal{D}|} \sum_{(u,i) \in \mathcal{D}}^{|\mathcal{D}|} \gamma_{u,i} \log(\hat{R}_{u,i}) + (1 - \gamma_{u,i}) \log(1 - \hat{R}_{u,i}) \tag{4}$$

However, because the true relevance probability $\gamma_{u,i}$ is unobservable, it is impossible to optimize this function directly. Therefore, we must define an alternative estimator using the available click variables, $Y_{u,i}$.

Inverse Propensity Score (IPS) Estimator

$$\hat{\mathcal{L}}_{IPS}(\hat{R}) = -\frac{1}{|\mathcal{D}|} \sum_{(u,i)\in\mathcal{D}}^{|\mathcal{D}|} \frac{Y_{u,i}}{\theta_{u,i}} \log(\hat{R}_{u,i}) + (1 - \frac{Y_{u,i}}{\theta_{u,i}}) \log(1 - \hat{R}_{u,i}) \qquad (5)$$

The IPS estimator is the first unbiased estimator in the pointwise loss function [8]; by taking the expected value, it aligns with the ideal loss function. This makes it an estimator that works even in the presence of data bias. Details of the IPS estimator are provided in [8]. In particular, for practical applications, it is necessary to estimate the exposure probabilities $\theta_{u,i}$ in advance.

$$\mathbb{E}_Y\left[\hat{\mathcal{L}}_{IPS}(\hat{R})\right] = -\frac{1}{|\mathcal{D}|} \sum_{(u,i)\in\mathcal{D}}^{|\mathcal{D}|} \frac{\mathbb{E}_Y[Y_{u,i}]}{\theta_{u,i}} \log(\hat{R}_{u,i}) + (1 - \frac{\mathbb{E}_Y[Y_{u,i}]}{\theta_{u,i}}) \log(1 - \hat{R}_{u,i})$$

$$= -\frac{1}{|\mathcal{D}|} \sum_{(u,i)\in\mathcal{D}}^{|\mathcal{D}|} \gamma_{u,i} \log(\hat{R}_{u,i}) + (1 - \gamma_{u,i}) \log(1 - \hat{R}_{u,i})$$

$$= \mathcal{L}_{ideal}(\hat{R}) \qquad \because \mathbb{E}_Y[Y_{u,i}] = \gamma_{u,i} \cdot \theta_{u,i}$$

Naïve Estimator

$$\hat{\mathcal{L}}_{naive}(\hat{R}) = -\frac{1}{|\mathcal{D}|} \sum_{(u,i)\in\mathcal{D}}^{|\mathcal{D}|} Y_{u,i} \log(\hat{R}_{u,i}) + (1 - Y_{u,i}) \log(1 - \hat{R}_{u,i}) \qquad (6)$$

The naïve estimator, which is commonly employed in practical settings, is defined above. However, the expected value of the naïve estimator does not align consistently with the ideal loss function and tends to overfit data characterized by large exposure probabilities. Therefore, from a statistical perspective, the IPS estimator is superior to the naïve estimator.

$$\mathbb{E}_Y\left[\hat{\mathcal{L}}_{naive}(\hat{R})]\right] = -\frac{1}{|\mathcal{D}|} \sum_{(u,i)\in\mathcal{D}}^{|\mathcal{D}|} \mathbb{E}_Y[Y_{u,i}] \log(\hat{R}_{u,i}) + (1 - \mathbb{E}_Y[Y_{u,i}]) \log(1 - \hat{R}_{u,i})$$

$$= -\frac{1}{|\mathcal{D}|} \sum_{(u,i)\in\mathcal{D}}^{|\mathcal{D}|} \gamma_{u,i}\theta_{u,i} \log(\hat{R}_{u,i}) + (1 - \gamma_{u,i}\theta_{u,i}) \log(1 - \hat{R}_{u,i})$$

$$\neq \mathcal{L}_{ideal}(\hat{R})$$

4   Issues with Prior Research and Potential Remedies

In the performance evaluation of the IPS estimator in [8], logistic matrix factorization (MF) was utilized as a machine learning model $\hat{R}_{u,i}$.

$$\sigma(x) = \frac{1}{1 + \exp(x)},\tag{7}$$

$$\hat{R}_{u,i} = \sigma(\mathbf{q}_i^\top \mathbf{p}_u + b_u + b_i + b).\tag{8}$$

MF is a technique commonly used in recommender systems because of its scalability and high performance [10]. However, MF may introduce bias in user and item interactions [6], resulting in only certain items being recommended, and widening the gap between items. To address this issue, we propose using an FM [7], which can incorporate user and item features to enhance the relevance and coverage of recommended items.

$$\hat{y}(\mathbf{x}) = w_0 + \sum_{i=1}^{n} w_i x_i + \sum_{i=1}^{n} \sum_{j=i+1}^{n} \mathbf{v}_i^\top \mathbf{v}_j x_i x_j \tag{9}$$

$$\hat{R} = \sigma(\hat{y}(\mathbf{x}))\tag{10}$$

5   Semi-Synthetic Experiment

We conducted experiments using semi-synthetic data to address the research question (RQ)[1].

RQ. Compared with MF, the use of FM can enhance both the relevance and coverage of recommendations from biased data.

5.1   Experimental Setup

4.1.1 Dataset. We utilized the Kuairec[2] [20] and Coat[3] [15] datasets for our experiments. Both datasets were selected on the basis of their characteristics, including biased training and uniformly observed test data, along with a comprehensive set of features. An overview of these datasets is presented below.

Kuairec Dataset. This dataset, sourced from the Chinese video platform Kuaishou, comprises two primary files: 'small_matrix.csv' and 'big_matrix.csv'. The former file, 'small_matrix.csv', contains nearly complete rating data for 1,411 users and 3,327 videos, providing a comprehensive snapshot of user preferences. The latter file, 'big_matrix.csv', documents naturally occurring interactions between 7,176 users and 10,728 video pairs, with a sparsity level of 16.3%, reflecting real-world engagement levels. This dataset was assumed to include various biases. Additional files offer anonymized user and item features, thus enriching the dataset's utility for bias analysis.

---

[1] Details on the experiment implementation are available at: https://github.com/tatsuki1107/Unbiased-Recommender-Learning-for-Enhanced-Relevance-and-Coverage.

[2] Kuairec: https://kuairec.com/.

[3] Coat: https://www.cs.cornell.edu/~schnabts/mnar/.

Coat Dataset. The Coat dataset, which was comparatively smaller in scale, categorized clothing items into five ratings. It includes two primary files: 'train.ascii' and 'test.ascii'. The 'train.ascii' file encompasses ratings provided by users for selected coats, introducing a selection bias, while the 'test.ascii' file represents unbiased user evaluations of randomly selected items. This dataset also incorporates additional attributes such as user gender and coat color, which were significant for our analysis.

4.1.2 Procedures for Creating Semi-synthetic Data.

To address data bias, this study required a population that is not typically observed. In other words, semi-synthetic data were created to assume the true relevance and exposure probabilities in the evaluation. The policy was to bias the training data with exposure bias and ensure that the test data were representative of the population. The procedure for creating these data was as follows.

Kuairec Dataset. Generate semi-synthetic log data using the 'small_matrix.csv' file. In this experiment, we assumed that the bias in the log data could be solely attributed to exposure disparity. We generated a log dataset $\mathcal{D}$ with a density of 7% of the evaluation value matrix using random recommendations. The size of the extracted log data is approximately 320,000. To generate the true relevance probability, we utilize the 'watch_ratio' column in 'small_matrix.csv'. This figure shows the ratio of viewing time to the total length of the video. If the 'watch_ratio' is high, we interpret that the user likes the video. If 'watch_ratio' is greater than 2, we transform the scale of the relevance probability, $\gamma_{u,i}$ to be within the range of $[0,1]$ by setting the maximum value of the relevance probability, $\gamma_{u,i}$ to 1. As for the true exposure probability, we assume that 'big_matrix.csv' contains various biases such as past recommendation policies and the degree of exposure, as mentioned earlier. We artificially created an exposure bias based on the observed frequency of items in 'big_matrix.csv', which is also included in 'small_matrix.csv'. The observation frequencies were then standardized, and a sigmoid function was applied to generate the exposure probability $\theta_{u,i} \in [0,1]$. These true probabilities were then used to generate binary random variables $Y_{u,i} \in \{0,1\}$ according to the click generation model defined in Sect. 3.1.

Coat Dataset. This dataset differs from the Kuairec dataset in that the biased training and test data representative of the population were already stored separately. However, the evaluation values are explicitly provided by the user and must be semi-synthetically transformed into implicit feedback such as click data. Therefore, we employed the method described in the literature [21] to transform the 5-level evaluation values into click probabilities and create click variables, $Y_{u,i}$. The exposure probabilities have already been estimated in the file, 'propensities.ascii' and are utilized in the experiments.

4.1.3 Feature Selection. Because feature selection was not the main focus of this experiment, multiple features were selected for both datasets. Please refer to experimental code [3] for further details.

4.1.4 Baselines and Proposed Model. The loss functions and recommendation models utilized in the experiments are as follows:

- **Random**: This model randomly selects user preferences from a uniform distribution. It doesn't involve optimization, resulting in low recommendation relevance but high coverage.
- **MF_Naïve, FM_Naïve**: A naïve method without correction for exposure bias. MF [10] and FM [7] are integrated with the Naïve estimator.
- **MF_IPS** (Rel-MF): As a conventional approach dealing with exposure bias, MF is integrated with the IPS estimator to learn the parameters [8]. In general, this model achieves high recommendation relevance. However, it suffers from low coverage and significant disparities among items.
- **FM_IPS**: In the proposed method, FM is combined with the IPS estimator to optimize the parameters. The objective extends beyond enhancing recommendation relevance to increasing the coverage ratio.

4.1.5 Model Training and Hyperparameter Tuning Criteria. The model was trained based on the generalization performance of the validation data, which were obtained by splitting the biased training data. The following description pertains to the learning method of the IPS estimator; however, the same procedure can be applied to a naive estimator.

The objective function when FM is applied is as follows: Note that the notation for FM is slightly different from that for MF because of the variance in the data retention methods.

$$\hat{\mathcal{L}}_{IPS}(\hat{R}) = -\frac{1}{|\mathcal{D}|} \sum_{t=1}^{|\mathcal{D}|} \frac{Y_t}{\theta_t^p} \log(\hat{R}_t) + (1 - \frac{Y_t}{\theta_t^p}) \log(1 - \hat{R}_t) \qquad (11)$$

Here, $p \in [0, 1]$ is incorporated as a hyperparameter to control for estimator bias and variance. The IPS estimator is unbiased. However, as Equation (12) shows, when the data sample size is small or the exposure probability θ_t is extremely small, the variance of the estimator increases, leading to an unstable estimation [8].

$$\mathrm{Var}_Y[\hat{\mathcal{L}}_{IPS}(\hat{R})] = \frac{1}{|\mathcal{D}|^2} \sum_{t=1}^{|\mathcal{D}|} \gamma_t (\frac{1}{\theta_t^p} - \gamma_t)(\log(\hat{R}_t) - \log(1 - \hat{R}_t))^2 \qquad (12)$$

When p is one, it is equal to the IPS estimator, and when p is zero, it is equal to the naive estimator. By setting p between zero and one, we introduce some bias into the estimator and reduce the variance to stabilize the learning process.

We observed a decrease in the loss and set $p = 0.5$ for the Kuairec Dataset and $p = 0.1$ for the Coat Dataset. In particular, for the Coat dataset, because of its small size, we believe that the IPS estimator will not function properly unless p is close to zero.

Here, the tuning criteria for the hyperparameters are described. For training, we used batch Stochastic Gradient Descent (SGD) as the optimization algorithm. The number of factors, batch sizes, and regularization parameters were fixed for each dataset, and only the learning rate was adjusted for each model and estimator. The learning rate was manually determined by observing the reduction in the pointwise loss in Equation (11). Learning stops when the following weighted discounted cumulative gain (DCG) at five [11] for the validation data is maximized out of a maximum of 500 iterations: The training was conducted based on these criteria.

$$\hat{R}_{IPS}(\hat{Z}_{u,i}) = \frac{1}{|\mathcal{U}|} \sum_{u \in \mathcal{U}} \sum_{i \in \mathcal{I}_u^{val}} \frac{Y_{u,i}}{\theta_{u,i}^p} \cdot \frac{\mathbb{I}\{\hat{Z}_{u,i} \leq 5\}}{\log_2(\hat{Z}_{u,i} + 1)} \tag{13}$$

where $\hat{Z}_{u,i} \in \{1, \ldots, |\mathcal{I}_u^{val}|\}$ denotes the predicted ranking of items for each user. In this case, pointwise loss was used for training, and the ranking was converted into one based on the predicted value of the association probability between the user and the item. That is, $\hat{Z}_{u,i} = 1$ for the highest predicted probability and $\hat{Z}_{u,i} = |\mathcal{I}_u^{val}|$ for the lowest probability.

$\mathbb{I}\{\cdot\}$ is an indicator function that returns 1 if the proposition in parentheses is true and 0 if it is not true.

4.1.6 Evaluation. The models were trained on biased training data and evaluated using test data representing the true distribution. DCG and Catalog Coverage were used as evaluation metrics to assess the performance of the recommendation system. DCG assesses the model's capability to recommend highly relevant items. Catalog Coverage assesses a model's ability to expose users to more items. Larger values for both metrics indicate better performance.

Given the trade-off relationship between DCG and Catalog Coverage, achieving a high value for only one of these metrics is insufficient. To evaluate the potential for simultaneous improvements in the relevance and coverage of recommendations from biased data, we assessed whether both metrics exhibited high values across the baselines and proposed FM_IPS model.

$$DCG@K = \frac{1}{|\mathcal{U}|} \sum_{u \in \mathcal{U}} \sum_{i \in \mathcal{I}_u^{test}:R_{u,i}=1} \frac{\mathbb{I}\{\hat{Z}_{u,i} \leq K\}}{\log_2(\hat{Z}_{u,i} + 1)},$$

$$CatalogCoverage@K = \frac{|\bigcup_{u \in \mathcal{U}} rec_u(K)|}{|\mathcal{I}|}.$$

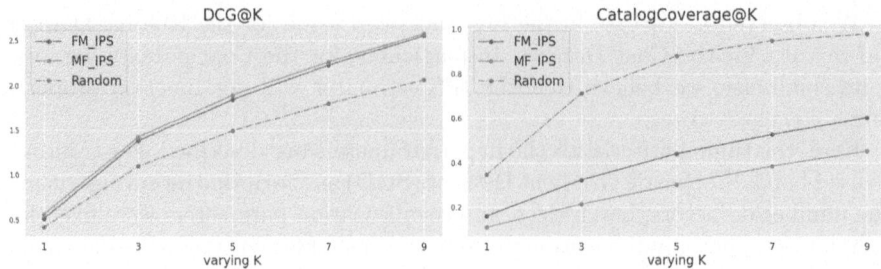

Fig. 3. Evaluation Metrics on the Kuairec Dataset

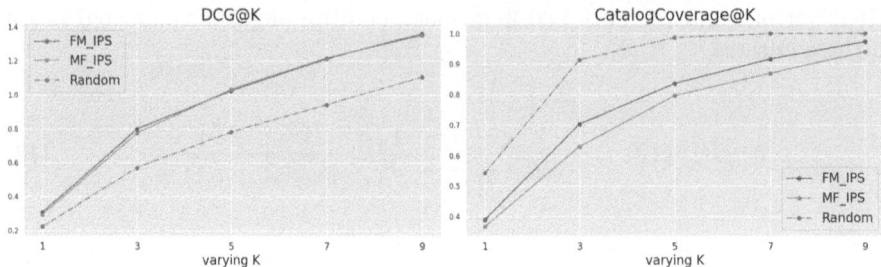

Fig. 4. Evaluation Metrics on the Coat Dataset

where $rec_u(K)$ represents the set of the top K items recommended to user u. The coverage is calculated based on the union of the set of recommended items $rec_u(K)$ for all users.

We then define the Mean Exposure (ME)@K to assess the functionality of the IPS estimator. Ideally, ME@K should have a constant value at any recommended position, K.

$$ME@K = \frac{1}{|\mathcal{U}|} \sum_{u \in \mathcal{U}} \sum_{i \in \mathcal{I}_u^{test}} \mathbb{I}\{\hat{Z}_{u,i} = K\} \cdot \theta_{u,i}$$

5.2   Results and Discussion

Results. Figures 3 and 4 show the experimental results for the Kuairec and Coat datasets. The DCG@K metrics for FM_IPS and MF_IPS surpassed those of Random, although FM_IPS deteriorated DCG@5 by 2.6% on the Kuairec dataset and 0.7% on the Coat dataset over MF_IPS. In terms of CatalogCoverage@K, Random exhibited the highest performance, with FM_IPS ranking second on both datasets. Specifically, FM_IPS improved CatalogCoverage@5 by 45.8% on the Kuairec dataset and by 5.0% on the Coat dataset compared to MF_IPS.

Figure 5 shows the ME@K performance for each dataset. Ideally, ME@K should demonstrate a constant value at any recommended position, similar to

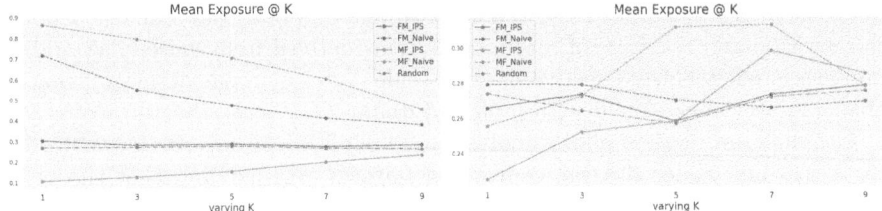

Fig. 5. (Left)Mean Exposure (ME)@K on the Kuairec Dataset. (Right)ME@K on the Coat Dataset.

Random performance. For the Kuairec dataset, we observed that the performance of the IPS estimator was closer to random than that of the naïve estimator, which tended to recommend items with high exposure bias at elevated recommendation positions. Additionally, it was demonstrated that using FM as the model within the IPS estimator leads to a performance that more closely mirrors that of random. In the Coat dataset, the ME@K performances when using either the IPS or Naïve estimators did not differ significantly.

Discussion. In conclusion, the research question was partially answered with a "Yes." Although FM_IPS exhibited a slight deterioration in DCG@K performance compared to MF_IPS for the conventional method, it significantly enhanced CatalogCoverage@K, particularly with the Kuairec dataset, which comprises a large volume of data. This improvement indicates a reduction in item bias, while concurrently preserving the high relevance of the recommendation. Despite Random achieving the highest CatalogCoverage@K, its DCG@K performance was notably poor. Consequently, FM_IPS offers a more balanced performance, suggesting that it is preferable in scenarios that prioritize both metrics. However, the ME@K performance results suggest that the use of the IPS estimator may not be necessary in smaller environments such as the Coat dataset. Given the pronounced popularity bias in large environments, we believe that FM_IPS delivers a more balanced performance and is the preferred choice in scenarios where both metrics are important. This choice enables more users to discover relevant content even in the presence of biased data and creates opportunities for broader content exposure. This is the value that platforms aim to provide when developing recommender systems.

6   Conclusion

In this study, we proposed a novel method that effectively recommends items despite the presence of exposure bias in log data. Drawing on the framework discussed in [8], we modeled the click generation process and derived a statistically unbiased IPS estimator with precision. Although prior research has predominantly utilized MF as a recommendation algorithm, this often resulted in biased interactions. By integrating the FM into our methodology, we enhanced both the relevance and coverage of recommendations derived from biased data. This approach is particularly effective in large-scale data environments, significantly enhancing user engagement with preferred items.

Although our method allows analysts to maximize relevance, it does not provide a mechanism for directly controlling fairness. We envision that the next phase of research will focus on designing a loss function that directly addresses both relevance and fairness in recommendations. Developing a statistically unbiased estimator based on this function will enable effective management of fairness.

Acknowledgements. We would like to express our gratitude to Chuo University for providing the grant for conference participation, which greatly facilitated the presentation and dissemination of our research findings. This support was invaluable in enhancing the impact and reach of our work.

References

1. Saito, Y., Aihara, S., Matsutani, M., Narita, Y. Open Bandit Dataset and Pipeline: Towards Realistic and Reproducible Off-Policy Evaluation. *arXiv preprint* arXiv:2008.07146 (2020)
2. Covington, P., Jay, A., Sargin, E. Deep neural networks for YouTube recommendations. In: Proceedings of the 10th ACM Conference on Recommender Systems (RecSys '16). Association for Computing Machinery, New York, NY, USA, pp. 191–198 (2016)
3. Mehrotra, R., McInerney, J., Bouchard, H., Lalmas, M., Diaz, F. Towards a fair marketplace: counterfactual evaluation of the trade-off between relevance, fairness & satisfaction in recommendation systems. In: Proceedings of the 27th ACM International Conference on Information and Knowledge Management (CIKM '18). Association for Computing Machinery, New York, NY, USA, pp. 2243–2251 (2018)
4. Chen, J., Dong, H., Wang, X., Feng, F., Wang, M., He, X.: Bias and debias in recommender system: a survey and future directions. ACM T. Inform. Sys. **41**(3), 1–39 (2023)
5. Baeza-Yates, R.: Bias on the web. Commun. ACM **61**(6), 54–61 (2018). https://doi.org/10.1145/3209581
6. Chaney, A.J.B., Stewart, B.M., Engelhardt, B.E.: How algorithmic confounding in recommendation systems increases homogeneity and decreases utility. In: Proceedings of the 12th ACM Conference on Recommender Systems, pp. 224-232. ACM (2018)
7. Rendle, S.: Factorization machines. In: *ICDM'10*, pp. 995-1000 (2010)
8. Saito, Y., Yaginuma, Y., Nishino, Y., Sakata, H., Nakata, K.: Unbiased recommender learning from missing-not-at-random implicit feedback. In: Proceedings of the 13th International Conference on Web Search and Data Mining, pp. 501–509 (2020)
9. Saito, Y.: Unbiased pairwise learning from biased implicit feedback. In: Proceedings of the 2020 ACM SIGIR on International Conference on Theory of Information Retrieval (ICTIR '20). Association for Computing Machinery, New York, NY, USA, pp. 5–12 (2020)

10. Koren, Y., Bell, R., Volinsky, C.: Matrix factorization techniques for recommender systems. Comput. **8**, 30–37 (2009)
11. Yang, L., Cui, Y., Xuan, Y., Wang, C., Belongie, S., Estrin, D.: Unbiased offline recommender evaluation for missing-not-at-random implicit feedback. In: Proceedings of the 12th ACM Conference on Recommender Systems (RecSys '18). Association for Computing Machinery, New York, NY, USA, pp. 279–287 (2018)
12. Cremonesi, P., Koren, Y., Turrin, R.: Performance of recommender algorithms on top-n recommendation tasks. In: Proceedings of the fourth ACM conference on Recommender systems (RecSys '10). Association for Computing Machinery, New York, NY, USA, pp. 39–46 (2010)
13. Bernardi, L., Mavridis, T., Estevez, P.: 150 successful machine learning models: 6 lessons learned at booking.com. In: Proceedings of the 25th ACM SIGKDD International Conference on Knowledge Discovery & Data Mining (KDD '19). Association for Computing Machinery, New York, NY, USA, pp. 1743–1751 (2019)
14. Marlin, M., Zemel, S., Roweis, S., Slaney, M.: Collaborative filtering and the missing at random assumption. In: Proceedings of the Twenty-Third Conference on Uncertainty in Artificial Intelligence (UAI'07). AUAI Press, Arlington, Virginia, USA, pp. 267–275 (2007)
15. Schnabel, T., Swaminathan, A., Singh, A., Chandak, N., Joachims, T.: Recommendations as treatments: debiasing learning and evaluation. In: Proceedings of the 33rd International Conference on International Conference on Machine Learning - Volume 48 (ICML'16). JMLR.org, pp. 1670–1679 (2016)
16. Ai, Q., Bi, K., Luo, C., Guo, J., Croft, W.B.: Unbiased learning to rank with unbiased propensity estimation. In: The 41st International ACM SIGIR Conference on Research & Development in Information Retrieval (SIGIR '18). Association for Computing Machinery, New York, NY, USA, pp. 385–394 (2018)
17. Dudík, M., Langford, J., Li, L.: Doubly robust policy evaluation and learning. In: Proceedings of the 28th International Conference on International Conference on Machine Learning (ICML'11). Omnipress, Madison, WI, USA, pp. 1097–1104 (2011)
18. Saito, Y., Joachims, T.: Off-policy evaluation for large action spaces via embeddings. In: International Conference on Machine Learning, pp. 19089–19122. PMLR (2022)
19. Li, S., Abbasi-Yadkori, Y., Kveton, B., Muthukrishnan, S., Vinay, V., Wen, Z.: Offline evaluation of ranking policies with click models. In: Proceedings of the 24th ACM SIGKDD International Conference on Knowledge Discovery & Data Mining (KDD '18). Association for Computing Machinery, New York, NY, USA, pp. 1685–1694 (2018)
20. Gao, C., et al.: KuaiRec: A Fully-observed Dataset and Insights for Evaluating Recommender Systems. *arXiv preprint* arXiv:2202.10842 (2022)
21. Saito, Y.: Doubly robust estimator for ranking metrics with post-click conversions. In: Proceedings of the 14th ACM Conference on Recommender Systems (RecSys '20). Association for Computing Machinery, New York, NY, USA, pp. 92–100 (2020)

AI Web Service Solution for Real-Time Forest Fire Prevention

Nuno A. Valente[1,2]([✉]), Eduardo J. Solteiro Pires[1,2], Arsénio Reis[1,2],
António Pereira[3,4], and João Barroso[1,2]

[1] Escola de Ciências e Tecnologia, Universidade de Trás-os-Montes e Alto Douro,
Quinta de Prados, Vila Real, 5000-811 Vila Real, Portugal
`al73891@alunos.utad.pt,{epires,ars,jbarroso}@utad.pt`
[2] INESC TEC - Instituto de Engenharia de Sistemas e Computadores,
Tecnologia e Ciência, Vila Real, Portugal
[3] Computer Science and Communications Research Center, School of Technology
and Management, Polytechnic of Leiria, Morro do Lena, Street, Alto do Vieiro,
Apartado 4163, 2411–901 Leiria, Portugal
`apereira@ipleiria.pt`
[4] INOV INESC INNOVATION - Institute of New Technologies of Leiria, Street,
Alto do Vieiro, Apartado 4163, 2411–901 Leiria, Portugal

Abstract. Forest fires in Portugal are a recurring tragedy, especially
during the summer, leaving a devastating trail affecting the environment and local communities. In addition to the loss of vast forest areas,
these disasters harm wildlife, pollute the air, and compromise soil and
water quality, contributing to environmental degradation and increasing
the risk of soil erosion and landslides. Furthermore, fires have significant
economic impacts, affecting communities that depend on the forest for
subsistence, tourism, and agricultural activities. To address this issue, an
innovative Web Service has been developed that uses artificial intelligence
algorithms to calculate real-time fire risk. This service integrates up-to-
date weather data with historical fire patterns, providing an accurate and
timely assessment of fire potential in specific areas. The machine learning model behind the service was trained with historical fire data from
mainland Portugal between 2017 and 2023, allowing for a more accurate
and predictive analysis of fire risk. The Web Service facilitates proactive
emergency prevention and decision-making response by integrating real-
time weather information with historical fire data. Authorities can use
the information provided by the service to implement preventive policies
to help elderly people.

Keywords: Web Service · Artificial Intelligence · Forest Fire
Prediction

1 Introduction

During the summer months and in extreme hot conditions, Portugal is recur-
rently affected by forest fires, which leave trails of destruction difficult to recover

H. Degen and S. Ntoa (Eds.): HCII 2024, LNCS 15382, pp. 246–255, 2024.
https://doi.org/10.1007/978-3-031-76827-9_14

in the short term every year. The impact of these tragedies goes far beyond the physical destruction of natural resources and local communities. In addition to the direct devastation of forests and wildlife, the long-term consequences of these fires include air and soil pollution, degradation of soil quality, and an increased risk of soil erosion and landslides. The economic implications are also considerable, especially for local communities that rely on the forest, both for agriculture, food, livestock farming, and tourism.

In recent years, technological advancements have allowed organizations to develop novel approaches for managing wildfires. The use of Internet Of Things (IoT), Artificial Intelligence (AI) and Unmanned Aerial Vehicles (also known as drones) has improved the accuracy of fire detection and prevention by analyzing fire behavior in real-time field situations [11]. Drones equipped with advanced cameras alongside thermal imaging can furnish up-to-date information to firefighters while they evaluate terrain conditions or release fire retardants in inaccessible areas. Additionally, AI algorithms analyze data from satellites, drones, and ground sensors to quickly identify potential fires, promptly notifying authorities for faster response against spreading blazes.

This paper proposes a real-time fire prediction system that integrates AI technology with web services for forest fire prediction. The system aims to give a real-time precise evaluation of the likelihood of a forest fire occurrence in a given area, allowing for proactive decision-making towards emergency responses, helping authorities and firefighting agencies make informed decisions and allocate necessary resources for proactive fire management and suppression. The integration of public Application Programming Interfaces (APIs) to obtain a variety of biophysical data such as temperature, humidity, precipitation, wind speed and direction, and vegetation density in real-time [9], along with the AI model and historical forest fire patterns, enables to analyze and predict fire risks with high accuracy. In addition, the web service will offer an API that can be integrated with other softwares or systems to access real-time wildfire risk evaluations by inputting geographical coordinates or areas and receiving immediate risk assessments.

The proposed system represents a promising effort to address the challenges of wildfires in Portugal. The application of AI and real-time data in forest fire prediction not only enhances the efficiency of early detection and response but also contributes to minimizing the environmental and economic impact of wildfires. The proactive approach enabled by the Real-Time Fire Prediction System will support sustainable forest management and aid in safeguarding the natural ecosystem and local communities from the devastating effects of forest fires.

2   Background and Related Work

Web services can be designed and implemented to provide accurate and timely results on wildfire risk. This can be achieved by combining various external weather data services to compute fire risk indications based on historical data in the form of measurements from meteorological weather stations, forecast data, or a combination of both. Such a system can use REST web services where a consumer provides longitude and latitude to trigger computation of a fire risk indication for the geographical location. The service can provide access to a variety of resources about locations, weather records, observations, lightning, sources (weather station metadata), elements (weather elements), climate normals, and frequencies [14]. Different weather services present their data in different formats, which need to be converted prior to being input into the model, as some services offer forecasts, measurements from a station, or interpolated data. The system can be developed as one monolith or several microservices, each of which needs to be configured and hosted in a suitable cloud service. The system must be scalable and able to handle increasing amounts of traffic [8].

In order to enhance the effectiveness of strategies for combating forest fires, it is essential to comprehend the latest developments in technologies used for fire prevention and how Web Services can be used for fire risk assessment. The research questions guiding this review are:

- How can Web Services be designed and implemented to provide accurate and timely results on wildfire risk?
- How can meteorological APIs and historical data be integrated into Web Services to predict wildfire risk?
- What are the main methods and technologies used in developing Web Services for wildfire risk analysis?

This study will focus on recent literature related to the application of Web-based systems to evaluate fire risk in real-time, with specific attention will be given to integrating meteorological data, historical fire patterns, and machine learning models to provide a comprehensive understanding of the current state of research in this area.

2.1   Methods and Materials

The research strategy involved conducting a thorough examination of academic databases, including Google Scholar, IEEE Xplore, Springer Open, MDPI and b-on. This process involved identifying and obtaining papers, conference papers, journal papers, and thesis using Web Services for real-time fire risk calculation. The search terms used were "web service", "restful API", and "real-time forest fire prevention" to ensure a comprehensive review of available literature. The study's criteria for inclusion were designed to align with the specific goals of this research, with a focus on recent publications to capture the latest developments in the field. The inclusion of studies published within the last ten years guaranteed the incorporation of the most current advancements in this area.

The data collection process involved a thorough review of selected studies to gather pertinent information for the analysis. Papers were selected based on an assessment of their titles, abstracts, keywords, and publication dates. This approach guaranteed the inclusion of only those studies that focused on forest fire forecasting models and methods while excluding those centered on unrelated subjects or different types of natural disasters. Furthermore, references from relevant studies and papers were reviewed to identify additional sources. The latest search was conducted on May 14, 2024, to ensure coverage of recent publications and research findings.

The data extracted from the selected studies provided invaluable insights into Web Services performance, integration of external meteorological data, historical fire patterns, and methodologies and technologies used in predicting forest fires. The comprehensive literature review allowed for a detailed understanding of the main trends and advances regarding the Web Services' effectiveness in real-time fire risk assessment, contributing to the development of a robust knowledge base for proactive and emergency response in forest fire management.

2.2   Results

The use of web services has enabled the seamless integration of external meteorological data, historical fire patterns, and AI technology for precise analysis and prediction of fire risks with high accuracy. This integration of technology and real-time data not only enhances the efficiency of forest fire management and suppression but also contributes to minimizing the environmental and economic impact of wildfires.

Poursanidis *et al.* [12] demonstrate the implementation of flood and fire risk assessment and Management (FLIRE) through a web-based information system (WIS). This system uses various data sources, including forest fuel maps, satellite data, in-situ observations, and weather forecasts, to model fire propagation and present results for specific user-defined periods. By conducting simulations to assess different fire development scenarios, this system serves as an important Decision Support Tool for planning fire mitigation efforts. The FLIRE WIS provides real-time access to any internet-enabled platform for predicting fire behavior using meteorological station data and numerical weather forecasts. It includes historical weather and fire data to initialize simulation models and manage calibration processes accurately if needed. Integration of weather data from national agencies or commercial providers is enabled through APIs, using server-side scripting languages like PHP and Python combined with frameworks such as Flask or Django while front-end development incorporates HTML, CSS, JavaScript alongside web mapping libraries.

A new framework has been proposed by Taktak *et al.* [15] for predicting wildfires. It aims to select the best data sources and adjust service instances using a machine learning-based approach at runtime. The focus is on integrating data services from various sources, selecting services with specific qualities based on wildfire context and expert requirements, and considering past observations of wildfires and expert feedback. The framework uses semantic web service technologies to represent the functionalities and capabilities of selected services, along with quality-of-service models to evaluate the services' quality dimensions in wildfire contexts. Additionally, it employs fuzzy logic-based approaches for inferring appropriate risk levels of wildfires in geographic areas based on environmental observation data obtained from service components.

A prototype software for indicating fire risk was designed and deployed by Stokkenes *et al.* [13]. The main concept was to offer the fire risk indication through a REST web service utilizing weather data REST services from the Norwegian Meteorological Institute and Netatmo. The primary service provided by the system is the Fire Risk Prediction Service, which operates as a REST web service where consumers input longitude and latitude to initiate calculation of fire risk indications for specific geographical locations. That triggers computation in the Fire Risk Model Service based on measurements and forecasts obtained through the Data Harvesting Service, with data stored in noSQL databases. For this fire risk indication system, two meteorological APIs were integrated into web services: Frost API from MET providing historical weather data resources such as location details, records, lightning information, station metadata, climate normals/frequencies; and Netatmo weather data API offering similar consumer grade weather station-based records outside private homes. Additionally, historical 2019 winter weather data from four selected locations was employed to validate the fire risk indication model. The software prototype utilized a micro-service-oriented approach with Spark/Java as its principal framework for implementing application services and components while leveraging cloud-based Amazon EC2 deployment alongside an Azure platform-hosted MongoDB database for storage purposes.

Halderaker and Evjenth [8] developed a software system for fire risk prediction that can provide an early warning to homeowners, building owners, and emergency services about the potential fire risk. The system is designed to calculate fire risks, gather weather data, and send notifications to subscribers, using key technologies such as Python, Flask, MongoDB, Docker, RabbitMQ, and React. The Fire Risk Services exposes a REST API with the Fire Risk Model as a library. This model is responsible for calculating the risk of fire based on incoming data. The Data Harvesting Service collects and stores weather data from various sources and formats it for use by the Fire Risk Services. Weather forecasts from various sources such as MET, along with historical measurements, are integrated through meteorological APIs and stored in a database for analysis and fire risk predictions. Moreover, future fire risks can be predicted by using weather forecast data as a measurement replacement. A collection of cloud-based micro-services allows stakeholders to access information on the risk of fires. Users can input specific locations into the platform, observe current and future risks displayed as a heat-map on a geographical interface, and choose to receive alerts regarding high-risk areas.

Strand *et al.* [14] described the implementation and experimental validation of a predictive fire risk model for wooden homes, utilizing cloud-provided weather measurements and forecasts to determine the indoor wooden fuel moisture content of houses that may catch fire, estimate time to flashover, and predict the near-future fire risk at given geographical locations. The study specifically focuses on the high and dense representation of wooden homes in Norway and their risk of fire during the dry and cold winter seasons. The system predict wildfire risk by using a three-component architecture: a Fire Risk Prediction

Service, a Data Harvesting Service, and a Fire Risk Model Service. The Data Harvesting Service is responsible for collecting weather data measurements and forecasts from the external weather data services and storing them in the associated database. The application uses meteorological APIs, such as Frost (MET) and Netatmo, as well as one external web service to obtain forecast weather data, as to predict the fire risk in the coming days, namely MET Norway weather API. The Fire Risk Model Service implements the fire risk indication model capable of computing fire risk indications based on historical data in the form of measurements from meteorological weather stations, forecast data, and a combination of the two. The Fire Risk Prediction Service is a REST web service where a consumer provides longitude and latitude to trigger computation of a fire risk indication for the geographical location. The system then uses the Data Harvesting Service and the Fire Risk Model Service to compute the fire risk indications for the location, resulting in accurate and timely predictions of wildfire risk.

In addressing the critical need for accurate and timely wildfire risk prediction, this research focused on three primary areas: the design and implementation of web services, the integration of meteorological APIs and historical data, and the methods and technologies employed in developing these services. This study provided an understanding of the latest advances and technologies used for forest fire prediction. Some of the study's key findings include the use of AI algorithms for calculating wildfire risk, the use of REST web services with micro-services architectures to ensure real-time data processing and provide up-to-date information on wildfire risk.

Accurate and timely wildfire risk prediction integrate diverse data sources, such as meteorological stations, satellite imagery, and in-situ observations [12, 15]. This integration enhances the comprehensiveness of risk assessments. Services that collect and store weather data from national meteorological institutes' APIs as well as weather stations ensure availability of historical and forecasted datasets.

Developing these web services involves using a micro-service oriented approach, ensuring scalability and flexibility in service deployment They are deployed on cloud platforms such as Amazon EC2 or Azure, leveraging scalable computing resources for high system availability and reliability. Modern programming languages like Python and Java, along with frameworks such as Flask, Docker, RabbitMQ, and MongoDB are used alongside cloud-based storage solutions to support efficient management and analysis of large volumes of data. These technologies enable the representation of service functionalities using semantic web technologies while creating RESTful APIs that facilitate real-time interaction between different components [8,13–15]. This results in effective Web Services highlighting the importance of integrating diverse source data with advanced computational methods leveraging modern web technologies for developing effective wildfire risk prediction and management.

3   Web Service Solution

This section explains the development and execution of a web service that uses various national and public APIs to gather meteorological data, in addition to incorporating a noSQL database for storage. The main objective of this service is to improve existing forest fire prediction systems by enhancing their accuracy and provide an architectural design that prioritize real-time effiencicy and reliability. To accomplish this goal, the service needs to offer a clear and consistent interface while being well-documented, enabling seamless integration with other systems that access fire risk assessments. Furthermore, security measures as well as authentication protocols are put in place to ensure secure communication among different machines.

The Forest Fire Prediction Web Service provides precise and timely risk assessments by analyzing weather data and historical fire incidents. The indicators used for predicting wildfire risk encompass temperature, humidity, wind speed and direction, precipitation, radiation, and the NDVI index. To gather these indicators from various public APIs in different formats, appropriate data transformation is integrated to maintain consistency and compatibility with the service. Subsequently, a machine learning model processes the information before storing results in the database.

3.1   Design

System Design. The service offers a range of RESTful endpoints for accessing real-time risk assessments. The API includes the following endpoints:

– /**predict**: Accepts POST requests with geographical coordinates.
– /**history**: Provides historical prediction data for given coordinates.

Users can use these endpoints to retrieve fire risk predictions and access historical data by inputting a single coordinate or a valid polygon of coordinates. The Web Service will then respond with the corresponding fire risk prediction and meteorological data in GeoJSON format.

System Architecture. The system comprises two components: the web service and the forest fire prediction model. These components communicate with each other to collect, process, and analyze data to create a high accuracy forest fire prediction. The component diagram of this system is represented in Fig. 1.

The web service exposes a RESTful API that is responsible for receiving user inputs, such as locations or geographical areas, based on coordinates and triggering the web service to collect real-time data from different APIs and send the data to the forest fire prediction model to generate a prediction for the given location.

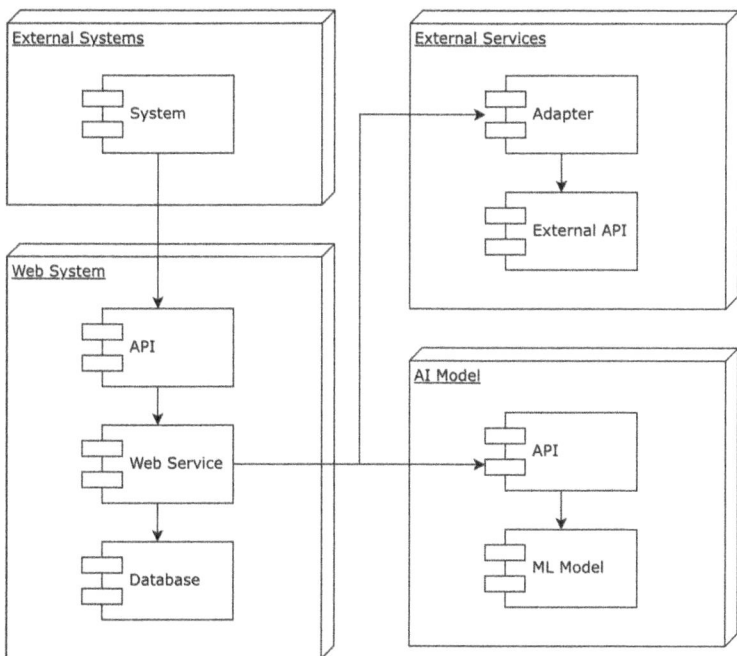

Fig. 1. Web Service component diagram

Machine Learning Model. The prediction model was trained using historical weather data from wildfires in Portugal over the last seven years [5]. The Random Forest model was selected and incorporates features such as temperature, humidity, wind speed and direction, precipitation, radiation and vegetation index (NDVI).

3.2   Implementation

For the system implementation, the Java programming language and the Spring-Boot framework were used for the Web Service implementation. Additionally, Spring Security was incorporated to ensure secure access. For model development, Python was employed due to its extensive libraries and tools. The database technology used was MongoDB that provided robust support for data storage and retrieval.

Multiple external data sources were used for developing and integrating the systems. Historical fire data from ICNF was processed for training, testing, and validating the model [5]. This was complemented with historical meteorological data specific to each location to achieve accurate fire risk assessment. In addition, real-time fire risk assessment relied on external APIs like IPMA, OpenMeteoAPI, WeatherAPI, and GeoAPI [1,2,6,10]. Data from these APIs were processed, formatted, sent to the model for calculating risk, and then stored in the database for future use.

An authentication system was implemented using JSON Web Tokens (JWT). Those tokens must be sent in the 'Authorization' header of the request. Since this system aims to be integrated with other systems, the communication is machine-to-machine. Two random keys must be generated for each client: one client ID and one secret key. The JWT must be generated by the external system using the client ID and the secret key, where a new key-value pair with the client ID must be inserted into the token header, and the signature must be done with the secret key using the HMAC SHA-256 algorithm. The token must follow the following structure:

Listing 1.1. JWT Token Structure Example

```
Header: {
    "alg": "HS256",
    "typ": "JWT",
    "kid": "client-id"    # client ID
}
Payload: {
    "aud": "/wildfire/",
    "exp": 1698852106,
    "iat": 1698851806
}
Signature: # Signature using the secret key
```

4 Conclusion and Future Work

The implementation of the AI web service for real-time forest fire prevention is a significant advancement in addressing the ongoing forest fire crisis in Portugal. This paper focuses on three key areas: the design and implementation of web services for forest fire prediction, the integration of meteorological APIs and historical data, and the exploration of the methods and technologies used in the development of these services.

The service developed provides a reliable tool for accurately assessing fire risk by leveraging AI and the integration of real-time meteorological data and historical patterns. This supports both rapid emergency response and long-term prevention strategies by identifying high-risk areas and signalling the implementation of specific interventions. It also brings economic benefits by protecting forest-dependent livelihoods, sustaining tourism, and maintaining environmental integrity.

This solution illustrates the potential of RESTful Web services combined with AI technology to make a significant impact in addressing environmental challenges and protecting natural resources and human communities.

Future work will test the effectiveness and reliability of the AI web service for real-time forest fire prevention through field operations. These extensive tests will include field trials and simulations in different forest areas to validate the accuracy of fire risk assessments and the service's ability to provide timely information for proactive actions.

Acknowledgement. This work was financed by national funds through the Portuguese Foundation for Science and Technology – FCT, under the Project "DBoidS - Digital twin Boids fire prevention System" Ref. PTDC/CCI-COM/2416/2021.

References

1. API, W.: Free Weather API. https://www.weatherapi.com
2. do Mar e da Atmosfera (IPMA), I.P.: IPMA API. https://api.ipma.pt
3. Brys, C., Navas-Delgado, I., Aldana-Montes, J.F.: Wildfire risk weighting and behaviour prediction using open geospatial data and ontologies. J. Inf. Sci. 01655515231202757 (2023)
4. Choi, S.E., Bang, J.H.: The design and implementation of mobile application solution for forest fire based on drone photography and amazon web service (AWS). J. Internet Comput. Serv. **21**(5), 31–37 (2020)
5. de Conservação da Natureza e das Florestas (ICNF), I.: geoCATALOGO. https://geocatalogo.icnf.pt/catalogo.html
6. geoapi: GEO API PT. https://geoapi.pt/
7. Ghibeche, Y., Sellam, A., Nouri, N., Khaldi, A., Harrane, A., Ghibeche, I.: Machine learning for forest fire prediction: a case study in north algeria. Ingénierie des Systèmes d'Information **29**(1) (2024)
8. Halderaker, E.D., Evjenth, A.: Development and Evaluation of a Software System for Fire Risk Prediction, Master's thesis, The University of Bergen (2021)
9. Novo, A., Fariñas-Álvarez, N., Martínez-Sánchez, J., González-Jorge, H., Fernández-Alonso, J.M., Lorenzo, H.: Mapping forest fire risk–a case study in Galicia (Spain). Remote Sens. **12**(22), 3705 (2020)
10. Open-Meteo: Free Open-Source Weather API. https://open-meteo.com
11. Pandey, S., Singh, R., Kathuria, S., Negi, P., Chhabra, G., Joshi, K.: Emerging technologies for prevention and monitoring of forest fire. In: 2023 International Conference on Innovative Data Communication Technologies and Application (ICIDCA), pp. 1115–1121. IEEE (2023)
12. Poursanidis, D., Kochilakis, G., Chrysoulakis, N., Varella, V., Kotroni, V., Eftychidis, G., Lagouvardos, K.: Web service tools in the era of forest fire management and elimination. In: Earth Resources and Environmental Remote Sensing/GIS Applications V. vol. 9245, pp. 255–266. SPIE (2014)
13. Stokkenes, S., Strand, R.D., Kristensen, L.M., Log, T.: Validation of a predictive fire risk indication model using cloud-based weather data services. Procedia Comput. Sci. **184**, 186–193 (2021)
14. Strand, R., Stokkenes, S., Kristensen, L., Log, T.: Fire risk prediction using cloud-based weather data services. J. Ubiquit. Syst. Pervasive Netw. **16**(1), 37–47 (2021)
15. Taktak, H., Boukadi, K., Zouari, F., Ghedira Guégan, C., Mrissa, M., Gargouri, F.: A knowledge-driven service composition framework for wildfire prediction. Clust. Comput. **27**(1), 977–996 (2024)
16. Zhang, A., Zhang, A.S.: Real-time wildfire detection and alerting with a novel machine learning approach. Int. J. Adv. Comput. Sci. Appl. **13**(8) (2022)

Adaptive Planning: Comparing Human and AI Responses in Premortem Planning

Elizabeth S. Veinott[✉] 🆔 and Betsy R. Lehman 🆔

Michigan Technological University, Houghton, MI 49931, USA
{eveinott,elehman}@mtu.edu

Abstract. Premortems are a structured analytic technique designed to evaluate a plan before it is implemented. They have been used to improve estimates and generate alternative predicted outcomes. One psychological mechanism that underlies the Premortem is prospective hindsight with people generating reasons for a plan's failure. The reasons reduce people's confidence and overconfidence in their plans relative to other plan critiquing methods. In this case study, we qualitatively compare student-generated responses for evaluating a plan and a large language model-generated (e.g., Chat GPT-4) evaluation of the same plan. To the extent that the reasons for failure generated by the large language model are similar or different to the human participants is the first step in a conceptual evaluation. The results have implications for a variety of structured analytic techniques to improve human-AI teaming in decision making. Furthermore, they provide initial suggestions for where adaptive systems could support collaborative intelligence.

Keywords: Adaptive Collaboration · Sensemaking · Large Language Models

1 Introduction

Evaluating a plan before it has been implemented is important for a variety of domains from design to disaster response [1, 2, 24]. Red teaming [12] or worst-case scenarios [25] are two common strategies for evaluating plans. Teams need adaptive methods that scale and support team processes [12, 13, 17, 37]. A generative AI tool may provide teams with this type of support in an adaptive way; the current paper explores this idea in the context of a plan evaluation process and existing epidemic plan.

Premortems [13] are a structured analytic method designed to support and improve what Hackman [10] describes as collaborative intelligence, the way groups can work together effectively to improve performance relative to a nominal team. In contrast, the collective intelligence of a team is the group's ability to perform a set of tasks and would be analogous to ensuring that teams share their unique information as much as the common information [8, 38]. The Premortem is designed to improve both the collaborative and the collective intelligence of teams by improving the information shared across the team [8, 33, 37].

© The Author(s), under exclusive license to Springer Nature Switzerland AG 2024
H. Degen and S. Ntoa (Eds.): HCII 2024, LNCS 15382, pp. 256–268, 2024.
https://doi.org/10.1007/978-3-031-76827-9_15

2 Background Research

2.1 Premortem

The Premortem [13] is a method that combines prospective hindsight [19] with team idea generation to improve overall plan evaluation. The basic steps of a Premortem include:

- Step 1. Review or Generate the Plan
- Step 2: Consider that it is in the future and the plan failed catastrophically.
- Individuals generate reasons why it failed.
- Step 3: Team systematically consolidates those reasons for failure. Step 4: Individuals generate solutions to the reasons for failure.
- Step 5: Team systematically consolidates those solutions. Step 6: Team revisits the plan and revises it as needed.

The Premortem supports a collaboration that goes beyond shared information and coordination. Managing the process between individual and group efforts is an important area for improving adaptive collaborative intelligence [17, 34]. Understanding where collaboration supports better team ideation is at the core of the collaborative intelligence concept [4, 10, 15].

2.2 Plan Evaluation Research

Plan evaluation research is limited, but includes a range of strategies from red teaming (Hackman 2017) to worst case scenarios [25]. While research showing that people underestimate their plans success [, far fewer have compared plan evaluation methods [24, 25, 32]. In Veinott et al., [33], researchers compared five different plan evaluation methods: critique, pro/con, con only, and Premortem to a no-evaluation control condition. They found that teams changed their confidence in the plan more in the Premortem condition, leading to better calibration than teams in the other plan evaluation conditions or the control condition.

2.3 Brainstorming Research and Generative AI

Being able to generate reasons why the plan failed is an important idea generation process in evaluating plans. DeRosa et al. [4] conducted a meta-analysis of 17 published papers that experimentally compared electronic brainstorming (EBS) and nominal brainstorming (each individual). For larger teams (> 8 people), EBS teams generated statistically more non-redundant ideas than nominal teams with a large effect size (r = 0.65). Also for larger teams, EBS teams also generated better ideas than the nominal teams with a large effect size (r = 0.55).

While brainstorming techniques have been studied for the last 80 years [23, 27], generative AI may provide some support for team brainstorming challenges related to production blocking and combining ideas, and refining ideas [15, 18]. For example, if generative AI could support teams by taking the large number of ideas generated and combining them into stronger ones or new ones [6], that would effectively support team brainstorming [4, 15, 31].

Generative AI is rapidly changing and improving and as a result it is changing the scope of human-centered computing. Research is needed to explore its use in these human centered contexts [3, 9] and to support divergent thinking and decision making [11, 34]. Eapen et al. [6] recently suggested several ways generative AI can be used to augment human creativity by a) promoting divergent thinking, b) challenging expertise bias, c) assisting in idea evaluation, d) supporting idea refinement, and e) facilitating collaboration. Generative AI can support divergent thinking, idea evaluation, refinement, and facilitate collaboration by connecting "remote" ideas in new ways and combining larger numbers of ideas to strengthen them. Idea refinement involves combining disparate ideas to create better solutions. It is also possible that a generative AI system could fill in the details on general ideas to assist in idea evaluation. While Eapen et al. [6] focus on the potential for generative AI, more research is needed to explore what these systems can do effectively. Therefore, the purpose of the current study is to explore the type of ideas a generative AI system develops during a Premortem process. For example, does the generative AI (i.e., ChatGPT-4) develop ideas that reflect the possibilities from Eapen et al. [6]?

There were three goals in this paper to extend the prior work. First, we were using a large language model as a team player to compare the responses of human team members to the large language model. Does the LLM (i.e., ChatGPT-4) provide different responses to the different plan evaluation instructions? Second, does the LLM provide different information to the human participants for the same plan? We compared a current LLM response to an archival set of data from a previous study [33]. Finally, we discuss whether the LLM generative AI provided useful insight and how it might be leveraged in plan evaluations. Our goal was to explore ideas about harnessing the collaborative intelligence of teams.

3   Methods

Participants. Human data consisted of a corpus of reasons and solutions generated during a previous Premortem study [33]. These human generated reasons were compared to a LLM plan evaluation response. We provided the plan evaluation instructions and plan text to an LLM, Open AI's ChatGPT (v4.0) (ChatGPT-4).

Task. The plan evaluation task included a fictional and involved a university lockdown to slow the spread of a H1N1 pandemic used in prior research (Veinott, Peabody). There were three parts to the plan, communication, containing the spread, and pivoting to remote learning.

Procedure. In the first method, we gave Chat GPT-4 the same instructions we gave human teams for the premortem process. We submitted the procedure introduction, plan to be evaluated, and response prompts as separate messages to the ChatGPT-4 system. This caused ChatGPT-4 to generate extraneous text in response to the introduction and plan, such as what a university's epidemic plan *should* look like. In the second method, we submitted the procedure introduction, plan to be evaluated, and prompt to generate reasons why the plan failed all as one initial message to the system. This limited the response from ChatGPT-4 and focused more on generating potential reasons for the plan's failure. Next, we submitted an additional message with the second prompt to generate potential solutions for these problems to the system. Overall, the second method was similar to a standard premortem process with human teams, with the background and plan presented simultaneously.

We then qualitatively compared the response length and content between the human data and ChatGPT-4 generated plan evaluation.

4   Results

In this section we explore the Chat GPT-4 generated reasons and solutions, then compare them to the human generated reasons for failure and solutions. The purpose is to evaluate the Generative AI tools evaluation of a plan qualitatively. The following reasons for failure when given the same instructions as humans.

4.1   Reasons for Failure

This is how ChatGPT-4 responded to the prompt, "No plan is perfect, now assume it is 6 months in the future and this plan catastrophically failed, explain why it failed":

"Assuming it's six months into the future and the State University's Lockdown Plan for dealing with an H1N1 epidemic has catastrophically failed, let's explore potential reasons for this failure. It's important to understand that this analysis is hypothetical and focuses on identifying possible areas of vulnerability in the plan.

Reasons for the Hypothetical Failure of the Plan.

1. Underestimation of the Epidemic's Severity and Speed: The plan might have failed to account for the rapid spread and severity of the H1N1 virus. This underestimation could have led to delayed implementation of the lockdown and insufficient preparation.
2. Communication Breakdown: The effectiveness of the plan heavily relied on the communication strategy. If the advisory network, media, and website couldn't handle the traffic surge or if messages were unclear or inaccessible to parts of the university community, critical information may not have reached everyone in time.
3. Inadequate Healthcare Resources: The plan may have underestimated the healthcare needs of residential students. Limited medical staff, insufficient isolation facilities, or a lack of necessary medical supplies could have led to inadequate care for infected students.
4. Technological and Logistical Challenges in Distance Learning: Transitioning to online learning requires robust IT infrastructure and training for both faculty and students. If this transition was poorly executed, it could have led to significant disruption in academic continuity.
5. Non-compliance and Enforcement Issues: The success of the quarantine relied on student and staff compliance. If the rules were too strict or not adequately enforced, it could have led to non-compliance, further spreading the infection.

6. Neglect of Mental Health and Emotional Well-being: The psychological impact of a prolonged lockdown and epidemic fears might have been underestimated. Lack of adequate mental health support could lead to widespread emotional distress and impact the overall well-being of the university community.
7. Challenges for Non-residential Students: Given the high ratio of non-residential students, failing to provide adequate support and guidelines for this group could have exacerbated the spread of the virus beyond the campus.
8. Economic and Financial Strain: The prolonged lockdown might have put financial strain on both the university and its students, leading to resource limitations and impacting the plan's sustainability.
9. Insufficient Collaboration with Local Authorities: If the university did not effectively collaborate with local health and emergency services, the response could have been disjointed, leading to gaps in managing the epidemic.
10. Lack of Flexibility and Adaptability in the Plan: If the plan was too rigid and did not allow for adjustments based on the evolving nature of the epidemic, it might have failed to address unforeseen challenges effectively.
11. This retrospective analysis highlights the importance of flexibility, comprehensive planning, and the need for a multifaceted approach in handling epidemic situations. It also underscores the importance of learning from such failures to improve future emergency response plans."

On first glance of the list above, the ChaptGPT-4 generated 11 unique reasons for failure that are reasonable. For example, the plan is flexible (#10). There are technological challenges with distance learning (#4). Furthermore, these 11 reasons were more reasons that any individual generated, and about the same as the number of unique reasons generated by a four-person team. Second, most of the ChatGPT-4 output overlapped with the human generated output at the topic level (Table 1). However, the core ChatGPT-4 responses were still tied to the hypothetical plan as can be seen above. This may be because ChatGPT-4 was able to systematically evaluate the plan based on the information provided, but was not as good at making inferences or possible failure scenarios as the human teams seemed to do.

Comparing the reasons generated between the human teams and the generative AI, they seem to be topically related. The reasons generated by ChatGPT-4 tended to be longer and focused on the problem (noncompliance), but not why it's a problem (e.g., too many ways to leave). There are several examples in Table 1 where the human teams were making additional inferences about the reasons for failure, while ChatGPT-4 was stating the problem, but not why. For example, teams identified the idea that the virus may spread because there are many ways to leave campus, whereas ChatGPT-4 simply described that the virus spread because people did not comply. The ChatGPT-4 lacked an explanation of why which would require an inference. As students at a university, some teams thought students might rebel or not follow protocol due to the quarantine.

When teams generate solutions to these reasons for failure, it requires them to have hypotheses for why the plan is failing, not simply that it is failing. In the next step in the Premortem, teams and the ChatGPT-4 listed of solutions for the failures. These solutions to the failures are explored next.

Table 1. Reasons for failure categories, examples, and percentages from the coded archived data vs. ChatGPT-4 examples by plan evaluation issue.

Issues	Human Generated Reasons	%	ChatGPT-4 Generated Reasons
Plan Phases	Administration initiates plan too late, or too early	13.7	Communicate early
Quarantine: Virus Spreads	Barriers fail because of many ways in and out of campus	57%	Inadequate Resources. Failure due to non-compliance
Quarantine: Logistics	Problems getting supplies onto campus		Security forces sensitive; Non-residential student movement
Quarantine: Emotion Response	Students rebel due to the lockdown	8%	Neglect students' mental health
Distance Learning	Professors do not post relevant information online	5%	Requires good IT infrastructure and training
Communicate Information	Students don't check their cell phones. No time to prepare for lockdown	12%	Multiple methods, Accessible, Effective. Early communicaion

4.2 Generated Solutions to Those Reasons for Failure

This is how ChatGPT responded to the prompt, "Based on these reasons for failure, how can this plan be improved? What are solutions for these failures?":

"Based on the identified reasons for the hypothetical failure of the State University's Lockdown Plan for an H1N1 epidemic, here are suggestions for improving the plan, addressing each point of vulnerability.

1. Enhanced Epidemic Monitoring and Rapid Response:

Solution: Implement a robust system for monitoring health trends and establish criteria for quicker activation of emergency protocols.

2. Robust and Redundant Communication Systems:

Solution: Develop multiple, reliable communication channels, including digital platforms, to ensure uninterrupted flow of information. Regularly test these systems for high-volume scenarios.

3. Scaling Healthcare Resources:

Solution: Create partnerships with local healthcare providers to expand available resources. Pre-plan for additional medical staff, isolation facilities, and necessary supplies.

4. Effective Transition to Distance Learning:

Solution: Invest in IT infrastructure and training for staff and students in advance. Have a contingency plan for students who lack access to necessary technology.

5. Enforcement and Compliance Strategies:

Solution: Implement a balanced approach to rule enforcement, combining clear guidelines with understanding and support. Engage student and staff leaders in promoting compliance.

6. Mental Health and Emotional Support:

Solution: Expand mental health services and provide easy access to counseling, online support groups, and stress management resources.

7. Support for Non-residential Students:

Solution: Develop specific guidelines and support systems for non-residential students, including remote learning resources and health advisories.

8. Financial and Economic Considerations:

Solution: Plan for financial contingencies to support the university's operations and provide financial assistance or flexibility for students in need.

9. Collaboration with Local Authorities:

Solution: Establish strong lines of communication and collaborative protocols with local health departments and emergency services.

10. Flexible and Adaptive Planning:

Solution: Design the plan to be adaptable, allowing for modifications in response to changing circumstances. Regularly review and update the plan based on new information and feedback.

- General Improvements:
- Regular Training and Drills: Conduct regular emergency response drills for both staff and students to ensure preparedness.
- Feedback Mechanisms: Implement systems to gather and incorporate feedback from the university community and external experts.
- Transparency and Trust Building: Maintain transparency in decision-making processes to build trust within the university community.
- Data-Driven Decisions: Use data and expert analysis to guide the response to the epidemic.
- Community Engagement: Foster a sense of community responsibility and involvement in epidemic response efforts.

These solutions generated by ChatGPT-4 and listed above are plausible and reasonable and share similar themes with the solutions generated by the human participants. For example, a direct comparison on one theme is shown below in Table 2. Some of the solutions generated were vague, however, or are not immediately actionable. While human-generated solutions may also be vague or non-actionable, they can be discussed and iterated upon by the rest of the team to become more useful or feasible within the plan.

There were also some surprising responses from the Generative AI. In the previous step of the process, one reason for failure given was a "communication breakdown" due to solely using digital means to communicate with personnel about the pandemic. One of the solutions generated by the Generative AI for this, however, suggested "multi-channel" communication, but only listed digital means (social media, email, and text messaging). It seems likely that human participants would notice this contradiction and not submit this response as a viable solution.

Table 2. Comparisons for distance learning

Participant	Reasonfor Plan Failure	Solution
Human	Distance Learning	"Online doesn't work, Distance learning/online classes do not work because students do not have network access or the distance learning tools are not sufficient or students/teachers are not well-trained on their use"
ChatGPT-4	Inadequate Infrastructure forDistance Learning	"The rapid shift to distance learning requires robust digital infrastructure, including reliable internet access for all students and faculty, training in digital tools, and effective online course delivery methods. If the university had not previously invested in these areas or if the transition was rushed, many students might have faced difficulties in accessing education, leading to a disruption in the academic calendar and student dissatisfaction."

Additionally, ChatGPT-4 generated a surprisingly familiar solution to plan inflexibility (#2 above), "Develop multiple scenarios with corresponding actions to allow for rapid response to unexpected developments." This suggestion sounds remarkably like the Premortem method. Overall, while the topical solutions overlapped between the humans and the generative AI, the level of actionable information seemed to differ. Human teams were adding inferences that ChatGPT-4 was not able to do at this time.

4.3 Premortem Interpretation: Comparing Generative AI to Human Teams

What does this mean for Generative AI and adaptive learning? Generative AI seem much better than it has been in previous years at producing reasonable plan evaluations and executing a premortem. ChatGPT produced more words than the individual team members and potentially more unique ideas, but not more than the teams. Nor did ChatGPT-4 produce more unique or better ideation than the team. This may be due to the fact that the teams evaluating the plans in this case would be the future recipients of the plan, therefore they may have had a unique perspective or more [relevant/specific] motivations. Furthermore, we saw no evidence that ChatGPT-4 was combining reasons for failure or solutions in unique ways as has been the reason generative AI can support creativity [6]. For these generative systems to be adaptive as intelligent tutoring systems are, they will need to be able to make inferences [35, 36].

If one thinks of the generative AI as a team member, not replacing the team but instead being one of the team members in the Premortem, then it could support the systematic evaluation of the information provided generally. However, as shown in Table 3 below, one can see that there are still key processes in the Premortem that cannot be supported by simply using ChatGPT-4.

Table 3. Comparing the Effectiveness of Generative AI as a Team Player and Standard Premortem Process

Generative AI	Premortem (Klein, 2007)
Divergent Thinking (Eapen et al. 2023)	Divergent Thinking from different experts on team
Avoids expertise bias (Eapen et al. 2023)	Identifies reasons for failure based on the unique expertise of team members
Finds typical plan assessment	Finds unusual problems with the plan based on the team's expertise. What Klein has called "weak signals" and potentially Black Swans
NA	Every voice on the team is heard in this process
NA	The team becomes aware of the challenges. Develops buy-in for the plan

There are several highlighted differences between the generative AI and. Human team responses. Both are expected to support divergent thinking and potentially counterfactual reasoning [16, 33]. ChatGPT-4 in this example plan avoided expertise bias, however it generated a typical or average plan assessment based on the plan provided [6]. The generative AI was unable to make inferences that the human teams did. This observation relates to the notion of explainable AI [5, 20, 21]. While it did support the divergent thinking in the plan assessment, the Premortem process also supports collective intelligence [37, 38] and collaborative sensemaking [33] by making sure every voice is heard, which in turn improves the plan assessment and the buy-in for those likely to have to execute the plan. Therefore, it makes sense to consider Generative AI as a team member, not a replacement for the team Premortem.

5   Discussion

ChatGPT-4 was effective for some aspects of plan evaluation, such as generating initial plausible reasons for plan failure and solutions to those problems. However, ChatGPT-4 stayed within the parameters of the information and seemed to focus on averages and typical evaluations. Therefore, it could not be used to find surprising failures or black swans using the Premortem the way that humans may [7].

In this exercise, ChatGPT-4 focused on breadth, rather than depth in plan assessment. It evaluated what was stated in the plan, but did not go beyond the bounds provided by the plan. In other words, it did not make inferences. If combined with the human teams as another team member, it might be able to iterate alternative explanations based on what the human teams generate. Future research might explore this option. One recent exploration found that human biases emerged from an LLM, but did not using ChatGPT-3 [11].

As a team member during the Premortem, Generative AI may support adaptive collaboration. Given the adaptive learning strategies, it could also encourage the human teams to question their initial theories and consider alternative explanations [16, 17]. While this exploration of the Generative AI evaluation of the plan using the Premortem instruction overlaps with the human generated evaluation, there are some distinct differences as noted.

One goal of the Premortem is to identify good reasons for a plan failure that can support teams by helping them develop better, more resilient plans [14]. However, there are also cognitive and social outcomes for teams as a result of conducting the Premortem that will not be present with a generative AI Premortem.

Cognitive Outcomes of a Premortem. The cognitive outcomes include changes for the individual and the team that cannot be replicated by using a Generative AI system such as ChatGPT-4. These are added benefits of the process that are related to the process of generating the reasons for failure and could be described as positive side effects of the process. For example, because teams will be executing the plan, any changes to their understanding, confidence in the plan, or mental model of the plan have positive ripple effects. Each of the reasons for failure generated during the premortem was an opportunity for the team to improve the plan, making it more resilient [13, 14].

Research has shown that using the premortem, individuals generate more reasons for failure than through common plan evaluation methods, such as critiquing, pros/cons, or worst-case scenario methods [24, 25, 26, 33]. This may help teams identify problems that they either did not anticipate or might have underestimated [14, 22]. Premortems help identify Black Swans (Gallop) and in our analysis, the Generative AI at this time would be unable to do this as it provides a systematic and prototypical evaluation of the plan [7]. A side effect of this failure generation process, team members reduce their confidence in the success of the plan [2, 17, 33] shift their focus [24, 25, 26], and have been shown to adjust their strategies [28]. Finally, team brainstorming done correctly will collaboratively building on each other's ideas [23, 27] generally, or with generative AI [30, 31]. Generative AI changing how people understand problems is a recent topic of interest [5]. In addition to cognitive changes, there are social changes in the team that would be difficult to replicate with ChatGPT-4.

Social Outcomes of a Premortem. The Premortem can help teams in several ways that have been shown in prior research to support better decision making. First, teams may develop a better shared understanding or mental model of the plan [14, 18, 22]. Second, the Premortem supports what has been called a team's collaborative intelligence [10] and collective intelligence [37, 38], by systematically capturing the diversity of ideas and unique perspectives each team brings [8] to support collaborative sensemaking [33]. Third, the Premortem gives everyone on the team an equal voice as each team member provides at least one reason for plan failure. This process also has the potential to reduce group tensions that may stem from conflicting beliefs. Finally, due to the above social mechanisms, it is expected that the Premortem process increases individual team members buy-in for the plan because they contributed to its evaluation and improved on it. Given teams need to execute their plans, these are important social outcomes of the Premortem. None of these social outcomes would be expected to result from using Generative AI to evaluate a plan alone because the social processes would not emerge.

Implications for Generative AI systems. To make Generative AI systems smarter would require better explanation on the part of the human-AI system. But as several researchers have suggested, the LLM is a tool, and not an equal team player. ChatGPT-4 can learn from what teams generate and potentially combine the ideas in new ways, but it is not currently able to generate ideas that are entirely novel [15, 29, 30]. Our exploratory study lines up with that interpretation as well.

6   Conclusion

In doing this exercise, several insights and gaps emerged that will help in future research and design focused on how Generative AI can support human creativity and ideation. First, the Generative AI (ChatGPT-4) produced surprisingly realistic and reasonable responses to the Premortem prompts. ChatGPT produced typical reasons for failure based on the text of the plan provided. It did not read between the lines and generate reasons for failure that might be related, but not stated in the plan. These unique reasons came from the human team members and their expertise in executing these plans. This idea of a typical response is consistent with the output of recent Generative AI responses in different domains from ideation [6] to supporting knowledge workers [5]. However, it is possible that ChatGPT could support divergent thinking if it iterated on some of the human Premortem responses [34].

The Premortem process supports switching to a failure frame to improve the plan evaluation methods and consider alternative explanations as a critical aspect of the process. It is possible that future generative AI systems can work with human teams as a team member to support the idea generation process as recently explored [34], but would not replace the human teams. The current effort was a first step toward thinking about adaptive systems in the new reality of generative AI and contributes to a growing body of research exploring how generative AI can support decision making.

Disclosure of Interests.   The authors have no competing interests to declare that are relevant to the content of this article.

References

1. Bettin, B., Steelman, K.S., Wallace, C., Pontious, D., Veinott, E.S.: Identifying and addressing risks in the early design of a sociotechnical system through premortem. In: Proceedings of the Human Factors and Ergonomics Society Annual Meeting, vol. 66, No. 1, pp. 1514–1518. SAGE Publications, Sage, Los Angeles, CA (2022)
2. Buehler, R., Griffin, D., Ross, M.: Exploring the "Planning fallacy": why people underestimate their task completion times. J. Pers. Soc. Psychol. **67**(3), 366–381 (1994)
3. Chen, X.A., et al.: Next steps for human-centered generative AI: a technical perspective. arXiv preprint arXiv:2306.15774 (2023)
4. DeRosa, D. M., Smith, C. L., & Hantula, D. A. (2007). The medium matters: Mining the long-promised merit of group interaction in creative idea generation tasks in a meta-analysis of the electronic group brainstorming literature. Computers in Human Behavior, 23(3), 1549–1581–239
5. Dell'Acqua, F., et al.: Navigating the jagged technological frontier: field experimental evidence of the effects of AI on knowledge worker productivity and quality (September15, 2023). Harvard Business School Technology & Operations Mgt. Unit Working Paper No. 24-013 (2023). https://ssrn.com/abstract=4573321 or https://doi.org/10.2139/ssrn.4573321
6. Eapen, T.T., Finkenstadt, D.J., Folk, J., Venkataswamy, L.: How generative AI can augment human creativity. Harv. Bus. Rev. **101**(4), 56–64 (2023)
7. Gallop, D., Willy, C., Bischoff, J.: How to catch a black swan: measuring the benefits of the premortem technique for risk identification. J. Enterprise Transform. **6**(2), 87–106 (2016)
8. Gigone, D., Hastie, R.: The impact of information on small group choice. J. Pers. Soc. Psychol. **72**(1), 132–140 (1997). https://doi.org/10.1037/0022-3514.72.1.132
9. Gupta, P., Ding, B., Guan, C., Ding, D.: Generative AI: aA systematic review using topic modelling techniques. Data Inform. Manage. (2024)
10. Hackman, J.R.: Collaborative intelligence: using teams to solve hard problems. Berrett-Koehler Publishers (2011)
11. Hagendorff, T., Fabi, S., Kosinski, M.: Human-like intuitive behavior and reasoning biases emerged in large language models but disappeared in ChatGPT. Nat. Comput. Sci. **3**(10), 833–838 (2023)
12. Hoffman, B.G.: Red teaming: how your business can conquer the competition by challenging everything. Crown business (2017)
13. Klein, G.: Performing a project premortem. Harvard Bus. Rev. **85**(9), 18–19 (2007)
14. Klein, G., Pliske, R., Crandall, B., Woods, D.D.: Problem detection. Cogn. Technol. Work **7**, 14–28 (2005)
15. Kohn, N.W., Paulus, P.B., Choi, Y.: Building on the ideas of others: an examination of the idea combination process. J. Exp. Soc. Psychol. **47**, 554–561 (2011)
16. Lehman, B., Veinott, E.S.: Changing perspectives: examining factors related to counterfactual thinking in ambiguous social judgments. In: Proceedings of the Annual Meeting of the Cognitive Science Society, vol. 44, no. 44 (2022)
17. McDermott, A.F., et al.: Developing an adaptive framework to support intelligence analysis. In: Sottilare, R., Schwarz, J. (eds.) 3rd International Conference for Adaptive Instructional Systems as part of HCI International (HCII) (2021)
18. Mosier, K.L., Fischer, U.M.: Judgment and decision making by individuals and teams: issues, models, and applications. In: Decision Making in Aviation, pp. 139–198. Routledge (2017)
19. Mitchell, D.J., Russo, J.E., Pennington, N.: Back to the future: Temporal perspective in the explanation of events. J. Behav. Decis. Mak. **2**, 25–38 (1989)
20. Mueller, S.T., et al.: Principles of explanation in human-AI systems. arXiv preprint arXiv: 2102.04972 (2021)

21. Mueller, S.T., Hoffman, R.R., Clancey, W., Emrey, A., Klein, G.: Explanation in human-AI systems: a literature meta-review, synopsis of key ideas and publications, and bibliography for explainable AI. arXiv preprint arXiv:1902.01876 (2019)

22. Orasanu, J., Fischer, U.: Finding decisions in natural environments: the view from the cockpit. In: Naturalistic Decision Making, pp. 343–357. Psychology Press (2014)

23. Parnes, S.J., Meadow, A.: Effects of 'brainstorming' instructions on creative pro lem solving by trained and untrained subjects. J. Educ. Psychol. **50**(4), 171–176 (1959)

24. Pearson, C.M., Misra, S.K., Clair, J.A., Mitroff, I.I.:. Managing the unthinkable. Organiz. Dyn. **26**(2), 51–64 (1997)

25. Peabody, M., Veinott, E.: Focus shift: differences in reasons generated using Premortem and Worst-Case Scenario plan evaluation methods. Naturalistic Dec. Mak. 259–261 (2017)

26. Peabody, M.: Improving planning: quantitative evaluation of the premortem technique. Unpublished Masters of Science Thesis. Michigan Technological University (2017)

27. Putman, V.L., Paulus, P.B.: Brainstorming, brainstorming rules and decision making. J. Creat. Behav. **43**, 23–39 (2009)

28. Sunstein, C.R.: Worst-case scenarios. Harvard Press (2009)

29. Roose, K.M., Lehman, B.R., Veinott, E.S.: Premortems in game development teams: impact and potential. In: Proceedings of the Human Factors and Ergonomics Society Annual Meeting, vol. 67, no. 1, pp. 1856–1861. SAGE Publications, Sage, Los Angeles, CA (2023). https://doi.org/10.1177/21695067231193936

30. Shaer, O., Cooper, A., Mokryn, O., Kun, A.L., Ben Shoshan, H.:. AI-augmented brainwriting: investigating the use of LLMs in group ideation. In: Proceedings of the CHI Conference on Human Factors in Computing Systems, pp. 1–17 (2024)

31. Shin, J.G., Koch, J., Lucero, A., Dalsgaard, P., Mackay, W.E.: Integrating AI in human-human collaborative ideation. In: Extended Abstracts of the 2023 CHI Conference on Human Factors in Computing Systems, pp. 1–5 (2023)

32. Valacich, J.S., Dennis, A.R., Connolly, T.: Idea generation in computer-based groups: a new ending to an old story. Organ. Behav. Hum. Dec. Proces. **57**, 448–467 (1994)

33. Veinott, B., Klein, G., Wiggins, S.: Evaluating the effectiveness of the premortem technique on plan confidence. In: 7th International ISCRAM Conference. Seattle (2010)

34. Veinott, E.S.: Adaptive collaborative intelligence: key strategies for sensemaking in the wild. In: Stephanidis, C., et al. (eds.) HCI International 2021 - Late Breaking Papers: Cognition, Inclusion, Learning, and Culture. HCII 2021. LNCS, vol. 13096. Springer, Cham (2021). https://doi.org/10.1007/978-3-030-90328-2_8

35. Wadinambiarachchi, S., Kelly, R.M., Pareek, S., Zhou, Q., Velloso, E.: The effects of generative AI on design fixation and divergent thinking. In: Proceedings of the CHI Conference on Human Factors in Computing Systems, pp. 1–18 (2024)

36. Whitaker, E., Trewhitt, E., Veinott, E.S.: Intelligent tutoring design alternatives in a serious game. In: Sottilare, R., Schwarz, J. (eds.) First International Conference for Adaptive Instructional Systems as part of HCII 2019, pp. 151–165. Springer, Cham (2019). https://doi.org/10.1007/978-3-030-22341-0_13. ISBN 978-3-030-22341-0

37. Whitaker, E., Trewhitt, E., Veinott, E.S.: Heuristica II: updating a 2011 game-based training architecture using generative AI tools. In: Sottilare, R.A., Schwarz, J. (eds.) Adaptive Instructional Systems. HCII 2024. LNCS, vol. 14727. Springer, Cham (2024). https://doi.org/10.1007/978-3-031-60609-0_23 (2024)

38. Woolley, A.W., Aggarwal, I., Malone, T.: Collective intelligence and group performance. Curr. Dir. Psychol. Sci. **24**, 420–424 (2015)

Neurosymbolic AI for Personalized Sentiment Analysis

Luyao Zhu[1][ID], Rui Mao[1][ID], Erik Cambria[1(✉)][ID], and Bernard J. Jansen[2][ID]

[1] College of Computing and Data Science, Nanyang Technological University, Singapore, Singapore
luyao001@e.ntu.edu.sg, {rui.mao,cambria}@ntu.edu.sg
[2] Qatar Computing Research Institute, Hamad Bin Khalifa University, Doha, Qatar
bjansen@hbku.edu.qa
https://www.sentic.net

Abstract. Sentiment analysis is crucial in extracting valuable insights from vast amounts of textual data generated across various platforms, such as social media, customer reviews, news articles, etc. Over the years, researchers and business professionals have worked hard to refine sentiment analysis algorithms, but there is a limit to how accurate any algorithm can be without considering personalization. In this work, we propose a framework for personalized sentiment analysis that performs automatic user profiling by modeling users based on different levels of personalization, before performing sentiment analysis. In particular, such framework leverages seven levels of personalization (from bottom to top), namely: Entity, to distinguish between humans and other intelligent agents; Culture, to take into account how different cultures perceive the same concept as positive or negative; Religion, to consider how specific religious beliefs may affect an individual's opinion about certain topics; Vocation, to better gauge people's opinion based on their job and education level; Ideology, to take into account political beliefs as well as social, economic, or philosophical viewpoints; Personality, to better classify certain concepts as positive or negative based on personality traits; finally, Subjectivity, to take into account personal preferences and experiences.

Keywords: Sentiment Analysis · Personalization · Persona · Personality · AI · NLP

1 Introduction

Sentiment analysis has evolved significantly from traditional survey methods, transitioning from structured, manual data collection to automated, unstructured text analysis in the early 2000 s. More advanced artificial intelligence (AI) techniques have been applied to the problem of automatically extracting people's opinions from text [14].

Recent advancements in sentiment analysis are shifting from document-level or sentence-level [8] to finer-grained aspect-level [35]. Most research relied on

H. Degen and S. Ntoa (Eds.): HCII 2024, LNCS 15382, pp. 269–290, 2024.
https://doi.org/10.1007/978-3-031-76827-9_16

supervised learning with annotated data. The ground truth labels were commonly identified by recruiting professional annotators and then taking the label agreed upon by majority voting among them [12]. This method works well in domains with consistent sentiment perception, e.g., interpreting the sentiment of product reviews. However, when it comes to understanding the sentimental perception of individuals, the task can be more challenging. For example, many sentiment analysis annotation tasks were achieved with imperfect agreement rates [23,54]. In other words, not all labels were agreed upon by all annotators. While using majority voting for labeling is acceptable in a probabilistic sense, it can be seen as overlooking the human-centric aspect of sentiment analysis.

Fig. 1. Conventional sentiment analysis vs. personalized sentiment analysis.

We introduce the task of personalized sentiment analysis, which focuses on analyzing individual sentiment perceptions. This approach is motivated by the observation that different individuals may perceive an identical statement differently regarding its sentiment polarity. In contrast, conventional sentiment analysis aims to predict the semantic sentiment of a statement, where the sentiment prediction remains the same for an identical statement. For instance, an introverted person may have a negative sentiment towards performing in front of a large audience, while an extroverted person may view the same situation positively (see Fig. 1). This variation in sentiment perception can be attributed to personality traits. While the distinction between introversion and extroversion is from personality theory, the variability in sentiment perception among individuals can also be influenced by other factors. The inconsistency in sentimental perception between individuals may originate from multiple sources. For example, as the adage suggests, *"the enemy of my enemy is my friend"*, the sentimental perception of a person can be driven by the relationship or the context of the situation. In this case, personalized sentiment analysis extends beyond traditional semantic and pragmatic understanding, incorporating a broader range of human subjective factors, such as persona information.

To this end, we propose a novel neurosymbolic AI framework that leverages seven levels of personalization (see Fig. 2) for personalized sentiment analysis. In particular, such a framework initially targets identifying whether the user is a human (e.g., male or female) or other intelligent agent, determining whether to consider typical human needs and beliefs. Secondly, the framework aims to identify the user's cultural background to discern whether a given concept is perceived as positive or negative based on different cultural beliefs. Next, a similar mechanism is applied to Religion. Vocation is considered an important factor in shaping users' views based on their job and education level. Following, the user's ideologies are modeled to consider political beliefs and social, economic, or philosophical viewpoints. Next, Personality is detected in order to better classify certain concepts as positive or negative based on the user's personality traits. Finally, Subjectivity aims to consider specific user preferences learned from historical or training data.

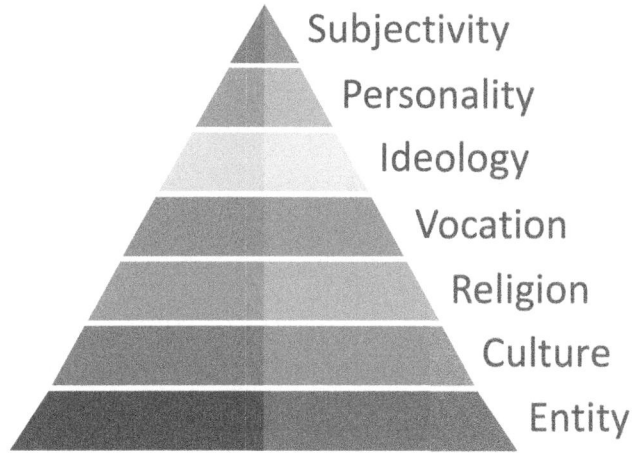

Fig. 2. Personalized Sentiment Analysis Pyramid.

This work aims to evaluate whether the framework of the identified seven levels of personalization can help improve the accuracy of sentiment analysis. We evaluate the framework based on a dialogue dataset [9] that originated from *Harry Potter* novels and large language models (LLMs). The dataset contains conversations between different characters in the *Harry Potter* novels and the associated sentiment perceptions between characters. Considering the advancement of LLMs in diverse domains [33], we leverage ChatGPT and GPT-4 to generate the seven-level persona information for each character by well-designed prompts. Finally, the utility of the persona information is evaluated with a neurosymbolic AI paradigm. The persona information is structured as tailored prompts, feeding into LLMs together with the conversations of the employed dataset. We analyze the variations in the sentiment analysis accuracy of AI after the inclusion or exclusion of different prompts.

We find that in the context of the conversations of *Harry Potter*, Culture, Vocation, and Ideology present the highest utility, resulting in the most accuracy gains in our research domain; All the seven aspects have positive utilities to the neurosymbolic AI system; Integration of personalized neurosymbolic knowledge into LLMs leads to biases towards the object and the subject on sentiment analysis task. It is reasonable that different types of persona information have different utilities in a specific domain because different individuals may prioritize certain aspects of persona information based on the context or the domain they are in. The sentiment perception reasoning may rely on different background knowledge in different scenarios.

The contribution of this work is threefold. (1) It introduces the novel concept of personalized sentiment analysis, designed to enhance AI's understanding of the varied sentiment perceptions between individuals. (2) It presents a comprehensive framework derived from an analysis of literature, delineating seven levels of personalization for personalized sentiment analysis. (3) It performs an empirical study to assess the effectiveness of various persona information types within a conversational domain.

2   Literature Review

2.1   Sentiment Analysis with AI

Recently, there have been notable advancements in sentiment analysis, characterized by several key trends. Initially, the focus was on lexicon-based approaches to identify sentiment polarities such as positive, negative, and neutral in sentences or documents. The field then evolved by introducing concept-level sentiment analysis systems like pSenti [44] and SenticNet [8]. These systems represented a shift towards more advanced methods that combined lexicon-based and learning-based approaches. They presented greater accuracy in tasks such as sentiment polarity classification and sentiment intensity prediction, surpassing the capabilities of traditional lexicon-based systems [43].

Later, with the development of neural networks, the research focus of sentiment analysis shifts towards developing different learning frameworks to improve accuracy. Convolutional Neural Network-based supervised learning [24], transfer learning [11], adversarial training [15], meta-learning [17], prompt-based [38] algorithms were proposed for sentiment analysis. These research efforts address learning challenges in sentiment analysis, e.g., pattern discovery with label data, efficient learning from few-shot examples, robust representations, and domain adaption. During this period, research in multimodal [55] or cross-lingual [56] sentiment analysis was dynamic because it expanded the scope of sentiment analysis beyond English text. Recently, there has been a significant enrichment in the task setups of sentiment analysis. Researchers are no longer satisfied with simply predicting a sentiment polarity for an input text; they are extending the scope of sentiment analysis to include different levels of granularity and contextual awareness, e.g., aspect-based sentiment analysis [35] and opinion mining [40], emotion detection [1], conversational sentiment analysis [28], sentiment analysis from electroencephalography (EEG) signals [25], facial expressions [10] or speech [30]. Another trend in sentiment analysis is that researchers paid more attention to the linguistic phenomena that likely affect sentiment analysis, e.g., metaphors [36], sarcasm [53], and ambiguous word senses [58]. Considering the impact of sentiment in broad domains, there are research papers studying sentiment analysis in different science domains, e.g., nature disaster [13], mental health [22], finance [31,32], legislation [48] and education [2].

To sum up, previous research has addressed sentiment analysis by tackling learning challenges, enhancing sentiment analysis granularity, improving natural language understanding in learning systems, and grounding sentiment analysis in different downstream tasks. However, sentiment perception can vary subjectively in different contexts. There is limited research on personalized sentiment analysis that integrates various types of persona information. This motivates us to bridge this gap by forming a framework to identify the sources of subjectivity in sentiment analysis and developing a neurosymbolic system to process the task of personalized sentiment analysis.

2.2   Sources of Diversity in Sentiment Perception

The theory of mind (ToM) suggests that individuals understand that others may hold beliefs, desires, intentions, emotions, and thoughts that differ from their own [3]. Thus, we believe that multiple factors can influence individual sentiment perceptions. According to the theory of appraisal [41], opinions and sentiments arise not as direct responses to stimuli but as complicated evaluations incorporating subjective judgments across multiple levels. We assume that the factors influencing sentiment perception are hierarchically structured. This hierarchical structure ranges from general factors affecting large populations to specific factors influencing individuals. To explore this idea further in the context of sentiment analysis, we reviewed the following theoretical research.

ToM research is subject to humans and other species or intelligent agents. Early research found that chimpanzees may possess a preliminary form of ToM. The ability allows them to infer the mental states of others, like humans [47]. This ability to attribute intentions, knowledge, and beliefs to others suggests that chimpanzees possess the basic forms of social cognition. However, the following research has shown that there are great differences between humans and animals in terms of the depth and complexity of ToM [7]. For example, while chimpanzees can understand others by a perception-goal psychology, they do not have a fully developed belief-desire psychology like humans. With the development of LLMs, e.g., ChatGPT, researchers also extended ToM tests to AI. ChatGPT and GPT-4 were tasked with difficult questions that required inferring the counterfactual effects of actions on mental states [5]. The findings show that GPT-4 demonstrated strong abilities in these scenarios, possessing an advanced level of ToM.

Cultural norms, values, and beliefs significantly impact how people perceive and understand the world. Researchers compared students from Western

(American) and Eastern (Indian) cultural backgrounds and discovered that Western participants had an independent self-construal and saw themselves as considerably more different from others [39]. Indian participants, on the other hand, perceived themselves as somewhat more alike to others, suggesting an interdependent self-perception. Additionally, studies show that different languages have different conceptions of emotion, with variations in the causes, evaluations, outcomes, modes of management and display, and even physiological responses linked to particular notions [45]. Sentiment perception can also be impacted by religious factors. The theory of cognitive dissonance suggests that individuals might adjust their opinions to match their religious beliefs in order to mitigate psychological discomfort [16]. This process can strengthen existing beliefs while eliminating conflicting opinions. Affirming religious beliefs can reduce the negative affect and emotional discomfort that occurs when individuals experience cognitive dissonance [6].

Individuals gain a sense of identity and self-esteem from association with various groups, including those based on occupational and educational backgrounds [50]. To maintain a positive social identity, individuals often adopt perspectives consistent with the norms and values of these groups. Related research also shows that people in high-status occupations tend to show more liberal attitudes toward social issues than people in low-status occupations [29]. Individuals may interpret information in a way that is consistent with their beliefs and values. This bias may lead individuals to view information that aligns with their ideology as more credible and trustworthy, while ignoring conflicting information [26]. Individuals with different ideologies may interpret identical information in divergent ways, thus delivering different opinions on the same target. For example, those with conservative ideologies often emphasize individual responsibility and individual rights, influencing their stance on welfare and healthcare-related policies [49]. In contrast, individuals with liberal ideologies often prioritize social justice and equality, leading to opposing opinions.

The way people construct their ideas is also influenced by certain personality traits [21]. For example, people who are open to new experiences are more likely to be receptive to new ideas and have flexible, open-minded perspectives [42]. On the other hand, those with higher conscientiousness typically base their beliefs on carefully analyzing the available data, leading to more thoughtful viewpoints. Additionally, research indicates that although intuitive thinkers depend more on heuristics and intuition, possibly producing subjective and prejudiced ideas, analytical thinkers often use deliberate, reflective thinking, leading to objective and evidence-driven judgments [46]. Sometimes, sentiment perceptions can be influenced by individuals' subjectivity, e.g., individuals who have had positive interactions with dogs are more likely to view dogs positively, contrasting with those whose experiences have been negative [51]. People tend to focus on information that aligns with their personal preferences and beliefs, potentially distorting their perception of emotions [4].

This tendency, termed confirmation bias, can impact how individuals interpret emotional events. Moreover, varied experiences and subjective feelings can influence using metaphorical language among individuals to express their opinions [27]. For example, financial analysts may employ different metaphors in their reports under different market conditions [34]. The public's perception of different types of weather disasters is also reflected in their metaphorical expressions [37]. To sum up, theoretical research and empirical studies support that individuals' sentiment perceptions are subject to multiple factors, including entity diversity that distinguishes between humans and other intelligent agents like animals and AI; culture, religion, vocation, ideology, personality, and subjectivity. These factors may impact personalized sentiment analysis in different scenarios. However, their collective impacts generally represent the complex interplay of individual characteristics and contextual influences on sentiment perception. These factors not only influence how individuals perceive and interpret the sentiment of a target but also alter the language they use to express subjective feelings. In sentiment analysis, understanding these factors is necessary for developing more personalized and context-sensitive systems.

3   Methodology

After reviewing relevant literature in psychology and cognitive science in Sect. 2.2, we define a hierarchical framework, containing factors that can impact individual sentiment perception and personalized sentiment analysis. This hierarchical framework is termed Personalized Sentiment Analysis Pyramid (see Fig. 2), including persona aspects, e.g., entity, culture, religion, vocation, ideology, personality, and subjectivity. Entity refers to the differentiation between human genders and other intelligent agents. Culture represents how various cultures perceive concepts as positive or negative. Religion involves considering how specific religious beliefs can influence an individual's opinions on certain topics. Vocation aids in understanding people's opinions based on their occupation and educational background. Ideology involves political beliefs and social, economic, or philosophical viewpoints. Personality assists in categorizing concepts as positive or negative based on personality traits. Finally, subjectivity considers personal preferences and experiences. At the bottom of the pyramid, personalization is more general, e.g., entities of the same gender and species, such as males, females, AI, or other creatures, can share the same persona information. Personalization is more specific at the top layer, e.g., subjectivity level. The persona information can be tailored for individuals. Next, we use an LLM, i.e., GPT-4 Turbo, to analyze the persona information of our subjects related to the above seven aspects. LLMs were trained with broader sources. It has shown superior knowledge in diverse domains, including natural language understanding and generation, multilingual capabilities, commonsense, reasoning, and scientific task processing [33]. It was also suggested as a useful tool for survey research and persona information generation [20]. Thus, it is eligible for analyzing the personalities of a subject from different aspects.

Finally, we test LLM performance on personalized sentiment analysis tasks. The obtained persona information in the former step is used as symbolic knowledge, guiding the sentiment inference of an LLM. Since we combine the symbolic knowledge and the reasoning ability of neural network-based LLMs together, the methodology is neurosymbolic. The structured symbolic knowledge provides a clear and understandable reasoning basis, enhancing the interpretability and explainability of the system's decisions. The testing data were sourced from novels, including dialogues with multi-turns. The task is to predict a speaker's sentiment perceptions towards another speaker involved in the conversation. We hypothesize that the additional persona information has different utilities in this scenario because the intensity of the influence of personal characteristics on sentiment perception changes as the scene changes. We aim to evaluate the utilities of the ensemble and each type of persona information.

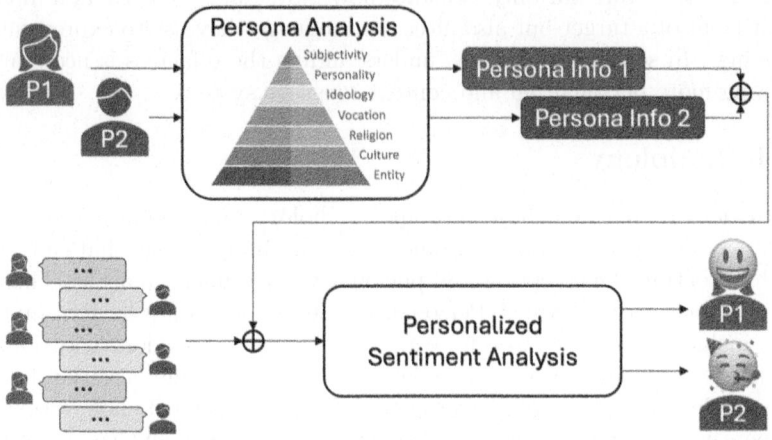

Fig. 3. Personalized sentiment analysis workflow. ⊕ denotes textual concatenation.

The overall workflow of our method can be viewed in Fig. 3. Our task setup and computing pipeline represent a novel approach for several reasons. First, we do not focus on analyzing the sentiment of a conversation based solely on its semantic content. Instead, our goal is to analyze how one person perceives another's sentiments. This means that even in a conversation that may seem neutral, there could still be negative sentiment if the individuals involved in the conversation do not like each other. Second, unlike traditional personalized AI techniques, such as user preference-based dialogue systems [59,60], personality trait-based recommender systems [52], or annotation-subjectivity-driven sentiment analysis [57], our approach considers persona information from multiple aspects. This allows our system to incorporate a broader range of factors that may be informative for personalized sentiment analysis. Finally, our system prioritizes user subjectivity by generating personalized outputs based on different types of persona information, even when presented with the same dialogue input. This approach to human-computer interaction is more human-centric.

3.1   Persona Information Acquisition

Since we have defined seven aspects for persona analysis and our analytical subjects are characters from *Harry Potter* novels, we can consult the persona information for GPT-4 directly. We formulate the query template as follows.

[Goal]: I want to categorize the given object according to their {aspect_term} in the Harry Potter book series. Please suggest a description, one in a line, starting with "-" and surrounded by quotes "". For example: - "{example_category}" Do not output anything else.
You may choose only one {aspect_term} from the following list: {category_list}
Please categorize {sample_in_prompt} into one {aspect_term} according to their {aspect_term} in the Harry Potter book series.

For each persona aspect, the *Harry Potter* persona analysis-tailored definition can be viewed in Table 1.

Table 1. Persona aspect term for analyzing the characters in Harry Potter novels

Aspect	Aspect Term
Entity	specie type and gender
Culture	cultural background
Religion	religious beliefs
Vocation	strong feeling of suitability for a particular career or occupation
Ideology	ideologies from aspects of political, social, epistemological, and ethical
Personality	MBTI personality type
Subjectivity	preferences and hobbies

Table 1 shows the aspect terms for the seven aspects we used to analyze the characters in the Harry Potter book series. To prevent overlap among the seven aspects and ensure that the LLM fully understands the meanings of the aspect terms, we provide a list of categories for the first six aspects (shown as follows) for the LLM to reference during inference. For "subjectivity", we provide examples such as "Quidditch Seeker" and "Painting", allowing the LLM to generate relevant answers openly.

– Entity: [specie type] Wizards and Witches, Muggles, Werewolves, Dragons, Hippogriffs, Basilisks, Trolls, Hags, Giants, Ghosts, House-elves, Goblins, Centaurs, Veela, Merpeople, Dementors, Vampires. [gender] male, female, or, inapplicable.
– Culture: Gryffindor, Slytherin, Hufflepuff, Ravenclaw, England, Scotland, Wales, Irish, French, Bulgarian, India, African, Romani, Middle Eastern, USA.
– Vocation: Auror, Healer, Transfigurers, Charms Experts, Diviners, Professor, Magizoologist, Potion Master, Curse Breaker, Metamorphmagi, Animagi,

278 L. Zhu et al.

Occlumens, Legilimens, Runes Experts, Patronus Charm Casters, Unspeakable, Wandmaker, Broom Maker, Quidditch Player, Journalist, Shop Owner, Ministry Official, Librarian, Herbologist, Arithmancer, Servants, Metalworkers, Bankers, Underwater Dwellers, Companions or Pets.
- Religion: Good vs. Evil, Love vs. Indifference, Acceptance_Death vs. Fear_Death vs. Bravery_Death vs. Denial_Death vs. Honor_Death, Sacrifice vs. Selfishness, Redemption vs. Condemnation, Impartiality vs. Prejudice, Tolerance vs. Intolerance, Courage vs. Cowardice, Faith vs. Skepticism, Responsibility vs. Irresponsibility.
- Ideology: Equality and Inclusivity vs. inequality and exclusivity, Reform vs. Satus Quo, Utilitarianism vs. Moral Absolutism, Knowledge vs. Ignorance, Loyalty and Community vs. disloyalty and individualism, Pragmatism vs. Idealism.
- Personality: ESTJ, ENTJ, ESFJ, ENFJ, ISTJ, ISFJ, INTJ, INFJ, ESTP, ESFP, ENTP, ENFP, ISTP, ISFP, INTP, INFP.

3.2 Personalized Sentiment Analysis

We conduct personalized sentiment analyses using the information obtained from the persona and an LLM. Given the collection of the persona information (p_i) of a person related to the seven aspects $(p = \{p_1, p_2, ..., p_i, ..., p_7\})$, the scene illustration (e) where the conversation happens, the dialogues with multi-turns (d), the interlocutors (m, n), and task description (t), the task aims to predict the mutual sentiment perceptions, e.g., the sentiment perception of m (a perceiving subject) towards n (a perceiving object) $(s^{(m \to n)})$ and the sentiment perception of n towards m $(s^{(n \to m)})$. We fit all the aforementioned textual information into a prompt template $(template(\cdot))$, then ask an LLM to predict the sentiment perceptions $(LLM(\cdot))$ from the prompt $(prompt)$.

$$prompt^{(m \leftrightarrow n)} = template(e^{(m,n)}, d^{(m,n)}, p^{(m)}, p^{(n)}, m, n, t) \tag{1}$$

$$s^{(m \to n)}, s^{(m \leftarrow n)} = LLM(prompt^{(m \leftrightarrow n)}) \tag{2}$$

The prompt template $(prompt^{(m \to n)})$ for inferring the sentiment perception of m towards n can be viewed below. In the prompt box, the content after [Goal] refers to the task description (t) that directs an LLM to deliver desired predictions, following a fixed structure. scene (e) is the background illustration in which the conversation takes place. dialogue_sample is the dialogue with multi-turns (d). character_1 and character_2 correspond to the interlocutors (m, n). persona_1 and persona_2 denote their persona information $p^{(m)}$ and $p^{(n)}$ that was obtained in Sect. 3.1.

[Goal] I want to classify the sentiment scores between the two characters in the Harry Potter book series based on their dialogue and persona.
Please suggest a sentiment score, one in a line, starting with "-" and surrounded by quotes "". For example:
- "<Harry to Hermione> 1"
- "<Hermione to Harry> 2"

The following shows the different meanings of the sentiment scores.
Please select the sentiment score from the following options: -5: Vendetta; -4: Intentionally inflict harm; -3: Maliciously targeting and harm; -2: Deliberately bullying/deliberately targeting; -1: Rude/Frivolous/Mean characters; 0: Stranger/Neutral; 1: Normal/Polite; 2: Friendly; 3: Kind; 4: Close; 5: Devoted.
[Scene] {scene}
[Dialogue] {dialogue_sample}
[Persona] {character_1}: {persona_1}. {character_2}: {persona_2}.
Please classify the sentiment scores between the two characters {character_1} and {character_2} based on the given dialogue and their personas.

4   Experiment

4.1   Research Questions

In this work, we aim to explore the following research questions:

1. What is the utility of using the ensemble of the seven levels of personalization?
2. What is the utility of using individual personalization?
3. How does personalization impact sentiment analysis accuracy across different types of entity and culture factors?

These research questions are explored in Sects. 5.1–5.3, respectively.

4.2   Dataset

Our personalized sentiment analysis uses the Harry Potter Dataset (HPD) [9]. It was developed to enhance the alignment of conversation agents with fictional characters from Harry Potter novels. It includes annotating relationships and character attributes that evolve over the storyline. HPD includes background information, such as conversation scenes, speaker identities, and character attributes, to enable dialogue agents to generate replies consistent with the Harry Potter universe. In contrast to our structured persona analysis, the character attributes in the dataset were not derived from the same set of analytical aspects. Thus, we did not use their character attribute descriptions. We leverage their affection labels that indicate the sentiment intensity of a perceiving subject to another perceiving object as our sentiment intensity labels. In our classification task, positive labels correspond to the sentiment intensity, ranging from –5 to –1; negative labels correspond to the sentiment intensity, ranging from 1 to 5. A neutral label corresponds to the sentiment intensity of 0. Our method is evaluated using the English version of the original HPD. The statistics of our employed data and the sentiment intensity distribution are shown in Fig. 4.

4.3   Large Language Models

The persona information was queried from GPT-4 Turbo. The personalized sentiment analysis was evaluated with GPT-4 Turbo and GPT-3.5 Turbo (i.e., Chat-GPT), respectively. GPT-4 Turbo is an upgraded version of GPT-3.5 Turbo.

Item	No. of samples
Dialogues	1,191
Positive sentiment	4,932
Negative sentiment	730
Neutral sentiment	8
Interlocutors	94

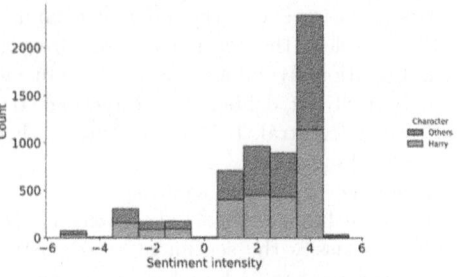

Fig. 4. Dataset statistics and sentiment intensity distribution

Both LLMs were developed by Open AI, pre-trained with Transformer-based deep neural networks and a large number of corpus resources. By a preliminary test, we found that these LLMs have rich knowledge about *Harry Potter* novels.

4.4   Evaluation Metrics

We evaluate the personalized sentiment analysis performance using two types of metrics. The F1 score and accuracy are used to evaluate the accuracy of sentiment polarity classification. In this task, LLMs aim to predict whether the sentiment perception is positive, negative, or neutral. Mean Squared Error (MSE) is used to evaluate the accuracy of sentiment intensity prediction. Considering the potential failure of LLMs to respond in the required format, the Answer Rate is also integrated into the evaluation. It measures the percentage of queries successfully answered by the LLM. In this task, LLMs aim to predict the sentiment intensity, ranging from –5 to 5. Since the sentiment intensity between the same perceiving subject and perceiving object is identical across all dialogues in the dataset, we combine all dialogues between two identical interlocutors as a united input. A correct prediction is defined as the predicted sentiment label (either a sentiment polarity or a sentiment intensity score) of a perceiving subject towards a perceiving object matching the ground truth label.

5   Results

5.1   The Ensemble Utility of the Seven Levels of Personalization

We compared the sentiment analysis results of GPT-3.5 and GPT-4 with and without the ensembled seven levels of personalization in Table 2. The ensemble utility of seven levels of personalization improved the performance of GPT-3.5 on sentiment analysis. For GPT-4, the inclusion of the seven levels of personalization seems to contribute to a slight improvement in F1(p:=pos) and accuracy and mean-square error(MSE) or even a marginal decrease in F1(p:neg) and Macro F1. Taking into consideration the answer rate, however, we found the accuracy of GPT-4 on the whole dataset turns into $0.8977 \times 0.8155 = 0.7321$ while the one of GPT-4 w/ p1:7 becomes $0.9058 \times 09492 = 0.8598$. Thus, the adjusted accuracy increase of 0.1277 demonstrates the ensemble effectiveness of the seven levels of personalization on sentiment analysis task.

Table 2. Personalized sentiment analysis. p:=pos means the positive sentiment is defined as positive labels for computing F1; p:=neg means the negative sentiment is defined as positive labels for computing F1

	F1 (p:=pos)	F1 (p:=neg)	Macro. F1	Acc.	MSE	Answer Rate
GPT-3.5	0.9381	0.5340	0.4907	0.8686	0.3586	0.6522
w/ $p_{1:7}$	0.9484	0.5859	0.5114	0.8936	0.3293	0.6860
Delta	0.0103	0.0519	0.0207	0.0250	-0.2036	0.0338
GPT-4	0.9569	0.7372	0.5704	0.8977	0.1860	0.8155
w/ $p_{1:7}$	0.9631	0.7092	0.5630	0.9058	0.1812	0.9492
Delta	0.0062	-0.028	-0.0074	0.0081	-0.0048	0.1337

5.2   The Utility Analysis of the Individual Personalization

Table 3 shows the positive influence of each individual personalization on the performance of GPT-3.5 in the personalized sentiment analysis tasks. Among them, Culture, Vocation, Ideology, and Subjectivity strengthened the performance of GPT-3.5 by a significant margin, while Entity, Religion, and Personality contributed to a relatively less improvement. There may be a thought-provoking rationale for such a discrepancy. The Harry Potter book series is deeply rooted in a rich culture, ideology, and subjectivity backdrops, thereby offering a rich tapestry of themes and narratives that resonate deeply with readers' or even sentiment intensity annotators' own values. For example, someone who values loyalty and friendship may possibly echo characters like Harry and Ron. Hence, they may easily capture Harry's negative sentiment towards Peter Pettigrew, who betrayed his friends, James and Lily Potter. Consequently, an LLM knowing these factors (culture, ideology, and subjectivity) may understand characters' sentiments more precisely by resonating with characters' values.

5.3   The Personalization Utility Analysis by Entity and Culture

The results presented in Sect. 5.2 are readily comparable, as the growths in F1, Macro. F1, accuracy, and answer rate are consistent. Unlike Sects. 5.1 and 5.2, performance summarized by different categories of entity and culture aspects is

Table 3. Personalized sentiment analysis by persona types

	F1 (pos = pos)	F1(pos = neg)	Macro. F1	Acc-all	MSE	Answer Rate
GPT-3.5	0.9381	0.5340	0.4907	0.8686	0.3586	0.6522
w/ p1	0.9478	0.5553	0.5010	0.8825	0.3200	0.6769
w/ p2	0.9508	0.5793	0.5138	0.8926	0.2941	0.6801
w/ p3	0.9413	0.5403	0.4939	0.8841	0.3736	0.6713
w/ p4	0.9504	0.5542	0.5015	0.8886	0.3055	0.7171
w/ p5	0.9456	0.5532	0.4996	0.8884	0.3419	0.6938
w/ p6	0.9490	0.5619	0.5073	0.8868	0.3108	0.6667
w/ p7	0.9502	0.5722	0.5074	0.8897	0.3046	0.6780

more sensitive to the answer rate, since we investigate the results by breaking down the characters into finer-grained groups instead of treating them as a whole. Therefore, we calculated the evaluation metrics based on all the query samples in Tables 4 and 5, by setting the missing result with a fixed value (100 in this paper) out of the scope of ground-truth labels. Moreover, we detailed the sentiment analysis results by presenting the metrics of each category group, both as subjects (conveying sentiments to Harry) and objects (receiving sentiments from Harry).

In general, including seven levels of personalization completely enhanced the performance of groups Ghosts, Acromantula, Veela, Centaurs, and French. For entity breakdowns, the negative effects on GPT-4 of including seven aspects occur only in the cases where the entity groups (Muggles, Wizards and Witches, House-elves, and Goblins) play as an object. For culture breakdowns, the negative impacts of including seven aspects on GPT-4 are primarily observed when the entity groups (England, Gryffindor, Ravenclaw, Slytherin, and Hufflepuff) function as objects. However, effects related to these breakdowns are observed in only two cases (Ravenclaw and Hufflepuff) when they serve as subjects. For both breakdowns (entity and culture), the negative effects on GPT-3.5 of including seven aspects occur relatively more often and mainly when the entity group plays as a subject. The above observation highlights the bias of LLMs (such as GPT-3.5 and GPT-4) towards the subject and the object on sentiment analysis, especially when these models address personalized neurosymbolic knowledge. Additionally, comparing the results of GPT-3.5 and GPT-4, we observed that GPT-3.5, when integrated with personalized neurosymbolic knowledge, achieved comparable or even superior performance to GPT-4. This is validated by the results from several Entity or Culture groups including Muggles, Ghosts, Acromantula, Veela, and England.

Table 4. Personalized sentiment analysis by entity breakdowns (adjusted by answer rate). * denotes the inclusion of persona information lowers the performance

Entity	Perc.	Model	F1(p:=pos)	F1(p:=neg)	Macro. F1	Acc.
Muggles	Sub.	G3.5	0.16	0.5203	0.2268	0.3208
		w/ p1:7	0.2105	0.6119	0.2742	0.4057
		G4	0	0.4833	0.1611	0.2736
		w/ p1:7	0.1111	0.6277	0.2463	0.4151
	Obj.	G3.5	0.0909	0.0833	0.0581	0.0566
		w/ p1:7	0.32	0.1237	0.1479	0.1321
		G4	0.0952	0.198	0.0978	0.1038
		w/ p1:7	0.2069	0.1237*	0.1102	0.0849*
Giants	Sub.	G3.5	0.875	0	0.2917	0.7778
		w/ p1:7	0.8529*	0	0.2843*	0.7436*
		G4	0.9646	0	0.3215	0.9316
		w/ p1:7	0.9957	0	0.3319	0.9915
	Obj.	G3.5	0.8641	0	0.288	0.7607
		w/ p1:7	0.8529*	0	0.2843*	0.7436*
		G4	0.9646	0	0.3215	0.9316
		w/ p1:7	0.9957	0	0.3319	0.9915
Wizards and Witches	Sub.	G3.5	0.7468	0.578	0.4416	0.5941
		w/ p1:7	0.7837	0.6724	0.4853	0.6483
		G4	0.865	0.7664	0.555	0.7644
		w/ p1:7	0.9521	0.82	0.6027	0.9061
	Obj.	G3.5	0.7497	0.2465	0.3321	0.5713
		w/ p1:7	0.7793	0.2189*	0.3328	0.6146
		G4	0.8679	0.6435	0.5079	0.7483
		w/ p1:7	0.9543	0.6323*	0.5331	0.8836
House-elves	Sub.	G3.5	0.7727	0.5714	0.4481	0.6176
		w/ p1:7	0.6829*	0.375*	0.3526*	0.5*
		G4	0.9412	0.9231	0.6214	0.8824
		w/ p1:7	0.9615	1	0.6538	0.9412
	Obj.	G3.5	0.6818	0.1538	0.2786	0.4706
		w/ p1:7	0.6818	0.1538	0.2786	0.4706
		G4	0.875	0.5882	0.4877	0.7647
		w/ p1:7	0.8148*	0.1538*	0.3229*	0.6765*
Ghosts	Sub.	G3.5	0.88	0	0.2933	0.7857
		w/ p1:7	0.9231	0	0.3077	0.8571
		G4	0.9231	0	0.3077	0.8571
		w/ p1:7	0.963	0	0.321	0.9286
	Obj.	G3.5	0.8333	0	0.2778	0.7143
		w/ p1:7	0.88	0	0.2933	0.7857
		G4	0.963	0	0.321	0.9286
		w/ p1:7	0.963	0	0.321	0.9286

continued

Table 4. continued

Entity	Perc.	Model	F1(p:=pos)	F1(p:=neg)	Macro. F1	Acc.
Acromantula	Sub.	G3.5	0.6667	0	0.2222	0.5
		w/ p1:7	0.6667	0	0.2222	0.5
		G4	0	0	0	0
		w/ p1:7	0	0	0	0
	Obj.	G3.5	0	0	0	0
		w/ p1:7	0	0	0	0
		G4	0	0	0	0
		w/ p1:7	0	0	0	0
Veela	Sub.	G3.5	0.5161	0	0.172	0.3478
		w/ p1:7	0.7895	0	0.2632	0.6522
		G4	0.6471	0	0.2157	0.4783
		w/ p1:7	0.7568	0	0.2523	0.6087
	Obj.	G3.5	0.5625	0	0.1875	0.3913
		w/ p1:7	0.7895	0	0.2632	0.6522
		G4	0.6471	0	0.2157	0.4783
		w/ p1:7	0.7568	0	0.2523	0.6086
Centaurs	Sub.	G3.5	1	0	0.3333	1
		w/ p1:7	1	0	0.3333	1
		G4	1	0	0.3333	1
		w/ p1:7	1	0	0.3333	1
	Obj.	G3.5	1	0	0.3333	1
		w/ p1:7	1	0	0.3333	1
		G4	1	0	0.3333	1
		w/ p1:7	1	0	0.3333	1
Werewolves	Sub.	G3.5	0.0571	0.5	0.1857	0.0541
		w/ p1:7	0*	0.8	0.2667	0.0541
		G4	0.1111	1	0.3704	0.1351
		w/ p1:7	0.1111	1	0.3704	0.1351
	Obj.	G3.5	0	0	0	0
		w/ p1:7	0	0.3333	0.1111	0.027
		G4	0.1176	0.5714	0.2297	0.1081
		w/ p1:7	0.1176	0.75	0.2892	0.1351
Goblins	Sub.	G3.5	0.5455	0	0.1818	0.3333
		w/ p1:7	0.3333*	0.3333	0.2222	0.2222*
		G4	0.4444	0.4	0.2815	0.3333
		w/ p1:7	0.5714	0.5714	0.381	0.4444
	Obj.	G3.5	0.7273	0	0.2424	0.4444
		w/ p1:7	0.5455*	0	0.1818*	0.3333*
		G4	0.8	0.6667	0.4889	0.6667
		w/ p1:7	0.7143*	0*	0.3571*	0.5556*

Table 5. Personalized sentiment analysis by culture breakdowns (adjusted by answer rate). * denotes the inclusion of persona information lowers the performance

Culture	Perc.	Model	F1(p:=pos)	F1(p:=neg)	Macro. F1	Acc.
England	Sub.	G3.5	0.5135	0.5362	0.3499	0.3889
		w/ p1:7	0.4762*	0.6104	0.3622	0.4306
		G4	0.6087	0.4776	0.4227	0.3819
		w/ p1:7	0.597	0.6133	0.4451	0.4722
	Obj.	G3.5	0.4752	0.0971	0.1908	0.2014
		w/ p1:7	0.4808	0.1321	0.2043	0.2222
		G4	0.5833	0.2456	0.2763	0.2431
		w/ p1:7	0.5854*	0.1651*	0.2502*	0.2292*
Gryffindor	Sub.	G3.5	0.7609	0.1798	0.3135	0.614
		w/ p1:7	0.7985	0.2985	0.3657	0.664
		G4	0.8772	0.2593	0.3788	0.7805
		w/ p1:7	0.9632	0.3478	0.437	0.9276
	Obj.	G3.5	0.7705	0.1282	0.2296	0.623
		w/ p1:7	0.8042	0.1017*	0.302	0.6694
		G4	0.8802	0.4667	0.4592	0.785
		w/ p1:7	0.9652	0.4364*	0.4847	0.9303
Ravenclaw	Sub.	G3.5	0.6443	0	0.2148	0.466
		w/ p1:7	0.5775*	0.069	0.2155	0.4078*
		G4	0.8047	0	0.2682	0.6602
		w/ p1:7	0.7976*	0.2	0.3325	0.6602
	Obj.	G3.5	0.5913	0.15	0.2471	0.3592
		w/ p1:7	0.6461	0.1081*	0.2514	0.4272
		G4	0.8125	0.3256	0.3794	0.5728
		w/ p1:7	0.8593	0.3111*	0.3901	0.6311
Slytherin	Sub.	G3.5	0.5143	0.6981	0.4041	0.543
		w/ p1:7	0.32*	0.7966	0.3722*	0.6471
		G4	0.5143	0.8822	0.4655	0.7692
		w/ p1:7	0.6061	0.933	0.513	0.8643
	Obj.	G3.5	0.3111	0.2797	0.1969	0.2127
		w/ p1:7	0.2281*	0.2712*	0.1664*	0.2036*
		G4	0.6667	0.7352	0.4673	0.6018
		w/ p1:7	0.5763*	0.7152*	0.4305*	0.5882*
Hufflepuff	Sub.	G3.5	0.6897	0.8572	0.5156	0.5542
		w/ p1:7	0.7333	0.75*	0.4944*	0.6024
		G4	0.7937	0.9333	0.5757	0.6867
		w/ p1:7	0.8905	0.7778*	0.5561*	0.8193
	Obj.	G3.5	0.6316	0.2857	0.3058	0.4578
		w/ p1:7	0.7097	0.1538*	0.2878*	0.5422
		G4	0.748	0.5	0.416	0.6024
		w/ p1:7	0.8467	0.4*	0.4156*	0.7349

continued

Table 5. continued

Culture	Perc.	Model	F1(p:=pos)	F1(p:=neg)	Macro. F1	Acc.
Bulgarian	Sub.	G3.5	0.4286	0	0.1429	0.2727
		w/ p1:7	0.4*	0	0.1333*	0.2273*
		G4	0.4	0	0.1333	0.2773
		w/ p1:7	0.6207	0	0.2069	0.4091
	Obj.	G3.5	0.625	0	0.2083	0.4545
		w/ p1:7	0.5806*	0	0.1935*	0.4091*
		G4	0.5806	0	0.1935	0.4091
		w/ p1:7	0.625	0	0.2083	0.4545
French	Sub.	G3.5	0.5	0	0.1667	0.3333
		w/ p1:7	0.7692	0	0.2564	0.625
		G4	0.6286	0	0.2095	0.4583
		w/ p1:7	0.7368	0	0.2456	0.5833
	Obj.	G3.5	0.5455	0	0.1818	0.375
		w/ p1:7	0.7692	0	0.2564	0.625
		G4	0.6286	0	0.2095	0.4583
		w/ p1:7	0.7568	0	0.2456	0.5833
Irish	Sub.	G3.5	0.5455	0.2	0.2485	0.2667
		w/ p1:7	0.4*	0.2	0.2*	0.2*
		G4	0.4286	0.2	0.2095	0.2667
		w/ p1:7	0.6316	0.2	0.2772	0.4667
	Obj.	G3.5	0.5455	0.2	0.2485	0.2667
		w/ p1:7	0.4*	0*	0.1333*	0.1333*
		G4	0.4615	0.2	0.2205	0.2667
		w/ p1:7	0.6316	0.2	0.2772	0.4667

6   Conclusion

In this work, we studied the task of personalized sentiment analysis. Personas were widely studied in commercial domains and web research [18, 19]. Unlike conventional sentiment analysis tasks that aim to analyze sentiment by the meanings of the text, personalized sentiment analysis targets to analyzing the individual sentiment perception.

The difference is that an identical statement can yield the same sentiment prediction by its meaning. In contrast, different people may perceive the message differently based on their own personal preferences, personality traits, beliefs, background, etc. To this end, we devised a framework, termed the Personalized Sentiment Analysis Pyramid, for tackling all these different facets through seven different levels of personalization, namely: Entity, Culture, Religion, Vocation, Ideology, Personality, and Subjectivity.

We evaluated the framework with a dialogue dataset sourced from *Harry Potter* novels. The evaluation showed that personalized neurosymbolic knowledge, i.e., seven levels of personalization, augmented LLMs' performance on sentiment analysis. We also analyzed the utility of each persona aspect and found that each individual persona aspect can augment sentiment intensity classification results. Finally, we investigated the influence of persona information on several character groups in the *Harry Potter* novels. Results showed that including persona information elevated the performance of groups Ghost, Acromantula, Veela, Centaurs, and French. Furthermore, a bias of LLMs fed with personalized neurosymbolic knowledge towards subject and object groups is observed.

In future work, we plan to develop more robust persona information parsers and classifiers to extract information related to the defined persona aspects from different modalities. With persona information, we will also conduct a wide range of personalized cognitive computing tasks, including investigating how different people use different metaphors to communicate different perspectives, experiences, and emotions, revealing the nuanced ways in which language shapes and reflects cultural, social, and individual identities.

Acknowledgments. This research/project is supported by the Ministry of Education, Singapore under its MOE Academic Research Fund Tier 2 (STEM RIE2025 Award MOE-T2EP20123-0005) and by the RIE2025 Industry Alignment Fund - Industry Collaboration Projects (IAF-ICP) (Award I2301E0026), administered by A*STAR, as well as supported by Alibaba Group and NTU Singapore.

References

1. Abdul-Mageed,M., Ungar, L.: EmoNet: fine-grained emotion detection with gated recurrent neural networks. In: Proceedings of ACL, pp. 718–728, Vancouver, Canada. Association for Computational Linguistics (2017)
2. Altrabsheh, N., Gaber, M.M., Cocea, M., et al.: SA-E: sentiment analysis for education. Frontiers Artifi. Intell. Appl. **255**, 353–362 (2013)
3. Apperly, I.A., Butterfill, S.A.: Do humans have two systems to track beliefs and belief-like states? Psychol. Rev. **116**(4), 953 (2009)
4. Bower, G.H.: Mood and memory. Am. Psychol. **36**(2), 129 (1981)
5. Bubeck, S., et al.: Sparks of artificial general intelligence: Early experiments with GPT-4. arXiv preprint arXiv:2303.12712 (2023)
6. Burris, C.T., Harmon-Jones, E., Tarpley, W.R.: by faith alone': religious agitation and cognitive dissonance. Basic Appli. Soc. Psychol. **19**(1), 17–31 (1997)
7. Call, J., Tomasello, M.: Does the chimpanzee have a theory of mind? 30 years later. Trends Cogn. Sci. **12**(5), 187–192 (2008)
8. Cambria, E., Zhang, X., Mao, R., Chen, M., Kwok, K.: SenticNet 8: fusing emotion AI and commonsense AI for interpretable, trustworthy, and explainable affective computing. In: Proceedings of International Conference on Human-Computer Interaction (HCII) (2024)
9. Chen, N., et al.: Large language models meet Harry Potter: a dataset for aligning dialogue agents with characters. In: EMNLP Findings, pp. 8506–8520 (2023)
10. Dagar, D., Hudait, A., Tripathy, H.K., Das, MN Automatic emotion detection model from facial expression. In: ICACCCT, pp. 77–85 (2016)
11. Dong, X.L., De Melo, G.: A helping hand: transfer learning for deep sentiment analysis. In: Proceedings of ACL, pp. 2524–2534 (2018)

12. Cuc Duong, Qian Liu, Rui Mao, and Erik Cambria. Saving earth one tweet at a time through the lens of artificial intelligence. In *IJCNN*, pages 1–9, 2022
13. Duong, C., Raghuram, V.C., Lee, A., Mao, R., Mengaldo, G., Cambria, E.: Neurosymbolic AI for mining public opinions about wildfires. Cogn. Comput. **16**(4), 1531–1553 (2024)
14. Fan, C., Lin, J., Mao, R., Cambria, E.: Fusing pairwise modalities for emotion recognition in conversations. Inform. Fusion **106**, 102306 (2024)
15. Fedus, W., Goodfellow, I., Dai, A.M.: MaskGAN: better text generation via filling in the _. In: ICLR (2018)
16. Festinger, L.: A Theory of Cognitive Dissonance. Stanford University Press (1957)
17. He, K., Mao, R., Gong, T., Li, C., Cambria, E.: Meta-based self-training and reweighting for aspect-based sentiment analysis. IEEE Trans. Affect. Comput. **14**(3), 1731–1742 (2023)
18. Jansen, B.J.: Understanding user-web interactions via web analytics. Springer Nature (2022)
19. Jansen, B.J., Jung, S.-G., Nielsen, L., Guan, K.W., Salminen, J.: How to create personas: three persona creation methodologies with implications for practical employment. Pacific Asia J. Associat. Inform. Syst. **14**(3), 1 (2022)
20. Jansen, B.J., Jung, S.-G., Salminen, J.: Employing large language models in survey research. Nat. Lang. Process. J. **4**, 100020 (2023)
21. Jansen, B.J., Salminen, J., Jung, S.-g., Guan, K.: Data-driven personas. Springer Nature (2022)
22. Ji, S., Li, X., Huang, Z., Cambria, E.: Suicidal ideation and mental disorder detection with attentive relation networks. Neural Comput. Appl. **34**(13), 10309–10319 (2022)
23. Kenyon-Dean, K., et al.: Sentiment analysis: It's complicated! In: Proceedings of ACL, pp. 1886–1895 (2018)
24. Kim, Y.: Convolutional neural networks for sentence classification. In: Proceedings of EMNLP, pp. 1746–1751 (2014)
25. Kumar, S., Yadava, M., Roy, P.P.: Fusion of EEG response and sentiment analysis of products review to predict customer satisfaction. Inform. Fus. **52**, 41–52 (2019)
26. Kunda, Z.: The case for motivated reasoning. Psychol. Bull. **108**(3), 480 (1990)
27. Lakoff, G., Johnson, M.: Metaphors We Live by. University of Chicago press(1980)
28. Li, W., Zhu, L., Mao, R., Cambria, E.: SKIER: a symbolic knowledge integrated model for conversational emotion recognition. Proc. AAAI **37**(11), 13121–13129 (2023)
29. Lipset, S.M.: The Confidence Gap: Business, Labor, and Government in the Public Mind. The Johns Hopkins University Press (1987)
30. Lu, Z., Cao, L., Zhang, Y., Chiu, C.-C., Fan, J.: Speech sentiment analysis via pretrained features from end-to-end ASR models. In: ICASSP, pp. 7149–7153 (2020)
31. Ma, Yu., Mao, R., Lin, Q., Peng, W., Cambria, E.: Multi-source aggregated classification for stock price movement prediction. Inform. Fusion **91**, 515–528 (2023)
32. Ma, Yu., Mao, R., Lin, Q., Peng, W., Cambria, E.: Quantitative stock portfolio optimization by multi-task learning risk and return. Inform. Fusion **104**, 102165 (2024)
33. Mao, R., Chen, G., Zhang, X., Guerin, F., Cambria, E.: GPTEval: a survey on assessments of ChatGPT and GPT-4. In: Proceedings of LREC-COLING, pp. 7844–7866 (2024)
34. Mao, R., Du, K., Ma, Y., Zhu, L., Cambria, E.: Discovering the cognition behind language: Financial metaphor analysis with MetaPro. In: ICDM, pp. 1211–1216 (2023)

35. Mao, R., Li, X.: Bridging towers of multi-task learning with a gating mechanism for aspect-based sentiment analysis and sequential metaphor identification. Proc. AAAI **35**, 13534–13542 (2021)
36. Mao, R., Li, X., He, K., Ge, M., Cambria, E.: MetaPro online: computational metaphor processing online system. Proc. ACL **3**, 127–135 (2023)
37. Mao, R., Lin, Q., Liu, Q., Mengaldo, G., Cambria, E.: Understanding public perception towards weather disasters through the lens of metaphor. In: Proceedings of IJCAI, pp. 7394–7402 (2024)
38. Mao, R., Liu, Q., He, K., Li, W., Cambria, E.: The biases of pre-trained language models: an empirical study on prompt-based sentiment analysis and emotion detection. IEEE Trans. Affect. Comput. **14**(3), 1743–1753 (2023)
39. Markus, H.R., Kitayama, S.: Culture and the self: implications for cognition, emotion, and motivation. In: College Student Development and Academic Life, pp. 264–293. Routledge (2014)
40. Marrese-Taylor, E., Velásquez, J.D., Bravo-Marquez, F.: A novel deterministic approach for aspect-based opinion mining in tourism products reviews. Expert Syst. Appli. **41**(17), 7764–7775 (2014)
41. Martin, J.R., White, P.R.: The Language of Evaluation, vol. 2. Springer (2003)
42. McCrae, R.R., Costa, P.T.: Validation of the five-factor model of personality across instruments and observers. J. Personal. Soc. Psychol. **52**(1), 81 (1987)
43. Medhat, W., Hassan, A., Korashy, H.: Sentiment analysis algorithms and applications: a survey. Ain Shams Eng. J. **5**(4), 1093–1113 (2014)
44. Mudinas, A., Zhang, D., Levene, M.: Combining lexicon and learning based approaches for concept-level sentiment analysis. In: ISDOMW (2012)
45. Pavlenko, A.: Emotion and emotion-laden words in the bilingual lexicon. Bilingualism: Lang. Cognition **11**(2), 147–164 (2008)
46. Pennycook, G., Cheyne, J.A., Barr, N., Koehler, D.J., Fugelsang, J.A.: On the reception and detection of pseudo-profound bullshit. Judgment Dec. Making **10**(6), 549–563 (2015)
47. Premack, D., Woodruff, G.: Does the chimpanzee have a theory of mind? Behav. Brain Sci. **1**(4), 515–526 (1978)
48. Proksch, S.-O., Lowe, W., Wäckerle, J., Soroka, S.: Multilingual sentiment analysis: a new approach to measuring conflict in legislative speeches. Legis. Stud. Q. **44**(1), 97–131 (2019)
49. Taber, C.S., Lodge, M.: Motivated skepticism in the evaluation of political beliefs. Am. J. Political Sci. **50**(3), 755–769 (2006)
50. Tajfel, H., Turner, J.C., Austin, W.G., Worchel, S.: An integrative theory of intergroup conflict. Organizat. Identity: Reader **56**(65), 9780203505984–16 (1979)
51. Tyrer, P., Reed, G.M., Crawford, M.J.: Classification, assessment, prevalence, and effect of personality disorder. Lancet **385**(9969), 717–726 (2015)
52. Yang, H.-C., Huang, Z.-R.: Mining personality traits from social messages for game recommender systems. Knowl.-Based Syst. **165**, 157–168 (2019)
53. Yue, T., Mao, R., Wang, H., Zonghai, H., Cambria, E.: KnowleNet: knowledge fusion network for multimodal sarcasm detection. Information Fusion **100**, 101921 (2023)
54. Yue, T., Shi, X., Mao, R., Hu, Z., Cambria, E.: SarcNet: a multilingual multimodal sarcasm detection dataset. In: Proceedings of LREC-COLING, pp. 14325–14335 (2024)
55. Zadeh, A., Chen, M., Poria, S., Cambria, E., Morency, L.-P.: Tensor fusion network for multimodal sentiment analysis. In: Proceedings of EMNLP, pp. 1103–1114 (2017)

56. Zhang, X., Mao, R., Cambria, E.: Multilingual emotion recognition: Discovering the variations of lexical semantics between languages. In: Proceedings of IJCNN (2024)
57. Zhang, X., Mao, R., Cambria, E.: SenticVec: Toward robust and human-centric neurosymbolic sentiment analysis. In: Proceedings of ACL, pp. 4851–4863 (2024)
58. Zhang, X., Mao, R., He, K., Cambria, E.: Neurosymbolic sentiment analysis with dynamic word sense disambiguation. In: EMNLP Findings, pp. 8772–8783 (2023)
59. Zhu, L., Li, W., Mao, R., Cambria, E.: HIPPL: hierarchical intent-inferring pointer network with pseudo labeling for consistent persona-driven dialogue generation. IEEE Comput. Intell. Mag. 19(4), 63–78 (2024)
60. Zhu, L., Li, W., Mao, R., Pandelea, V., Cambria, E.: PAED: zero-shot persona attribute extraction in dialogues. Proc. ACL 1, 9771–9787 (2023)

An Exploratory Study of Conventional Machine Learning and Large Language Models for Sentiment Analysis

Cui Zou[1]([✉]) [iD], Jingyuan Cai[2] [iD], Langtao Chen[3] [iD], and Fiona Fui-Hoon Nah[2] [iD]

[1] University of Oklahoma, Norman, OK 73019, USA
tracyzou@ou.edu
[2] City University of Hong Kong, Kowloon Tong, Kowloon, Hong Kong SAR, China
jingyucai2-c@my.cityu.edu.hk, fiona.nah@cityu.edu.hk
[3] The University of Tulsa, Tulsa, OK 74104, USA
langtao-chen@utulsa.edu

Abstract. Sentiment analysis is the use of natural language processing to identify affective states and determine people's opinions in various analytical applications such as customer reviews and social media analyses. Large language models (LLMs) such as GPT-4o demonstrate impressive performance in text generation tasks. Despite numerous studies in the extant literature, few have compared the performance of conventional machine learning models with LLMs for sentiment analysis. This study aims to fill this gap by conducting an evaluation of these models using a balanced dataset of 2,000 IMDb movie reviews. Our study shows that GPT-4o achieves the highest performance, while GPT-3.5 and FLAN-T5 models also show strong performance, being slightly below that of GPT-4o. Advanced LLMs outperform conventional machine learning models. Our findings highlight the advanced capabilities and user-friendliness of LLMs compared to conventional machine learning models. This research underscores the rapid evolution of LLMs for sentiment analysis.

Keywords: Sentiment Analysis · Large Language Models · GPT · FLAN-T5 · Machine Learning · IMDb · Movie Reviews

1 Introduction

Sentiment analysis (SA) has been a critical component of the machine learning (ML) landscape for many years. Whether analyzing movie reviews or social media posts, SA plays a vital role in natural language processing (NLP) by evaluating and quantifying human emotions expressed in text. The IMDb dataset, in particular, has been widely used as a benchmark for developing and testing models for SA. Numerous models have been developed and tested on this dataset, and they demonstrate varying performance[1].

---

[1] https://paperswithcode.com/sota/sentiment-analysis-on-imdb (accessed on 2024/05/19).

© The Author(s), under exclusive license to Springer Nature Switzerland AG 2024
H. Degen and S. Ntoa (Eds.): HCII 2024, LNCS 15382, pp. 291–300, 2024.
https://doi.org/10.1007/978-3-031-76827-9_17

The advent of large language models (LLMs), such as GPT, has revolutionized the domain of NLP. Several studies (e.g., Zhang et al. 2023) have started to utilize LLMs for conducting SA, leveraging the advanced capabilities of LLMs in understanding text. Although LLMs are mainly developed for other purposes such as machine translation and text generation, these models have shown significant promise for SA. However, the research community has largely focused on evaluating individual model performance rather than conducting a comprehensive comparison of LLMs versus conventional methods for SA.

Little research has provided a comprehensive comparison of performance across the latest LLMs and conventional ML methods. This research gap is notable given the rapid advancement of LLMs and the introduction of new versions, such as GPT-4o (OpenAI, n.d.). A comprehensive comparison of the performance of these models on a common testbed offers implications for selecting the best or appropriate methods for SA tasks.

Furthermore, the workflows associated with these models can vary widely for SA. Conventional ML techniques often require extensive preprocessing, feature extraction, and hyperparameter tuning. In contrast, LLMs, such as GPT, streamline the data analysis workflow. However, they also introduce new challenges such as prompt engineering. Some pre-trained LLMs, such as those hosted on Hugging Face, strike a balance by offering robust performance with relatively less preprocessing compared to the conventional methods.

Our study aims to bridge the aforementioned gaps by comparing these models and their workflows. We evaluate the performance of these models, with a particular focus on the advancements brought by the latest LLMs.

2 Literature Review

2.1 Overview of Sentiment Analysis

SA refers to the use of NLP methods to computationally analyze human emotions, sentiments, and opinions embedded in text (Zhang et al. 2023). The ability to effectively capture underlying emotions and attitudes from textual content is a critical step towards human-level intelligence (Zhang et al. 2023). Therefore, SA has always been a crucial and dynamic research area in the field of NLP. Approaches to SA have evolved alongside the development of NLP. SA methods can be categorized into lexicon-based approaches, conventional ML approaches, and deep learning approaches (Wankhade et al. 2022; Birjali et al. 2021).

Lexicon-based methods are based on a collection of tokens or terms that are labeled with predefined sentiment scores corresponding to their categories and/or intensity of emotions (Wankhade et al. 2022; Yuan & Siau 2017b). Corpus and dictionaries such as SentiWordNet and SenticNet were built by collecting a list of opinion words and evaluating their emotion polarity and intensity (Baccianella et al. 2010; Cambria et al. 2010). To analyze the sentiment of a given text, the valence of emotions, such as positive, negative, and neutral, are calculated based on the pre-defined lexicons, with the emotion category having the highest score selected as the overall polarity (Yuan & Siau 2017a; Adeborna & Siau 2014). Lexicon-based approaches require no training data, making their applications simple to implement at a low cost. However, given that the same word may have different meanings in different contexts, lexicon-based methods typically have low generalizability and accuracy.

With the rise of ML models and their proven capabilities in text mining, the performance of SA has been significantly improved by using ML approaches (Zhao & Siau 2017). ML methods enable a deeper level of sentiment classification by capturing the linguistic features (Birjali et al. 2021) and have played an important role in the early stage of SA. For instance, logistic regression as a classical linear classifier has been used to model the probability of a text belonging to a certain sentiment category. Despite its simplicity, logistic regression can often achieve state-of-the-art performance (Joulin et al. 2016). Other ML models, such as support vector machines (SVM), naive Bayes, and random forests, are also widely applied in SA (Ravindran & Nah 2017). The performance of conventional ML models largely depends on feature engineering (Domingos 2012), which requires manual extraction and selection of important data features related to sentiment. Such a manual feature engineering procedure often requires a deep understanding of the SA context and data, and is therefore difficult to generalize to other domains (Birjali et al. 2021).

Compared to conventional ML, deep learning can automate the feature engineering process by allowing the algorithm to learn complex features and representations from raw data. Therefore, deep learning models such as convolutional neural networks (CNN) and recurrent neural networks (RNN) have been employed in SA tasks (Yadav & Vishwakarma 2020; Kim 2019; Li et al. 2020). CNN automates feature extraction with convolution layers and it can capture local patterns in the text to understand the sentiment (Kim 2019). RNNs, such as long short-term memory (LSTM), use memory cells to connect early-stage information in previous layers with current information, which enables the model to process long texts and capture long-range sentiment features (Li et al. 2020).

2.2 Large Language Models for Sentiment Analysis

More recently, transformer-based LLMs such as GPT-3 (Brown et al., 2020), GPT-4 omni (i.e., abbreviated as GPT-4o) (OpenAI n.d.), and FLAN-T5 (Chung et al. 2024) have set new benchmarks for SA (Zhang et al. 2023). With their impressive capabilities in content creation and text processing, LLMs have been recognized as a significant milestone on the way to artificial general intelligence (Nah et al. 2023a; Pan et al. 2023). The most prominent characteristics of LLMs include the transformer mechanisms and large-scale pre-training. The transformer architecture uses self-attention mechanisms to focus on important parts of a sentence so that the model can effectively capture the global context regardless of the input sequence (Vaswani et al. 2017). Further, attention mechanisms enable parallel computation, significantly increasing the efficiency of data processing. Current LLMs are pre-trained on large-scale textual data using techniques such as instruction fine-tuning and reinforcement learning from human feedback (Zhang et al. 2023). The large scale of model complexity and training data helps LLMs achieve state-of-the-art performance in multiple tasks, although the training process is computationally expensive and time-consuming. Current popular LLMs can be categorized into encoder-decoder models (e.g., FLAN-T5) and decoder-only models (e.g., GPT-4 omni).

Encoder-decoder models capture context bidirectionally, enhancing the overall understanding of sentiment. Decoder-only models efficiently utilize large-scale pre-training data, improving generalizability for zero-shot tasks (Fu et al. 2023; Acheampong et al. 2021).

Recent studies have tested LLMs for SA. Zhong et al. (2023) compared GPT-3.5 with BERT in SST-2 SA task and found that the two models achieve similar performance. Wang et al. (2023) compared GPT-3.5 with a fine-tuned BERT model in sentiment classification, opinion mining, and sentiment cause analysis. They found that GPT-3.5 exhibited impressive zero-shot ability in aspect-based sentiment analysis (ABSA) and polarity shift detection. Zhang et al. (2023) found that LLMs performed better in simple sentiment classification tasks but were less effective in complex tasks such as ABSA, compared with domain-specific small language models that identified sentiment in specific aspects and entities (e.g., consumer reviews for products may contain different attitudes towards different product dimensions).

In summary, the powerful capabilities of LLMs in semantic understanding and reasoning have significantly raised the benchmarks for deep learning models in SA by capturing more complex semantic nuances and richer contextual cues associated with underlying emotions. However, there is a need to empirically compare LLMs with conventional ML models and to test the performance of LLMs with different architectures. Such efforts will offer important insights toward selecting the most appropriate models for SA tasks.

3 Research Method

3.1 Data

The IMDb movie reviews dataset was utilized in this study to compare different SA methods. The IMDb movie reviews dataset has been extensively employed in SA, text classification, and opinion-mining research. Specifically, we retrieved both the training and testing datasets from the transformers Python package (version 4.35.2). Each dataset comprises 25,000 reviews, with sentiments evenly distributed between positive and negative labels[2].

We implemented GPT models for SA using OpenAI's application programming interface (API). Due to the prolonged evaluation time for GPT models and OpenAI's API daily usage restrictions[3], we sampled 2,000 reviews (1,000 positive and 1,000 negative) from the original testing dataset for the study. This subset was used to assess the performance of different conventional ML models and LLMs.

3.2 Conventional Machine Learning Models

To predict whether movie reviews have positive or negative sentiment using conventional ML models, standardized text preprocessing was performed on both the training

---

[2] Https://huggingface.co/docs/datasets/en/index (accessed on 2024/05/19).

[3] Https://platform.openai.com/settings/organization/limits (accessed on 2024/05/19).

and testing datasets. The preprocessing procedure included tokenization, removing stopwords, stemming, and vectorizing the text using TF-IDF (Kadhim et al. 2014). Multiple conventional ML models were then trained using the default hyperparameters when applicable. The models included logistic regression, naive Bayes, decision tree, random forest, gradient boosting, AdaBoost, and CatBoost. Finally, all trained models were evaluated using the 2,000-sample testing dataset. The following is an example of a positive movie review:

"One of the other reviewers has mentioned that after watching just 1 Oz episode you'll be hooked. They are right, as this is exactly what happened with me. The first thing that struck me about Oz was its brutality and unflinching scenes of violence, which set in right from the word GO. Trust me, this is not a show for the faint hearted or timid. This show pulls no punches with regards to drugs, sex or violence. Its is hardcore, in the classic use of the word. It is called OZ as that is the nickname given to the Oswald Maximum Security State Penitentiary. It focuses mainly on Emerald City, an experimental section of the prison where all the cells have glass fronts and face inwards, so privacy is not high on the agenda. Em City is home to many..Aryans, Muslims, gangstas, Latinos, Christians, Italians, Irish and more....so scuffles, death stares, dodgy dealings and shady agreements are never far away. I would say the main appeal of the show is due to the fact that it goes where other shows wouldn't dare. Forget pretty pictures painted for mainstream audiences, forget charm, forget romance...OZ doesn't mess around. The first episode I ever saw struck me as so nasty it was surreal, I couldn't say I was ready for it, but as I watched more, I developed a taste for Oz, and got accustomed to the high levels of graphic violence. Not just violence, but injustice (crooked guards who'll be sold out for a nickel, inmates who'll kill on order and get away with it, well-mannered, middle-class inmates being turned into prison bitches due to their lack of street skills or prison experience) Watching Oz, you may become comfortable with what is uncomfortable viewing thats if you can get in touch with your darker side."

The following is an example of a negative movie review:

"Basically, there's a family where a little boy (Jake) thinks there's a zombie in his closet & his parents are fighting all the time. This movie is slower than a soap opera... and suddenly, Jake decides to become Rambo and kill the zombie. OK, first of all when you're going to make a film you must Decide if it's a thriller or a drama! As a drama the movie is watchable. Parents are divorcing & arguing like in real life. And then we have Jake with his closet which totally ruins all the film! I expected to see a BOOGEYMAN similar movie, and instead i watched a drama with some meaningless thriller spots. 3 out of 10 just for the well playing parents & descent dialogs. As for the shots with Jake: just ignore them."

3.3 FLAN-T5: Pre-trained Model from Hugging Face

A pre-trained FLAN-T5 model[4] was loaded from Hugging Face using the AutoTokenizer and AutoModelForSeq2SeqLM classes. These tools were used to load the tokenizer for the FLAN-T5 model and retrieve important settings such as the model architecture, vocabulary size, and input length limits[5]. To test the performance of the pre-trained FLAN-T5 model, each movie review from the 2,000-sample testing dataset was tokenized and converted into PyTorch tensors, including both 'input_ids' and 'attention_mask'. These tensors were then placed on the GPU for processing, facilitated by the.to('cuda') method. The model then generated output tokens, which were subsequently decoded back into readable predictions.

3.4 GPT 3.5 and 4o

Various prompts were tested for all GPT models. The following prompt was adopted due to its ability to return a single word, either "positive" or "negative":

"Analyze the following movie review and determine if the sentiment is: positive or negative. Return the answer in a single word as either positive or negative: {text}"

This prompt, along with each movie review from the 2,000-sample testing dataset, was passed to the client.completions.create method in the OpenAI GPT API[6]. By specifying the model version (see Table 1), the responses were generated as either "positive" or "negative."

4 Results

As shown in Table 1, GPT-4o (version gpt-4o-2024-05-13) demonstrated the highest performance among all the models in the evaluation. GPT-3.5 (version gpt-3.5-turbo-0125) and FLAN-T5 also showed strong performance, being slightly below that of GPT-4o. Conventional ML models without hyperparameter tuning showed reasonable performance but were outperformed by advanced pre-trained LLM models. Logistic regression outperformed other conventional models like naive Bayes, decision tree, random forest, gradient boosting, AdaBoost, and CatBoost.

Our results show that LLMs performed better than conventional ML models. The Transformer architecture enables the models to comprehensively capture the underlying semantics and context to generate more accurate predictions. While conventional ML models, such as logistic regression, are cost-friendly, their performance lags behind the LLMs by around 10%. Despite variations in model size and pre-training cost, the higher performance of GPT models suggests that advanced decoder-only models have an edge in NLP tasks such as SA.

---

[4] https://github.com/M-Taghizadeh/flan-t5-base-imdb-text-classification   (accessed   on 2024/05/19).

[5] https://huggingface.co/google/flan-t5-base (accessed on 2024/05/19).

[6] https://platform.openai.com/docs/api-reference/ (accessed on 2024/05/19).

Table 1. Performance Comparison of Models

Model	Version	Accuracy	Precision	Recall	F1-score
GPT 4o	gpt-4o-2024-05-13	0.950	0.950	0.950	0.950
GPT 3.5	gpt-3.5-turbo-0125	0.930	0.930	0.930	0.930
FLAN-T5	Hugging Face	0.930	0.930	0.930	0.930
Logistic Regression		0.876	0.876	0.876	0.876
CatBoost		0.862	0.862	0.862	0.861
Random Forest		0.833	0.833	0.833	0.833
Naive Bayes		0.810	0.815	0.810	0.809
Gradient Boosting		0.804	0.806	0.804	0.803
AdaBoost		0.795	0.795	0.795	0.794
Decision Tree		0.708	0.708	0.708	0.707

5 Discussion

5.1 Rapid Evolution and Performance Improvement of Large Language Models

The progression from GPT-3 to GPT-3.5, and then to GPT-4o, showcases significant performance improvements. Initially, GPT-3 (text-curie-001) was assessed in our pilot study and it showed relatively limited performance, with an accuracy of 83.5% and a precision rate of 78%. Despite our use of a specific prompt that requested only a "positive" or "negative" response (i.e., "Analyze the following movie review and determine if the sentiment is: positive or negative. Return the answer in a single word as either positive or negative"), we observed that GPT-3 sometimes generated ambiguous outputs without providing a positive or negative prediction. The introduction of GPT-3.5 brought substantial improvements, yielding more precise and reliable SA. The most recent upgrade to GPT-4o further enhanced these capabilities, delivering superior performance across various benchmarks. These advances are attributed to increased model complexity, improved training data, and more sophisticated algorithms that enable the model to capture more nuanced aspects of language and sentiment. This rapid development underscores the continuous evolution of AI technologies, providing increasingly better tools for SA and other NLP applications.

5.2 User-Friendliness and Accessibility

Prompt engineering is crucial for the accuracy of sentiment predictions when using GPT models. In this study, a specific prompt was used to request returning a single-word sentiment (positive or negative) and to maintain consistency and clarity in the model's responses. As shown in Table 2, one of the significant advantages of using GPT models is their user-friendliness, particularly for individuals who may not have knowledge of text preprocessing and model training. Such knowledge, often necessary for conventional ML models, is not required when working with GPT models, making them accessible to a broader audience including non-technical users.

Table 2. Workflow of Models

Model Type	Text Preprocessing	Model Training	Prompt Engineering
Conventional ML	Yes	Yes	No
Pre-trained Models from Hugging Face	Yes	No	No
GPT	No	No	Yes

5.3   Cost and Efficiency Considerations

In terms of cost implications, using commercial GPT models, which require a paid API, presents a financial consideration compared to the cost-free nature of conventional ML models and Hugging Face models. This information is crucial for researchers and organizations with budget constraints, as it affects the cost-efficiency of SA tasks, especially when dealing with large datasets. Open-source GPT models, however, are available for free and can serve as an alternative option.

5.4   Transparency and Bias Concerns

One potential issue with using LLMs is the lack of transparency (Nah et al. 2023b), which creates uncertainty in the robustness of the results of SA analyses. Due to the probabilistic nature of the LLMs, it is hard to guarantee consistent output. Furthermore, whether the IMDb dataset was part of the training data for LLMs is unclear. If the dataset had been used for training, it could potentially bias the model's performance, leading to overly optimistic performance. Future studies should seek more transparency into the training datasets used for pre-trained models.

5.5   Future Research Directions and Practical Implications

For future research, extending the comparison to include time cost for training and operational speed in production environments would provide a more comprehensive understanding and comparisons of the application of these models. Evaluating models on additional datasets and exploring other metrics, such as computational resource requirements and scalability, could offer valuable insights into the practice of SA. Given their capability to extract contextual information, LLMs could be relatively easy to apply to ABSA, which poses challenges for conventional ML. A more comprehensive evaluation approach will provide more in-depth insights into choosing appropriate models for SA tasks, with considerations that balance competing metrics such as performance, scalability, cost, and ease of use.

References

Acheampong, F.A., Nunoo-Mensah, H., Chen, W.: Transformer models for text-based emotion detection: a review of BERT-based approaches. Artif. Intell. Rev. **54**(8), 5789–5829 (2021)

Adeborna, E., Siau, K.: An approach to sentiment analysis – the case of airline quality rating. In: Proceedings of the Pacific Asia Conference on Information Systems. Chengdu, China (2014)

Baccianella, S., Esuli, A., Sebastiani, F.: SentiWordNet 3.0: An enhanced lexical resource for sentiment analysis and opinion mining. In: Proceedings of the International Conference on Language Resources and Evaluation, pp. 2200–2204 (2010, May)

Birjali, M., Kasri, M., Beni-Hssane, A.: A comprehensive survey on sentiment analysis: approaches, challenges and trends. Knowl.-Based Syst. **226**, 107134 (2021)

Brown, T., et al.: Language models are few-shot learners. In: Larochelle, H., Ranzato, M., Hadsell, R., Balcan, M.F., Lin, H. (eds.) Advances in Neural Information Processing Systems, vol. 33, pp. 1877–1901 (2020)

Cambria, E., Speer, R., Havasi, C., Hussain, A.: SenticNet: a publicly available semantic resource for opinion mining. In: Commonsense Knowledge: Papers from the 2010 AAAI Fall Symposium. Fall Symposium Series Technical Reports, FS-10-02. Arlington, VA (2010)

Chung, H.W., et al.: Scaling instruction-finetuned language models. J. Mach. Learn. Res. **25**(70), 1–53 (2024)

Domingos, P.: A few useful things to know about machine learning. Commun. ACM **55**(10), 78–87 (2012)

Fu, Z., et al.: Decoder-only or encoder-decoder? Interpreting language model as a regularized encoder-decoder. arXiv preprint arXiv:2304.04052 (2023)

Joulin, A., Grave, E., Bojanowski, P., Mikolov, T.: Bag of tricks for efficient text classification. arXiv preprint arXiv:1607.01759 (2016)

Kadhim, A.I., Cheah, Y.N., Ahamed, N.H.: Text document preprocessing and dimension reduction techniques for text document clustering. In: 2014 4th International Conference on Artificial Intelligence with Applications in Engineering and Technology, pp. 69–73. IEEE (2014)

Kim, Y.: Convolutional neural networks for sentence classification. arXiv preprint arXiv:1408.5882 (2019)

Li, W., Qi, F., Tang, M., Yu, Z.: Bidirectional LSTM with self-attention mechanism and multi-channel features for sentiment classification. Neurocomputing **387**, 63–77 (2020)

Nah, F.F.H., Cai, J., Zheng, R., Pang, N.: An activity system-based perspective of generative AI: challenges and research directions. AIS Trans. Hum.-Comput. Interact. **15**(3), 247–267 (2023)

Nah, F.F.H., Zheng, R., Cai, J., Siau, K., Chen, L.: Generative AI and ChatGPT: applications, challenges, and AI-human collaboration. J. Inform. Technol. Case Appl. Res. **25**(3), 277–304 (2023)

OpenAI. Hello GPT-4o. https://openai.com/index/hello-gpt-4o/. Accessed 19 May 2024

Pan, S.L., Nishant, R., Tuunanen, T., Nah, F.F.H.: Literature review in the generative AI era-how to make a compelling contribution. J. Strat. Inf. Syst. **32**(3), 1–4 (2023)

Ravindran, S.K., Nah, F.F.H.: Prescriptive analytics: a game changer for business. Cutter Bus. Technol. J. **30**(10/11), 11–17 (2017)

Vaswani, A., et al.: Attention is all you need. Adv. Neural Inform. Proces. Syst. **30** (2017)

Wang, Z., Xie, Q., Feng, Y., Ding, Z., Yang, Z., Xia, R.: Is ChatGPT a good sentiment analyzer? A preliminary study. arXiv preprint arXiv:2304.04339 (2023)

Wankhade, M., Rao, A.C.S., Kulkarni, C.: A survey on sentiment analysis methods, applications, and challenges. Artif. Intell. Rev. **55**(7), 5731–5780 (2022)

Yadav, A., Vishwakarma, D.K.: Sentiment analysis using deep learning architectures: a review. Artif. Intell. Rev. **53**(6), 4335–4385 (2020)

Yuan, B., Siau, K.: A research stream on sentiment analysis. In: Proceedings of the Americas Conference on Information Systems. Boston, MA (2017)

Yuan, B., Siau, K.: Lexicons in sentiment analytics. In: Proceedings of the Twelve Annual Midwest Association for Information Systems Conference. Springfield, IL (2017)

Zhang, W., Deng, Y., Liu, B., Pan, S.J., Bing, L.: Sentiment analysis in the era of large language models: a reality check. arXiv preprint arXiv:2305.15005 (2023)

Zhao, W., Siau, K.: Machine learning approaches to sentiment analytics. In: Proceedings of the Twelve Annual Midwest Association for Information Systems Conference. Springfield, IL (2017)

Zhong, Q., Ding, L., Liu, J., Du, B., Tao, D.: Can ChatGPT understand too? A comparative study on ChatGPT and fine-tuned BERT. arXiv preprint arXiv:2302.10198 (2023)

Author Index

H. Degen and S. Ntoa (Eds.): HCII 2024, LNCS 15382, pp. 301–302, 2024.
https://doi.org/10.1007/978-3-031-76827-9

The manufacturer's authorised representative in the EU is Springer
Nature Customer Service Centre GmbH, Europaplatz 3, 69115 Heidelberg,
Germany. If you have any concerns regarding our products, please
contact ProductSafety@springernature.com

Printed and bound by CPI Group (UK) Ltd, Croydon, CR0 4YY
30/04/2026
02100208-0001